D0933480

CIVIC LITERACY

Civil Society: Historical and Contemporary Perspectives

BRIAN O'CONNELL
Civil Society: The Underpinnings of American Democracy

PHILLIP H. ROUND
*By Nature and by Custom Cursed: Transatlantic Civil Discourse and
New England Cultural Production, 1620–1660*

BOB EDWARDS, MICHAEL W. FOLEY, AND MARIO DIANI, EDS.
*Beyond Tocqueville: Civil Society and the Social Capital Debate
in Comparative Perspective*

KEN THOMSON
From Neighborhood to Nation: The Democratic Foundations of Civil Society

HENRY MILNER
Civic Literacy: How Informed Citizens Make Democracy Work

CIVIC
LITERACY

How Informed Citizens Make

Democracy Work

Henry Milner

Tufts University
PUBLISHED BY UNIVERSITY PRESS OF NEW ENGLAND
HANOVER AND LONDON

Tufts University

Published by University Press of New England, Hanover, NH 03755

© 2002 by Henry Milner

All rights reserved

Printed in the United States of America

5 4 3 2 1

Library of Congress Cataloging-in-Publication Data
Milner, Henry.
  Civic literacy : how informed citizens make democracy work / by Henry
Milner.
    p. cm.
  ISBN 1–58465–172–5 (cloth)   ISBN 1–58465–173–3 (pbk.)
    1. Political participation. 2. Civil society. 3. Civics—Study and teaching.
4. Social capital (Sociology) I. Title.
  JF799 .M55 2002
  306.2—dc21   2001004979

Contents

Preface   vii

Introduction   1

I   Civic Engagement and Social Capital   11

1   The Uses and Abuses of Social Capital   13

2   Civic Engagement and Political Participation   25

3   Political Participation and Political Knowledge   38

II   Sources of Civic Literacy   51

4   Civic Literacy in Comparative Context   53

5   Political Participation and Political Institutions   66

6   Civic Literacy and Political Institutions   78

7   Civic Literacy and the Media   90

III   Policy Choices Promoting Civic Literacy   105

8   Promoting Civic Literacy through Political
    Institutions and the Media   107

9   Promoting Civic Literacy through Adult Education   117

10   The Case of New Zealand   134

IV Civic Literacy and Socioeconomic Outcomes   **145**

11   Economic Outcomes: Combining Growth
     and Fair Distribution   147

12   Civic Literacy and the Foundations of the Sustainable
     Welfare State in Sweden   161

13   Civic Literacy and the Sustainable Welfare State   170

14   Conclusion: The Future of the Sustainable Welfare State 178

Appendixes

I   The CSES Questions on Political Knowledge   191

II   The International Adult Literacy Survey   194

III The TV Dependency Scale: Data and Sources   200

IV   A Survey of New Zealand Candidates   203

     Notes   209
     References   263
     Index   287

Preface

This book comes at the end of an intellectual journey over the last two decades of the twentieth century. Though the focus and perspective have evolved through various stages and publications, my intended destination has not changed: I have sought to understand what makes equitable welfare states able to survive and adapt—what makes them sustainable. The path of the journey has thus never strayed very far from lived experience—from the content, causes, and effects of key policy choices in the industrial democracies and, especially, the Scandinavian countries. The path has taken me through and beyond the empirical literature, and into a search for a satisfactory theoretical framework for understanding these choices and explaining their causes and effects.

In hindsight, it is clear why a conceptual framework suitable for this purpose emerges only with this book. This is the point in my journey when the analysis of the Scandinavian social-democratic welfare state is set in comparative context. At the theoretical level, the task has been to develop a framework that takes into account a great deal of information about many countries. The ambitious comparative project undertaken in this book is based on international data assembled over four years. Completion of this task was facilitated by the possibilities opened by developments of two kinds, electronic and geographical. The first of these, access to sophisticated electronic sources of data and documentation, is hardly unique to me, though it is still fully made use of by far fewer social scientists of my—Boomer—generation than one might expect. So, unlike my younger colleagues, I remain in awe of what electronic data retrieval makes possible.

The Internet and related technologies take us well beyond the confines of our own field of specialization. A moderate investment of time and effort yields results that enable one to travel if not to the frontiers then at least to the mainstreams of hitherto closed-off worlds of intellectual pursuit. With documentation relevant to the subject of this book fragmented by academic discipline, ideological perspective, and geography, the electronic journey was one that had to be taken.

But virtual exploration is only one side of comparative research: hands-on-the-keyboard is no substitute for feet-on-the-ground exploration. Due to the generous support of research grants from the Social Science and Humanities Research Council of Canada and the Quebec Department of

Research, Science, and Technology (FCAR), as well as a fellowship from the University of Melbourne, and kind invitations to lecture, carry on research, and teach from a number of the people listed below, I have been able to spend much time in countries other than my own. In working on this book I have had the opportunity to live for periods at least several months long in New Zealand, Australia, and Sweden,[1] as well as make shorter visits to the United States, Switzerland, and several other European countries.

As a result, the comparative research underpinning this book goes against the current trend in international research. Comparative analysis in social science increasingly consists of assembling the work of research teams, with members confining their contribution to their home countries. This trend might be termed the academic side of globalization. Such globalization has served social science research but also distorted it. Funding has moved from national to multinational research, especially to research corresponding to the territory of multinational organizations. In the European Union, researchers in one nation are offered powerful cash incentives to team up with similar groups in some or—preferably—all Europen Union member countries. Not to be outdone, American, Australian, Canadian, and other non-European OECD researchers have formed their own teams, which tend to span to larger and larger number of countries.

These developments have the welcome effect of bringing otherwise excluded countries—and their scholars—into the mainstream of comparative research, increasing the breadth and scope of knowledge to be gained. Yet there is a downside. Intrastate comparative research has stagnated.[2] More profoundly, research based on national teams is necessarily pluralistic in nature, and is subject to pressure pushing downward toward the lowest common denominator. No matter how uncompromising the original research design, once co-equal national teams become involved, the dynamic inexorably changes: to achieve consensus, variables that are trickier to research in specific countries give way to ones acceptable to everyone.

That is the trade-off. More countries and more data, but a process that makes it harder to ask the most interesting questions in comparing outputs and outcomes, because such comparisons inevitably make some participants' countries look worse. We shall see this quite clearly in relation to the theme of this book, namely, the causes and consequences of differences in political knowledge. The proliferating teams of political scientists seeking to explain voting behavior pose a wide range of standardized questions that get at attitudes; few questions, however, get at knowledge (i.e., have a right or wrong answer), and those that do usually leave it to the national research team to decide just what questions to ask. It thus becomes impossible to compare countries systematically and directly on the basis of some measure of aggregate political knowledge.

Because of this, a main objective of my electronic and geographical voyages has been to track down sources of information on the basis of which to compare levels of political knowledge in industrial democracies. Explaining the causes and consequences of the differences so identified is at the core of what this book is about and how it fits into the intellectual journey toward understanding what makes social-democratic welfare states sustainable.

The process of getting to this point has been a long one, and much ground has been covered—as graphically manifested by the oceans dividing the many friends and colleagues who have contributed useful suggestions. In Europe: Rune Åberg, Eric Åsard, Pertti Ahonen, Ewe Becker, Hans Bergström, Buno Cautrés, Klas Eklund, Heikki Ervasti, Olle Findahl, Elmire af Gejerstam, Gullan Gidlund, Gunnel Gustavsson, Torstein Hjellum, Kimmo Kuusela, Andreas Ladner, Jan-Eric Lane, Donald Lavery, Anders Lidström, Tomas Lunden, Pierre Martin, Ingrid Munck, Richard Murray, Anders Nordlund, Huib Pellikaan, Bo Rothstein, Yves Schemeil, and Stefan Svallfors.

In North America: Keith Banting, André Blais, Robert Campbell, Patrick Fafard, Paul Howe, Ronald Inglehart, Richard Katz, Tom Kent, Gordon Laxer, Martin Lubin, Louis Massicotte, Tom Moran, Jack Nagel, Richard Niemi, Francois Petry, Rob Richie, Dietlind Stolle, Hugh Thorburn, Eric Uslaner, Axel van den Berg, and Reg Whitaker. In Australia and New Zealand: Jonathan Boston, Brian Galligan, Paul Harris, Bruce Headey, Ian Marsh, Elizabeth McLeay, Raymond Miller, Nigel Roberts, Bob Stephens, David Tucker, and Jack Vowles.

If the above—and I apologize to those I missed—heeded the call of duty, several people went beyond the call, and I end by expressing my special gratitude to them. John Richards and Peter Aimer each read one or more of the chapters that follow and offered useful suggestions and criticisms. Arthur Milner and Svante Ersson read the entire typescript: their invaluable contribution cannot be adequately acknowledged. Frances Boylston also read—and reread—the typescript; more than that, she shared the experience "on the ground" in the countries visited in researching and writing this book. Her insights find their way into every aspect of the pages that follow.

Introduction

There is an upheaval taking place in the world of ideas. It is a discussion that knows neither ideological nor geographic bounds; a debate that has transcended academic disciplines, indeed scaled the walls of academia—a debate about citizenship. The popular and scholarly press, almost daily, write of the decline and possible reawakening of community, or civil society, speculating about the causes and consequences of apparently eroding civic engagement and political participation.

In the United States—but not only the United States—this debate over the renewal of citizenship has been stimulated most of all by the writings of political scientist Robert Putnam around the concept of social capital, most recently in his much-discussed book *Bowling Alone*. Yet despite all the ferment, the work has left a gap that impedes our weaving together the strands of the philosophical debate over citizenship and community to with the empirical findings of social scientists about social capital and political participation. Missing in the discussion is a clear conceptualization of the knowledge needed to exercise the responsibilities of citizenship as we enter the twenty-first century.

That is what this book is about. The point of entry into the discussion, both conceptually and empirically, is the idea of civic literacy—the knowledge and ability capacity of citizens to make sense of their political world. Our goal is to shed light on what William Galston, a leading American contributor to this the philosophical inquiry (1991: 227), terms the specific political virtue of citizenship "the willingness and ability to engage in public discourse and evaluate the performance of those in office." We do so by, in effect, operationalizing these two aspects of citizenship as measurable dimensions of civic literacy: ability manifesting itself in the form of political knowledge, and willingness in the form of political participation.

Through political participation, as John Stuart Mill taught, people ensure that their interests are taken into account in the decision-making process. In so doing, they gain the skills and knowledge to act effectively as

cite
John S. mill

members of the community—such skills and knowledge then contribute to the well-being of the community.[1] Taking this approach refocuses our interests and research efforts from voluntary associations and trust—on which the current social-capital literature is focused—to the relationship between political participation and political knowledge. In posing the empirical question of what produces and sustains civic literacy, we shall look at the role of political and especially electoral institutions to provide voters with a clear and meaningful "map" of political alternatives.

Beyond the conceptual and empirical is the practical. We are shall be concerned with developments that may inhibit civic literacy, such as increased television viewing, not so much for their effect on individuals' engagement in voluntary associations and trust in people and politicians—as the current literature is wont to do—but for their impact on political knowledge. We shall go from the big picture—comparing trends in fifteen Western democracies—to the micro-level, to manifestations of civic literacy in a Swedish community. And we consider a number of possible measures for promoting civic literacy, such as subsidization of newspapers, the informational activities of political parties, and the encouragement of public broadcasting and adult and civic education.

Institutions and policies promoting civic literacy, we shall show, can produce a virtuous circle by themselves fostering informed political participation. These, in their turn, can lead to more equitable socioeconomic outcomes. Such outcomes encourage citizens to keep well informed of governmental decisions—beginning the cycle once again. Civic literacy is thus both end and means.

Civic Literacy as End and Means

In contrast to the standard works on political participation, we emphasize voter turnout in local elections. Casting one's ballot is a measurable expression of informed citizenship, and it is local political decisions that are closest to the citizen's everyday activities. The degree to which citizens regularly participate politically by voting in local elections, thus, provides a kind of barometer of the level of the "civic" component of civic literacy. The word *civic* is chosen because it combines in one word the notion of exercising one's role as citizen and of being a member of a local community.

No single indicator exists for the "literacy" component of civic literacy. But a combination of partial measures allows us to compare nations and communities along this dimension. The word *literacy* is chosen because it implies that there is a known quantity that is attainable by each individual that cannot be "stocked"—unlike, say, knowledge or capital which can. A minority can build up a community's stock of physical capital and, by implication, social capital. However, though one person may read much more than another, both contribute equally to the overall literacy rate of their community. While the available indicators do not always allow us to make the distinction as finely as we would wish, the intent behind our choice of the term *civic literacy* is clear: to compare societies on the basis of the proportion of their inhabitants demonstrating the knowledge and skills to act as competent citizens.

One important similarity between the conceptualization of civic literacy in this book and the way social capital is used in the work of Robert Putnam is that in both cases the concept serves as both indicator and explanatory factor. For Putnam, levels of associational participation and interpersonal trust are indicators of social capital; they also explain how the stock of social capital comes to be built up and depleted. While less than ideal for the purposes of theory building, the duality inherent in this kind of analysis has proven extremely fruitful in practice, spawning wide-ranging research into the manifestations and consequences of associational density and trust. It is this vital contribution made by social scientists operating within the social-capital framework to the contemporary discussion of citizenship and community that opens the way to the civic-literacy-centered approach taken here.

Apart from its stress on knowledge, my approach departs from the main thrust of the work on social capital by viewing civic literacy as a condition for attaining certain social outcomes—not only an end in itself but also as means to an end. That end is explored in the last part of this book analyzing the relationship between levels of civic literacy and socioeconomic equality, taking up the discussion in my previous work on Scandinavia. In so doing, it addresses the often-heard contention that, with the advent of globalization, all societies must sacrifice egalitarian outcomes to be competitive.

The relationships among the key variables are illustrated in figure 0-1. The first three parts of this book concentrate on the quite complex relationships in which civic literacy is an end in itself, illustrated in the center and left of the chart. The chapters set out and investigate various indicators of civic literacy, illustrated in the circle at the lower left of figure 0-1, as well as the policy choices that enhance it. These choices are both direct, as depicted by the arrows leading to indicators of civic literacy—for example, policies promoting newspaper reading—as well as indirect, depicted by the arrow leading to consensual political institutions.

But civic literacy is not only an effect, it is also cause; in scientific terms, it is both dependent and independent variable. The arrow going from civic literacy suggests that high civic literacy is conducive to optimal policy choices, both as a "virtuous circle" reinforcing civic-literacy-enhancing choices and also, as illustrated by the arrow to the right side of the chart, contributing to the society's capacity to combine equity and efficiency in its outcomes. The stress on adaptation is deliberate. An institution-based

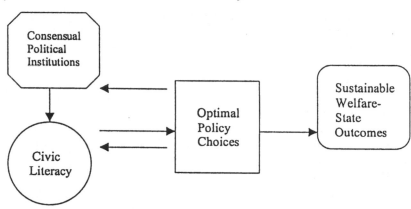

FIGURE O–I

analysis such as this one has a clear historical dimension, but it is not deterministic. Policy choices that strengthen civic-literacy-enhancing institutions are still human choices, and thus predetermined neither culturally nor historically. Empirical data differentiating comparable countries serve to show that there is a real connection between choices of policies and institutions and outcomes. Still, ultimately, the argument does not rest on the data. While most effort is spent on describing aspects of different trees, the goal is always to improve our understanding of what kind of forest we are in.

It could not be otherwise. Using aggregate data of this kind for sixteen (and often fewer) industrial democracies makes it impossible to control every possible relevant factor. True, individual-level data are drawn upon, especially, in those chapters dealing with political participation, and constitute a rich source of information about the attributes of voters and nonvoters, their interest in politics, knowledge of public affairs, partisanship, media use, as well as age, gender, race, and level of education. Yet, though helpful at pointing toward possible explanatory factors, findings based on such individual-level relationships cannot be used to confirm aggregate-level hypotheses, to explain, for example, why average turnout is higher in some countries than others.

To see why, consider the effect of education on turnout. In the United States, education accounts for a 40 percent difference in individual voter turnout levels, yet there are several countries with much higher average turnout that have lower average levels of education than the United States (Franklin 1996: 218–19). Indeed, there is no relationship between OECD countries' average length of education and average voter turnout—despite the fact that, individually, more highly educated people are more likely to vote. In comparing aggregates, the effect of individual variables like education must be set in the context of other—potentially intervening—variables, for which we cannot, as with individual data, readily control. One such intervening variable (investigated in this book) affecting turnout is media consumption. Education, it is suggested, can only partially compensate for the overall negative effect on civic literacy of high television and low newspaper consumption.

Plan of the Book

Part One

Chapter 1 is an account of the contemporary scholarly discussion around social capital and its relationship to citizenship and civil society, focusing on what Robert Putnam terms civic engagement. For Putnam, the stock of social capital underpinning civic engagement is built up through participation in voluntary organizations. Such participation results in increased interpersonal trust, which, in turn, fosters participation. A review of the literature briefly delineates what we know about the relationship between these two main indicators of social capital. It concludes that, though useful for historical developments in a given country, the indicators travel poorly. Trust is too culturally embedded and subjective to serve adequately the purposes of comparative analysis, while voluntary organizations play different roles in different institutional settings. Church-based organizations prove especially difficult when it comes to assessing and comparing their contribution to the "stock" of social capital.

In search of objective indicators of civic engagement suitable for comparative analysis, Chapter 2 explores one indicator that, unlike trust and associational membership, does not rely on self-reporting, namely, voter turnout. Turnout is in fact used by Putnam, but seldom explored in the literature on social capital, despite the wide acknowledgement that voting is an inescapable component of civic engagement in contemporary pluralistic societies. After briefly surveying what we know about political participation in the industrial democracies, chapter 2 sets out the results of my own efforts at assembling the data for average levels of turnout in municipal elections from the different countries. We then move to the relationship between the more traditional indicators of social capital and average local turnout. A weak correlation with organizational density is found, but none is found with trust, leaving us unconvinced as to the usefulness of the standard indicators of civic engagement for purposes of comparative analysis.

Chapter 3 presents an alternative approach to explaining differences in civic engagement by shifting emphasis from trust to knowledge. Starting from the universal findings of individual-level studies that more informed people vote more, it suggests that at the aggregate level two factors combine to explain variations in turnout. Comparative measures of political knowledge, albeit incomplete, indicate that there is higher turnout in those countries where the average levels of knowledge of public affairs are higher. This is the "demand" side of political knowledge. But there is also a second, "supply," side, identified by political scientists as the "effort" of political actors—especially political parties—to get out the vote by informing potential voters. The nature and intensity of such efforts are seen to be a function of institutionalized incentives; in other words, political institutions matter when it comes to the accessibility and intelligibility of political information.

The chapter goes on to survey the large, mainly American, literature on individual political knowledge and its relationship to political participation. Irrespective of education, it reveals, more politically informed people vote more. This points toward the evidence of an ongoing decline in aggregate political knowledge, with age as a key factor. Though today's young people can be expected to vote more as they get older, a significant change seems to be taking place, at least in the United States. Despite spending more years at school than their parents' or grandparents' generation, and being somewhat more willing to volunteer for community service than their parents, young people today vote less and know less about politics.

Part Two

Chapter 4 begins by refining the concept of civic literacy, first setting it against alternative expressions found in the literature. A society's level of civic literacy reflects the proportion of adults possessing the knowledge required for effective political choice, a proportion that changes over time and varies among countries. The international contours of civic literacy are traced by setting out what we know of differences among countries on the factual as well as cognitive dimensions of political knowledge. The number of countries involved and the questions asked in existing international surveys of political knowledge are too small to allow for the development of any kind of standardized civic literacy scale. Nevertheless, their results do correlate strikingly with comparative levels of our indicator of "civicness," average turnout in local elections. Findings at the aggregate level correspond to those at the individual level: low levels of political knowledge correlate with low turnout—even more in local than in national elections.

Chapter 5 brings political institutions into the analysis, with a summary of the literature linking differences in political institutions to variations in voting turnout. The most important institutional factor affecting party strategies is the electoral system, and the aggregate data on turnout in local elections confirm findings from comparative studies of national elections: voting turnout is higher under proportional systems (PR). In addition, using turnout in local elections in countries employing more than one electoral system, namely, Switzerland, Australia, and Norway, allows us to control for national cultural differences that may affect such turnout. In each, we find a strong positive relationship between turnout in local elections and the use of PR, a relationship that does not disappear even when we control for the presence and number of political parties emphasized in the literature. Something is at work here other than the extra efforts of parties to attract voters whose votes are wasted under non-PR systems. That something, it is argued in chapter 6, is civic literacy.

Chapter 6 probes the relationship between political, and especially electoral, institutions and civic literacy. It compares "consensual" institutions based on proportional electoral systems typical of Europe with majoritarian systems common in the English-speaking democracies. As a general rule, by more fairly translating votes into seats, consensual institutions based on PR systems bring more sectors of the community in under the umbrella of democratic institutions. Moreover, in contrast to majoritarian electoral systems, which exaggerate a party's weakness and thus create a disincentive against its investing resources in regions and municipalities where it is weak, PR fosters political party involvement in local politics. This adds a vertical dimension to broadened involvement under consensual institutions.

The chapter explores the effects on political information costs of consensual political institutions in both their horizontal and vertical dimensions. An indirect reduction of information costs lies in the incentive structures faced by political actors. Under PR, political parties have to cooperate to govern, and the effective horizontal transmission of information among parties is necessary for effective cooperation. Moreover, under PR, parties' costs of making the electorate more aware of alternative policy positions are seen to be lower than in a majoritarian electoral system with its high winner-take-all payoffs. Overall, it is concluded, consensual institutions contribute to the "supply side" of civic literacy by, in effect, providing citizens with a more coherent and stable political map.

Chapter 7 returns to the "demand side" of civic literacy, identifying the factors directly affecting the level of factual political knowledge and relevant cognitive capacities of individuals, starting with patterns of media use. It begins with Putnam's controversial contention that television is the culprit behind the "disappearance" of social capital in the United States because television watching takes time away from "bowling leagues" and projects a mean world. The problem is that little time is needed to vote, and intensified use of television in political campaigning should—if anything—raise turnout. Moreover, Americans are not nearly as low in their degree of organizational involvement and social trust as their television-watching levels would imply. Why is it only when it comes to voter turnout that America's numbers are as low as their television consumption is high?

The puzzle is resolved by replacing social capital by civic literacy. A careful review of what is known about the effects of TV watching on public-affairs knowledge reveals that, at a certain point, commercial television, by replacing other, more effective sources of political information, has a negative impact on civic literacy. To test this assertion, a TV dependency index is created, combining countries' relative ratings on commercial television and newspaper consumption. A high score indicates that a relatively large proportion of people watch a great deal of commercial television, which, for many, constitutes their only source of political information. A close negative correlation is established between aggregate scores on TV dependency and average turnout in local elections. By then using TV dependency as a second indirect indicator of civic literacy, part two ends with a graphic depiction ranking countries on these two indicators combined: the Scandinavian countries followed by the Dutch and German-speaking countries fall into a high-civic-literacy category.

Part Three   on✖ media

Part three turns to the policies that may account for the observed variations in civic literacy. Chapter 8 begins by comparing media-related policies, specifically subsidies to newspapers, and restrictions on commercialization of television. It then surveys the rules governing the various activities by parties and other political actors related to the dissemination of political information. The high-civic-literacy European countries differ sharply from the United States in their publicly funding such activities. A link is thus drawn between low civic literacy, in the United States in particular, and the combination of a winner-take-all electoral system with dependence on privately funded television commercials to disseminate political information about parties and policies.

Chapter 9 looks at the effects of policies related to education, especially adult education, and information technology. When it comes to civic literacy, the evidence points to the importance of learning acquired after formal schooling is completed. Hence special attention is paid to study circles and other adult education programs in the high-civic-literacy countries—especially Sweden. Within formal schooling, the acquisition of sophisticated reading comprehension skills is suggested to have a more lasting impact on civic literacy than the content of civics courses. The chapter proceeds from statistics about study circles and civics classes to more descriptive accounts of the "real world" of civic literacy woven into the fabric of community life.

The northern Swedish city of Umeå serves as case study. We follow the thread from the emergence of discussion groups in the temperance lodges in the nineteenth century to the development of contemporary civic-literacy-enhancing institutions: study circles, libraries, local newspapers, and the network of associations linked to them. The story is taken into the future with a glimpse of the network's integration into the region's information-society project, an example of how Sweden, and nearby Finland, play a leading role in information-society developments. Central to the Nordic approach are found to be collaborative efforts to develop ways of narrowing what American social critics have aptly called the "digital divide." The chapter concludes that a growing digital divide between the "wired" and "unwired" is perhaps the greatest threat to civic literacy, raising the frightening possibility that the new technology will further exclude those already lacking access to the knowledge necessary to be active informed citizens.

Part three ends with an analysis of institutions and policies in another insufficiently known country. Chapter 10 presents a case study of New Zealand, a small homogenous country in many ways similar to Finland, Norway, or even Sweden, but recently transformed into a kind of "anti-Scandinavian model." In the mid-1980s, this remote country was among the most protected and regulated of democratic regimes; it is now among the most market-oriented. Most interesting for our purposes is the effect of privatization and deregulation of television broadcasting on media consumption and, thus, on civic literacy. Accompanying, and partly in reaction to, these developments was a change in political institutions. The adoption of the German form of proportional electoral institutions appears to have modestly boosted informed political participation and may, to some degree, counteract the civic-literacy-reducing effects of broadcasting privatization and other reforms of the 1980s and 1990s.

Part Four

Of course, no analysis of New Zealand can ignore the changes in socioeconomic outcomes associated with the reforms, the discussion of which serves as a transition to part four, which explores the relationship between levels of civic literacy and socioeconomic outcomes. Chapter 11 begins with an overview of what we know about the effects of distributional equity relationships on economic growth. Evidence that high levels of redistribution need not be incompatible with solid economic growth leads to the suggestion that, under appropriate institutional arrangements, reinforcing outcomes associated with the modern welfare state can be a matter of rational self-interest.

The appropriate institutional arrangements are those favoring civic literacy. These are explored in Chapter 12 through a brief account of some of the ideas underlying the policies and achievements of the welfare state in Scandinavia. I argue that policy choices fostering civic literacy have long been one of its key—if unheralded—features. Such thinking is seen as central to the approach of two leading policy intellectuals, Gunnar Myrdal and Gösta Rehn. This view is contrasted with certain "new leftist" ideas that emerged in the 1970s, whose adoption, it is suggested, helps explain why Sweden—and not Denmark or Norway—suffered economic reverses in the 1980s and 1990s. Nevertheless, the chapter concludes, the overall resilience of the Scandinavian "model" illustrates the effects of the "virtuous circle" associated with civic literacy: an informed population supports policies that reinforce egalitarian outcomes and also contribute to keeping the population informed, which in turn sustains consensual institutions that enhance political participation and thus civic literacy.

Chapter 13 adds the final element to the comparative analysis of the industrial democracies, linking the institutions and policies underlying civic literacy with the outcomes of the sustainable welfare state. Using Gini coefficients of disposable income distribution and other indicators of socioeconomic equality, it draws a clear correlation between a country's civic literacy levels and its willingness and capacity to distribute resources equitably. The explanation offered is twofold, quantitative and qualitative. The quantitative explanation is straightforward: by drawing into the political process people from the lower strata (who in low-civic-literacy societies are excluded from effective citizenship), these societies assure that their needs enter the decision-making process and its outcomes. More profoundly, it is added that only a high-civic-literacy democracy is qualitatively endowed with the possibility of getting right the complex trade-offs that make it possible to attain relative equality without sacrificing efficiency (particularly in a globalizing economic environment).

Chapter 14 concludes on the question of how and where to apply what has been learned: how to maintain the virtuous circle of high civic literacy and generous socioeconomic outcomes where it exists, and what steps might be taken by societies where it is incomplete. In the former case, in Scandinavia in particular, the prospects for adapting the trade-offs to meet new policy challenges are seen as promising—as long as existing institutional arrangements are in place. And the main threat they will face will be external, in the form of the challenge of further integration into the European Union. The most acute threat to the "virtuous circle" lies not in the economic constraints imposed by monetary union but in a set of political institutions in which the basic features of consensualism are absent. Over time, this could undermine civic literacy and break the circle. The chapter ends with a discussion of the prospects for societies with lower levels of civic literacy, drawing on Canada for specific examples. This is a country that could significantly improve civic literacy through practical policies affecting media consumption and adult education, and—especially—through reforming its electoral institutions.

I

Civic Engagement and Social Capital

For the first two-thirds of the twentieth century a powerful tide bore Americans into ever deeper engagement in the life of their communities, but a few decades ago—silently, without warning—that tide reversed and we were overtaken by a treacherous rip current. Without at first noticing, we have been pulled apart from one another and from our communities over the last third of the century.

ROBERT PUTNAM, *Bowling Alone*, 2000

1

The Uses and Abuses of Social Capital

In the summer of 2000, as I was writing the conclusion to this book, the final report of the International Adult Literacy Survey was released. (The IALS test assesses the extent to which people in twenty countries possess the literacy needed to function as an effective citizen and is described in chapter 4.) In it appeared a particularly striking chart, one that dramatizes the close relationship between income inequality and functional literacy. By reproducing it here—as figure 1-1—I start at the end, with a graphic illustration of a key relationship this book seeks to establish and explain. Its message is dramatically clear: *democratic societies that more equally distribute intellectual resources also more equally distribute material resources.*

That relationship fully emerges only toward the end of this book, in part four. It follows upon an argument that can also be strikingly illustrated in a chart using the same IALS data, this time combined with voter turnout averages in local elections (from chapter 3). Figure 1-2 shows that *democratic societies that more equally distribute intellectual resources attain higher levels of political participation.* The reader will have to await later chapters for explanations as to just how functional literacy, voter turnout in municipal elections, and income inequality are measured. But it is useful, right at the outset, to get a taste of the kind of data that is used and how it is displayed.

The reader should not read too much into the variance (Rsq) and statistical significance (F) indicators provided with the charts; they are there essentially to show numerically the relationship which is illustrated in the scatter diagram.[1] As noted in the introduction, the argument ultimately cannot rest on the data. When using aggregate data from often fewer than fifteen countries,[2] it is always possible that factors other than those identified may explain the relationship uncovered. However significant the correlations between the independent and dependent variables—and, as we shall see, many are strikingly so—the small number of cases and the impossibility of controlling for every possible relevant factor make it impossible to rule out other possible interpretations. In the end, the reader will have

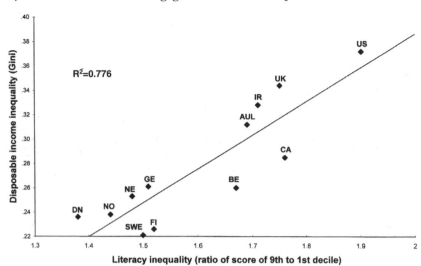

FIGURE I-I   **sig F = 0.001**

to be persuaded of the plausibility of the explanation advanced as to why, as displayed in figure 1-2, the proportion of functionally literate adults varies with voter turnout, and how this helps explain why, as we see in figure 1-1, higher levels of functional literacy correspond to income inequality. To put the argument bluntly: because they promote higher levels of

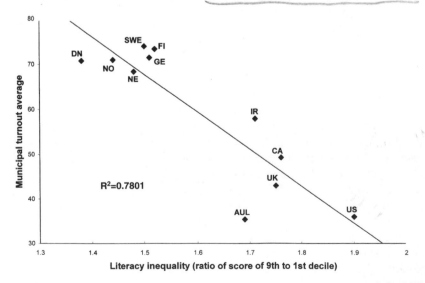

FIGURE I-2   **sig F = 0.000**

political participation, societies that more equally distribute intellectual resources—high-civic-literacy societies—will also be those that, over the
long term, more effectively redistribute material resources.

It is the first relationship, that between civic literacy and political participation, that is at the core of the contribution that this book seeks to make.
This constitutes a novel approach to a question that is central to the contemporary concerns of political scientists and public opinion leaders,
namely, that of civic engagement and how to promote it. So the task of this
first chapter is to set the analysis within the framework of the contemporary discussion, both academic and popular. As noted in the introduction, if
there is one concept around which that discussion has taken place more
than any other, it is that of social capital.

Social Capital: Tocqueville at the End of the Twentieth Century

The publication, in the summer of the year 2000, of Robert Putnam's book
Bowling Alone marks a high point in a public discussion that had begun with
the publication of an article under the same title five years earlier (Putnam
1995a).[3] The original article led to what Putnam himself terms "a deluge."
He had "unwittingly articulated the unease that had already begun to form
in the minds of many ordinary Americans" (2000: 506). Yet, though *Bowling Alone* brought to bear an impressive quantity of data not before assembled for this purpose, there was nothing fundamentally new in the argument. The ideas flowed from conceptions that had been developed in
Putnam's previous work and that of his predecessors, especially sociologist
James Coleman.[4]

Coleman had treated social capital as an asset based in social-structural
resources: for example, living in a safe rather than unsafe neighborhood.
Like other forms of capital, social capital is productive, making possible the
achievement of certain goals that in its absence would not be possible; but,
unlike the other forms of capital, social capital is found in the structure of
relations between actors rather than in actors themselves or in physical im-
plements of production.[5] Putnam and other political scientists and economists writing on social capital have shifted this emphasis from the structure
of relations between actors to the characteristics of the actors themselves.
This has generated a fair amount of criticism to the effect that empirical
tests of social capital using such "exogenous" indicators invite selective use
of data and ad hoc procedures.[6]

There is some truth in these charges. Yet Putnam's approach is more
subtle than that of some political scientists and, especially, economists,
who have effectively reduced social capital to trust. Putnam's work owes
much to the profound insights of the nineteenth-century French observer

of American life Alexis de Tocqueville, at the core of whose understanding is the role of the voluntary association. Where in France or Britain one looks to the state or the gentry to take initiative, Tocqueville insisted, "in the United States, you are sure to find an association."

> If some obstacle blocks the public road halting the circulation of traffic, the neighbors at once form a deliberative body; this improvised assembly produces an executive authority which remedies the trouble before anyone has thought of the possibility of some previously constituted authority. . . . An association, be it political, industrial, commercial, or even literary or scientific, is an educated and powerful body of citizens which cannot be twisted to any man's will or quietly trodden down, and by defending its private interests against the encroachments of power, it saves common liberties. (Tocqueville 1969: 189, 513)

For Tocqueville, it is primarily through interaction in such voluntary organizations that citizens learn the skills of democratic participation and the civic virtues of trust and reciprocity.[7] Putnam elaborates: social capital is a "public good" inherent in the community in the form of a "stock" from which all the members can draw. The components of social capital reinforce each other; their use builds up and their disuse diminishes the stock of social capital. Generalized reciprocity is produced through associational activities that stimulate interpersonal trust, which, in turn, fosters participation in voluntary organizations. A high-social-capital community is one that fosters mutual cooperation, honest and effective government, and entrepreneurship, which in turn promotes economic development. "When economic and political dealing is embedded in dense networks of social interaction, incentives for opportunism and malfeasance are reduced (2000: 21). "For a variety of reasons . . . life is easier in a community blessed with a substantial stock of social capital" (1995: 6).

Putnam first applied and developed his conceptualization in a study investigating the creation of twenty regional governments in Italy in the 1970s. Some of these governments were clearly failures; others "remarkably successful in satisfying their constituents" (1993: 81). Yet political institutions were basically the same, while economic conditions seemed not to be decisive. The single decisive factor that seemed to distinguish success from failure was the presence of voluntary associations. To test this insight, Putnam constructed a "Civic Community Index," taking into account such factors as community organizational density, newspaper readership, and voter turnout. The "civicness" of a region, he found, corresponded more closely with effective government performance than economic development or any other predictor. In such "civic" areas, concentrated in the North, politics concerns citizens; in the others, it is for "bosses" (1993: 147). Moreover, the distinction turned out to have profound historical roots. High-social-capital regions were those which had inherited traditions of civic engagement from medieval guilds and associations; low-social-capital regions were those which had been ruled by one or another form of "boss" for centuries.

When he turned his attention to his native country, and to longitudinal comparison, Putnam found that social capital had declined significantly over the last forty years, amounting to the "strange disappearance of social capital in America" (1996: 3). He based this conclusion on a wide range of indicators of voluntary group membership and participation, similar to, but more complete than, those used in the Civic Community Index, as well as on voting turnout data from U.S. national elections. In addition, he drew on time-series data accumulated over fifty years by polling agencies tracing the proportion of respondents agreeing that "most people can be trusted." All these indicators revealed a parallel steep decline. For example, interpersonal trust plummeted from 58 percent in 1960 to 35 percent in the mid-1990s.

Perhaps in response to the criticism that greeted his earlier articles,[8] Putnam, in *Bowling Alone*, blunts the Tocquevillian edge of the analysis, defining social capital in wider, indeed fuzzier, terms. "Some forms [of social capital] involve repeated, intensive, multistranded networks—like a group of steelworkers who meet for drinks every Friday after work and see each other at mass on Sunday—and some are episodic, single stranded, and anonymous, like the faintly familiar face you see several times a month in the supermarket checkout" (2000: 22). In ranking American states, he uses a Social Capital Index composed of fourteen indicators that—apart from indicators of participation and membership in various kinds of associations, of levels of social trust, and of voter turnout in presidential elections—includes two "measures of informal sociability": "spend a lot of time visiting friends"; and "average number of times entertained at home in the last year" (2000: 291). Nevertheless, given that nine of the fourteen indicators in some way measure participation in organized forms of voluntary activities, it is fair to say that Tocquevillian concerns remain at the core of the social capital project.

Comparing Voluntary Associations and Their Effects

Despite a number of legitimate misgivings, social capital as operationalized by Putnam and those who have followed him has proven heuristically rich. It is via this conceptualization of social capital that social scientists as social scientists have most effectively entered the contemporary discussion of citizenship and community. Putnam's work, more than that of anyone else, has placed social capital onto the research agendas of scholars (and funding agencies) in many countries and given rise to a wide though informal international network sharing a common understanding. We can see this in the debt to Putnam in the World Bank's *World Development Report* definition of social capital as "the informal rules, norms, and long-term relationships that facilitate coordinated action and enable people to undertake cooperative ventures for mutual advantage" (1997: 114).[9]

The quantity and quality of applications of the social capital framework have, as noted in the introduction, resulted in acceptance of an ambiguity inherent in Putnam's conceptualization, namely, that the main indicators of social capital, associational density, and interpersonal trust also serve to explain how social capital comes to be built up and depleted, making the attribution of causality all the more difficult. This conceptualization has also given rise to more specific concerns among critics who have taken issue with the conclusions Putnam derives from the data. A main theme concerns the effect of religion on social capital. Suggesting that Putnam's assessment is influenced by the Catholic Church's apparently negative effect on social capital in Italy,[10] Uslaner (1998) argues that the United States is fundamentally different. While the former, on balance, discourages people from becoming involved in their communities, he contends, the more democratic American churches and synagogues have the opposite effect. Greeley (1997) is even more critical, arguing that Putnam's characterization of Americans as bowling alone is misleading in ignoring the significance of church-related organized activities, implying Putnam to be "deliberately blind . . . to ignore religion as a source of social capital or deal only with its negative effects."[11]

Greeley cites the World Values Survey, which showed American volunteer rates to have actually increased during the 1980s, adding that the phenomenon is a wide one and that, in almost all the countries included in the survey, church attendance went hand in hand with volunteer service.[12] Though Putnam does not engage in international comparisons based on indicators of social capital, Greeley and Uslaner are typical in using data from the World Values Survey to make such comparisons. Unfortunately, relying on the WVS for this purpose is problematic. In relation to religion, positive responses to questions about membership in religious institutions do not distinguish between members of religious groups that encourage their congregations to become involved in their community and those which discourage other forms of civic engagement by sowing distrust of outsiders. Since membership in religious organizations contributes more to total memberships in some countries than in others, this distinction needs to be incorporated into any comparative analysis using the WVS figures.[13]

In the World Values Survey, samples of the population in over fifty countries were shown or read a list of sixteen types of voluntary associations[14] and asked, "to which, if any, of these organizations do you belong?" The

1991 results (displayed in figure 1–3) for the advanced industrial societies considered in this book show the United States to rank fifth (behind the Netherlands, Sweden and Norway) in associational memberships (per 100 people). We know, however, that treating participation in every kind of organization as contributing equally to the stock of social capital is inappropriate. For example, New Zealand surveys[15] found a positive relationship between political knowledge and interest and membership in professional associations, trade unions, service and community organizations, and, of course, political parties—but not sports clubs and church organizations. No doubt, this distinction applies to many of the other types of organizations.

While this drawback is not serious if one is comparing historical periods or regional differences for one country—as is Putnam—it is important when international comparisons are being undertaken.[16] Any calculation that does not distinguish organizations that contribute to social capital from those that do not must affect comparative rankings—unless we assume that the two types of organizations are equally present in different countries. But, we have seen with regard to religious associations, this is not the case.[17] In different contexts, similar types of associations can have different effects on social capital. For example, consider the "gated communities" estimated to house 50 million Americans in 1997 (Puro 1998).[18] The voluntary organizations that operate to provide services within such communities contribute differently to social capital than similar associations operating in "open" communities. More widely, the need for particular

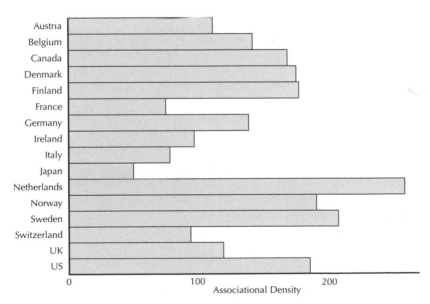

FIGURE I–3   (1991 WVS)

kinds of organizations differs in different societies, depending on the societal rules regarding service delivery. A case in point is the fact that the Scandinavians' high level of participation in voluntary organizations is concentrated in cultural, recreational, and labor-market-related activities in contrast to the United States and even Germany, with their less universalistic welfare systems, where health- and social-welfare-related activities stand out (Lundström and Wijkström, 1998). A specific example of how such selective incentives distort membership levels is provided by the Netherlands, with its very high associational density. In the past, this high rating was explained by the presence of social action groups, especially those promoting international solidarity and the environment.[19] But there is another factor peculiar to the Netherlands. Associational density there is inflated by the large memberships of a number of cultural and educational associations who gain access to television time based on the size of their membership. No real participation is involved, but by signing up the "member" receives the television listings at a fraction of the cost.

Another, more subjective aspect of this problem enters here: to what extent does the focus on organizations in the WVS and similar survey instruments impose a North American and Scandinavian bias? In Scandinavia and North America, social life is associational life because there is not much opportunity for social communication outside organizations. In the southern European (Latin) countries especially, and less so in Germany, the Benelux countries, Britain, Ireland, Australia, and New Zealand, there is a pub or cafe or even town-square life that is not "organized" but may serve a similar purpose.[20]

Apart from the difficulties associated with comparing different countries' associational densities, the fact that we must rely on subjective assessments stands in the way of any attempt to develop an objective comparative indicator of group participation analogous to level of electoral turnout. Unlike some of Putnam's longitudinal American data on actual group membership levels, existing comparative measures like the World Values Survey rely on subjective assessments, which are notoriously sensitive to culturally specific, normative expectations, which, we know, are more salient in certain countries. Yet, for all these limitations, there is still an objective dimension to comparisons based on associational density. This is, however, not the case for the most common standard comparative indicator of social capital, interpersonal trust.

Interpersonal Trust: An Uncertain Guide

Putnam, following Tocqueville, places emphasis on participation in voluntary associations as building trust although, over time, he sees causality as bidirectional, suggesting that current levels of civic engagement in Italian regions arise out of a level of social trust or distrust itself the product of earlier experiences of organizational participation.[21] Economists interested in social capital tend to go further, making trust almost interchangeable with social capital.[22] Interpersonal trust readily serves as a numerical measure of social capital to match standard economic indicators and thus allows, for example, for simple statistical tests of the effect of social capital on economic growth.[23] Figure 1–4 sets out the 1991 World Values Survey results for interpersonal trust, the percentage of people agreeing that "most people can be trusted."

Unlike alternate indicators, however, the standard measure of trust is even further from objective reality than is the standard measure of associational density based on statements of membership in voluntary organizations. We have no independent empirical referents apart from the subjective responses, and thus no way to know whether the words mean the same thing in different times and places.[24] Not unexpectedly, a recent exhaustive review of the trust/social capital literature concluded: "trust . . . is not the universal lubricant that oils the wheels of cooperation wherever it is applied. . . . The use of generalized social trust . . . as the primary focus of attention in political scientists' work on social capital [is] a dead-end."[25]

Clearly, how we respond to a question about the trustworthiness of others reflects the institutional setting in which the question is asked. Without controlling for various contextual factors, something impossible to do when one asks the question on one occasion in many different countries,

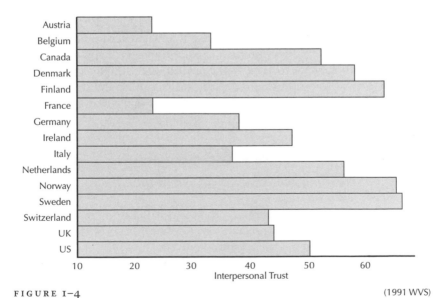

FIGURE 1–4   (1991 WVS)

we simply do not know what weight to give to the statistical differences reported. Grounds for some skepticism are to be found in the responses obtained in the international surveys themselves. A case in point: a question concerning trust has been asked in the Eurobarometer survey at irregular intervals starting in 1976 and ending in 1993.[26] The World Values Survey asked a very similar question.[27] In comparing the outputs of the 1991 WVS with those of a Eurobarometer survey taken in the same year, which used quite comparable samples, Newton found unexpected variation: there were significant differences, not only absolutely but also relatively. For example, Belgium, Portugal, and France were at the top of one and the bottom of the other (Newton 1997: 13).[28]

We know further that differences in the role of voluntary organizations in different countries will lead to differences in the relationship between organizational participation and social trust. For example, Uslaner (1998) argues that, in an individualistic culture like that of the United States, interpersonal trust is more important for collective projects than in Canada, a society that, in comparison, emphasizes group rights and a strong state. Similar results were found by Stolle (1998), who analyzed comparable groups in the United Sates, Germany, and Sweden. Very important differences in the relationship between membership in these groups and the trust exhibited by members versus nonmembers in each country were linked, she concluded, to differences in national political institutions.[29] Even within a single country the relationship proves elusive: Cusack compared the level of associational life in thirty German communities and found that Putnam's predictions were not borne out: "there is no relationship between associational density and the level of trust that the citizenry have" (Cusack 1997: 39).

Such results, plus the existing evidence that whatever causality exists is largely in the expected direction (from associational participation to interpersonal trust) leads us to look more toward associational participation rather than trust for appropriate measures of social capital. However, we shall seek measures that better control for institutional factors and are not dependent on self-reporting. First, though, there is one aspect of trust that must be considered.

Trusting and Distrusting Political Institutions

One dimension of trust has featured prominently in the political science literature. Indeed, it is relatively recently that political scientists have become interested in interpersonal trust; traditionally, the focus has been on political trust, that is, trust in political leaders and institutions. Questions of this sort have been posed in the U.S. National Election Survey since 1952. Political trust is nowadays often referred to as vertical trust, to distinguish it from interpersonal, or horizontal, trust. In general, satisfaction with the functioning of democracy correlates more with satisfaction with one's own life than with anything else (Abrial and Greffet 1997).[30] Unlike horizontal trust, where the picture is mixed (Newton and Norris 2000), vertical trust is declining in most countries. The United States is among the minority with a marked decline in both forms. A lack of consistency is, in fact, to be expected from a Tocquevillian perspective, which views participation in voluntary associations as challenging state power and thus, potentially, undermining trust in political institutions.[31] Canadian data bear out this conclusion. An analysis of the WVS data for Canada found that French-speaking Quebeckers are higher in political trust yet markedly lower in interpersonal trust than (English-speaking) Canadians in all other regions (Johnston and Soroka 1999: 17).

Declining vertical trust has drawn significant public attention and concern in countries as dissimilar as the United States and Sweden (Holmberg 1999)—though it should be kept in mind that Sweden is rather the exception among the Nordic countries.[32] The situation in Sweden is worth looking at here since it bears directly on the more general propositions advanced in later chapters. Exit polls conducted on election day in 1998 revealed that 60 percent of respondents were distrustful of politicians, a rise from an already high 54 percent in both 1991 and 1994. Yet, the distrust was targeted primarily at more distant, national-level politics.[33] In light of our emphasis on political participation at the local level, it is noteworthy that voters valued more highly their relationship to local council lors than to higher-level elected officials, and judged the former positively on their honesty and respect for due process (Petersson 1998: 130–31). In addition, despite the low levels of vertical trust, a high proportion of respondents expressed interest in following politics in the media (102–3).[34]

It would appear, then, that relatively low levels of vertical trust are compatible with interest in politics, and with what this book argues to be a crucial component of social capital, namely, political knowledge or civic literacy. But we are getting ahead of the story. As far as participation in voluntary associations is concerned, the data do not show any clear relationship with political trust (Kaase 1999). For example, a number of recent studies look at the effects of service and volunteering experiences that, as noted, have recently grown more frequent among American high school and college students. The weight of evidence appears to be that, as one of the studies concluded, "service experiences did not affect students' assessments of the value of elections, the objectiveness of public officials, and the attentiveness of public officials to the public" (Hunter and Brisbin 2000: 625). For some, like those surveyed in the Dutch study cited above, participation in community action organizations is an expression of lack of trust in the traditional institutions of political participation. Generally speaking, as far as political participation is concerned, the data are inconclusive. Despite expectations that people who trust their political institutions would be more likely to participate in them and vice versa (e.g., Rosenstone and Hansen 1993; Teixeira 1992), an analysis of 1990s data from the American National Election Surveys (Popkin and Dimock 1999) found no correlation whatsoever between political distrust and nonparticipation and found as well as substantial fluctuation in levels of political trust.

More widely, levels of vertical trust appear to have less effect on people's views on politics and policies than one might expect. For example, people low in political trust are no less open to state intervention. Comparing Norway and the United States, Edlund (1999) found that trust in the political system has hardly any impact on views on government intervention, and fails to explain the very large differences in views on government intervention between the two countries. Svallfors (1999) found lower levels of trust in political institutions in Sweden than in Norway, but no correlation whatsoever with support for government intervention in either. In sum, though we cannot ignore possible antisocial effects of declining trust in government, it is clear that including a vertical trust dimension does not usefully contribute to our understanding of social capital and its effects. As Inglehart succinctly put it,

> Politics is a peripheral aspect of most people's lives: and satisfaction with this specific domain can rise or fall over night. In contrast, satisfaction with one's life as a whole is far more conducive to political legitimacy than is a favorable opinion of the way the political system is currently functioning. . . . If one feels that one's life as a whole has been doing well under democratic institutions, it gives rise to a relatively deep, diffuse and enduring basis of support for those institutions. Such a regime has built up a capital of mass support that can help the regime weather bad times. (Inglehart 1997: 176)

If trust in politics does not shed much light on the causes and consequences of differences in social capital, we are left with the task of choosing other indicators that are also closely linked to civic engagement. The most appropriate place to look is at the substantive body of work on political participation. What we find is that the literatures on social capital and political participation overlap less than one might expect, a failing we try to help correct in the chapters to follow.

2

Civic Engagement and Political Participation

Having set out the key elements of the scholarly literature around the rather abstract term *social capital*, we can now focus on *civic engagement*, a term that more clearly denotes what the debate is really about.[1] The goal is to identify indicators for comparing countries' level of civic engagement that overcome the limitations inherent in measures of trust and associational participation. In this chapter I argue that one such indicator is voting turnout: civic engagement is closely linked to political participation, and we have no more suitable indicator of political participation than voter turnout. Comparatively passive though it may be, voting is the only activity that serves the purpose of comparing broad and long-term trends in political participation in different societies. Indeed, in a complex, pluralistic world, it is inconceivable that civic engagement be dissociated from the most basic expression of democratic citizenship, the exercise of the franchise.

Yet, while no one disputes this relationship per se, political participation is given rather short shrift in the social capital literature. Putnam, though including the steady decline in turnout in national elections in his litany of the symptoms of shrinking social capital in America,[2] expends little analytical effort on factors affecting voter turnout.[3] This is in keeping with the Tocquevillian approach in which participating in a voluntary organization is an act of a qualitatively different order than supporting a political party. The political participation literature, in contrast, makes no such distinction: voting is a form of participation, different in intensity but not substance from more active forms directed at the political choices of others, such as passing out campaign literature.

Voting is a visible, readily identifiable, and quantifiable act, for which we have objective as well as subjective measures. Studies of political participation over the generations show that—apart from a typically very small minority of political activists of an anarchist bent who consciously reject all forms of electoral politics—voting is the sine qua non of political participation. People who do not vote do not take part in more active forms of politics.[4] Moreover, unless built into the institutional structure so as to become effectively passive (as with membership in certain interest organizations that automatically entails party membership and financing), the more active forms of participation are, as a rule, limited to a small minority of the population. If civic engagement is not to be restricted to elites, then political participation must be something open to and, under normal circumstances, practiced by the majority of the population. In addition, of course, voter turnout is an objective indicator that can be operationalized for the purposes of international comparison, something we have seen to be fraught with difficulty with regard to the other, standard measures of levels of social capital.

Still, voter turnout is not quite the simple phenomenon it appears to be. In democratic countries, individuals vote to select representatives to a variety of legislative and administrative offices. Comparative studies of voter turnout typically consider only participation in elections for national legislatures. But the potential is far richer, and if we are interested in voting as an expression of civic engagement, we cannot limit ourselves to elections to positions that, by definition, are remote from people's immediate experience. And while not all countries have intermediate or regional elected assemblies, the election of local or municipal councils has effectively become universal in democratic societies. In our search for a comparative indicator of civic engagement, therefore, the level of turnout in local elections is a logical place to start. In doing so, we will be comparing national aggregates. Individual-level differences drawn from largely American data will be brought to bear to better explain variations at the aggregate level—being careful not to draw unwarranted inferences.

Rationality and Participation

With such considerations in mind, we begin by looking at what is known about why some people vote and others do not. One seemingly simple and straightforward way to pose the question—why do people bother to vote at all?—takes us down what turns out to be a not especially rewarding path. In recent years, some political scientists influenced by, or critical of, the standard economic model of behavior (e.g., Green and Shapiro 1994) have taken it to imply that there is something irrational or "paradoxical" about the "effort" put into voting. Yet, this "economic model of democracy" turns out to be a straw man, the result of a faulty application of the model of analysis used by economists. Economists are not interested in the "effort" people put into going to buy or sell, that is, to participate in the market: this is simply taken for granted. What is of interest is the effort they make to inform themselves so that they can make efficient choices. It was in relation to his discussion of the costs of informing oneself that the father of the economic model of democracy, economist Anthony Downs, raised the question of "rational ignorance" in relation to voting.

Downs stressed the contradiction between, on the one hand, rational citizens wanting democracy to work well so as to gain its benefits and knowing it to work best when citizens are well informed, and, on the other (their knowing) the fact that the benefits to individuals of informing themselves are outweighed by the costs they must bear. According to Downs, the existence of thousands or millions of other voters does not affect the decision to vote per se. What differentiates the "political market" from product markets is its effect on the decision to invest in relevant information. The existence of other voters reduces the incentive to pay the costs of that information. As Downs put it,

> [The citizen's vote] is not decisive: it is lost in a sea of other votes. Hence, whether he himself is well-informed has no perceptible impact on the benefits he gets. If all others express their true views, he gets the benefits of a well-informed electorate no matter how well-informed he is; if they are badly informed, he cannot produce these benefits himself. . . . Since all men do this, the election does not reflect the true consent of the governed." (Downs 1957: 246)

If producers and consumers in product markets based their choices on insufficient information, the market would never reach an efficient equilibrium. But this is not normally the case, since individuals gain benefits from investing in relevant information. It becomes the case when it comes to elections, since voters base their decision on incomplete information.[5] This is what Downs referred to as the "voter's paradox."[6] To the extent that Downs's economic framework is relevant to the overall discussion, it is in relation not to the choice over whether to vote,[7] but whether to acquire the requisite political information—a fundamental concern of this book.

According to Fishkin, it is in fact the existence of social capital that resolves the voters' paradox.

> I can be a "free rider" and save the costs of doing my share but still reap the benefits. . . . Why should I invest in acquiring political information to produce the benefits of a better public decision when those benefits, in all reasonable probability, will be provided—or not—regardless of my actions? But citizens in a civic community, one with high social capital, have many reasons to participate in politics together and to stay informed. They are part of a dense network of civic associations, both political and nonpolitical, which provides them lots of reasons to read newspapers, to stay informed, to participate in community activities. They internalize norms that motivate

them to participate and to join with others—norms that give them satisfaction regardless of any calculation about the effects of their individual actions. And, as Tocqueville noted, these habits of association, the widespread acceptance of working together, make it far easier for each individual to participate, to combine with others for some cause of mutual interest. (Fishkin 1995: 148)

As we shall see in chapter 3, this picture of Tocquevillian activism in a high-social-capital community doesn't correspond to the United States of the high-social-capital early 1960s, let alone contemporary America. The massive empirical data about the American voter confirm Downs's expectation of "rational ignorance." In a famous essay of that earlier period, Converse (1964) concluded that the average American citizen lacked a stable orientation toward politics and exhibited a low level of knowledge, lack of consistency between attitudes, attitude instability, and vacuous answers to open-ended questions. Since that time, American students of politics have systematically retested his assertions, gauging citizens' knowledge of American political institutions, processes, and leaders, with the result that, as one observer summarized the situation (Bartels 1996: 184), "the political ignorance of the American voter is one of the best documented data in political science."[8]

Chapter 3 shows that there is no real debate as to the overall accuracy of such assessments but much disagreement as to what, if anything, should be done. Some, like Fiorina, simply take rational ignorance as inevitable, indeed trivial.[9] But what of the "paradox" of such rationally ignorant citizens losing out on the benefits to be gained from an informed electorate? Here the cause is taken up by, among others, Lupia (1994) and Sniderman, Brody, and Tetlock (1991), who maintain that the voters' paradox does not have the ill effects attributed to it, since politically uninformed people use heuristics by following social cues and rules of thumb. These, they argue, allow them to arrive at decisions—including the decision not to vote—resulting in outcomes similar to those that would have been attained through the participation of informed people.

Can we thus dispense with the concerns raised by Downs? Are the costs of rational ignorance in fact negligible? Is there evidence that knowledgeable voters vote sufficiently differently from uninformed ones to affect outcomes? This question is taken up in chapter 3 in the context of the exploration of the individual-level relationship between political participation and political knowledge. This is because it hinges on the question of who votes and who does not, the answer to which is in fact intimately linked to the answer to another question: who has the necessary political knowledge? In the remainder of this chapter we stay at the aggregate level of analysis, returning to our discussion of political participation, and voting in particular, as an indicator of social capital. What do we know of the relationship between voter turnout and the standard indicators of social capital?

Voter Turnout in Different Countries: What Do We Know?

We now have reasonably reliable standardized turnout figures for elections in most countries, compiled by reputable international organizations such as IDEA, the Stockholm-based Institute for Democracy and Electoral Assistance. Official voter turnout data of this kind free us from relying on subjective self-reported assessments. We know that expectations based on cultural norms affect responses not only to such commonly used indicators of political involvement as "do you discuss politics at home?" but also "did you vote in the last elections?"[10]

We begin with the national data on voter turnout, in this case using IDEA figures for national legislative elections (presidential elections in the United States) since 1945. These figures, unlike most previous compilations, take into account differences in rates of registration by using as base age-eligible citizens rather than registered voters. I do not include countries with compulsory voting, even though one could subtract from their overall turnout rate the average additional turnout attributable to compulsory voting—estimated to be around seven percent (Franklin 1996: 226). This would be highly inappropriate since there are major variations[11] due to, for example, the severity of enforcement procedures triggered by failure to vote.[12]

The turnout figures for the countries surveyed in this book—and excluding those using compulsory voting—are presented in figure 2-1. Displayed are the average percentages of citizens of legal voting age (VAP)[13] who turned out to vote in legislative elections—presidential elections in the United States—as calculated by IDEA (1997: 17-18). One advantage of using VAP as base is that it brings the data from other countries into line with the way turnout is calculated for American national elections. This avenue is not open to us when it comes to calculating local turnout, since the national sources from which it is obtained, as a rule, use registered voters as base.

Using the numbers from figure 2-1, we can test for an aggregate relationship between levels of voter turnout and interpersonal trust at the beginning of the 1990s in countries participating in the World Values Survey and not using compulsory voting. The chart in figure 2-2 challenges the presumption that people in high-trust societies are more likely to vote than those in low-trust ones. The absence of any relationship parallels the findings of studies using individual data in countries as disparate as the United States and Sweden (Teorell and Westholm 1999). As Norris (1996: 475)

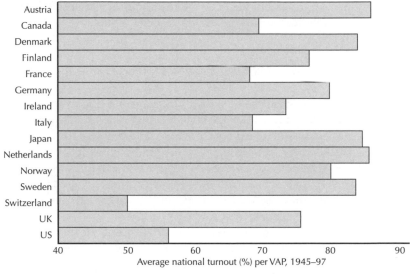

Average national turnout (%) per VAP, 1945–97

FIGURE 2–1   (IDEA, 1997)

concludes, "trusting citizens are not more likely to vote, engage in campaign activities, or be interested in politics."[14]

What of the relationship between such overall levels of voter turnout and organizational density? Replacing interpersonal trust with the WVS data on associational participation (in figure 2–3), we see that countries with higher levels of secular organizational inclusion tend to average

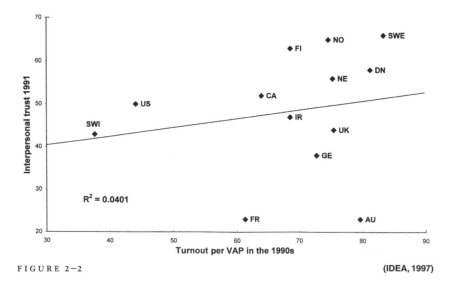

FIGURE 2–2   (IDEA, 1997)

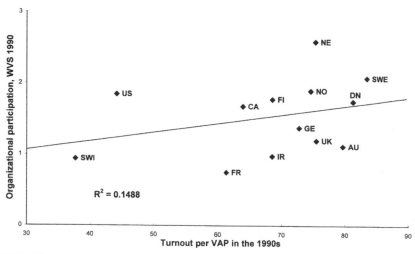

FIGURE 2-3

slightly higher turnout, but nowhere near enough to suggest a statistically significant relationship. This corresponds to individual-level findings in the American Citizen Participation Study that there is only a low correlation between membership in voluntary groups and voting, as opposed to a significant one with more active forms of political participation.[15] Another indicator of the lack of fit between trust and turnout is the fact that Americans trust local government most but turn out least at that level. The June 2000 Kaiser/Harvard poll for National Public Radio, for example, found that 14 percent more of the 1,557 respondents voiced confidence in local as opposed to national government. Let us look more closely at voter turnout at this level.

Comparing Turnout in Municipal Elections

Unfortunately, neither IDEA nor any other international organization assembles comparative local voting averages. Hence it has required considerable effort to seek out this data from the relevant authorities and specialists in each country. This effort is more than justified by the value of such data for the comparative analysis of civic engagement. For reasons elaborated by John Stuart Mill among others, more than at other, more distant levels, voting in local elections is understood to be a reflection of—and a spur to—more active forms of involvement.[16] Moreover, local elections are less prone to being distorted by the "noise" of emotion-laden[17] television campaigns designed to bring uninformed voters to the polls, since local elections seldom offer sufficient incentives for incurring the high costs of such campaigns. Hence it is at the local level that casting a ballot and being well informed about relevant issues can be expected to be most closely linked. This is borne out in individual-level surveys. For example, in her study of political participation and political knowledge at different levels, Junn (1995) found that political activity at the local level correlates positively with knowledge about local leaders—though it has no relationship with the amount known about national leaders. Similarly, Bean (1989) found a close interrelationship between turning out to vote, taking part in the campaign, and being involved in some effort to deal with a local problem.

It is at the local level, thus, that voting and more active forms of political participation appear to go hand in hand most often. It is also reasonable to expect that higher turnout in local elections will usually be reflected in higher levels of participation in nonpolitical, local organizational activities. While voting in local elections does not meet the standards of the active participation in New England towns described by Tocqueville, it does offer a greater potential of living up to the Rousseauian ideal of political participation as an act of political learning. Mill put the case simply: local politics best affords opportunities for learning about democracy, since holding local—as opposed to national—office is a reasonable aspiration for ordinary citizens. Moreover, though the impetus to participate is to ensure that their own interests are taken into account, in so doing, people learn to define their interests effectively in the context of the interests of the wider community for which they also have responsibility (Mill 1910: 346–59).

As an indicator, then, voting in local elections is less likely than voting in national elections to be a merely passive act, and more likely to be a reflection of civic engagement. Of course, institutional considerations affect voting at this level as at other levels. The effects of the electoral system will be considered separately, in chapter 5, when we look at the effect of institutional arrangements on turnout. Here (in figure 2–4), I present the aggregate averages for municipal-level turnout for elections that took place in the 1980s and 1990s for the countries under consideration here and for which such data are available.[18] Countries with compulsory voting at the local level are excluded. The technical reasons for doing so were already noted; in addition, there is something contradictory about treating the action of individuals who vote simply to avoid paying a fine as an expression of civic engagement.[19]

Compulsory voting, though probably the most significant, is only one of many institutional factors affecting local turnout. In some cases, there is as much variation within countries as among them. Moreover, the relevant regulations change fairly frequently since it is typically far easier to enact such changes at the local level. The best that can be done is to try to bring such factors to the reader's attention when relevant to particular cases.

Among relevant rules are the extent to which the elections are simultaneous across the region or country, or with elections at another level; whether noncitizens, or nonresident property owners, are permitted to vote; the use of postal ballots; the day of the vote and length of voting hours; the ease of registering to vote.[20]

There is, however, no reason to think that, apart from compulsory voting, any of these factors systematically distorts outcomes to the extent of making overall aggregate relationships suspect. Indeed, differences on certain of these features within the more pluralistic countries to some extent cancel out differences among those countries. Significant variations in important features of local elections and politics have been noted in Germany, Australia, and, especially, Canada (Goldsmith 1992). There is one exception: that is when local elections occur simultaneously with national elections, which bring a certain number of people to the polls who would not otherwise have voted. Only one country among those considered here uses such a system, namely, Sweden. (To take this factor into account, the Swedish turnout results have been reduced by 10 percent.)[21]

One aspect of local elections—at least when nonproportional electoral systems are used and (thus) parties play less of a role—is the substantial number of acclamations. These can either be treated as elections with a turnout rate of zero or simply be excluded from overall numbers. Neither solution is ideal, but the latter, typically used in such cases, distorts reality less than the former. Another dilemma is posed by the fact that most countries, especially the unitary ones where the elections are simultaneous, such as France and the Nordic countries, calculate turnout by simply setting the total number of voters participating over the potential number of voters. This is not done, however, in the federal states or other countries where local elections are not simultaneous. In several, such as Germany, Austria, and Britain, we use average municipal turnout per region; and in most of the rest, we use average turnout per municipality, effectively treating all municipalities as contributing equally to the aggregate, whatever the population. A related problem presents itself in the case of the few countries for which there are incomplete data, typically limited to dwellers of cities over a certain population size. To get our indicator of average turnout in municipal elections, we try to adjust for such considerations where obviously relevant, but we do not wish to give more attention to the phenomenon than it merits given that the overall effect of the size of municipality on turnout is rather modest, as we see in chapter 5's detailed analysis of turnout in Swiss municipalities.

For the smaller unitary countries where figures are provided by central government agencies, incomplete data are rare. Potential problems arise with the federal states that leave it to the regional units to collect municipal data and where these, in turn, leave it up to the municipalities themselves.

Fortunately, except for the United States and Switzerland and a few Canadian provinces, this practice has recently been abandoned. It does mean, however, that even where we have complete data for these countries they are only for recent elections. For Canada, it means that we are limited to partial data. We use the mean turnout in contested municipal elections in the two largest provinces, Ontario and Quebec, as well as the fourth largest, Alberta.[22] However, it is only recently that the two English-speaking provinces began to assemble the data, while Quebec provides only the raw data, city by city.[23]

In the case of Australia, such data are now collected by all the states, but several have only recently begun to do so. Three such states are Tasmania, South Australia, and Western Australia, which are of particular interest to us in that they are the only ones where municipal voting is voluntary. Australian data used in this study are thus limited to those three states and only to the last two elections (see table 5–3). And because all other elections are compulsory, we cannot be sure whether our average derived from turnout in these three comparatively small Australian states is representative of the country at large—though there is no specific reason to think not. The 34 percent average arrived at is low by international standards but corresponds to an earlier estimate by Goldsmith and Newton (1986: 146) of 25 percent, once we take into account the turnout boost in elections during the 1990s due to the introduction of postal ballots and other administrative reforms designed to foster participation (discussed in chapter 6).

We face fewer problems in Europe in part because the European Union now gathers such data for member states.[24] This has proven especially helpful for gathering and adjusting the figures for federal Germany and Austria.[25] In the case of Britain, I rely on 1995 figures, though these correspond very closely to numbers for the previous decades.[26]

For New Zealand we have complete information for elections that took place in the 1990s.[27] This is brings us to the two countries for which acquiring information from regional or national authorities is most difficult, the United States and Switzerland. The former is especially disappointing, given the immense amount of electoral data collected by American researchers. It has proven impossible to find any comprehensive municipal turnout data in the various American databases. Nor have I been able to identify specific state government agencies that collect such data on a statewide basis. Lacking, as a result, are systematic analyses of turnout in American municipal elections. There are only two partial and dated sources in the published literature (Morlan 1984; Alford and Lee 1968) on which I am forced to rely. In both cases the data were acquired through a mailed survey of officials of municipalities with over 20,000 population. Fortunately, a recent paper adds substantially to our knowledge. Schuckman (1998) wrote to the city halls of the seventy-nine cities with over 200,000 population, requesting information about the results of the last mayoral election held before spring 1998. He then calculated totals (from the sixty-five cities that responded) against the estimated number of potential voters.

My starting point for the United States is a 23.5 average, calculated from Schuckman's figures and the 31.5 percent average cited by Morlan. However, the data place the United States at a comparative disadvantage in two ways. First, they are based on potential rather than registered voters, and, second, they leave out the small municipalities. I have attempted to correct for these disadvantages. Using available newspaper reports, I was able to note the results of fall 1997 local contests in Connecticut as well as in a number of counties in central New York State. Based on a commonly made—and probably still conservative—assumption that 25 percent of eligible voters do not register in the United States, the 43 percent average of registered voters that turned out in both cases corresponds to 31 percent of potential voters, 8 to 9 percent above the big-city totals provided by Schuckman. This corresponds roughly to the apparent effect of size on turnout in Ontario[28] and Quebec.[29] To compensate for these factors, I have chosen to base the U.S. percentage on registered rather than potential voters by reducing the base by the estimated 25 percent of potential voters that do not register. Hence the U.S. figure goes up from 27.5 (the average of Morlan and Schuckman's figures)[30] to 36.5 percent.

Switzerland presented an equally difficult problem, since there are no official records assembling the results of all local elections in any canton, let alone for Switzerland's over three thousand municipalities (*Kommunes*) as a whole. Fortunately, a research project conducted at the Institute of Sociology at the University of Zurich surveyed the communal secretaries of all Swiss municipalities to which 81.6 percent of the communes responded, providing an especially rich source of turnout and related data—examined in detail in chapter 5.

Learning from Comparative Turnout in Local Elections

Keeping the limitations of the data in mind, we see, in figure 2–4, a family portrait of average turnout for local elections. If we compare it to the data on national turnout in figure 2–1 (from which Australia is excluded due to compulsory voting in national elections), we see a fairly close relationship—especially if Switzerland is eliminated. (The relative autonomy, observers agree, of Swiss communes is the main reason that, unlike in every other country, turnout is no lower in Swiss local than national elections.)[31]

It is worthwhile to stress that the numbers in these figures are meaningful in no absolute sense but only as part of an overall comparative aggregate. This is due both to the partial data and to the artificial manner in which we

Civic Engagement and Social Capital

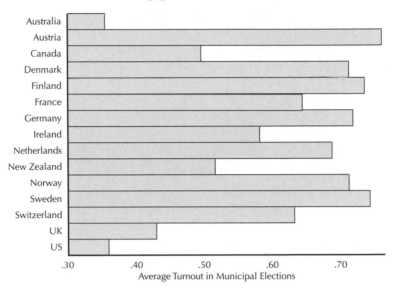

FIGURE 2-4

were forced to alter existing figures to take into account specific factors in
the cases of the United States and Sweden. This said, it is nevertheless true
that compared to the existing alternatives, aggregate comparisons of average local turnouts are both meaningful and useful as comparative indicators of countries' levels of civic engagement. We see this by posing about
turnout in local elections the questions asked above in relation to turnout
at the national level. In relation to the more traditional indicators of social
capital, in local as in national election turnout, there is no relationship with

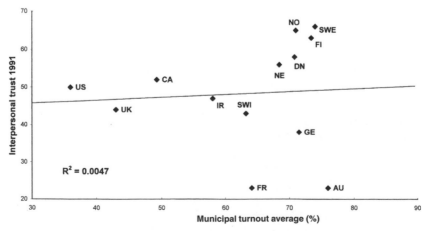

FIGURE 2-5

interpersonal trust. And, as we can see in figure 2–5, the weak relationship between associational participation (from the World Values Survey) is not strengthened when local electoral turnout is considered.[32]

If a country's average level of interpersonal trust does not predict the level at which its citizens will turn out to vote in the elections closest to their "civic" lives, and its level of organizational participation does so only weakly, there is a link missing between these indicators and civic engagement. The missing link, we shall argue, is none other than that identified in the discussion on rational ignorance early in this chapter.

3

Political Participation and
Political Knowledge

Why is it that people in countries with higher rates of associational participation are hardly more disposed to vote in national and even local elections
than people in less "civic" countries? Plainly, a chapter is missing in the
much-told social capital story of how organizational membership builds
trust, which, in turn, fosters civic engagement.

What else might account for the variations in voting turnout that we
have seen? What is it beyond interpersonal trust and involvement in voluntary associations that brings some citizens to the voting booth and not others? One possible candidate is political interest, which is frequently probed
through survey questions such as "how interested are you in politics?" or
"how often do you discuss politics?" Unfortunately, it adds little to our
understanding to learn from such surveys that people who express greater
interest in politics are more likely to vote. Indeed, all conclusions relying
on such subjective assertions must be taken with a large grain of salt. This
includes even an expressed intention to vote.[1]

If political knowledge is an explanatory factor, as we argue it to be, it can
be backed up by objective survey questions, that is, questions for which
there is a right and wrong answer distinct from the respondent's preference. A unique insight into the very real difference between hard
knowledge-data and soft interest-data is provided by a series of experi-
ments in which the order of political interest and political knowledge was
changed. When first asked about their interest, 75.9 percent reported following politics most or some of the time; however, when first asked political knowledge questions, the percentage expressing interest dropped to
57.4 percent (Schwarz and Schuman 1997).[2] The message is clear: little
weight can be given interest that rests on ignorance.

The same logic, I suggest, applies to all subjective indicators, including
interpersonal trust. There are two aspects to the expression of trust: one is

38

a superficial and fleeting statement very much influenced by contextual factors, including the wording and ordering of a questionnaire; the second is something deeper, very much akin to knowledge.[3] Trust, to endure, must be based on knowledge, since trust based on ignorance is doomed to eventual disappointment. Indeed, the first step to genuine trust is reciprocal knowledge. Generalized reciprocity, Putnam's "touchtone of social capital," is—as he phrases it: "I'll do this for you now . . . confident that somewhere down the road you or someone else will return the favour" (Putnam 2000: 134).[4] If associational participation does indeed build trust, this suggests that the process is one of acquiring the knowledge required for the generalized reciprocity underlying civic engagement. Political knowledge, it seems, lies in the background in any discussion of these indicators of civic engagement, as well as our own indicator, that of turning out to vote; it is time to bring it to the foreground.

Comparing Levels of Political Knowledge

What exactly do we know about the relationship between knowledge and political participation? Research at the individual level (described in the next section) bears out the truism that knowledge is power, that the competent, active citizen is the knowledgeable citizen. But what of the aggregate level? Is turnout higher in countries with more politically informed citizens? To answer this we need data allowing us to compare levels of political knowledge in different countries. In principle, gathering such data is a straightforward matter, since, in contrast to trust and interest, knowledge can be tested through objective measures. We might reasonably expect that existing research would have developed standardized public-affairs knowledge scores for the mature democracies based on the responses of large representative samples to a battery of political knowledge-oriented questions—selected and pretested to minimize bias in favor of any particular country. Unfortunately, for reasons suggested in the introduction, and taken up in chapter 4, such an instrument does not exist. This may change somewhat in 2001 when the results of the IEA Civic Education Study of sixteen- to eighteen-year-olds (discussed in chapter 9) are made known. For now, however, starting in chapter 4, we are forced to try to fill the void by assembling data from existing comparative surveys of political knowledge. Since these studies are, in and of themselves, inadequate in either or both the number of countries surveyed and the comparability or applicability of the questions used, we will complement this data by developing indirect indicators of political knowledge.

Fortunately, clues as to where to look for such indirect indicators of differences in aggregate public-affairs knowledge are to be found in numerous studies of the relationship between political knowledge and political participation at the individual level. There is a large and rapidly growing literature (or rather overlapping literatures) delving into what accounts for some individuals being more politically knowledgeable than others, and whether and how this translates into differences in political participation. Because the debate has taken place preponderantly among and about Americans, we shall have to be especially careful in applying its findings— however otherwise interesting—to comparative analysis. Fortunately, we can draw on several relevant studies that contrast the United States with Sweden, a comparison that complements the overall approach taken here.

We noted above that Fishkin's portrait of the high-social-capital civic community, in which politically active citizens stay informed of the issues through civic associations and newspaper reading, was already unrealistic in the United States of the early 1960s and is now quite distant from reality. Let us look more closely at this fact in light of the suggestion by Fiorina that such rational ignorance is universal. There are comparative data that suggest that rational political ignorance is not the universal phenomenon it is made out to be, and that this may be linked to, in Putnam's terms, the "disappearance of social capital in America." A good illustration of this is provided by changes in the consistency of support for political parties. While partisanship has been generally declining over the past forty years, in the United States in particular, this has occurred primarily among voters lacking knowledge about politics (Dimock 1998).[5]

Looking comparatively at the relationship between party identification and attitude consistency, we find some interesting contrasts. In the early 1960s, Granberg and Holmberg (1986) found significantly greater attitude consistency among Swedish than American respondents. A later study found a significant difference in the effect of political campaigns related to this: "In the United States, the switchers tend disproportionately to be those who are apathetic and who are poorly informed. . . . In Sweden it is not necessarily the apathetic and ignorant citizens who are most susceptible to being influenced to change their party selection during a political campaign"[6] (Granberg and Holmberg 1988: 217–18). This difference helps explain why, despite declining voter turnout over the last twenty years, political knowledge levels had slightly increased,[7] in contrast to the United States, where turnout and levels of political knowledge have been declining together.

Education, Age, and Political Knowledge

In part two we shall look to political institutions to help explain this divergence. Here we concentrate on individual attributes. We know that the decline in political knowledge and voter turnout has coincided with a rise in educational level, a surprising fact since more educated persons tend not only to be more knowledgeable but to vote more (e.g., Nie, Junn, and Stehl-Barry 1996: 34). If we control for socioeconomic class, we know that more highly educated strata generally earn higher incomes, and the better off vote more (e.g., Dopplet and Shearer 1999: 18); we also find that education has less of an effect on participation than age (e.g. Coulson 1999): people vote more as they grow older. But age includes at least two distinct elements: life experience and generation. We first address the former as plainly related to knowledge.

Civic competence,[8] defined as "knowledge and habits of knowledge acquisition relative to politics,"[9] has been found to be very closely related to aging. "Life experiences . . . have the effect of dampening the biases in patterns of political participation attributable to socioeconomic status" (Strate et al. 1989: 456). Political participation of Americans increased from age eighteen to sixty-five only marginally for the best-educated, but significantly (from 20 to over 50 percent) among the least well-educated (Wolfinger and Rosenstone 1980: 60). Rosenstone and Hansen (1993: 242) interpret this phenomenon as a result of political mobilization: "When political leaders offset the costs of political involvement—when they provide information, subsidize participation, occasion the provision of social rewards— they make it possible for people who have few resources of their own to participate."[10] In other words, there is a political education process associated with the mobilizing activities of political leaders and parties, the effectiveness of which raises not only the proportion of citizens who vote but also the relative proportion of the lower classes among them.

Certain observers (e.g., Teixeira 1992)[11] downplay the effects of this process, maintaining that the absence of nonvoters from the voting pool little affects government policies, since nonvoters' views, when tested, turn out not to differ substantially from those of voters.[12] Lijphart (1997), however, raises an important objection to this line of reasoning, namely, that the nonvoters polled in such surveys have not given the issues much thought, which they could be expected to have done had they been mobilized to vote. Hence their informed votes could very well have been different enough to affect outcomes. A number of studies provide support for this contention,[13] suggesting that in a significant number of cases, uninformed people in the United States would make different political judgments if they were well informed.[14]

Individual-level analysis cannot help us resolve this issue, since we ultimately cannot know what uninformed nonvoters would do if they became informed voters, and thus cannot prove that their absence translates into suboptimal political decisions. It is at the wider comparative level of analysis that this argument can most usefully be engaged. Lijphart marshals data showing a strong link between turnout and support for left-of-center parties, citing, in particular, an analysis of national election results from 1950 to 1990 in nineteen industrial democracies that showed that the left's share of the total vote increased by almost one-third of a percentage point for every percentage point of added turnout (Pacek and Radcliff 1995). Stated in individual terms, an American's contact with the mobilizing activities of parties would likely be boosted were she a citizen in a European country. There she would encounter what Rosenstone and Hansen refer to as the "more intense exertions" by European political actors to promote citizen participation,[15] through, among other things, being provided with political information.

We should not be misled by the expression "more intense exertions:" the intentions or energies of individual actors are immaterial. It is rather a matter of institutions. Or, to use the language of Gordon and Segura, a matter of decisions, not capabilities.

> Lack of sophistication need not indicate an inherent weakness of mass publics; this shortcoming may, instead, be a product of the systems—and the individual choices structured by those systems—within which it emerges. . . . Assessing capabilities by measuring performance, therefore, is problematic since the measure assumes the availability of accurate information and is driven both by genuine cognitive capacity as well as by the existence of variations in the value and accessibility of information. Capable people, in environments where information is available may choose to be uninformed if that information is expensive and difficult to accumulate, or if the use of that information is of limited utility. Measures of political sophistication, then . . . are really products of both capabilities and decisions. (Gordon and Segura 1997: 129)

In other words, the relationship between political knowledge and political participation in a society is affected by two kinds of factors, one having to do with the characteristics of the potential voters, the other having to do with the characteristics of those institutions which either encourage or discourage "effort" on the part of political actors to get voters to the polls. The efforts include, evidently, informing citizens of the issues at stake in the election. The capabilities of the system, the authors add, are a function of its political institutional structures, in particular, its electoral institutions, which have an impact on the accessibility, intelligibility, and usefulness of political information.

We shall emphasize differences in such institutions operating at the capability or "supply side" of political knowledge in explaining international differences in aggregate levels of voter turnout and political knowledge in chapters 5 and 6. Since institutions have not changed, however, we are no closer to uncovering the parallel decline in voter turnout and political knowledge in the United States, a decline we have good reason to believe is anything but benign in its consequences. To do so we need to return to the individual level and look more closely at the capability or "demand" side of this relationship.

Information and Turnout

A number of studies in countries other than the United States have ad-dressed the relationship between political knowledge and voter turnout, and we begin with these. One rich source of relevant information is the research commissioned by the New Zealand Electoral Commission, which was established in 1994 by the New Zealand government to inform voters about upcoming changes in their electoral system. Since its establishment, the commission has regularly polled New Zealanders on matters related to its mission, including knowledge about relevant aspects of New Zealand politics. In its report after its first year of operation, the commission noted that of the 328 respondents who described themselves as having little knowledge, 20 percent stated that they had not voted in the previous election, while, of the 186 and 246 who described themselves as having some or much knowledge, 6.5 and 3 percent, respectively, said they had not voted.[16] Similarly, Coulson's (1999) analysis of the results of the 1997 Canadian Election Study found the highly informed 9 percent more likely to have voted, a percentage higher than for all the other nineteen variables (including level of education and political interest) except age.[17] A 1997 study found that of EU citizens who knew neither the name of commission president Jacques Delors nor that of a commissioner from their own country, only 41 percent had voted in one or both of the previous national or EU elections, compared to 62 percent of those who could identify one or both (Blondel, Sinnott, and Svensson 1997). Similar findings emerge from the studies of young people.[18]

Australian research has delved into the underlying relationship between political knowledge and the predisposition to participate politically.[19] Using responses to political knowledge questions in the 1996 Australian Election Study, McAllister concluded that "political knowledge increases political literacy, in the sense of enhancing other forms of basic knowledge about the operation of political institutions. Those who possess political knowledge are significantly more likely to know the name and party of their local MP; such information would, it is reasonable to assume, make it easier for a citizen to contact their MP and, in turn, enhance his or her sense of political efficacy. . . . Political knowledge [also] increases political competence" (McAllister 1998: 21). Overall, he found that while knowledge of political history was adequate, familiarity with the operation of the political system was low.[20] Somewhat similar questions asked in British and Canadian surveys elicited only slightly better overall responses. Of respondents to the 1997 British election survey, 71 percent agreed that "MPs from different parties are on parliamentary committees;" 57 percent knew that Britain's electoral system is not based on proportional representation; and 64 percent knew that the longest time allowed between general elections is not four years (Curtice and Shiveley 2000). A Canadian citizenship survey that same year found that only 62 percent could name the three levels of government (cited in Gwyn 1997: 21–22).

Turning to the United States, parallel results emerge from a survey of the political knowledge of 1,500 respondents by the *Washington Post*, Kaiser Foundation, and Harvard University in late 1995. The study found "those in the highest third of the survey in terms of political knowledge were twice as likely to have voted in the 1994 presidential election as those in the lowest third" (Morin 1996: 7). This is also true, indeed more so, when it comes to off-year legislative elections (Popkin and Dimock 1999: 137). Junn summarizes the situation: "There is near universal agreement [that]. . . more knowledgeable people participate at a much higher rate" (1995: 9).[21] Popkin and Dimock (1999: 142) put it more dramatically: "The dominant feature of nonvoting in America is lack of knowledge about government. . . . Nonvoting results from a lack of knowledge of what government is doing and where parties and candidates stand."

Can we say that the situation is the same in the United States as elsewhere, that we are witnessing a universal decline in political knowledge and (thus) participation, that the United States is merely ahead of, if not typical of, "advanced" democracies?[22] We do not know. We do know, as will be elaborated in chapter 4, that national differences in voter turnout reflect the fact that political knowledge figures for Britain, Australia, New Zealand, and Canada, though low, appear to be considerably higher those for similar surveys in the United States. For example, the *Post*-Kaiser-Harvard survey found that only one-third of U.S. respondents knew the name—and just one-half knew the party—of their representative in the House (Morin 1996: 6)—a response barely better than chance in a two-party system. In Australia, in comparison, 70 percent correctly named their member in the House of Representatives, and 61 percent correctly named his or her party (McAllister 1998). An even better score was attained in New Zealand, where 67 and 73 percent were able to identify their representative's name and party (Vowles and Aimer 1993). A recent report comparing countries that participated in CSES election surveys (Curtice and Shiveley 2000) placed New Zealand first, followed by Germany, Norway, Britain, Australia, and the United States among the countries here analyzed, in the proportion of respondents able to identify a candidate in the last election.

Of course, aggregating individual-level political knowledge data for the purposes of international comparison is of limited value since it fails to take into account differences in size as well as relevant institutional differences between a parliamentary and presidential system, as well as (in the case of New Zealand) unitary versus federal constitutions and unicameral versus bicameral legislatures.

Still, without drawing unfair comparisons, we can say that the portrait of a comparatively low level of American knowledge is supported by evidence from many American surveys that portray American citizens as "hazy about any of the principal political players, lackadaisical regarding debates on policies that preoccupy Washington, ignorant of facts that experts take for granted, and unsure about the policies advanced by candidates for the highest political offices" (Kinder and Sears 1985: 664). This portrait emerges from many sources, since it has become almost commonplace for American political surveys to include some form of knowledge indicator. Most important are the recent wide-ranging studies of political participation that tested political knowledge. Best known perhaps is the American Citizen Participation Study (Verba, Schlozsman, and Brady 1995), a questionnaire administered to the 15,000 respondents that usefully distinguishes such knowledge from the other, more subjective, components of political engagement (interest in politics, tendency to discuss politics or follow politics in the media). Knowledge is assessed through a political information scale, which sums up the score on a battery of questions made up of nine items, three of which required naming public officials and six of which tested knowledge of government and politics.[23] An earlier survey very much in the same mold, reported on by Nie, Junn, and Stehl-Barry (1996), asked twelve questions in three categories: knowledge of principles of democracy (3 questions); knowledge of leaders (5 questions); questions other political knowledge (4 questions).[24] Table 3–1 summarizes the results (by what percentage of respondents answered how many questions correctly in each category).

TABLE 3–1

U.S. Political Knowledge Survey

	Number of Correct Answers (%)					
	0	1	2	3	4	5
Category 1: Principles	5	13	44	38		
Category 2: Leaders	26	20	21	18	11	5
Category 3: Other	4	19	36	30	11	

Source: Nie, Junn, and Stehl-Barry 1996: 23–25.

TABLE 3-2

U.S. National Election Survey

	'58	'60	'62	'64	'66	'68	'70	'72	'74	'76	'78	'80	'82	'84	'86	'88	'90	'92	'94	'96
Party with most members of congress (% correct)																				
Before election	47	64	—	64	69	70	50	64	—	61	59	71	32	55	33	59	49	59	70	73
After election	77	55	—	79	21	49	54	56	—	58	40	15	54	51	—	—	—	—	—	—
Party more likely to favor a strong government (%)																				
Democrats				51	—	40	—	23	—	26	25	35	—	28	—	26	—	28		
No difference				27	—	35	—	45	—	53	52	42	—	48	—	45	—	53		
Republicans				11	—	16	—	26	—	14	18	19	—	20	—	28	—	19		
Don't know, no interest				11	—	8	—	7	—	7	5	4	—	3	—	2	—	1		
Is one party more conservative? (%)																				
Yes, Democrats							16	15	—	17	—	—	15	—	—	12	18	12		
Yes, Republicans							51	57	—	54	—	—	53	—	—	57	44	57		
No, Both Same, Don't Know							33	28	—	29	—	—	32	—	—	31	38	31		

The results of these tests confirmed the low levels of knowledge already visible in the answers to the standard political knowledge questions posed in the U.S. National Election Survey (see table 3–2). For many years, the NES has been asking respondents which party had the most members of Congress before and after the election and, more interestingly, which party is more likely to favor a strong government. As we can see, only in 1964 were more than half the respondents able to answer correctly.[25] The percentage declined to the 20s in the 1970s, rose to 35 percent with Reagan in 1980, but fell back to the 20s in the 1980s and 1990s. Finally, a slightly better result—but still averaging only just over 50 percent—chose the Republicans on the question added in 1970: Is one party more conservative?

Given that some election results were closer than others and that party policies evolved during this period, it is possible to infer but difficult to prove a decline in political knowledge from these numbers—though there can be no doubt as to the general inability to identify political actors or parties with positions on issues or ideological stance.[26] To delve further into the relationship between declining political knowledge and political information, we need to return to the specific effects of age—in this case as a generational phenomenon.

Political Ignorance and Age: The Effects of Generation and Education

A number of recent studies have revealed a worrisomely low level of both political knowledge and voting turnout among younger Americans. We know, of course, that part of this is simply a life-experience effect, that, as with earlier generations, as they get older, more experienced, and, presumably, wiser, people become concerned with political matters and thus more likely to vote. But that is not all; there is also a generational factor at work. In comparison to young Americans of their parents' and grandparents' generation, young Americans at the end of the twentieth century were voting significantly less. The data from the National Election Surveys estimate voter turnout among those aged eighteen to twenty-four at 32 percent in the 1996 presidential election, compared with 50 percent of that age group who voted in 1972.[27] The data also show that a parallel development has been taking place with regard to political knowledge. A national survey of six hundred teenagers[28] found that while 74 percent could name Al Gore as vice-president, only 33 percent could name House speaker Newt Gingrich, 21 percent knew that there were one hundred senators, and 2 percent could name Supreme Court chief justice William Rehnquist. And in the *National Geographic* test reported on in the next chapter, while the United States placed sixth overall, its eighteen- to twenty-four-year-olds placed tenth and last, behind even Mexico, in geographical knowledge.

One useful source of information about political knowledge and the factors affecting it is to be found in the Pew News Interest Index. Looking at the results of one Pew survey, Parker and Deane (1997) point out that

> generation gaps in knowledge are . . . substantial. The great divide seems to be between those over 30 and those under 30. On average, 36% of those under 30 answered the information questions correctly, this compares with 45% of those age 30–49 and those 50 and over. Generation gaps can be seen on questions dealing with campaigns and elections and national politics. Only 26% of young people answered our campaign-related questions correctly, this compares with 38% of those 30–49 and 42% over those 50 and over. On national politics, young people averaged 32% correct, compared to 44% of middle aged Americans, and 48% of those 50 and older. . . . Big gaps also exist on international politics and policy, domestic policy, and military and terrorism. The gaps are smaller on crime, scandal and personality issues. Young people are nearly as well informed as their older counterparts when it comes to business and finance. . . .

Similarly, the Pew Research Center Biennial News Use Survey (of 4,002 adults taken in spring 1998) revealed that only 33 percent of Americans aged eighteen to twenty-nine made an effort to keep up with the news, compared to 68 percent of seniors (Bennett 1998). The lack of knowledge is attributed to lack of attentiveness. "Americans over age 50 are much more attentive to a variety of types of news, particularly when compared with those under age 30. This comes across clearly in the attention paid to politics and policy. Those over 50 are almost twice as likely as members of Generation X to say they follow national politics and domestic policy very closely, and 10 percentage points more likely to follow election campaigns and international politics."

It would be comforting to ascribe these differences to life-experience effects. The reality is otherwise. A 1990 study by the Times-Mirror Center reported that young people have not always trailed in political knowledge. Survey results from the 1940s through the 1970s reveal that previous generations of young people knew as much as, if not more than, their elders. Thus, something has happened that is generational, something that goes well beyond the age replacement taking place among adult Americans. A clue is provided by a study of first-year college students (reported in the *New York Times*, 12 January 1998: A10), which found "a record low of 26.7 percent [who] thought that 'keeping up to date with political affairs' was a very important or essential life goal, compared with 29.4 percent in 1996 and a high of 57.8 percent in 1966."

Clearly the political realm is less relevant to young people today than was the case with earlier, less educated generations. So we find ourselves with a historical paradox parallel to that identified earlier, namely, that the positive relationship at the individual level is washed out at the aggregate level. This latter puzzle, as suggested in chapter 2, is in part attributable to institutional or "supply side" factors to be considered in chapters 5 and 6. But there is more. And this is revealed by the fact that the puzzle reemerges in comparing American generations: earlier generations were less educated but more politically knowledgeable (and voted more); yet individually, more highly educated people are still better informed and more likely to cast a ballot.

It would seem that there are two potential effects of education: one directly tied to factual political information, the other to cognitive proficiency. In chapter 9 we shall look at these two aspects of the educational system in detail. It seems clear, however, that we cannot today count on the formal educational system to supply the former. But what about the latter? What do we know of the effects of education on cognitive proficiency, that is, the ability to comprehend relevant information to which one has access, typically in written form?[29] Fortunately, we know a fair amount thanks to the International Adult Literacy Survey (IALS), the comprehensive comparative study mentioned in chapter 1.

Beginning in chapter 4, we shall make intensive use of the results of the IALS. Relevant here is the finding, in the section on age and literacy (OECD 1997: 68–71), that functional literacy is significantly lower among Americans sixteen to thirty years old than for those between thirty and fifty, the opposite of what is found for the five other countries compared in that section.[30] This would help account for the striking generational drop in political knowledge and, in part, political participation.

For now, we seem to be on the track toward reconciling the results of American individual-level and aggregate data. Controlling for all other relevant factors, it is true, in the United States as elsewhere, that for an individual, an added year of education has a positive effect on political knowledge and, thus, political participation. Nevertheless, in some countries more than others, and especially in the United States, for which we have the needed individual-level data, the generational effect is in the other direction. Independent of other factors that also have a negative effect on political knowledge and, thus, political participation, the education being provided to current generations—even though it is educating more of them longer—is not doing the job it once did. In later chapters we explore the implications of this disturbing development.

II

Sources of Civic Literacy

If you could see what I see every day in my job, you would understand where all the guns and gangs and violence come from . . . TV is the whole existence for a new class of silent people. Look all around you in the Southwest; most of the buildings you see are mobile homes. Inside most of these homes are filthy people who can't read who don't talk to each other. . . . The little money they have is used to install cable TV.

CAYCE BOONE,
cable TV installer (quoted in Kaplan 1999: 181)

4

Civic Literacy in Comparative Context

Part one set the stage by outlining the conceptual and empirical landscape of our investigation. It is now time to give shape to this outline—beginning with our conceptual framework. Up to now, the terms most commonly used to denote the key variables in our argument were civic engagement and political knowledge. Both, it was argued, find expression in political participation—especially that which takes the form of voting in local elections. While some illustrative data were presented, there was little effort at systematic comparative analysis. To undertake such analysis we need first to concretize our conceptual framework and make explicit to which purposes our concepts will be put. To begin, we need a single term that clearly and unmistakably identifies what it is we are investigating.

Why Civic Literacy

So far we have referred to political knowledge. Conceptually, it is easy to grasp what is meant by this term. Knowledge is information that is (presumed to be) accurate. For an individual, having political knowledge constitutes being aware of, for example, the prime minister's name and party affiliation and that party's policy on deficit spending or abortion. It is fairly easy to test which of two individuals has greater political knowledge. But comparison at the aggregate level is problematic: what does it mean to say, for example, that political knowledge is higher in New Zealand than in the United States? Obviously, given the plethora of books about politics and the quantity and quality of political scientists in the United States, it cannot mean that the "stock" of political knowledge is higher in New Zealand.

This, as already noted, is what makes the concept of social capital problematic. If social capital can be stocked, it suggests that its overall quantity in a given community is in effect independent of the number or proportion of individuals in which it is invested. This is the real implication of Putnam's including in his social capital index a majority of indicators that are "stockable."[1] Taken to its logical extreme, it means that an individual bowling in five leagues adds five times as much to the "stock" of social capital as an individual bowling in only one.

In theory at least, the term *knowledge* invites the same inference: that one person reading five books is the equivalent of five reading one. Hence, despite its being used by many scholars working in this field,[2] it is nevertheless inferior to a term that carries a clear inference that the variable under investigation cannot be compounded or stocked. The concept of literacy serves this purpose extremely well. In normal usage, one is either literate or one is not. When used as an aggregate for comparative purposes, it is clearly understood that a society's level of literacy refers to the percentage of the population corresponding to whatever criteria are used to determine literacy. You cannot build up a "stock" of literacy by having a "very literate" minority.

To say this is not to fall into absolutism on the other side. When we go beyond the simple capacity to read and write—and even there, there is a gray area—no existing or even hypothetical test of political or any other knowledge allows for a simple black-and-white distinction. The increasingly authoritative functional literacy scale of the International Adult Literacy Survey (IALS) provides three such points (on three separate scales), leaving it up to the user of the data to choose which criterion for functional literacy is to be adopted.[3] This serves as a reminder that when used for aggregate purposes, even the most sophisticated indicators remain crude devices, and one should not be misled by the precise mathematical expression of the results of such tests in making comparisons.

With these caveats in mind, we return to the search for the appropriate term for comparing countries according to the proportion of persons having the information and capacity to be competent citizens. Westholm, Lindquist, and Niemi (1989) refer to *political literacy*, which is accurate but is insufficiently identified in the public mind as closely linked with citizenship and civic engagement.[4] The solution is to use the term *civic literacy*,[5] the roots of which lie in the Latin term for community, *civis*, from which the word citizen is derived. (Hence courses of instruction in the political information required for effective citizenship are known as civics courses.[6] *Civic* is the adjective that best corresponds to the kind of knowledge and information we are concerned with, that relevant to exercising one's role as a citizen, as a member of the community.[7] In addition, the term has an additional dimension of meaning, one conveyed by the expression "civic engagement," and connected to the particular approach taken here. Our own focus on voting at the municipal or local level is evoked in the association of the term with the local municipality or "civic community."

Civic literacy[8] is thus at the center of what this book is about. It is both an attribute of the individual and an aggregate indicator allowing for the comparison of societies according to the proportion of civically literate individuals, that is, possessing the knowledge required for effective political choice. Given that innate abilities are distributed roughly equally in the societies under consideration, a country's level of civil literacy is an indicator of the efficacy of its political knowledge-enhancing institutions. Of course, comparisons based on empirical measures are always tentative, since it is reasonable to suppose that the quantity of political knowledge needed to be a competent citizen in the United States is somewhat greater, given the size differences and the complexity of American institutions, than, say, in New Zealand.[9]

Having established what is meant by civic literacy, the next step is to operationalize the concept, to identify what we shall use as indicators. In entering this terrain we confront a problem already encountered in the debate of indicators of social capital: just what is the relationship between the indicator and that which it is indicating the presence of? Only by treating social capital as purely exogenous—by eschewing indicators tied to individual characteristics or attitudes not built into the institutional relationships in question—can we resolve the problem that the indicators signal both the presence of civic literacy and point to its cause. But this comes at too high a cost, for it means that the kinds of comparisons here envisaged are rendered impossible. Hence to engage in analytical work of this kind means living with and within these constraints as we apply our concept to the realities of the countries being compared.

Indicators of Civic Literacy: Comparing Factual Knowledge

As noted, compared to the standard indicators of social capital, civic literacy has the advantage of being objectively testable; that is, one can use questions with right and wrong answers. Unfortunately, this advantage cannot be optimally exploited, since we do not have available the required instrument to be used for such purposes. There is no country-neutral battery of political knowledge-oriented questions comparable to those devised for and extensively used in the American studies discussed in chapter 3. Instead, the proliferating teams of social science researchers administering the same surveys in different countries have tended to avoid political knowledge-oriented questions.

Standardized questions are common when it comes to attitudes and opinions probed by the many political scientists collaborating in the international groups seeking to explain different aspects of voting behavior. It has now become automatic to pose a number of political efficacy and horizontal trust-related questions, such as: "do you agree that 'politicians don't care about ordinary people like me?'"[10] Concern with political efficacy originated in the 1958 National Election Studies (NES) based at the University of Michigan, which remains at the center of international academic networks conducting voter surveys. The current (1999) NES Guide reports on the longitudinal results in answers to thirteen questions asked in each of its surveys: five about trust in government; four about the respondents' sense of political efficacy; and four addressing their assessment of government responsiveness. In comparison, the four dealing with political knowledge—the results of which were presented in chapter 3—make for rather small change.

Of course, the relative infrequency of questions getting at political knowledge is understandable. Apart from the effort required to agree on the content of such questions given differences in political institutions, researchers are reluctant to embarrass the subject by posing questions that may reveal the subject's ignorance and may bring the interview to a sudden end (Lambert et al. 1988: 360). Posing such questions in international projects can also raise problems with funding organizations, perhaps even running the risk of having certain countries pull out of the projects. Whatever the reason, researchers avoid seeking cross-cultural validity for questionnaire data on political information.

I write from firsthand experience. The obvious choice for devising and posing a country-neutral battery of political knowledge-oriented questions is the CSES (Comparative Study of Electoral Systems) group (see Rosenstone 1995), based at the University of Michigan. CSES was formed to devise a common instrument to be used by national election surveys in its roughly fifity participating countries. The original intent was to include common political knowledge questions, but this was rejected.[11] Instead, the teams were asked to put three political information questions to their respondents, but the content was left up to them. The only stipulation was that they be designed so that, respectively, they could be answered correctly by roughly two-thirds, one-third, and one-half of respondents, a condition that could not always be fulfilled.[12] (The content of the questions and the breakdown of the responses for Australia, Canada, Denmark, Germany, Great Britain, New Zealand, and the United States are to be found in appendix I. These are the countries here being analyzed for which data were available in summer 2000 for elections that took place since 1996, when the CSES project was formally initiated.) Unfortunately, as appendix I reveals, the questions are far too varied for any systematic comparative analysis. Moreover, a few of the participating countries, Australia for example, use a self-completion survey. While this is unlikely to affect significantly responses to other questions, this is not the case with factual questions, which, though they avoid embarrassing the respondent, run the risk that the answers reflect the knowledge of more than one person.

In the absence of the required instrument, we have no comparative indicator of political knowledge comparable to our measure of average local voting turnout.[13] Yet there is no intrinsic reason why an instrument that meets the requisite criteria of reliability could not be developed. A possible starting point would be for teams in each country to begin by identifying the (say, four) most important political positions in their country (prime minister, finance minister, etc.) in order, and asking respondents the names and political affiliations of the persons occupying those positions.[14] Another series of questions could test knowledge of major party positions on key issues and of basic constitutional and institutional practices such as the time lapse between general elections, the composition of legislative committees, or the specific powers of local governments.[15] To these could be added a set of questions testing familiarity with the role, structure, and leadership of international institutions, such as the United Nations and World Trade Order. Over time, through a number of pretests, an appropriate battery would emerge.

Given the absence of the requisite instruments, we are forced to rely on existing studies that in some way gauge and compare political knowledge. These are typically deficient in one or both of two ways: either the number of countries is too small or the questions are skewed toward subjects of greater salience in some countries than in others. Typical of studies with the latter deficiency are the Eurobarometers, a series of surveys carried out regularly under the auspices of the EU Commission since 1970. Almost all of the more recent surveys include a knowledge component. With, now, fifteen member states, the EU surveys draw samples from a reasonably large number of countries. Unfortunately, the questions concern only EU-related events or institutions, since they are designed to test—and thus aid in fostering—people's involvement and interest in the union. Apart from being less than ideal for wider comparisons, the questions attract responses that reflect not only differences in civic literacy among the member countries but also differences in length of membership in the European Union, the extent to which EU activities take place within the country's borders, and, of course, the legitimacy of the European integration project.

With these caveats, we can consult the least unsuitable of the Eurobarometer studies, those with a comparatively large and varied battery of questions. The most useful was administered in 1996 and reported in Eurobarometer #45. Respondents were queried on ten items concerning the European Union, including the name of the president of the European Commission, the number of commissioners from their country, the then recently chosen name for the European currency, the country holding the presidency of the European Union, and the city in which most of the EU institutions are located. Essentially the pattern is one of Germanic Europe and Scandinavia being more knowledgeable about the European Union than southern Europe, Britain, and Ireland. From the numbers, however, we cannot discern to what extent the differences reflect greater interest in the European Union as opposed to higher civic literacy. Response patterns to a question posed in one of the series of "Continuous Tracking Surveys" conducted for the European Commission[16] sheds some light on this. Positive responses to "have you read something about the EU in a daily newspaper in the past three months?" correspond reasonably well to knowledge levels identified by the Eurobarometer. One would expect that levels of people reading newspaper accounts of the European Union would even more closely reflect levels of interest in the European Union. That, however, is not the case as, reflected in responses to questions of interest in various aspects of the European Union: citizens' rights, the European currency, the powers and responsibilities, and the aims and objectives of the European Union, the functioning of its institutions, and its enlargement to include more countries. Overall, only the Danes were above average both in interest in the European Union and in having read about the European Union in a newspaper.

If, as argued in chapter 7, there is a close relationship between levels of daily newspaper reading and civic literacy, the results suggest that higher levels of civic literacy are the main factor accounting for the differences in knowledge of the European Union identified in the 1996 Eurobarometer, and that Scandinavia and Germanic Europe may be higher in civic literacy. But to go any further we need to combine the results of European surveys with those used in other countries. Here we confront the problem of questions chosen to meet specifically European (or rather EU) concerns, as well as parallel problems raised by a number of studies that compare only English-speaking industrial democracies. One such study (Baker et al. 1996) asked samples in Canada, the United States, and Britain a number of questions testing their knowledge of their countries' legislatures, and found, as we might expect from chapter 3, that the differences were significant enough to conclude the Americans were less politically knowledgeable.[17]

The first international study in recent years to draw public attention to important differences in levels of knowledge relevant to civic literacy was conducted for the *National Geographic* magazine (December 1989: 816–18). It asked samples of the populations in ten countries to locate sixteen places on the world map. (Sweden came first with 11.6 average right answers, followed by Germany with 11.2. Japan, France, and Canada followed with 9.6, 9.3, and 9.2 respectively, followed by the United States, U. K., and Italy with 8.6, 8.5, and 7.6. Mexico and Russia came last at 7.4.) A study conducted in January 1994 by the Times-Mirror Center for the People and the Press also used representative samples in countries on both sides of the Atlantic. Though the number of countries was few, the questions were more political in content. The differences in responses to

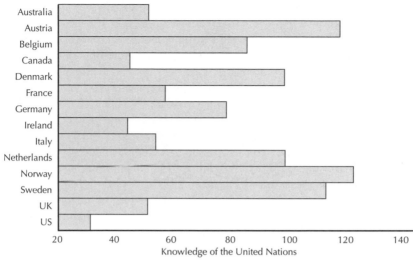

FIGURE 4-1   (Millard, 1993)

the five questions about current international affairs[18] proved striking: the U.S. respondents scored lowest (with an average of 1.67 right answers), then those of Canada (1.90), Britain (2.07), and France (2.13). The German respondents (with an average of 3.58 right answers) were far and away the most knowledgeable (Bennett et al. 1995: 43).

Overall, the impression so far is that people in (northern) continental European countries are more politically informed than people in the Atlantic English-speaking countries; the Americans are the least informed—at least concerning knowledge of international politics. This impression is reinforced by a survey even more skewed toward international politics—and thus, unfortunately, away from the kind of knowledge associated with civic competence—but with many more (fourteen) participating countries. The survey tested respondents' ability to identify the UN secretary general (from a list of five) and to name a UN agency (Millard 1993). As figure 4-1, which combines the percentage of correct answers on each question, illustrates, the results correspond reasonably well to the impressions gained from the above studies. The small countries of northern Europe had the highest awareness, followed by Germany, France, Italy, Australia, and the U.K., Canada, Ireland, and, finally, the United States brought up the rear.

Indicators of Civic Literacy: Comparing Cognitive Proficiency

There are no doubt other comparative studies of political knowledge, but none, to the best of this writer's knowledge, adds much substance to what has so far been reported. Given the potential that exists for comparing factual political knowledge, the actual state of affairs can only be described as disappointing. Indeed, were we to limit ourselves to these direct indicators, our capacity to compare countries would be impoverished indeed. Fortunately, there is another dimension to literacy. We have already drawn attention to comparative tests of cognitive—as opposed to factual—knowledge in the previous chapter. And here the data are richer, due in large part to the contribution of the International Adult Literacy Survey. This highly sophisticated cognitive proficiency test was developed jointly by Statistics Canada and the OECD. After the results from twelve countries were published (OECD 1997), eight more followed in the summer 2000. In what follows, I include the results for fourteen of the twenty: I exclude Poland, Portugal, Hungary, Slovakia, Chile, and the Czech Republic for reasons set out in the introduction. In addition, the IALS provides separate results for German and French Switzerland, which I have combined, weighing the former at two-thirds and the latter at one-third. Finally, the IALS figures for Belgium, it should also be noted, are in fact only for Flanders.

The IALS seeks to assess the extent to which people over sixteen years of age in each country possess the kind of literacy needed to be effective citizens in today's world. The study tests the level of comprehension of three types of written materials: narrative prose, documents such train schedules, and those requiring application of basic arithmetic skills. The IALS's descriptions of the three types of literacy, sample questions from each, and the definition of the five levels of literacy for each scale are set out in appendix II. Before going deeper into what the IALS has to teach us about the literacy side of civic literacy, it is worth drawing attention to a finding from the first round in the IALS (OECD 1994a), which highlights the relationship between functional literacy and the civic engagement side of civic literacy. In table 4–1 A (on the first page of appendix II) we see a clear positive relationship between participation in voluntary associations and functional literacy for each country taking the test, as well as indications of a positive aggregate relationship between countries' overall level of organizational participation and their level of functional literacy.

We can already see quite clear differences in functional literacy levels. Additional information is provided in figure 4–2, which displays for each country the average percentage of those scoring in the lowest category in the three tests (there are five categories in all). The level-one score from Figure 4–2 is an especially useful comparative indicator of functional literacy,[19] since level one leaves little doubt about the functional illiteracy of those so classified.[20]

As we can see, the ranking in figure 4–2 corresponds fairly well to differences in levels of factual political knowledge. The outstanding countries turn out to be those of Scandinavia, followed by the Netherlands and

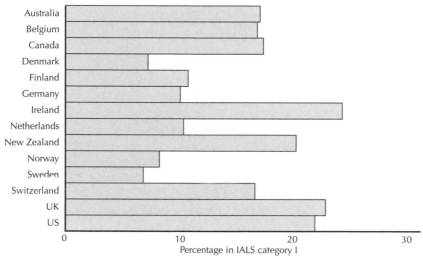

FIGURE 4-2 Functional Illiteracy Level

Germany. Australia fits into a wide middle category along with Belgium, Switzerland, and Canada and above those at the bottom: the United States, Britain, New Zealand, and Ireland.

While there have been a number of tests comparing the performance of students at similar levels in various countries over the past twenty years, the only recent study testing older students in the countries relevant here is a 1998 study limited to skills in mathematics and science, given, in this case, to students in the final year of secondary school (TIMSS 1998), and briefly mentioned in the preceding chapter. (Figure 4-3 sets out the combined average score in the two tests by country, while figure 4-4 sets out the average score for those at the bottom, i.e., at the 5 percent level.)

Of the countries included (Finland did not take part in TIMSS), those we have identified as having high levels of political participation—the Scandinavian countries and the Netherlands, but not Germany—score highly not only in average scores on math and science literacy but also, and especially, in the average score of students who placed lowest.[21]

As we see in figure 4-5, though the number of countries that participated in both surveys is too small to produce a statistically significant relationship, both clearly manifest the same tendency. Simply put, countries with lower levels of functional illiteracy among their adult populations are those with the highest levels of scientific literacy among the lower stratum of secondary students. This latter group consists of those who, we can assume, are nearing the end of their formal academic studies.

It is not unreasonable, therefore, to draw from figure 4-5 tentative confirmation of the point first raised in chapter 3, that a contributing factor to

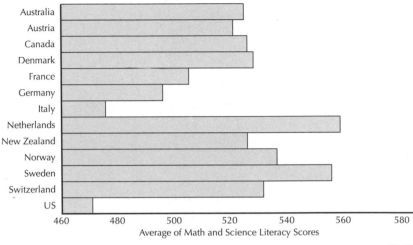

FIGURE 4-3   (TIMSS)

a society's level of civic literacy is the capacity of the schools to bring students at the bottom to a level of cognitive proficiency making possible the comprehension and retention of the factual knowledge required for civic competence. Of course cognitive capacity does not necessarily lead to factual knowledge. What happens in school is only a part of the story of civic literacy, and probably not the main part. This matter is taken up in chapter 9 when we examine civics courses in schools and adult education outside formal schooling, finding schooling to help create a disposition toward civic literacy, but one that must be reinforced in adult life.

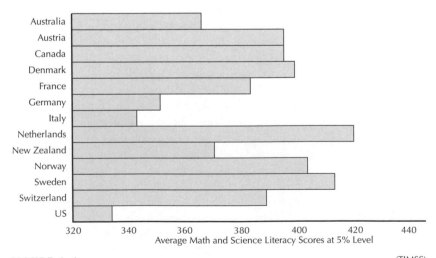

FIGURE 4-4   (TIMSS)

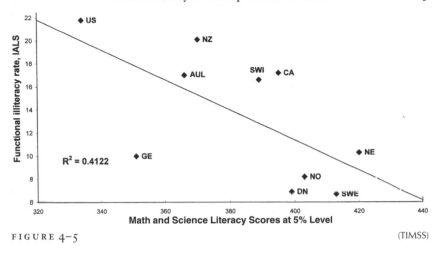

FIGURE 4-5 (TIMSS)

One aspect of the earlier (1997) IALS report highlights this fact. Breaking down the results on the document test by level of education attained and only for respondents with less than upper secondary level, the overall mean (for the eleven countries) is 238 (the cutoff point for level one is 225), with the United States lowest at 200 and Sweden (the only Nordic participant) highest at 281. The difference is due to a combination of schooling, mobility, and economic inequality. "In Sweden . . . youth whose parents had completed only the 8th grade, scored on average 13 percent above the international average; whereas in the United States, the country with the greatest inequalities, youth with similar family backgrounds scored 60 percent of a standard deviation below the international mean" (OECD 1997: 75).

Civic Literacy: What We Know So Far

By combining our limited knowledge of differences on the factual and cognitive dimensions of political knowledge, we are getting a better, if still incomplete, picture of differences in civic literacy in our effort to compensate for the absence of a standardized test of political knowledge. Let us see if the results on the best of the comparative factual knowledge indicators available to us correspond to those on our indicator of cognitive proficiency. Indeed they do: figure 4–6 shows a very high positive relationship between functional literacy and knowledge of the United Nations for the countries participating in both surveys.

For the time being, we provisionally use levels of functional literacy and knowledge of the United Nations as proxy indicators of the literacy

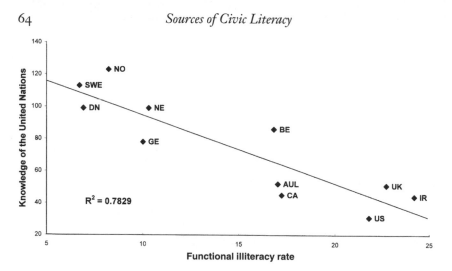

FIGURE 4-6   **F= 32.718, sig F= 0.000**

dimension of civic literacy. To complete this chapter, it remains only to test the relationship between these proxy measures and our indicator of the civic dimension of civic literacy, namely, average turnout in local elections. To restate the logic in using turnout in this way: more politically informed people, other things being equal, are seen as more likely to vote than those ill informed, especially at the local level. Hence average levels of turnout in such elections reflect the proportion of people with both the capacity and knowledge to be active citizens.

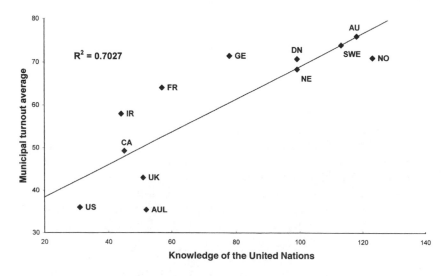

FIGURE 4-7   **F= 23.637, sig F= 0.0007**

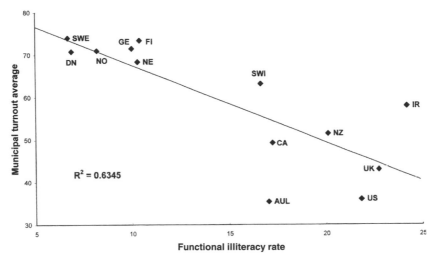

FIGURE 4-8   F= 18.902, sig F= 0.001

If this is true, there should be a correspondence between the two proxy indicators of the literacy side of civic literacy with what we know of average turnout in local elections as set out in chapter 2. Figures 4–7 and 4–8 chart the relationship between municipal turnout to knowledge of the United Nations and to functional literacy (the proportion of the population with the basic literacy skills needed for competent citizenship, i.e., those above IALS level one). The unambiguously positive correlations more than meet our expectations.

Of course, the deficiencies of our test of political knowledge and the limited number of cases inhibit our reading too much into these figures. Still, the strong negative relationship of average turnout with the proportion of adults lacking the basic literacy skills to exercise informed citizenship suggests that our approach to civic literacy is on the right track. We have in this chapter stressed the literacy side; it is time to return to the civic side, to the factors associated with political participation.

5

Political Participation and
Political Institutions

Addressing the British Labour Party Conference in September 1998 on the results of the local elections that had just taken place in which some 12,000 Labour councillors were elected, Sir Jeremy Beecham pointed out:

> Most of us couldn't claim to have been elected on a 40 percent ballot! In my own ward this year I was returned with 75% of the vote on a pitiful turnout of 16%. But then not a door was knocked on nor a leaflet delivered by the Conservative or Liberal Democrat candidates, neither of whom even turned up to the count! One can hardly blame the electorate for failing to vote when the result appears to be a foregone conclusion.

Indeed. The blame for low turnout does not lie with the voters; but it also does not lie with the candidates. In chapter 3, we noted that while turnout reflects the efforts on the part of political actors to get voters to the polls by supplying them with information, underlying that effort—or lack of it—are institutionalized incentives. Why campaign against someone with a 50 percent lead in a single-member district? Political institutions matter, and they matter particularly with regard to local political participation.

Hence, if we are interested in turnout, and especially turnout in local elections, we cannot look only at the effects of variations in political knowledge or capabilities, at the literacy side of civic literacy stressed in chapter 4. The extent to which voters are informed on matters relevant to the decision to vote is in fact closely linked to the political institutions in which elections take place. We must consult another, extensive, literature in political science that addresses the effects of political institutions on voting behavior. The findings from this literature, we shall see, raise the civic literacy concerns. Interestingly, these concerns are seldom explicitly addressed in this literature[1]—something we shall try to change. Put schematically, there is a three-way relationship between civic literacy, political (especially electoral) institutions, and political participation. We have so far considered the relationship between voter turnout, and civic literacy. This chapter delves more deeply into explanations for voter turnout bringing into focus the institutional dimension. In chapter 6 attention shifts to the third duo, the relationship between civic literacy and political institutions.

In the earlier discussion about why people "bother" to vote, it was noted that the economic model of the "rational voter," when correctly applied, draws our attention to the information needed and the costs of attaining it. This is not to deny the cost of the physical act of voting: making registration easier or imposing a fine on failing to vote can and does affect turnout. Franklin (1996: 226–30) estimates the average boost to turnout at about 4 percent for postal voting and 5 to 6 percent for weekend voting.[2] Similarly, Wolfinger and Rosenstone (1980: 88) claim that turnout in the United States could be increased by an average of up to 15 percent if registration were made the responsibility of the state, as it is in most democratic countries,[3] though Wattenberg (1998: 6), testing for the difficulties associated with registration in different American states, finds their impact to be "relatively minor."[4] Another institutional factor is the frequency of elections. Observers have noted that Americans are called on to vote more frequently than people in every other democratic country (except Switzerland); hence "voter fatigue" may help explain the low turnout in these two countries.[5]

At the municipal level, institutions that link politics to administration have an important effect. For example, Bridges (1997: 98) sets out a litany of the features of what she terms "Big-city Reform" systems, which, by the 1960s, characterized nearly every big city in the American Southwest. "The institutions of local politics, ambitions of the leaders of big-city reform growth machines, the desires of their middle-class residents, and the near exclusion of other residents from participation and representation worked together to create political orders of almost unassailable strength and durability." Apart from institutional barriers to voting such as registration restrictions, poll taxes, and literacy tests, and the placement of polling stations, which discouraged voting by the poor and racial minorities, there was also the effect of institutional arrangements associated with reform politics, nonpartisanship, nonconcurrent elections, and the noncompetitiveness of elections. As a result, turnout was highest in affluent neighborhoods, and incumbents were regularly reelected. But overall turnout was much lower than in cities that were not "machine descendant," such as New York, Chicago, and New Haven. For all their flaws, these machine-descendant systems had strong party organizations, substantial patronage resources, and concurrent elections, which often combined to bring the majority of citizens to the polls.[6]

It is a well-documented fact that United States congressional elections known to be close contests generate significantly higher turnout.[7] This is not fully explained by the increased chance of the voter affecting the outcome, since, in reality, the likelihood of affecting the outcome remains minuscule. There must be an indirect effect, that of parties investing more effort and money in close contests.[8] A Canadian study found a similar, though weak, association between both the closeness of elections and party spending in the constituencies and turnout in the 1980 and 1984 Canadian elections.[9] A recent study of political participation in American states suggests that party investment of resources, if it is to boost political participation, must include "direct party contact [which] is a strong predictor of levels of political and community engagement, even when we control for the competitiveness of state political competition" (Weinstein, 1999: 1).

A related matter explored in the literature links voting turnout to the relative importance or "salience" of elections, thus explaining, for example, lower turnout in both European parliamentary elections and local, state, and off-year U.S. congressional elections compared to national elections. Elections at these levels have been termed "second-order elections," that is, elections in which less is at stake than in those affecting who will control national executive power (Reif and Schmitt 1980). Salience does account for the fact that the average levels of turnout in local elections in the countries here being studied (with the notable exception of Switzerland) are lower than for national elections. But it does not seem to account to any significant degree for differences in average levels of local turnout. Countries high in turnout at national levels tend to be so at local levels, largely irrespective of the degree of "second-orderness" of local government.[10]

Only if understood subjectively can salience account for low turnout in these "second-order" elections. For example, although turnout for European Parliament (EP) elections is always lower than for national elections, there are significant variations by country. Turnout in the 1994 EP elections averaged 58.3 percent (Smith 1995), but both the British and Dutch turned out at less than 40 percent. The fact that the well-informed Dutch know how little the EP actually does may explain their low turnout, while negative feelings toward the European Union must be taken into account in explaining the equally low turnout of the relatively poorly informed British.[11]

Salience is thus mainly in the eyes of the beholder, a measure of the ability of local political leaders to get the attention of the voter above and beyond their actual administrative clout. Indeed, some members of the British government presented their May 1999 proposal to extend the direct election of mayors beyond London as a way of increasing voter turnout. In sum, turning out to vote in local elections seems more to reflect the level of public attention given to civic political activity than the actual administrative clout of local officials.

The most important institutional factor, one that has been analyzed at great depth, has to do with the electoral system used, especially the degree to which it assures that outcomes in terms of seats are proportional to support for parties expressed in the vote. Instead of here entering the debate over the effects of electoral systems on government performance, I start from Lijphart's (1999) assessment, based on many years of looking at the effects of electoral systems in democratic societies: there is no trade-off between proportionality and government efficiency; but there is a positive relationship between proportionality and the representation of women and ethnic minorities. Thus the discussion of the effects of electoral systems is limited to the relationship between proportionality and turnout.[12]

Lijphart (1997) in his 1996 presidential address to the American Political Science Association summarized the comparative literature, arriving at an estimated turnout boost of 9 to 12 percent due to proportional representation (PR). A somewhat similar estimate is offered by Franklin, who calculates a boost of 0.6 percent in turnout for every percent by which the distribution of seats in the legislature approaches proportionality with the distribution of votes (Franklin 1996: 226). But there are problems with using aggregate data of this kind. The turnout boost is a statement of a statistical and not necessarily causal relationship. It could be that higher turnout is due to aspects of the national political cultures of the higher turnout countries, which favor both political participation and the selection of proportional, that is, "fair" electoral systems. A potential further advantage from studying turnout in local elections is thus that it can potentially overcome such problems inherent in cross-national comparisons. Comparing subunits in the same country more readily allows us to isolate the influence of a single variable by keeping others—that is, those associated with the particularities of the national culture—constant. If local turnout levels vary significantly within the same country, we can be more confident of an explanation based on identified differences in political institutions.

This is a field of research with great potential that has so far been little developed. Indeed, there is practically no comparative literature purporting to explain different levels of turnout in local elections. While it is admittedly difficult to find countries that have both significant institutional variation in local electoral systems and sufficiently differentiated data, at least three serve the needed purpose.[13] The following section shows the potential richness of such an exploration, making use of data assembled from Norway, Australia, and, especially, Switzerland.

Norway

The relevant Norwegian data are historical, since all elections in Norwegian municipalities have used PR since the 1960s. But Norway has remarkably complete historical data on local elections going right back to the advent of electoral democracy. It is these data that prompted Rokkan's influential analysis of the relationship between political participation, proportional elections, and the presence of political parties (Rokkan et al. 1970, 191–99). The only systematic examination of the turnout data is to be found in a little-known paper by Hjellum (1967). Table 5–1 is drawn from figures Hjellum collected based on local election results from 1913 to 1961 in western Norway, the region where proportional elections were slowest to arrive. Overall, for the election years he looks at, turnout averaged 60 percent in municipal elections in western Norway contested under PR and 42 percent in those contested under the majority system. The increase, he concludes, was due primarily to voters under the PR system being able to vote for candidates from lists presented by organized groups and that those groups would be represented proportionately on the municipal councils. The increase specifically due to the national parties presenting such lists, he suggests, are fairly minor (Hjellum 1967: 83–84).

Hjellum's findings also raise questions as to the effect of the size of the municipality. The literature on political participation offers two alternate theses on the effect of size (Verba and Nie 1972). According to the "mobilization model," participation increases with the size of the community as larger cities have more and more powerful political organizations to mobilize citizens and politicize decision-making. According to the "decline-of-community model," participation is lower in the more anonymous cities than in smaller towns because the city dwellers are less integrated into

TABLE 5–1

Turnout in Local Elections in Western Norway (Majority versus PR)

Year	Non-PR Elections (%)	Majority Turnout (%)	PR Turnout (%)
1913	83.3	30.0	54.0
1919	49.3	36.5	55.0
1925	26.2	37.4	56.0
1931	23.0	31.7	54.0
1937	5.7	47.2	62.0
1955	7.3	51.2	64.0
1959	6.0	50.9	65.0
1963	5.9	52.2	71.0

Source: Hjellum 1967.

TABLE 5–2

Turnout in Norwegian Local Elections

	1913		1916	
	Avg. Turnout	(N)	Avg. Turnout	(N)
Communes using PR	.554	(337)	.524	(375)
Under 400 population	.582	(26)	.531	(23)
Over 4,000 population	.642	(17)	.603	(26)
Communes not using PR	.339	(241)	.296	(238)
Under 400 population	.381	(39)	.279	(199)

community life. To test these, I retrieved the original data from the National Data Archives in Bergen for the 1913 and 1916 elections, a period when both kinds of elections were still common. Table 5–2, which sets out the turnout figures under each type of electoral system for all Norwegian municipalities, reveals differences in favor of PR even slightly greater than for western Norway. Table 5–2 controls somewhat for size, by giving separate figures for small towns, with less than 400 population, and cities, with more than 4,000 (of which all seventeen used PR). Like Hjellum, we find little impact due to size—the mobilization and decline-of-community factors apparently canceling each other out.

It is clear that politicization of local politics was taking place in Norway in the first half of this century. The adoption of PR was itself a result of that politicization, but PR contributed independently to increased turnout. It is not possible, though, looking back over a process so far back and over so many years, to say to just what degree. To do so we need to look at countries using more than one electoral system in local elections today.

Australia

While unitary Norway universalized the system used in local elections, federal Australia has not. A partial form of PR is used to elect Australia's Senate as well as the upper houses in all six states except Tasmania, where it is used to elect the lower house. We noted earlier that compulsory voting in these elections means that we cannot fairly compare turnout in Australia with that of jurisdictions without compulsory voting. Fortunately, there are three states in which municipal voting is voluntary, Tasmania, South Australia, and Western Australia, one of which, Tasmania, uses PR.[14] Unlike Norway and Switzerland (see below), however, municipal politics is typically contested by individual candidates and local organizations with few formal or public links to the national political parties.

TABLE 5–3

Average Turnout in Recent Local Elections

Year	Tasmania Avg. Turnout	Western Australia Avg. Turnout	South Australia Avg. Turnout
1993		14.1	17.3
1994	55		
1995		15.8	18.8
1996	59		
1997		25.0	34.4
1999	55		

Data from the electoral commissions or local government departments in each of the three states (see table 5–3) show, for South Australia and Western Australia in the most recent three rounds of municipal elections, overall turnouts of about 17.3, 18.8, and 34.4 percent in South Australia, and 14.1, 15.8. and 25.0 percent in Western Australia.[15] These compare poorly to the 55, 59, and 55 percent turnout in Tasmania. Since Tasmania used a form of postal ballot in all three of the elections, it is fairer to compare the outcomes only to the most recent (1997) elections when the other two states did the same.[16] Even so, there is still a large discrepancy, as we can see in table 5–3.[17] These figures support the above findings that PR boosts turnout even in the absence of formal involvement by political parties.[18]

Switzerland

Switzerland is the country allowing us to test these hypotheses most fully since voting is not compulsory and both majority and proportional elections take place at the municipal level. As noted earlier, Switzerland's potential would have been left untapped if research were restricted to data from official public sources, since no agency assembles the data from the over three thousand communes (municipalities). It is access to information from the 1988 survey conducted by Andreas Ladner and his colleagues,[19] which produced comprehensive data on 81.6 percent of the Swiss communes (see Ladner and Milner 1999), that makes what follows possible.

TABLE 5–4

Electoral Systems in Swiss Communes

	Percentage	Number of Communities
Majority voting	1.6	1695
Proportional system	28.4	671

TABLE 5–5

Voting System for Communal Executives

Canton	Majority System (%)	PR System (%)	Communities (N)
Valais	2	79	123
Solothurn	26	74	104
Jura	42	58	71
Fribourg	47	53	191
Bern	60	4	341
Basel-Land	83	17	65
Thurgau	95	5	106
Graubünden	99	1	151

While PR elections[20] have become the norm at higher levels, a large number of communes use majority systems to elect their communal executive.[21] Table 5–4 sets out the overall data. As in the case of the Australian states, legislation in eighteen cantons governs the electoral system: two impose PR (Zug and Tessin), while sixteen impose the majority system. Of particular interest here are the remaining eight cantons (Bern, Fribourg, Solothurn, Basel-Land, Graubunden, Thurgau, Valais, and Jura) where some communes use PR and some use majority systems. As we see in Table 5–5, while the latter is found in large numbers of communes in all eight, PR is commonly used only in five: Valais, Solothurn, Jura, Fribourg, and Bern.

Breaking the communes down by size (in table 5–6), we find that only 15 percent of the smallest communities use PR, a figure that rises to 70 per cent of those with 5,000 or more inhabitants. The connection between size of municipality and voting system chosen was already noted with regard to Norway: smaller communes find it harder to attain the degree of political organization needed to put together the lists required under PR.[22]

TABLE 5–6

Voting System and Turnout at Elections for Communal Executive in the Five Cantons

Population	Majority		PR		Diff. (%)	Sig.
	Average (%)	N	Average (%)	N		
All communities	50	341	71	432	21	**
1–499	56	216	78	109	22	**
500–1,999	38	101	75	180	37	**
2,000–4,999	39	20	67	93	28	**
5,000–9,999	51	2	58	30	7	n.s.
10,000+	48	2	52	20	4	n.s.

** = significance (F) 0.001

As we see in table 5–6, the overall average turnouts in communal elections in the over twenty-three hundred municipalities in the survey conforms to expectations. Participation averaged 71 percent in the 28 percent of communities using PR, compared to only 50 percent in those using a majority system. Such a difference is, of course, statistically highly significant. It remains significant—58 percent in majority communities compared to 73 percent in PR communities—after we eliminate the approximately 15 percent of the (as a rule, very small) communities in which executive elections take place not at the polls but at a communal assembly.

Moreover, the data better fit the "mobilization" than the "decline-of-community" model: on average, participation is significantly lower in Swiss cities than in the towns. To see the real influence of the electoral system on turnout we thus need to control for size. In addition, to control for possible regional cultural differences, we begin by limiting our observations to Bern, Fribourg, Solothurn, Valais, and Jura, the cantons in which both voting systems are used by at least 20 percent of communes. Without controlling for size, the differences in the rate of participation conform to our overall finding. As we see in table 5–6, the average turnout for majority elections is 50 percent, while for PR elections it is 71 percent.

In the five cantons there are altogether fifteen cities with over 5,000 inhabitants, and only four use a majority system. While turnout is higher in the eleven PR cities, unlike in the smaller communities, the difference is not statistically significant due to the low number of cities. Table 5–7 provides the data for all communes in the five cantons, excluding only those with communal assembly voting. Because majority communities are concentrated among the high-turnout small towns and villages, and PR systems in the low-turnout cities, the average difference in turnout between majority communities and PR communities is only 5 percent. But if we compare communities of more or less equal size, the differences

TABLE 5–7

Voting System and Turnout for Communal Executive Elections in the Five Cantons (excluding communes using communal assemblies)

Population	Majority Average(%)	N	PR Average (%)	N	Diff. (%)	Sig.
All communities	67	185	72	428	5	**
1–499	69	134	78	107	9	**
500–1,999	63	35	75	178	12	**
2,000–4,999	56	12	67	93	13	*
5,000–9,999	51	2	58	30	7	n.s.
10,000+	48	2	52	20	4	n.s.

* = significance (F) 0.05; ** = significance (F) 0.001

TABLE 5–8

Voting System and Number of Political Parties, by Size of Community (only communities with elections at the polls)

Population	Majority		PR		
	Avg. No. Parties	N	Avg. No. Parties	N	Sig.
All communities	1.5	199	2.9	442	**
1–499	1.2	144	1.8	112	*
500–1999	1.8	38	2.7	187	**
2,000–4,999	3.2	12	3.4	93	n.s.
5,000–9,999	5.5	2	4.4	30	n.s.
10,000+	6.7	3	6.6	20	n.s.

* = significance (F) 0.05; ** = significance (F) 0.001

remain substantial—at least for the communes smaller than 5,000 inhabitants, where the differences are between 9 and 13 percent.

Using these figures we next test the effect of politicization. In PR systems, the hurdles that must be overcome to win a seat are lower, making it easier for more political groups to compete under PR (Katz 1980). This proves to be clearly the case when one looks at Swiss communes. Table 5–8 shows that, on average, there are almost twice as many parties in PR as in majority communities. Yet, interestingly, the positive effect of the PR system on the representation of smaller parties holds only in smaller communities. As we see in table 5–8, the relationship between the number of parties and the electoral system vanishes once a certain threshold of size is attained.

Thus it appears that proportional systems do have a positive influence on voter turnout. Moreover, this effect is also linked to the party system through the mobilization effect—but only in smaller communities. From this we infer that the extra turnout boost associated with PR in the smaller communities is through party politicization, while the more limited boost

TABLE 5–9

Voting System, Turnout at Communal Executive Elections, and Number of Parties

Population	Majority			PR				
	Average Participation (%)	Avg. No Parties	N	Average Participation (%)	Avg. No. Parties	N	Diff. (%)	Sig.
10,000+	42	6.9	61	50	6.6.	34	8	**

** = significance (F) 0.001

in the cities is related to the effect of PR itself irrespective of its effect on parties.[23]

Our analysis of the effects of PR on voter turnout in the larger communities is marred by the small number of cities—especially majoritarian ones—in the five mixed cantons. To rectify this, table 5–9 assembles the data on turnout in all Swiss communities over 10,000 in population. The overall difference between PR and majoritarian cities corresponds to the lower end of the expectations from the cross-national literature, namely, an average of 8 percent.

Before going further, as Swiss society is culturally, linguistically, and religiously diverse, and this is reflected in the profiles of the cities, we need to ascertain to what extent these factors are intervening variables. Fortunately, the richness of the Swiss data affords us a means of so testing since it includes the national and the canton election participation rates of each commune as well as the results of the communal executive elections.

If cultural diversity is the prime explanation for turnout differences between the cities, then this should show up in different turnout rates not just for the communal elections but also for the cantonal and national elections. (Only at the communal election do we have diverse electoral systems; at the cantonal and national level the same system is employed throughout the country.) The numbers in table 5–10 suggest that there is something going on beyond the "cultural" factor, since voter participation is greater at every level in communities using PR to elect their communal executives.

We are not in a position here to pinpoint the basis of this difference or to rule out any difference reflecting language or religion. It may be it is a "spillover effect," that the tendency toward higher participation at the communal level caused by PR has found its way into the political culture surrounding voting at the other levels. To be certain, though, if we wish to use numbers to capture the "pure" effect of PR, we must subtract the variation at the cantonal level (which is greater than at the national level) from

TABLE 5–10

Voting System and Turnout at Communal, Cantonal, and National Elections

Population	Level	Majority (%)	N	PR (%)	N	Diff. (%)	Sig.
<10,000	communal	43	90	60	46	17	**
	cantonal	41	89	51	42	10	**
	national	43	88	50	43	7	**
≥10,000	communal	42	61	50	34	8	**
	cantonal	41	61	46	32	5	*
	national	43	60	47	33	4	*

*= significance (F) 0.05; **= significance (F) 0.001.

that at the communal level. As we see in table 5–10, the average difference in turnout at the national and cantonal level is not as great as at the communal level. In the 5,000 to 10,000 population category, the average difference is 10 and 7 percent versus 17 percent, while it is and 4 and 5 percent versus 8 percent in the over 10,000 category. We can thus conclude that, at a minimum, PR itself boosts turnout between 3 and 10 percent, or an average of 5 percent.

In sum, the Swiss numbers have allowed us to isolate the minimal or "pure" effect of proportional elections on turnout that we were unable to isolate in our analysis of Norwegian and Australian data. PR seems to bring something like an additional 5 percent of citizens to the polls beyond its indirect effect through enhancing party politicization. Yet, while it is easy to understand the indirect effect, how PR makes it easier for organized parties to be present, and how their activities can raise turnout, we are still left unclear as to just what the direct effect might be. How are we to explain that extra 5 percent, the "pure" effect of PR elections on turnout? That explanation, chapter 6 will show, lies in the missing link between political institutions and voter turnout, namely, civic literacy.

6

Civic Literacy and Political Institutions

How can it be that even when we control for the presence of political parties and levels of participation at the level of the canton and the nation, Swiss citizens in PR communes vote more? Can it be that citizens of the same canton can be more politically informed simply because they live in towns using PR? If so, there is something specific about the use of PR that contributes an element of coherence or comprehensibility to the political process of the particular local setting distinct from the general level of political knowledge or civic literacy. This suggests that there are thus two aspects of civic literacy: a general political informedness linked to citizenship, and a specific "civic" or local expression or application of that knowledge.

Chapter 5 showed how, beyond facilitating their mere presence, PR makes it easier for political parties to maintain a consistent identity in the local political arena. In this context, local voters are in a position to develop relatively clear and stable orientations both in terms of the local issues and personalities, and of the relationship of those issues and actors to matters of wider political concern. They are, in effect, able to develop more accurate political maps to navigate the political landscape. Such maps enhance the capacity of citizens to acquire political knowledge and, by reducing the cost of information, bring more potential voters to the polls more often. This chapter compares the political processes associated with PR and majoritarian systems as to their respective "mapping" qualities.

Consensual Democracy and Electoral Institutions: The Vertical Dimension

Henceforth we shall, as a rule, compare experience in one or more high- and low-civic-literacy societies, most frequently, given the information available, the United States and Sweden. In this chapter, we once again bring insights gained from the micro comparisons to our macro-level analysis, starting

from the variation in attitude consistency identified in the comparative research. We noted in chapter 3 the greater attitudinal consistency in Sweden
than in the United States in both the early 1960s and mid-1980s discovered
by Holmberg and his colleagues at the University of Gothenburg. This has
not changed—despite the substantial fall in the level of trust in Swedish politicians (reported in Holmberg 1999). An exit poll of nine thousand voters
was taken for Swedish public television by the Gothenburg team on election
day in September 1998.[1] One result of the poll was to confirm a feature of
Swedish (and, to a lesser extent, all European) voting patterns too often
overlooked in the wider discussion of increasing voter volatility. While, as
elsewhere, Swedish voters have shown signs of increasing volatility in their
choice of party, it turns out that their roving rarely crosses the divide separ-
ating the left and right blocs (Gilljam and Holmberg 1995: 32).

Indeed, this is only what we would expect from an informed voter under
normal circumstances. Only in the relatively infrequent event of a profound change in ideological orientation can we expect that disappointment
with a particular party or politician would lead an informed voter to support a party of an opposing ideological stripe. Instead, in the normal course
of events—if the political institutions allow for such alternatives to manifest themselves—one moves to a party not far away on the ideological spectrum but with different priorities and, seemingly, more competent leaders.
Empirical confirmation that the absence of volatility across the ideological
divide is a reflection of a politically knowledgeable electorate is provided
by the responses to other questions in the exit poll. When asked to rank
the parties, the second and third most popular choices of supporters of
one of the parties of the center-left (Social Democrats, Left Party,
Greens) were the two others; similarly for supporters of one of the "bourgeois" parties of the center-right (Conservatives, Liberals, Christian
Democrats)—with the Center party placing fourth for each group.[2] The
responses to two other questions also suggest that the ideological consistency of the Swedish electorate reflects a high level of civic literacy. Those
surveyed in the poll were asked to place themselves from right to left on
the political spectrum as well as to state their position on European monetary union, a major issue dividing the parties. The researchers found a remarkably close correspondence between the voters' profiles on both items
and the positions of the parties they favored.

What is the connection between such attitude consistency, or more profoundly, civic literacy, and the political—especially electoral—institutions
of Sweden? To put it simply, some political institutions are better than others at clarifying political choices. In his analysis of the development of
Australia's political institutions, Ian Marsh stresses a concern with "policy
learning" in the Australian colonies and commonwealth,[3] a concern that
diminished once the two-party system took hold.

How do multi-party politics encourage political learning and the mobilization of political consent? In championing their agendas, Labor, protectionists and free traders were all shaped by the formal political and policy making process through which they operated. By contrast with the two-party period (after 1909), multi-party politics in a colonial parliament and in federal politics up to 1909 were characterized by the substantial role of Parliament and of MPs in policy-making. Parliament and parliamentarians played a specific role in setting the medium-term agenda, determining the detail of legislation, and refining and building public understanding of the strategic agenda. The medium-term agenda was agreed when governments formed. The detail of legislation was finally determined through the process of legislative inquiry and legislative voting. The strategic agenda was also markedly influenced through legislative inquiry. . . . The turbulence associated with these developments reflected the large interests with stakes in the opposing purposes. But the turbulence played a positive role. The turbulence constituted a drama through which public attention was engaged and public understanding molded. (Marsh 1995: 301)

In the terms to be used here, Australian citizens during this period had access to a comprehensible political map. At the core of this comprehensibility lie those institutions linking "ordinary" citizens to the structures of government in their community, namely, the system by which they elect their representatives: on one side are (various forms of) PR, on the other FPTP (first-past-the-post) and other majoritarian or nonproportional systems.[4] Each system has its own distinct, long-term representational logic and it is via this logic, that the citizen makes sense of the political choices available. Candidates in majority systems are primarily oriented toward the median voter in the electorate, while those under PR are more oriented toward the median voter of their party (Wessels 1996). This means that, right from the moment of entering politics, the pressure on political actors to misrepresent their ideas is stronger under FPTP. Little wonder that PR systems outperform majoritarian ones in "quality of representation," the correspondence between citizen and legislative medians on the left-right scale (Powell and Vanberg 1998).

As we work our way through the representational logic, we shall see an overall pattern explaining why, in advanced industrial democracies, political institutions based on PR (as those in Sweden) result in higher levels of civic literacy, and—therefore—voter turnout. A good place to start is with a recent comparative study linking the effects of the difference in representational logic to satisfaction with democracy. Anderson and Guillory (1997), using the Eurobarometer cross-sectional survey data for eleven countries, divided their respondents into two groups, those who supported a winning party (i.e., one that became part of the government) the previous election, and those who favored one that lost. They then compared each group's responses to a question asking respondents how they felt about the way democracy worked in their country. They found that under majoritarian (FPTP) systems, democratic satisfaction came from being on the winning side—far more than under PR-based consensual systems.

> Losers who live in consensual systems show a higher level of satisfaction with the way democracy works than do those who live in a majoritarian system. . . . The more consensual the democracy, the less satisfied are winners with the workings of the system. Conversely, the closer the democracy to a pure majoritarian type, the more satisfied are winners (76–77).[5]

Unlike here, where societies are categorized by their electoral system, Anderson and Guillory apply a complex scale developed by Lijphart (1984),[6] going from consensual to majoritarian democracy in which the proportionality of a country's electoral system is one of several interrelated elements.[7] Though indebted to Lijphart overall approach to the effect of political institutions, the analysis here does use his scale. The main reason for this is that I view federalism, one of his major criteria for consensualism, as more contradictory rather than complementary to consensualism—a view that in fact tallies with Lijphart's recent reassessment of his own typology and is consistent with his finding that "federalism is associated with lower instead of higher turnout"(Lijphart 1997a).[8]

Having thus jettisoned the federalism dimension, Lijphart does not offer an alternative indicator for capturing the vertical dimension of consensual institutions, that is, the relationship between institutions at the local (and regional) level with those at the center. But this dimension remains central to the preoccupations of this book, focusing as we do on the citizen's relationship with—and knowledge of—the political institutions that are closest to his/her everyday concerns. I argue that, in their vertical manifestation, consensual systems are not, as Lijphart's original scheme predicted, characterized by decentralization or federalism, but rather by the degree to which party and other political networks directly link political activities oriented toward (macro level) national politics to those concerned with (micro level) local matters. In spite of this, I do not add a vertical dimension, since, as I shall show, the proportionality of elections is a crucial factor in a country's position on this vertical dimension. For these reasons, a complex scale compounding several elements that are assigned the same weight—when in reality one element, the electoral system's proportionality, weighs much more heavily than the others[9]—is likely to cause more problems that it solves. Instead, therefore, I use a single indicator of consensualism: whether the electoral system is proportional or not.[10]

The electoral system's relationship to the horizontal dimension of consensualism is well known. This is due to the simple fact that PR systems use lists from which—unlike winnable single-member districts—it is hard to exclude women or members of minorities such as the Maori in New Zealand. This is revealed by the distribution of New Zealand MPs (under the MMP system, see chapter 10) in tables 6-1 and 6-2. New Zealand results are especially edifying because, under MMP, parties nominate both single member district candidates, as in FPTP, and from lists used in PR systems.

Beyond fostering greater political participation on the part of members of underrepresented groups, proportional systems are more representative and fairer both in translating votes into seats and in bringing sectors of the community in under the umbrella of democratic institutions (Powell 1989; Karp and Banducci 1998).[11]

As noted above, the proportionality of a country's electoral system also affects the vertical dimension of consensualism, that is, the degree of vertical continuity in its party system. It has to do with the investment choices among limited resources. Because FPTP exaggerates a party's weakness as well as strength, it creates a disincentive against investing in regions and municipalities where a party is weak. Over time, this has the effect of eliminating parties from effective if not real presence in more and more regions and localities. With parties less present at the base, vertical political links are weakened and vertical communication flows disrupted. Citizens find themselves with a map from which side roads that connect the small communities to the main centers have been erased.

As noted in the case study of Norway in chapter 5, once PR is adopted for national legislatures, its use tends to spread to other levels, with the result that PR becomes embedded in a system of vertically integrated relationships centered on the political parties. In Sweden, for example, the introduction of proportional representation in the cities in 1910 went hand in hand with the Social Democrats' active involvement at that level, which forced their "bourgeois" opponents to do likewise—a process gradually

TABLE 6-1

Women Elected to 1996 New Zealand Parliament

Party	N	% of Party's MPs	District	List
National	8	18.2	4	4
Labour	13	35.1	6	7
NZ First	4	23.5	0	4
Alliance	7	53.8	0	7
ACT	3	37.5	0	3
Total	35		10	25

Source: Arseneau, 1999.

TABLE 6–2

Maori Elected to 1996 New Zealand Parliament

Party	N	% of Party's MPs	District	List
National	1	2.3	0	1
Labour	4	10.8	0	4
NZ First	7	41.2	6*	1
Alliance	2	15.4	0	2
ACT	1	12.5	0	1
Total	15		6	9

* Five of these were elected from the 5 districts reserved for Maori voters.

extended to the rural communes over the next decades. With the municipal amalgamation reforms, completed in 1974, full "party politicization" took place, with virtually all parties presenting platforms in even the smallest municipalities (Strömberg and Westerståhl 1984). In contrast, in the majoritarian countries, except for Britain, the national parties are largely absent from local politics.[12] In the United States, where parties were traditionally present in local politics, about three-quarters of municipalities now use nonpartisan elections to select their public officials (Schaffner and Streb 2000: 2).

A useful empirical indicator of the effect of the vertical dimension of consensualism on turnout can be found in the disparity between local and

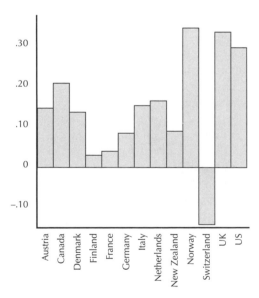

FIGURE 6–1 Difference between Average National and Municipal Turnout

national turnout levels. Municipal turnout levels reflect both the horizontal effect of the proportionality of the electoral system as well as the vertical effect of the degree of integration of political institutions; on national turnout the vertical factor has only a marginal effect. Hence the relative gap in turnout levels can be seen as reflecting the level of integration of the system. In figure 6-1 (which sets out the differences between average national and average local turnouts), we see a significantly larger gap in the countries where national parties play little or no role in local politics, such as the United States, Canada and New Zealand, than in the European countries where they are very much involved.[13] Interestingly, the gap is also high in Britain where the national parties do run candidates in local elections but FPTP is used throughout with the result, as noted at the beginning of chapter 5, that only a minority of seats are in any real doubt.[14]

Thus, as figure 6-1 graphically displays, by using average turnout in local elections as indicator, we are, in one measure, incorporating both dimensions of the representational logic of consensual democracies: the horizontal one of proportionality, and the vertical one of structural continuity of political activity from the local to central levels. We can now explore how the contrasting representational logics of the consensual/proportional system and the majoritarian/FPTP system are related to civic literacy.

Civic Literacy and Consensual Political Institutions

Franklin, Van der Eijk, and Oppenhuis (1995), in their analysis of turnout variations in elections to the European Parliament, conclude that "turnout seems above all to be affected by voters' awareness of the consequences of their decisions. Proportionality enhances the predictable consequences of the voters' choice." Gordon and Segura (1997) show that nationally competitive elections among a larger number of parties, which we know to be associated with PR elections, increase the availability of information to potential voters. Let us look more carefully at how this happens. We begin from the simple fact that in the two-party system usually resulting from FPTP, voters can find themselves having to cross to the other side of the traditional ideological divide to meaningfully express dissatisfaction with the performance of the party they have supported, something, as illustrated in the Swedish results, seldom required under PR. In addition, in making people's satisfaction with democracy less dependent on the success of one's preferred party, PR reduces polarization, thus clearing the way toward greater consensualism. Generally speaking, students of electoral systems in industrial democracies agree that, over time, experience of stable coalition government tends to promote political cooperation and consensus.[15] Missing in the literature, however, is a clear link between the operations of these consensual institutions and politics, beyond the fact that, under PR, parties are more motivated to solicit support by providing information to voters whose votes are "wasted" under FPTP.

A key feature is the relative stability of the features of the political map under PR. The representational logic of PR-based multiparty systems is to inhibit precipitous changes to a party's principles and identity, that is, the elements that constitute its place on the political map. Political actors, and the voters themselves, can thus count on a relatively clearly drawn and stable political map on which to plot their own paths. For political actors, this includes reliable expectations (underlying choices) about which other actors to cooperate with and over what issues. In these ways, consensual institutions enhance the "supply side" of civic literacy by rendering political reality easier to comprehend.[16] They gain greater benefits and face fewer institutional obstacles (costs) to supplying political information under consensual than under majoritarian institutional arrangements. With disparities in their support not exacerbated by the electoral system (as under FPTP), political parties have to cooperate to govern;[17] and unimpeded horizontal transmission of information between parties is necessary for effective cooperation.

Let us elaborate. In comparison to FPTP, under PR there is less incentive for political leaders, who may very well need their opponents' support after the election, to inhibit the awareness of the electorate of alternative positions on the issues of the day. In contrast, FPTP-based political actors in the legislature (and the parliamentary press) form a picture of the political world outside parliament influenced by what they experience in the chamber, that of a single-party government with the support of a solid majority. In reality, this latter aspect is almost always misleading, the majority being an artifact of the electoral system.

Nevertheless, the numbers are such that the governing party is expected to implement its program as if a majority of the population was behind it, and not seek broad-based multipartisan support for needed, but controversial, reforms. It knows, moreover, that such support is rarely forthcoming, since other parties, with no chance of entering the government between elections, have nothing to gain by cooperating. Their political interest lies in resisting, denouncing, and exaggerating unpopular policies, even ones they know to be necessary. These tendencies are exacerbated by the political rewards under FPTP since parties know that the choices of a relatively small number of voters can make the difference between monopolizing political power and having none whatsoever. With politics as a ruthless zero-sum game—you lose; I win—distorting the opponent's position (through appeals to emotion, negative advertising, and the like), while keeping one's own policies vague, pays off (see Amy 1989). The result, whatever the intentions of the individuals involved, is a public less informed than it needs to be.

In contrast, under PR, where compromise and coalition are visible, built-in features of the political process, it is only to be expected that opponents collaborate even when they disagree. One overall result of this pattern is greater continuity and thus stability in state policy,[18] rather than the cyclical pattern under FPTP where opposition parties seek—and are expected to carry out—mandates[19] for visible change from volatile electorates.[20]

Moreover, a parallel logic operates at the level of the electoral district, where the crucial distinction is the reliance on single-member constituencies in majoritarian systems. It is well known that such constituencies provide incentives for catering to narrow local interests. But the effect is very subtle. FPTP overvalues the behavior of the least partisan citizens, those who can make the difference between winning and losing marginal seats—since that is what counts for winning power—at the expense of traditional party supporters. The effect is to erode the usefulness of the party to the electorate. In the long run more and more voters become volatile, that is, they loosen their ties to the political party, which purports to be "everybody's instrument." Such a party is, in fact, "nobody's instrument" (Irvine 1979: 77).

Further, the resulting rapid turnover among legislators in a single-member system makes it difficult for individuals to envisage a political career through continuous service to the party and the electorate.[21] Lacking local party activists to serve as representatives, antennae, and organization builders between elections, the party turns to "experts" and pollsters to tell it how to appeal to the voters, thus further alienating traditional supporters.[22] Yet even the party whose candidate was successful in the FPTP district is not spared by this process: the party relies on its elected MP as its link with its supporters at the base, but the MP needs the party organization only to assure renomination. In between, what counts is the sympathy of local voters not aligned with the party. Thus the normal, everyday activities of the local MP contradict the basic message and undermine the continuity of the party. Just as the signals the governing party under FPTP receives from its parliamentary environment mislead it into thinking that it has the mandate of the majority of the population, so the members elected by plurality in a single-member district see a world in which they reflect the whole political spectrum. In contrast, under PR, parties have reason to build faithful voting blocs around individuals advancing their political careers. Legislators elected along with candidates of other parties on a proportional basis in a multimember district are not prone to lose sight of the fact that it is the party that links them to the electorate, just as a governing party elected under PR does not lose sight of the fact that majority support is not supplied by elections but may have to be rebuilt for each important legislative initiative.

Parallel to these horizontal information-cost reduction tendencies are those linked to the vertical dimension. Information-cost reduction derives from the functioning of vertical political networks linking political activities at the national level to those attuned to regional and local concerns. This takes place mainly through the channels of political party organizations complemented by the career patterns of individuals.[23] We can see the results of this process, for example, in the conclusions drawn by Eldersveld and his colleagues from interviews of 250 to 400 local leaders in fifteen to twenty comparable municipalities in the majoritarian United States as well as consensual Sweden and the Netherlands in the latter 1980s. They reported that

> in both European systems local elites have much more contact with national administrators than US elites do. . . . European leaders are also more in touch with party leaders at the local and the national levels. In Europe, for example, over 80 percent of local councilors report that they initiate contacts with the local party organizations (93 percent in Sweden, 83 percent in the Netherlands, compared to 27 percent in the US). In addition, approximately one third of European councilors are in touch with the national or provincial party leaders. Thus there is a strong vertical structuring of the party relationships in Europe among policy leaders, from the bottom to the top of the system, unlike in the US. . . . The role of the political party as a very relevant, powerful, integrative institution for the entire system is very distinctive in Europe, in contrast to the US. (Eldersveld, Strömberg, and Derksen: 1995:239)[24]

The horizontal and vertical information-cost reduction effects of PR are manifested in the kind of attitude consistency noted at the outset of this chapter. We can see this by applying the data derived from a study by Dalton (1996). Using the most recent World Values Survey, Dalton calculated the participating countries' average correlation between left/right attitudes and the party preference of respondents (who expressed such a preference), that is, the higher the correlation, the more closely the average voter's views correspond to his or her party preference. Not surprisingly, the more consistent countries turned out to be the high-civic-literacy northern European ones.

In these various ways, consensual institutions enhance the "supply side" of civic literacy by rendering the political world more intelligible. Political participation is fostered, especially at the lower end of the income and education ladders where information is at a premium. A recent finding based on American data illustrates how class differences matter when it comes to the effect of party identification on voting. Testing the extent that the decline in turnout in U.S. elections between 1964 and 1988 was related to class, Darmofal (1999) found the decline to be three times as great among those in the lowest income and education groups: while all socioeconomic groups experienced diminished levels of identification with a political party during this period, only among the poor did this translate into lower turnout.

Conclusion

I cannot, at this point, resist pointing out that those public-choice analysts who relentlessly apply economic reasoning to the study of political institutions have shown remarkable timidity with regard to the logic of electoral systems.[25] An economic approach to the "political market" and its imperfections should favor PR. The golden rule of applied economics is "do not—unless clearly justified by market imperfections—institutionally distort the signals of informed consumer choice." Translated to political science, it would read "do not—unless clearly justified by political market imperfections—institutionally distort the signals of informed citizen choice." Since we know that the overwhelming majority of citizens vote for the party not the person, FPTP, by its very nature, violates this principle, rewarding the leading party with many extra seats and, quite often, a four-year monopoly of power. This is analogous to fiscal arrangements that give tax breaks to monopolists and oligopolists at the expense of small enterprises. Economists have no trouble articulating the

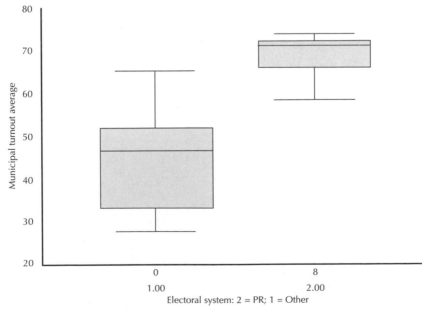

FIGURE 6-2 Local Voting Turnout under Different Electoral Systems

suboptimal outcomes when firms make choices under a system that skews rewards in this manner, but I have yet to come across any one of the growing number of economists writing about political institutions applying the analogy to the institutional incentives under FPTP for parties to exaggerate, distort, and polarize.

To conclude, then, other things being equal, there is good reason to believe that the "average" citizen is better informed under consensual institutions associated with PR than under the majoritarian ones of FPTP—both directly and indirectly. Directly because there is simply more accurate political information at the citizen's disposal at negligible cost; indirectly because, with a clearer, more complete political map, the political landscape is more comprehensible horizontally and vertically. As a simple test I have calculated the average municipal turnout for consensual countries and for majoritarian countries not using compulsory voting. Figure 6–2 provides summary plots with boxes that contain the turnout values falling between the 25th and 75th percentiles, as well as lines indicating the medians and the highest and lowest values. As we can see, the average under PR is roughly 70 percent, compared to less than 45 percent under FPTP: with the lowest PR country almost as high in turnout as the highest FPTP.[26]

In sum, it is clear that the three-way relationship identified in the introduction and illustrated in figure 0–1 is a real one. We can say with some confidence that when it comes to comparisons between countries, and within countries using more than one electoral system, political institutions do affect political participation, and they do so in no small part through enhancing or diminishing civic literacy. While consensual institutions based on proportional elections and vertical political integration do affect turnout directly, a crucial link is via civic literacy, and the higher turnout in local elections especially reflects this. Aggregate turnout in local elections thus serves our purposes as the best single indicator of the civic side of civic literacy—and will be used for that purpose in the chapters to follow. We can now turn to the institutions and policy choices that impact especially on the literacy side of civic literacy.

7

Civic Literacy and the Media

Consensual political institutions indirectly facilitate civic literacy by making the political map more comprehensible, but the capacity of the citizen to assimilate political knowledge is directly affected primarily by the educational system and the media. In chapter 9, we shall set out and compare what is known about the effects of education—especially civics education and programs directed toward adults—on civic literacy in the different countries. In the next two chapters, we focus on the media.

In introducing the discussion of social capital upon which our investigation began, we noted that the newspaper readership rate was a key element in Putnam's "Civic Community Index" for testing levels of social capital in the Italian regions. When he went on to record evidence of declining social capital in America, Putnam at various points treated declining newspaper readership as both indicator and cause.[1] Not all media are created equal, however: "Newspaper reading is associated with high social capital, TV viewing with low social capital" (Putnam 1996: 14). Putnam makes a very sharp distinction between newspaper reading and television viewing—the latter emerging as the culprit in the declining social capital case—citing data highlighting the rise in television watching at the expense of newspaper reading in the United States.

This transfer in media consumption is also reflected in attitudes. Hepburn (1990) shows, based on data from the Roper organization,[2] that for a solid majority of Americans (55 versus 21 percent), television and not the press is the most credible news source.[3] This is compared to the early 1960s, when newspapers were still 5 percentage points ahead of TV[4] and when, we should add, 71 percent—as opposed to 50 percent today—responded affirmatively to Gallop pollsters asking if they had read a newspaper on the previous day.[5] In the 1960s, less than 20 percent of Americans said they usually obtained news of the world from "TV only. . . . This percentage rose roughly 10 percent per decade, reaching 50 percent in 1986" (Clark and Rempel 1997: 24).

In Putnam's view, the replacement of newspaper reading by TV viewing as the prime medium of information has a compound negative impact since television watching actually reduces social capital. His argument draws a historical pattern of parallel steep decline between the 1950s and 1990s: as TV watching rose in the United States,[6] the various indicators of social capital, interpersonal trust, voting turnout, and, most importantly, group membership and participation fell. After examining other possible explanations, Putnam sums up the evidence against television:

> First, the timing fits. The long civic generation was the last cohort of Americans to grow up without television, for television flashed into American society like lightning, in the 1950s. In 1950 barely 10 per cent of American homes had television sets, but by 1959, 90 per cent did. . . . Most studies estimate that the average American now watches roughly four hours per day (excluding periods in which television is merely playing in the background). Even a more conservative estimate of three hours means that television absorbs 40 per cent of the average American's free time, an increase of about one-third since 1965. (Putnam 1996: 13–14)

Television, Putnam suggests, destroys social capital by taking time away from civic engagement—what Uslaner calls a "time crunch"—and by making viewers less trustful of the world outside their homes.[7]

> Putnam's case against television rests on two foundations. The first is a direct cause of waning participation in civic affairs: Television viewing eats up time. If you are hooked in front of your television set, you can't be out and about partaking in civic life. The second part gets to civic participation through television's effect on personality. Television dramas bring us violence and bad guys. The news highlights crime, war, disease, and other plagues. A viewer might reasonably think that the real world is cruel as well. If you watch a lot of TV, you are likely to believe that the "television world" is the real world. And it is a "mean world," where people don't trust each other, would try to take advantage of each other, and are looking out primarily for themselves. (Uslaner 1998: 442)

Putnam adds a third effect, though admitting the evidence is not in. Children who watch a lot of television become more aggressive and less achievement-oriented; heavy watching "is statistically associated with psychosocial malfunctioning" (Putnam 1996: 14). Indeed, we are only beginning to understand the long-term effects of large-scale exposure to TV starting at a young age. Fifty percent of American children average six or more hours of television exposure daily.[8]

Of course, television has defenders who reject Putnam's critique and who have sought alternative explanations.[9] Uslaner (1998) argues that the figures from the General Social Survey cited by Putnam offer no support for either a time-crunch or "mean world" explanation of declining social trust and civic participation. Unlike other researchers,[10] he finds no relationship between the amount of television viewing and either group membership or social trust. But other data suggest just such a relationship. For example, a mid-1970s study compared the one-third of adults who watched more than four hours of TV daily to those who watched two or fewer hours.[11] The heavy viewers were 35 percent more likely to respond "can't be too careful" to the question "can most people be trusted?" and 33 percent more likely to expect to be involved in some kind of violence (Gerbner and Gross 1976). These findings have been replicated in many different settings.[12] Clearly, as the amount of television watching rises, at some point civic engagement declines.

Commercialism, News Watching, and Civic Literacy

The American debate over the effects of television has stressed the relationship between media consumption and civic engagement: in our terms, it has focused on the civic side, to the detriment of the literacy side of civic literacy. This is a serious deficiency since the literacy side adds an important, and neglected, dimension to the discussion. This dimension emerges when we focus on the fact that television viewing—and commercial television viewing in particular[13]—has replaced newspaper reading.

This has not been just a case of substituting one means of information acquisition for another. A number of studies have found that what is learned is qualitatively different in the two types of media. Studies have shown that adults remember more from a print account than from a comparable television presentation.[14] More generally, as reported in a wide-ranging American study, a high amount of TV viewing is linked to low concentration and cognitive effort, and is thus inimical to learning (Kubey and Csikszentmihaly 1990). Another relevant finding emerges from interviews conducted by Sanders (1998), based on the 1996 National Election Study. Sanders found that the more television they watched, the more respondents tended to talk of candidates in terms of personalities and character rather than issues. A British study by Newton (1999: 592) finds that "the more general television people watch, the less they know about politics, though the regression coefficient is relatively weak." In their interpretation of the results of the Times-Mirror test (see chapter 4), Bennett and his collaborators are quite definitive: "One finding stands out: the more people watch popular entertainment shows on television, the less they know about foreign affairs, even when other predictors are taken into account" (1995: 32).

These effects of television consumption are unexplained and, indeed, unexplainable by Putnam's time-crunch and mean-world account. We can see this with regard to voting turnout. Though Putnam cites declining electoral turnout as a symptom of disappearing social capital in the United States, he never tries to explain this relationship. Indeed, why should watching more television lead to people voting less? Little time is needed to vote, and, with ever more intensified use of television in American campaigns, one would—if anything—expect the opposite. Such anomalies led Norris (1996) to conclude—despite confirming Putnam's empirical expectations about the connection between high TV watching and low political participation—that it may simply be a case of getting the direction of causality reversed: nonparticipators simply watch more television. Similarly, we might also be tempted to exonerate Putnam's culprit based on the comparative social capital indicators cited above: Americans watch at least as much television as anyone, yet "America is already high as a generation of joiners, with a dense network of civic associations" (Norris 1996: 479). The United States is nowhere nearly as low on the two main indicators of social capital as its high TV-watching figures would lead one to expect. And Putnam's expectation that TV watching[15] varies inversely with trust and associational participation is only very weakly supported by the aggregate data here assembled.[16]

Yet when it comes to local voting turnout averages, as we see in figure 7-1, the correspondence with TV watching is clear-cut. In sum, when applied comparatively, Putnam's expectation that high TV watching results in low social capital is not confirmed by measures of community involvement

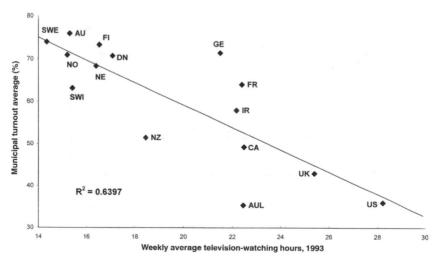

FIGURE 7–1   F = 23.085, sig F = 0.003

and interpersonal trust—where the argument is plausible—but is confirmed in relation to voting turnout, for which he provides no plausible explanation.

The paradox is resolved if we see social capital as based on civic literacy rather than trust. Norris (1996: 478) found that, even controlling for social background, "the hours people spent watching television was negatively correlated . . . people who watch a great deal of television know less about politics."[17] And the opposite appears to be the case with newspaper reading: individuals who read newspapers daily invariably average significantly higher rates of knowledge than those who do not. Newspaper reading, as opposed to television watching, correlates positively and strongly with correct answers on the five questions used in the Times-Mirror study (Bennett et al. 1995: 32).[18]

What do we know of the effect of watching TV programs with political content?[19] What of news and public-affairs television programs, that is, programs at least claiming to provide, and thus contribute to, political knowledge? Norris found that those who watched more televised news and public-affairs programming were somewhat more knowledgeable than those who watched less. A clearer positive relationship was found in Britain. Using data from the 1997 British General Election Campaign Panel Study, Norris and her colleagues found that those attentive to news on television as well as in the press "were significantly more knowledgeable about than the average citizen about party politics, civics and the parliamentary candidates standing in their constituency" (Norris et al. 1999: 113). In contrast, McLeod and Perse found a *negative* relationship between their subjects' score on fourteen questions testing public-affairs knowledge and their watching of TV news and public-affairs shows, as opposed to a very positive relationship between such scores and newspaper reading. One reason for this, they speculate, is the particular content of American public-affairs programs. Nightly news programs are in competition with newsmagazines, which quite openly place entertainment above information, with few scruples about paying sources, staging events, and so forth. In competing for scarce advertising dollars, they sensationalize, oversimplify, and exaggerate, seeking out "stories about crimes, accidents and disasters that have little public affairs information" (McLeod and Perse 1994: 440).[20] And, note Gilliam and Iyengar (2000: 560): "local television news is the public's primary sources of public affairs information. News stories about crime dominate local newsprogramming." This is due to the nature of television, argues Scheuer (1999): a "one-dimensional" medium relying on sentimentality, visceral "sound bites," and "photo ops."

Perhaps the best snapshot of the situation in the United States is provided by a study by Hartley and Dautrich (1998). The authors tested five hundred voters' knowledge of campaign issues in a four-wave panel study in the ten months before the 1996 election. The panel form of the study allowed them to control for the possible effects of background or prior knowledge. They found, as expected, that voters who frequently read newspapers were more informed than those who did not; but they also found that television news watching had no effect.[21]

The issue may be increasingly moot since television news watching appears to be in precipitous decline in the United States, in part due to the fact that in the 1980s and 1990s network television lost a great many viewer hours to cable-based networks. A study by the Times Mirror Center for the People and the Press (1990) found the American public's appetite for national and international news to be waning, with viewership of nightly network news in continuing decline.[22] Bennett (1998: 535), using the results of more recent Pew studies as well as the 1997 National Election Study, concludes that roughly half as many American adults under thirty watch television newscasts and read newspapers as those over thirty.[23] At the end of the 1980s there were on average thirty-eight minutes less per day of foreign news on combined U.S. network news programs than at the beginning of the decade (*Harper's Index*, July 1993).

Why Public-Service Television Is Different

The reduction in foreign news content in the United States reflects the chasm between news and information programs in the United States and these in most European countries. Of course, insofar as television is concerned, the situation in the United States is quite atypical. We know that practically all other comparable countries have more significant sectors of public-service television than the United States—despite the trend toward deregulation and privatization. This trend can be seen by comparing the present situation in western Europe with that prevailing in 1980. At that time, all countries operated publicly owned television channels, with only Italy and the U.K. having privately owned channels alongside. In Belgium, Denmark, Norway, and Sweden the only source of revenue for telecasters was license fees. By 1990, this restriction had been removed, and by 1997, only Austria, Ireland, and Switzerland limited ownership of television channels to the public sector (De Bens and Østbye 1998: 27; Blömgren and Blömgren 1999).

Yet important differences remain. In Germany the public broadcasting companies ARD and ZDF are largely funded through the license fees, whereas the private companies are financed by advertising revenue alone.[24] In Canada and France the public channels depend heavily on advertising, whereas in Great Britain the BBC carries no advertising whatsoever. Similarly, the Australian ABC is funded solely from taxes rather than through advertising or a license fee. In contrast, New Zealand (like Luxembourg) has no publicly financed television network, though state subsidies are available so that television companies can make programs of public interest that could not otherwise be funded from advertising (Hoynes 1994).[25]

With the possible exception of New Zealand,[26] no similar society has such a weak public-service broadcasting sector as the United States. And nowhere is the effect of television news watching the same as in the United States. For example, in Britain TV news watchers were more knowledgeable about the issues in the 1997 campaign than were those who did not watch the news (Norris et al. 1999). It is reasonable to suppose that the difference has to do with the more substantive news coverage by British television and especially the BBC, which attracts a significant part of TV news watchers and contributes to setting a standard for the private (commercial) sector.[27] American Public TV has a budget amounting to less than US$4 per capita, compared to US$27 in Canada and US$38 in Sweden (Hoynes 1994). The Swedish money seems to have been well spent. A Swedish study before and after the 1991 election found that daily TV news watching was significantly related to higher political knowledge, reflecting the fact that (at the time) all the television news was provided by high-quality public-service channels.[28] The most beneficial effect of media use was on those at the lower levels of education and, presumably, on those who had least access to alternative sources of information (Findahl 1993).[29] In the concluding chapter we report on the encouraging results of an ongoing study of the evolving content of Swedish public television. Similarly, the above-observed higher level of political knowledge of Germans as compared to Americans has been attributed not only to the Germans' reading newspapers more but also to the importance of public-service TV networks. Semetko carefully studied the content of election campaign coverage in news programs in four countries: "Substantive issues were most important in Germany, followed by Britain and Spain, and then the US. . . . The public service channels . . . aired more substantive issue stories than the private channels" (Semetko 1996: 11).[30]

A number of studies have compared the content of commercial and private television. Holtz-Bacha and Norris (2001), controlling for education, attitudes toward the EU, and other relevant characteristics, found Eurobarometer respondents who preferred public television to be significantly more informed about the EU than those who chose private TV. A Dutch study that began in the early 1990s when private television entered the market indicates that an average of 38 percent of public television broadcasting time, and 33 percent of viewing time, is spent on information programs, while for private television it is 26 and 23 percent (Euromedia Research Group 1997: 166).[31] A 1986 investigation cited by Findahl (1991) breaks down European telecasters into private, public with advertising, and public without advertising, estimating that the percentage of shows classified as entertainment averaged around 80 percent for the first, 60 percent for the second, and 45 percent for the third. More specific data along these lines have been gathered for the Nordic countries, where commercial television now has close to half the market share.[32] In Denmark, the private channel, TV3, devotes only 15 percent of program hours to news and information compared to 50 percent for Danish Radio; in Sweden, the private channels average 24 percent compared to 54 percent for SVT; In Norway, it is 30 percent versus 48 percent for NRK, and in Finland, 33 percent versus 46 percent for YLE (Carlsson and Harrie 1997: 222–25).

While the distinction between entertainment and information is generally accepted (even though it is not always easy to apply), there is greater controversy surrounding the interpretation of the difference. Defenders of commercial television assert that, through market forces, they are in fact providing consumers the information they want. The question posed is whether information is in fact just like any other product in a competitive market. This seems unwarranted, to judge by what we know of (American) attitudes: people do not treat media information as another commodity; they have expectations of what the media should present quite distinct from their own inclinations as consumers. A study undertaken by the Pew Center for the People and the Press (Parker and Deane 1997) compares what kinds of information people see themselves as attentive to and what kinds of information they actually know, by testing knowledge of current events on a range of subjects from entertainment news to sports to world events. It found a significant difference between professed attention to, and knowledge of, stories involving entertainment, scandal, and crime.[33]

While respondents place "infotainment" stories at the bottom of the list of news stories to which they claim attentiveness, facts from such stories turn out to be at the top of their knowledge scale. And this is all that counts from a commercial point of view: if you are simply concerned about ratings in the market. "News" shows about the latest twist in the O. J. Simpson story are what people watch—whatever they may say they want. So the numbers cited above reflect the simple fact that, other things being equal, the more that commercial considerations enter into decisions on "news and public affairs" programming, the lower the actual public-affairs information content—and thus knowledge—we can expect. As a medium, TV is particularly susceptible to commercialism: "Every time a newspaper includes a feature which will attract a specialized group, it can assume it is adding at least a little bit to circulation. To the degree a television news program includes an item of this sort . . . it must assume that its audience will diminish" (Postman and Powers 1992).

The generations raised on commercial television, television's critics contend, have a reduced capacity to make fundamental distinctions between information and entertainment, between news and gossip, between fact and wishful thinking, and they are suggestive to the—usually hidden—claims of TV advertisers. A useful experimental confirmation of this tendency, and one that deals specifically with political advertising and political knowledge, is provided by Boiney. After surveying the existing literature, Boiney hypothesizes that while "we can retrieve meaning from televised communication . . . there's a trap . . . [since we] assume that pieces of information communicated . . . at the same time or in the same space, are consistent with one another." Because of this "multimodal" character, television is "a uniquely effective vehicle for communicating deceptive claims"—especially in political campaign advertising.

> Voters who do not know much about politics are less likely to recognize when an ad fails to refer explicitly to some piece of information upon which an invited inference turns. Without that information, they fill in the "blank" with the interpretation that best fits with the scenario the ad has created, via mood-inducing music, attractive visuals, word choice, editing, argument structure and many other factors." (Boiney 1993: 6–11)

Boiney showed his subjects[34] six campaign ads and then asked them to choose from among a series of statements as to the claim being made in the ad. In each case, the ads' visual content set up misleading claims.[35] The subjects were also tested for political knowledge.[36] As expected, those with low political knowledge were far more frequently misled.

In sum, there is sufficient evidence to say with reasonable confidence that, at a certain point, exposure to commercial television, by replacing other, more accurate sources of political information, has a negative impact on civic literacy. This displacement effect includes the effect on participation in voluntary organizations emphasized by Putnam[37] but, more importantly, gets at a reduction in direct exposure to more accurate sources of political knowledge through print media[38] and (potentially) study circles and the like.

The Television Dependency Scale

Newspapers

The above logic underlies our method for comparatively analyzing the relationship between media consumption and civic literacy in different countries. For each country for which we have the relevant data, we shall derive a *television dependency* rating to reflect the comparative impact of its media consumption pattern on civic literacy. While it is perhaps not ideal, *television dependency* is the best term available to us, as it highlights the approach taken here, which contrasts the extent to which people rely on commercial television—as opposed to newspapers—for information. The television dependency scale is based equally on the countries' relative ratings on commercial television consumption and newspaper reading. I begin with the latter, which is the simpler measure since we have recourse to a commonly used and objective indicator, daily newspaper circulation per capita. The data are presented in figure 7–2.

Of course, not all newspapers are the same. Indeed, certain countries have high-circulation tabloid newspapers that barely qualify as newspapers at all, given their pandering to gossip and scandalmongering, while ignoring what is normally considered news. We know that, overall, there is an important difference, with respect to contribution to the reader's knowledge, between the average U.K. tabloid and the average broadsheet.[39] Baker et al. (1996) suggested that the inclusion of tabloid readers explained the lack of a significant positive effect on political knowledge found for newspaper reading—as opposed to radio listening—in Britain (but not in the United States and Canada). Yet, despite being unable to control for quality,[40] we can nevertheless assert that over the entire set of

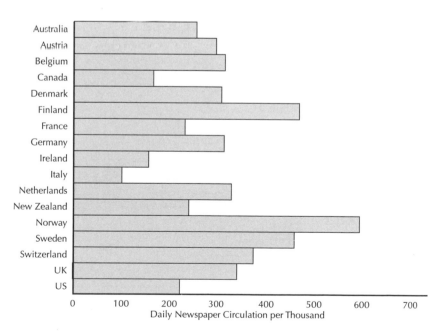

FIGURE 7–2   (UNDP 1998)

countries, gross per capita daily newspaper circulation reflects (and affects) civic literacy. The EU countries where more people said they read something about the European Union in a daily newspaper (see chapter 4) correspond reasonably closely with those with high circulation numbers in figure 7–2.[41]

Of course, other written materials contribute to civic literacy. The standard measure based on daily newspaper circulation does not take into account the relative importance of weekly newspapers, magazines, and books.[42] Yet doing so, it would appear, would not significantly change the situation. We know that Australia and Denmark are countries that have seen the proliferation of Sunday newspapers at the cost of readership on other days,[43] while the rank of both Denmark and Germany on minutes devoted daily to magazine reading compares favorably to that based on daily newspaper consumption.[44]

Television

The second element of the scale is television consumption, Putnam's "culprit" for the decline of social capital in the United States (see appendix III for details). I use a compound measure composed equally of two elements.

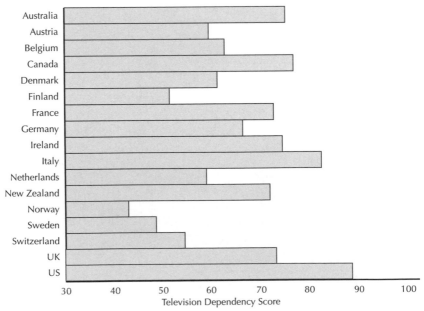

FIGURE 7–3

The first is average weekly television watching by country as set out above in figure 7–1.[45] The second element serves to incorporate the commercial dimension into the scale,[46] by using national per capita spending on television advertising.[47] (To standardize, in creating the composite, each indicator was recomputed to bring it to a score for which the maximum attained was close to 100.) With the exception of Japan, countries tend to be high in commercial television consumption or in newspaper circulation, but not both (or neither). Hence the countries under consideration here cluster into two polar types: in one, there are roughly four people for each daily newspaper, and commercial television watching is widespread and frequent; in the other, newspaper circulation is around one for every two people and there is less widespread recourse to commercial television. It is fair to add that in the former group, people lower down the economic and educational ladder are at the mercy of commercial television.[48] This theme will be taken up in part four.

Finally, in figure 7–3, we combine the commercial television consumption score with the newspaper reading score[49]—each given equal value— and we get a television dependency score for each country. From the chart we can discern a relatively large proportion of people, especially in the United States and Italy, who watch a great deal of commercial television which constitutes their only source of political information. In contrast, there is another group of people, found in Scandinavia more than elsewhere, who regularly read newspapers and seldom watch commercial television.

Television Dependency and Civic Literacy

We can now statistically test the relationship between television dependency and the indirect indicators of the literacy side of civic literacy examined in chapter 4 with a large enough number of countries to allow for statistical tests of significance. The most useful and important is the International Adult Literacy Survey (IALS).[50] Figure 7–4 plots the close relationship between TV dependency and the proportion of the population in fourteen countries scoring in the lowest category in the combined three IALS tests. There is nothing even slightly ambiguous about figure 7–5, which reveals a remarkably strong inverse relationship between the second such indirect indicator, knowledge of the United Nations, and TV dependency.[51]

Finally, we return in figure 7–6 to the "civic" side of civic literacy, and the relationship of TV dependency to voter turnout in local elections. While we must be careful in analyzing the relationship so as not to treat

Sources of Civic Literacy

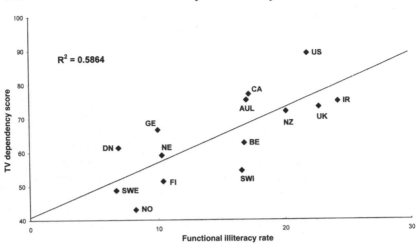

FIGURE 7–4   F = 17.013, sig F = 0.001

the numbers as anything more than indicative, it is clear from the high level of statistical significance in figure 7–6 that TV dependency also has the expected effect on local turnout, the civic side of civic literacy.[52] In part three, we look at the policy components of that effect, beginning with the policies influencing patterns of media consumption we have observed in this chapter.

One last consideration to end part two: TV dependency can serve as an

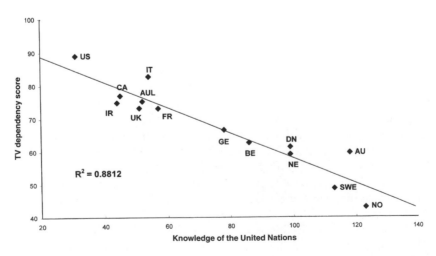

FIGURE 7–5   F = 89.025, sig F = 0.0000

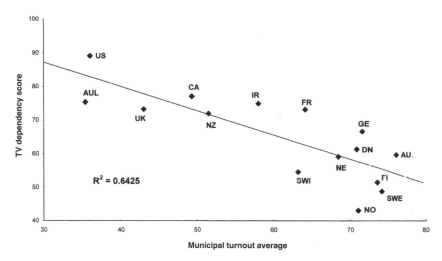

FIGURE 7–6

F = 23.362, sig F = 0.0003

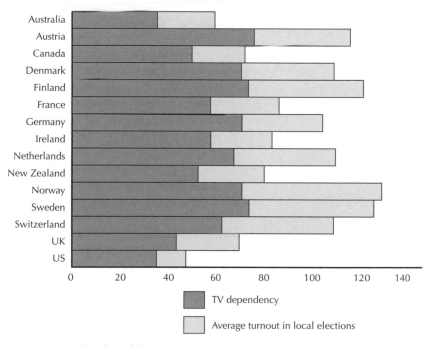

FIGURE 7–7 Combined Civic Literacy Score

indirect indicator of civic literacy according to a logic similar to that underpinning our use of turnout in local elections for that purpose. Figure 7-6 thus serves an added purpose, setting out the data that, combined, provide a composite indicator of civic literacy taking into account both the civic and the literacy dimensions—giving equal weight to each. Portrayed in the bar graph in figure 7-7, the scores on our composite indicator make more concrete the discernible pattern that has been emerging in this part of the book. The Scandinavian countries are in a high-civic-literacy category, along with the Netherlands and German-speaking countries. The low-civic-literacy category is dominated by the English-speaking countries plus Italy and perhaps France.[53]

III

Policy Choices Promoting Civic Literacy

Rather than a social democracy, I prefer to call our society a
"study-circle democracy."

OLOF PALME
(addressing the 1969 Congress of the Swedish Social Democratic Party)

8

Promoting Civic Literacy through
Political Institutions and the Media

Levels of civic literacy are not immutable; they can be altered by deliberate policy choices. But the effects of these decisions take place over time: the policy and institutional choices of one generation are manifested in the media consumption and voter turnout patterns of the next. In the rest of this book we will concentrate on comparing the high- and low-civic-literacy countries identified at the end of part two—and exploring the current and past societal choices that account for the observed differences.[1] In this chapter, we focus on choices affecting activities at the junction where political participation and media consumption meet. These include rules governing political party activities concerned with the dissemination of political information, and those affecting TV dependency on the political information disseminated through the media. In the next chapter we tackle the educational system and the wider framework of knowledge-enhancing institutions.

We begin where we left off in chapter 7—with the media. Part two ended with the suggestion that low television dependence in the Scandinavian countries was an important indicator—and cause—of their high civic literacy. The pronounced tendency to look for information in print finds roots in an inherited cultural tradition stressing reading. By the seventeenth century, the Lutheran State Church in Sweden (which then included Finland) had made it a moral obligation to be able to read from the Bible.[2] As the hierarchical structures of society both secular and ecclesiastical came under attack in the nineteenth century in the free church, temperance, and, later, labor movements, the concerns were gradually funneled into secular institutions. The folk high schools movement spread out from Denmark in the latter half of the century, providing secondary-level education to talented and ambitious young workers and peasants. In the process, the mantle of adult literacy was picked up by popular—

civic—associations, most frequently secular organizations tied to the labor movement and political parties, especially through the adult education movement discussed in chapter 9.

Clearly the Protestant religious heritage of Lutheran Scandinavia was more conducive to the spread of civic literacy than, say, the religious heritage of Catholic France or Italy. But the explanation is not a deterministic one:[3] potential remains only potential unless it is tapped by appropriate policy choices at key historical moments. Let us examine more recent reading-related choices, setting Scandinavia in comparative context.

Encouraging Newspaper Reading

There is no secret about how to avoid or reduce dependence on commercial television for information: encourage the development and use of alternate sources of public-affairs knowledge. It is a matter of identifying effective policies for reducing the comparative cost of newspapers and other printed sources of information as well as public-service television and radio versus that of commercial electronic media.

While most countries help newspapers and periodicals with some kind of special postal rates, Scandinavia stands out for its direct subsidies. Norway, Finland, and Sweden subsidize daily newspapers that are not leaders in their markets (Sanchez-Tabernero 1993: 229). Such newspapers benefit to an amount between 5 and 35 percent (averaging around 11 percent) of revenues, while the subsidies traditionally account for 3 to 4 percent of all newspaper revenues (Hadenius and Weibull 1999; Salokangas 1999).[4] Not surprisingly, then, among European countries, Norway, Sweden, and Finland rank first, second, and fourth in daily newspaper titles (Sanchez-Tabernero 1993: 40). While the Netherlands, Belgium, France, and Denmark offer some form of indirect press subsidies beyond fairly standard VAT exemption or reduction (De Bens and Østbye 1998: 14),[5] the only other country known to this writer with a direct subsidy program comparable to that of Norway, Finland, and Sweden is Austria.[6] It should therefore come as no surprise that there is an unambiguous positive relationship between such government efforts at encouraging newspaper reading and national circulation figures.[7]

In the 1990s, newspaper reading declined in the Nordic countries—as it did elsewhere—affected especially by cutbacks in public spending. The most significant decline in both took place in Finland.[8] In Sweden, circulation declined at more than 1 percent per year in the early 1990s (Hadenius and Weibull 1999),[9] though subsidies were kept fairly close to the SEK 435 million level (Carlsson and Harrie 1997). Norwegian subsidies were not reduced from their NRK 250–300 million (Høst 1999: 119) in the early

1990s, and during this period Norway witnessed the smallest reduction in circulation.[10] The second-largest decline in circulation took place in Denmark, which has never directly subsidized newspapers (Søllinge 1999) and started at a lower level to begin with, roughly 10 percent lower than the Scandinavian pattern, in which 80 to 90 percent of people over sixteen read at least one reasonably good daily newspaper,[11] with little variation by gender or even educational background (Hadenius and Weibull 1999: 149).[12]

Overall, despite the hard times, the policies continue to have the desired effect, evidence of the central place of civic literacy in the Scandinavian model.[13] The Nordic countries stand out as that corner of the developed world where reading daily newspapers remains an unquestioned part of everyday life.[14] In addition, concerted efforts are made to encourage the reading of books, both through subsidies to publishing and distribution and through programs offered by local public libraries (see chapter 9). Libraries in Sweden, for example, provide free home delivery for shut-ins and services to hospitals and homes for the elderly. There are also "book ombudsmen" in many local trade unions (see Milner 1989 and 1994). Finland and Denmark lead in book titles published per capita (along with the Netherlands and Switzerland), as well as in library book loans per capita, 16 and 14 per capita (in 1995) compared to the still high 8 and 5 for Sweden and Norway (*Mediebarometer* 1997: 188).

One other policy with a very pronounced positive effect on reading should be noted: all foreign-language television programs as well as films and videos are subtitled. This is due mainly to the small population of Nordic-language speakers, which makes dubbing very expensive. But it is also a matter of a conscious policy choice to promote language acquisition and reading, a technically—if not politically—easy and inexpensive policy choice that could be adopted by societies elsewhere to raise levels of functional literacy.[15]

As expected and noted, a direct parallel is to be drawn between an approach emphasizing newspaper reading and one that regards radio and television as in large part media of public-service information. In chapter 7 we learned that the high-civic-literacy countries invest more in public-service television channels. Despite the by now well-established presence of commercial television in the Nordic countries, and the often-made criticism of the lowest-common-denominator effect of commercial broadcasting, it is still fair to say that in all four Nordic countries public-service channels remain dominant, if not always in audience share, certainly in setting the standard in news and public affairs. While the contrast is not quite as clear as it is in the case of newspaper reading, the Nordic countries fall plainly on the public-service rather than commercially oriented side of the continuum. Here the starker contrast is between the United States, New Zealand,[16] and tiny Luxembourg and the other countries where public-service television continues to play an important, if somewhat diminished, role, and serious effort is made and money invested by public bodies to bring the informational content of television—and, of course, radio—to a level higher than would be the case if left to market forces.

While reading literacy has deep historical roots, it was not so long ago that radio and television arrived on the scene. With the British Broadcasting Corporation leading the way, the electronic media were primarily regarded and thus organized as instruments of public information—even education—rather than entertainment. During the crucial early days of radio in the first half of the twentieth century, the Swedish public broadcasting system (SR) was as much linked to the world of adult education as it was to journalism. From the outset, SR's charter included a clause mandating it to promote adult education (through educational programs and cooperation with the adult education societies) and provide "uplifting" entertainment. In 1931 one of the leaders of the Swedish adult education movement, Yngve Hugo of the ABF (see chapter 9), was appointed head of the educational division of SR. Swedish Radio took the leading role in the "listening circles" movement (initiated by the BBC), collaborating with the adult education societies to produce radio programs for use by study circles whose "foremost common denominator was their role as a school for citizenship" (Nordberg 1998: 377).

The content of radio and later television programming was very much shaped by its educational role, even after the formal link with the adult educational organizations was severed. (This relationship was so profound on both sides that the term *adult education* is too narrow to do justice to a whole range of activities that, as we shall see in chapter 9, went well beyond the classroom.) Of course much changed after television replaced radio as the main electronic medium: commercialization, which has come increasingly to mean globalization, has spread. As reflected in the TV dependency figures in chapter 7, most countries moved toward the American model, though stopping short of its almost entirely commercial character. The most common system mixes private and public ownership, with public-service channels usually partially dependent on advertising. (For example, in France, 50 percent of their revenues are from advertising, in Germany 25 percent, and in Italy and Canada about 35 percent.)[17] The exceptions, with little or no advertising revenues, are the public-service television channels in the Nordic countries, with roughly 50 percent of market share, the BBC, with 40 percent, and the ABC (Australia) with 15 percent. By more or less imitating the commercial channels' light entertainment strategy, Italy's RAI and France's F2 and F3 combined win 49 and 41 percent of market share respectively. Taking a middle road between infotainment and public information wins Germany's ARD and ZDF 39 percent, but only 12 percent for Canada's CBC.[18] These differences are reflected in television's share of overall advertising expenditures, which in Europe averaged 30 percent in 1995. (Switzerland was lowest at just under 10 percent; the Nordic countries and the Netherlands had slightly under 20 percent, Germany and Austria just over 20 percent, and Italy was highest at 53 percent—De Bens and Østbye 1998: 19.)

Promoting Civic Literacy through Political Institutional Choices

From policies directed toward the media, we go to policies affecting political institutions that foster civic literacy. Connecting the two are political parties, the prime organizational actors in disseminating political knowledge, which increasingly rely on the media to get their messages out. In chapters 5 and 6, we saw how proportional electoral systems enhance the overall capacity of political parties to carry out this role. It should come as no surprise that proportional systems tend also to feature laws and regulations other than electoral systems that facilitate the smaller parties' playing their representational role (Bowler, Carter, and Farrell 2000), thus promoting the political participation of, especially, people with low levels of education.[19]

Here we shall concentrate on laws and regulations that directly affect information dissemination and, thus, civic literacy. The most direct connection is through the newspapers themselves. While not as partisan as they used to be, Scandinavian newspapers generally still identify with a party: newspaper subsidies were established not simply to foster diversity in the media but also to facilitate the political parties' publicly presenting their views. In the case of television, the use of the media for transmitting partisan political information becomes more problematic, first, because of the cost and thus inequality of access involved and, second, because of television's greater potential for distortion. The Scandinavian countries are among the strictest when it comes to facilitating equal access to television. Sweden and Norway have, by and large, eliminated political-party television commercials,[20] while Denmark restricts campaign television commercials to the public-service channels with equal time allotted to all parties. In this, they are somewhat distinct. Most common is a policy of providing free time on the public-service channels but also permitting privately purchased advertising—though in most cases under restricted conditions (Holtz-Bacha and Kaid 1995). The exception is the United States, where money—and only money—gets a party or candidate TV time.

With television campaigning constrained, distributed written information remains a significant feature of Nordic politics. One manifestation is to be found in the political information kiosks set up during campaigns.

The visitor to any Swedish city or town square will encounter wooden huts reminiscent of the summer cottage *(stuga)* where parties distribute their programs and campaign literature and where candidates and party leaders meet electors. Further, each of the Swedish parties is associated with one of eleven adult educational associations that organize state-supported study circles for their member organizations. The political parties use these study circles most frequently to familiarize party members and sympathizers with party programs and strategies in the period before an election. During election years, such partisan study circles can account for up to half of the study circles offered.

In addition to these indirect measures, there is a generous system of direct subsidies to the political parties in the Nordic countries. These are not without their critics, who complain that too much of the money ends up in the hands of party bureaucrats whose very careers become dependent on the continuation of the subsidies. While such criticism appears justified in light of significantly declining party membership and identification, Pierre, Svåsand, and Widfeldt (2000) find no evidence of such a relationship. Moreover, from a comparative civic literacy perspective, these failings are still more than compensated for by the fact that the subsidies facilitate voters' getting information directly from the political parties with which they identify and thus make them less dependent on the mass media for political information. An indication that enhancing party identification through such measures contributes to civic literacy is provided by the results of a survey conducted during the 1994 referendum campaigns on EU membership in Finland, Sweden, and Norway. Voters with stronger party identification, and who shared their party's position on EU membership, had the greatest factual and conceptual knowledge of the European Union (Jenssen and Listhaug 1999).[21]

Measures promoting the capacity of parties to inform voters may also facilitate party members' and supporters' playing a more active part in party activities. This is suggested by Krouwel (1999), who examined the level of openness in the procedures used by European political parties to select candidates.[22] Krouwel's data show that the countries with the most open systems correspond essentially to those identified in part one as having high levels of both local voting turnout and organizational participation.[23]

Table 8–1 gives a sense of the extent of public support for political-party activities, setting out the Nordic countries' annual levels of support in the national currency for the political parties' operations at all levels (including the youth wings) for the latest year available. The table does not include public support tied to election campaign expenses,[24] nor for party-oriented study circles and other such quasi-educational party activities, nor for the party press, which in some cases is distinct from that going directly as press supports.[25] The Nordic approach is to use general grants from the appropriate levels of government to compensate the parties for expenditures for normal operations outside an election campaign.

The contrast here parallels that drawn with overall civic literacy: at one pole of a continuum on regulations affecting party funding are the Nordic countries; at the other is the United States. American voters are far more dependent on commercial television for political information because of both the structure of the media and the resources available to political parties.[26] In 1984, for example, the entire election campaign expenditures by Swedish political parties amounted to one-fourth of those of candidates for the California U.S. Senate seat.[27] The result, as a study comparing Sweden and the United States concluded, is that "low media users in Sweden, unlike those in the United States, . . . are utilizing sources other than the mass media for political information—most likely originating from direct involvement with partisan organizational activism" (Miller and Asp 1985: 249).

In the United States, the dependence on private funding, the importance of television advertising, and the incentives for exaggeration and negative campaigning built into winner-take-all electoral institutions go hand in hand. Much has been written on these features of American election campaigns, and there is no need to repeat them here. Instead we simply note certain quantitative manifestations of a process that effectively excludes parties and candidates unable to raise a great deal of money and, among other things, thus constrains the citizen's access to information about possible policy alternatives.

We can begin with figures gathered by the Center for Voting and Democracy in Washington, D.C. In 1998, and again in 2000, over 98 percent of incumbents in the House of Representatives were reelected; in 1998, 94 of 435 races were uncontested by one of the two major parties, and only 43 districts were won with less than a 10 percentage point spread. (The average victory margin was 43 points.) To the knowledge of this writer, the members of no other legislature in the democratic world face so little competition. Yet American legislators are ideologically deeply divided over

TABLE 8–1

Public Financial Support for Political-Party Activities

	Denmark	Sweden	Norway	Finland
Amount	DK 72.4 m	SEK 321 m	NRK 124 m	FIM 82 m
Year	1986–87	1991–92	1991	1989

Sources: Gidlund 1991; Svåsand 1991; Wiberg 1991; Pederson and Bille 1991.

In the period in question, the Swedish and Norwegian Crowns were valued at around 6 to a U.S. dollar, the Danish Crown at 8, and the Finnmark at 4.

major issues. The problem is unequal access to (money for) television in a winner-take-all electoral system. In a campaign story for the Associated Press (AP) on October 19, 1998, Kevin Galvin reported that "in two-thirds of House races, the incumbent holds a 10-to-1 fund-raising advantage over his or her challenger, or faces no challenger at all." An AP story after the election (by Jonathan D. Salant, December 29) tells us something about the amounts involved, and why they were needed.

> In one of every six congressional races this fall, at least one candidate's cam-
> paign cost $1 million or more. . . . The Federal Election Commission re-
> ported that Senate and House candidates spent $617.1 million between Jan.
> 1, 1997, and Nov. 23, 1998. . . . One factor in the increased spending by
> House candidates is the growth in the number of television and cable sta-
> tions. "There are no volunteer armies any more," Republican consultant
> Jack Cookfair explained. "The most effective way to reach large numbers of
> voters at a reasonable cost per thousands is television. Because of all the clut-
> ter that's out there, you need to have people see your spots so many more
> times to drive your message." Incumbents have the distinct advantage since
> they can use their office for fund-raising, "which begins anew as soon as the
> election ends."

According to the Center for Responsive Politics, a nonpartisan, non-profit research group, on its website the day after the 2000 U.S. election, the presidential candidates in total raised $350 million for the campaign, the most expensive Senate campaign (of thirty-four) raised $80 million, and the most expensive House campaign $10 million. Journalistic reports estimated the total spending of the candidates for national office at some-where around $3 billion,[28] not including the unregulated "soft money" contributions to political parties.

Indisputably, the failure of the United States to regulate the use of pri-vate money in electoral campaigns and, especially, in paying for television commercials feed into the lack of information available to voters, especially those with limited resources. Moreover, it also skews party strategy and, hence, government policy. Robert Reich, at the end of his account of four years in the first Clinton cabinet, describes the successful electoral strategy based on ignoring all categories of people lacking the resources to partici-pate politically, quoting Clinton's chief pollster, Mark Warren:

> We co-opted the Republicans of all their issues—getting tough on welfare,
> tough on crime, balancing the budget, and cracking down on illegal immigra-
> tion. . . . This election signals the end of the old Democratic coalition of blacks,
> the elderly and the downscale. It marks the emergence of a new Democratic
> coalition of women, Latinos, and, especially, middle-class couples.

The strategy worked, admits Reich, but he adds:

> The fact is few people voted. The turnout was the lowest percentage of the voting population since 1924—seven million fewer people than in 1992. And almost all of the new non-voters were from households earning less than $50,000 a year. (Reich 1997: 330–31)

There is much more detail that should be added to our discussion of the civic literacy effects of various regulations and programs affecting campaign spending and political-party activities, but the absence of any systematic comparative schema for portraying the situation in the different industrial democracies prevents our doing so here. What we do know suffices to add substance to a distinction drawn in part two; when it comes to measures affecting the contribution to civic literacy by political parties and the media, the Scandinavian countries are at one pole, and the United States, clearly and firmly, is at the other.

Transparency

There is a dimension to information dissemination in high-civic-literacy countries not yet captured in the discussion.[29] At its most profound, this transparency dimension[30] is etched into the functioning of local political institutions, which can be adequately described only at a micro-level (as in chapter 9) and cannot be captured in macro-level comparisons.

One macro-level manifestation of this concern is in the three Nordic EU members' demands for transparency in EU operations discussed in the final chapter. Each, following the Danish example, have special parliamentary committees where proposals to be brought before the European Council are discussed, in the full view of the media and the public.[31] At the national level, there are regulations governing the availability and accessibility of information related to the public interest. In this context, transparency has two basic policy thrusts: first, the requirement in Sweden (and other Nordic countries) that individual and corporate tax-return information be public[32] and, second, that public institutions open their books to interested citizens with ombudspersons appointed to ensure that this is done (Axberger 1996).[33] The underlying principle is well stated by Gunnar Myrdal, who, as we shall see in part four, was one of the founders of the contemporary Scandinavian welfare state. Myrdal wrote the following in the 1950s, after he had withdrawn from Swedish politics.

> Except in Sweden, a person's wealth and income is not a matter for public record, but is supposed to be entirely his own private affair—with the provi-

sion only that they must be disclosed in confidence, to the tax-assessing authorities. . . . In this undemocratic and protective social system a major role is
played by the formidable power of the communications industry to influence
people's attitudes and choices. . . . Under the influence of propaganda for private consumption of all kinds, which is not matched by any equally powerful
campaign for the consumption of services provided by organized society, the
voters tend to keep the public spending below the level that would be rational.
. . . Reforms in the interest of the effective implementation of the voters' true
inclinations . . . have everywhere to overcome tremendous inhibitions, created by the services of the communications industry. (Myrdal 1958: 80–81)

As Myrdal reminds us, the better individuals are informed, the better
they can identify the effects alternative policy options have on their own
interests and those of others. To overcome information asymmetries, the
Scandinavian welfare state developed a series of well-entrenched
information-enhancing policies. The underlying assumption is that, as the
opening section of the Swedish Social Democratic Party's official position
paper on EU membership[34] puts it, "everybody is both desirous and capable of playing a part in the running of society. . . . The individual is capable of acquiring knowledge and insights which will enable him to play a
part in the life of the community" (SAP 1993: 6).[35]

It is on this note that we end this chapter. I do not here provide, as I have
done elsewhere,[36] a picture of the wide range of measures used to support
noncommercial cultural activities in the Scandinavian countries. These
various measures have only a thin direct connection to civic literacy, but
form part of the cultural underpinning of the institutions and policies that
do contribute to civic literacy. Publicly supported cultural and educational
activities offer an alternative point of reference to that of commercial television, yet one that is largely invisible as it is woven into the fabric of civil
society. To see this, consequently, we need to move toward micro-level observation and away from the comparison of national aggregates.

9

Promoting Civic Literacy
through Adult Education

Modern systems of education tend to treat adult education as a phenomenon quite separate from the formal education of the young. And indeed, unlike education directed at young people, adult education is available to all and open-ended in content: its mission to disseminate knowledge at whatever level is appropriate for the recipient. As such, it is a form of education that is "continuing" or "permanent." In a sense, whatever the specific content, adult education is civic education; that is, it is education aimed at citizens, qua citizens.[1] Citizens by definition are capable of choice, including the choice of shunning adult education programs and informing themselves in other ways—or not at all.

Its voluntary and open-ended nature makes adult education distinct but also relegates it to a secondary place in societies' educational policy priorities. This is inevitable when it comes to investment of scarce public resources; but it typically applies also to low-cost choices that can nevertheless have a major impact. The reality is that adults generally know far better where to find information about educational services for their children than for themselves. The same applies to the educational research community. Compared to what we know about formal education systems for the young, there is a penury of basic information about adult education expenditures, levels of participation, performance criteria, or staffing.[2] What little we do know suggests, not surprisingly, that most nations underinvest in the civic literacy of their adult population. Yet, since no systematic comparative data are to be found, policy makers really have no comparative basis for assessing existing efforts. Lacking basic information on inputs, we are hardly in a position to assess outputs. Yet there is good reason to believe that, when it comes to civic literacy, the content of what is learned as an adult is more important than that learned in school in one's youth. Such learning is, of course, not limited to organized courses in the classroom; private activities like reading newspapers and visiting the library—manifestations of what the International Adult Literacy Survey (IALS) refers to as the "literacy habit"—matter greatly.[3]

Teaching "Civics" to Adolescents

While participation in adult education activities stimulates reading and other activities that comprise the "literacy habit," it is fair to say that the primary contribution to the development of such habits takes place earlier, during the period of compulsory schooling. Note, however, that this is a phenomenon largely distinct from course content, that is, from the extent to which formal schooling includes a civics component. Though there is some American and Swedish evidence that civics courses enhance the political knowledge of students,[4] it is uncertain that the information acquired in such courses is retained into adulthood so as to impinge on civic literacy.[5] At least in the latter decades of the twentieth century, adolescence is a stage in life little conducive to the kind of learning stressed in civics courses.[6] Hence, however well taught, the content of civics courses is expected to fade over time unless reinforced in organized educational or political activities in adulthood. In contrast, habits of general literacy acquired during formal schooling are more likely to prove lasting, since they are reinforced by private activities.

These are but suppositions because, as with adult education, there is no systematic information to be found about the quantity and variety of civics courses offered in different countries and their effects. "Civic education is a low-status subject and curricular aim" (Torney-Purta, Schwille, and Amadeo 1999: 31) despite the renewed interest in citizenship education signaled by the International Commission on Education for the Twenty-First Century established by UNESCO in 1993.[7] In recent years, a number of countries have set up task forces and investigatory commissions on citizen education. Fostering citizenship is a core objective of British Labour's "third way." The Blair government accepted the recommendation of the Advisory Commission on Citizenship (the 1998 "Crick Report") making citizenship education a statutory subject as of 2002. Crick sought to foster a "culture of active citizenship" by teaching the knowledge, skills, and values that comprise political literacy, going even further than the Australian Commission on Civics and Citizenship Education, which, in its 1994 report, elaborated a detailed proposal for eight levels of civics-related courses from primary school right through secondary school, with the greatest concentration on grades eight to ten (Civics Expert Group 1994).

The report also commissioned a survey of "international best practices" in civics education. But due to the dearth of comprehensive information the survey merely described the three basic approaches it identified as characterizing then-current practice in OECD countries, associated respectively with the U.S., Britain, and France.[8] It made no attempt to compare the benefits of the three, no doubt because recognized instruments for doing so do not exist. In the absence of hard international data needed to do the quantitative and qualitative comparisons required, we cannot know what, if any, effects on civic literacy are produced by differences in the approach taken to civics education for schoolchildren. From what we have seen about the low levels of political knowledge revealed in chapter 4, one cannot but be skeptical about any wider or long-term effects of civics courses, given that such courses—typically about U.S. government—are taken by the majority of high school students (Hahn 1998: 17).[9]

It is a reflection of renewed interest in civics education that the IEA (the International Association for the Evaluation of Educational Achievement), which is known for its comparative assessments of students' native-language and science comprehension, coordinates an ongoing comprehensive Civics Education Study. This ongoing study should add to our knowledge of the civic literacy of adolescents and the effects of civics-related courses directed toward them. The first phase assembled case studies in twenty countries based on the responses to fifteen questions posed to fourteen- and fifteen-year-old students, as well as to more detailed questionnaires given to teachers of civics-related courses (Torney-Purta, Schwille, and Amadeo 1999). Out of this process, three core international frames of reference were identified (as paraphrased from the IEA's project summary and guidelines) for in-depth study: (1) democracy, institutions, rights, and responsibilities,[10] (2) national identity,[11] and (3) social cohesion and diversity[12]—the first of which corresponds most closely to civic literacy.

Phase two recast these framing questions into a ninety-minute test of students' knowledge, skills, and attitudes, combined with a teachers' questionnaire dealing with civics course content and delivery, placing more emphasis on attitudes and values than on knowledge. Such questions are problematic since we do not know to what extent the answers reflect the students' understanding of what they are expected to say, rather than what they will actually do when given the opportunity to, say, vote upon reaching age eighteen. The results of an earlier and less ambitious IEA Civics Education Study (Torney-Purta et al. 1974), which tested students at ages ten, fourteen, sixteen, and seventeen in ten countries, though dated, are revealing in this regard. It found no relationship between knowledge of political institutions and positive attitudes toward civic participation.

Current IEA study results (Torney-Purta et al. 2001) were released as this book was being completed. They showed a clear relationship between the civic knowledge of fourteen- to fifteen-year-olds and their intention to vote. For purposes of this analysis, however, the findings raised more questions than they answered. The aggregate scores show little relationship between young people's civic knowledge and (adult) civic literacy. Unfortunately, we cannot draw any inferences about the comparative effects of socialization and civic education after age fourteen since the questions tested the capacity to comprehend how democratic institutions work rather than specific factual knowledge. A second group will be added to the main study (eighteen-year-olds), and new questions that directly get at political knowledge, though fewer countries will participate. The results should provide insight into civic literacy among young people and let us begin to link differences in effort invested in civics education with levels of civic literacy.[13]

In the meantime, I wish to stress the effect of formal schooling on promoting "habits of literacy." In chapter 4 we noted the fairly close correlation between countries' average scores (especially for students at the lower percentiles) in the TIMSS tests of sixteen-year-old students' literacy in mathematics and science, and the level of functional literacy among adults measured in the IALS study. This relationship suggests differences in the extent to which systems of formal schooling contribute to young persons' attaining the functional literacy required to (one day) comprehend the basic texts and documents associated with competent citizenship. The strong relationship between adult literacy and the average scores of students at the lower percentiles in TIMMS suggests that the key contribution has to do with inculcating habits of literacy in the overall student population. Some schools, and also the school systems of some countries, are better at encouraging a larger proportion of students to read newspapers and books, use libraries, make use of political maps,[14] write letters, and so on—habits retained into adulthood.[15]

Support for such a conclusion is found in the results of the IEA's Reading Literacy Study of 1991, which tested reading (narrative, expository, and document) skills of fourteen-year-old students in thirty-two countries. While the average scores do not correlate in any significant way with those

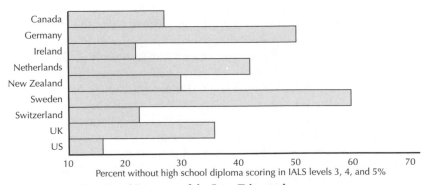

FIGURE 9–1 Functional Literacy of the Less Educated

of the IALS (Finland, France, Sweden, and New Zealand had the highest means), the dispersion rate, which was especially low in top-ranked Finland, fits into the pattern we have observed: "in all three domains, New Zealand, the United States and Canada (British Columbia) showed the widest range of achievement between the lowest 5% and the highest 5%" (Elley and Schleicher 1994: 59). Yet, even here, we can give too much importance to what happens in school.

The data from the 1997 IALS report set out in figure 9-1 show the high-civic-literacy countries—Sweden, the Netherlands, and Germany—do especially well among those with the lowest levels of schooling. Sweden distinguishes itself most of all in the performance of those with the lowest levels of formal education. This suggests that what matters most is the reinforcement of literacy habits acquired at school after formal schooling has been completed. Sweden stands out as a world leader in policies designed to encourage adults to acquire and use information especially through participation in adult education—to which we now turn.

Educating Adults

Let us look more closely at what we know of Swedish inputs into adult education. I have written previously about the role of study circles (Milner 1989 and 1994) in Sweden and the other Nordic countries, and here concentrate on those features relevant to our comparative analysis. We begin with current information from Sweden to illustrate what is generally accepted as Scandinavia's leading role in adult education. As the IALS concluded from its survey: "Countries fall broadly into three categories. The Nordic countries are in the first group where lifelong learning has become a reality for a large segment of the population. Over the 12 month period preceding the survey, Denmark, Finland and Sweden have overall participation rates over 50 percent . . . and Norway rates close to 50 percent" (OECD 2000: 42).[16]

Of course, these numbers tell us very little, since we know nothing of how much time was spent in such courses and what was taught. Moreover, apart from the limitations of all such subjective assessments, this one also weakens comparability by mixing adult education and retraining, since they are not alike in their relationship to civic literacy. Some countries, Germany especially, invest heavily and quite effectively on retraining. But such courses make less of a contribution to civic literacy than the study circles for which Sweden is famous. With over 2.8 million participants in study circles (in 1997)[17] out of a population of 9 million, with 10 percent of its education budget going to adult education (Rubensson 1994), and with an estimated 75 percent of adults having at least one time in their lives attended study circles (Lundström and Wijkström 1998: 215), we can say with some assurance—even in the absence of systematic comparative indicators of adult education, either by participation or by expenditure—that Sweden is a world leader in adult education.

One useful study casts light on the differences in adult education participation between top-ranking Sweden and Canada. Rubensson (1994) not only provides overall data of the proportion of adults participating in adult education, but also breaks down the figures by the participants' level of education (see table 9–1). As we can see, Olof Palme's "study-circle democracy" leads in all categories, while Canada's limited efforts are concentrated among university graduates. The ratio of university graduates participating in adult education compared to those with less than nine years of education is nine to one in Canada, but only three to one in Sweden. There is surely a correspondence between this ratio of these "inputs," and the "outputs" (in figure 9–1), revealing that of those who have not finished high school more than twice as many Swedes as Canadians score average or above in the IALS.

The extent to which countries gather data on adult education is in itself indicative of the importance of a program. An indication of its being a priority in Sweden lies in the establishment of a Royal Commission in the latter 1990s to investigate adult education services. The commission's report has much to teach us about adult education in Sweden. It found that, while there has been a slight decline during the 1990s, study circles and related activities still play a prominent role in the lives of citizens.[18] Overall, adult education turned out to be healthier than suspected due, it appears, to the fact that perceptions among opinion leaders tended to disproportionately reflect developments in the Stockholm metropolitan region, where there has been a continuing decline. A brief look at more specific figures is instructive.

There are eleven adult education associations in Sweden linked to organizations representing different sectors of society as well as the political parties. According to the Royal Commission report, there were a total of 336,037 study circles in 1997, lasting an average of thirty-five to forty hours, with a total of 2,844,356 participants. This was down from the

TABLE 9–1

Participation in Adult Education by Educational Background (1983)

	Canada (%)	Sweden (%)
Fewer than 9 years of schooling	5	21
Upper secondary school	19	46
University education	45	64

Source: Rubensson 1994.

decade's high of 343,732 (in 1990–91, before the recession) but higher than most years since. As usual, the largest number of study circles stressed improving skills such as music appreciation, foreign languages, computers, accounting, and safety, weapon use, and orienteering in the wilderness (required to obtain an elk-hunting license). Music appreciation was the most popular subject, followed by international affairs and media studies. Overall, about one-third of study circles centered on political-social issues, the number rising and declining according to the proximity of elections and referenda, and the salience of issues in public debate at the national or local levels. In addition, adult education societies in that year organized 165,000 miscellaneous popular cultural events (a number that has been rising steadily), as well as 38,000 noncourse pedagogical activities, such as conferences and lectures.

The great variety of these courses makes it impossible to state hard-and-fast rules about their contribution to civic literacy. We can get a better idea by focusing on concrete examples. The largest of the eleven adult education associations is the Workers' Educational Association (ABF), which is affiliated with the Swedish Labor Confederation (LO) and the Social Democratic Party (SAP). It merits special attention because of its size and importance but also because it has the most significant role in serving those whose educational backgrounds and occupations are in themselves least conducive to continuing education. Founded in 1912 by the SAP and a number of trade unions, cooperatives, and organizations representing women, retired persons, and tenants, ABF organizes about 100,000 study circles for over a million participants (roughly 30 percent of all study circles in Sweden).

The ABF program commits the organization "to educate the members of its affiliated organizations for positions in associations, working life and society; and to create conditions for everyone to participate in freely chosen education and cultural life." Study circles "seek to stimulate a critical attitude, to help clarify the difference between facts and opinions on crucial issues of the day." Courses concerned with civics education are thus given priority. While it organizes a wide variety of study circles—including those leading to the much sought-after elk-hunting permit—ABF places priority on those concerned with public policy issues and related developments. Over 50,000 people participated in ABF study circles on EU membership in the period preceding the 1994 referendum.

While all study circles are partially subsidized by state funds (the average is roughly 50 percent—Rubensson 2000: 22), such civics-oriented circles focusing discussion on important questions of the day are eligible for special state funding. These include local issues, such as threatened plant closings and access to green space in planned urban development, and national issues affecting public health,[19] economic prosperity, and social justice, such as nuclear power and the effects of computers (Oliver 1987: 49–51, 57–59).[20]

We shall see in part four how such programs complement the social and economic policies of the "Swedish model": how well-informed citizens acting on their interests in the context of appropriate government policies can encourage growth and the sharing in the fruits of that growth. Relevant information is disseminated through a network of institutions beginning with the study circles but extending to the traditional services to adults provided through the formal system of education and the institutions of the labor market. The former consist primarily of *komvux*, municipally run catch-up courses for completing compulsory and upper secondary education.[21] The latter comprise Sweden's famous labor-market training courses run in close collaboration with employers' organizations and trade unions. In between are the various programs offered annually to some 200,000 Swedish adults in the *folkhögskola*, the approximately 140 popular institutes of adult education that provide specialized courses in many areas of knowledge usually tailored to the needs of the economy in the regions where they are situated—including distance education in the remote regions.

Something should be said about civics education in Swedish schools at this point, given the close link between the educational system and adult education. In Sweden, civics courses are designed for the upper secondary school level. Education at this level is provided by separate institutions (*gymnasia*), attended by the overwhelming majority of sixteen- to eighteen-year-olds, as well as certain specialized institutions and the *komvux* centers. While, as noted above, we should not expect much of a direct impact on adult civic literacy from civics courses followed as adolescents, there is reason to believe that the impact in Sweden is likely to be higher than elsewhere due to the relative maturity (late teens) of Swedish students taking courses at the upper secondary level.[22] Hence the pronounced concern with civic literacy merits consideration.

I cite below from the official translation of the formal educational program at the upper secondary level.[23] The program not only defines the obligations the state places on the school but also the demands and expectations students may make on the school as well as those that the school makes on the students.[24] The curriculum sets out the basic values of the school (which are to a great extent common to the whole of the school system). The first excerpt is from the overall study program; the second is from the section setting out the content of the civics course taken by all students for a minimum of ninety hours (three hundred hours for social science students).

The school . . . shall strive to ensure that all pupils:

- further develop their ability to consciously adopt ethical standpoints based on knowledge and personal experience,
- respect the intrinsic value and integrity of other people,

- work against people being exposed to oppression and abusive treatment and are a source of help for other people,
- understand and respect other people and cultures,
- can empathize with and understand the situation other people are in and also develop the will to act with their best interests at heart and
- show respect and care for the . . . environment.

On completion of the [civics] course students will:

- be able to give an account of important political ideologies and their development, and how these ideologies influence views on various social conditions,
- have broader knowledge on how Swedish society has developed and currently functions, and be able to make certain comparisons with conditions in other countries,
- know what influences the economic conditions of the community, companies and individuals,
- be able to place economic, political and social development in a historical perspective,
- be able to consider international relations and global conditions from economic, political, legal and cultural aspects as well as being conscious of conditions for international cooperation, and the political goals and means of Swedish security policy,
- be able to use different sources of knowledge and tools to analyze and discuss social issues, using different approaches, and in such a manner that their own opinions are made clear.

Does exposure to such courses enhance civic literacy in Sweden? Judging by the content and age of the students, there is good reason to believe that it does on both the civic and literacy side. An example of the close link between school civics courses and the political process is found in the strategy adopted by the parliamentary commission mandated to take the issues raised at the EU's Intergovernmental Conference to the Swedish population. It targeted study circles and other activities associated with adult education, especially the civics-related classes and projects of senior upper secondary students. A micro-level concrete example of such courses enhancing the civic side of civic literacy is a program instituted in the 1990s in civics classes in the upper secondary schools of the northern Swedish city of Umeå. In order to provide a bridge from the classroom and to the channels of political organization and activity outside the school, and thus encourage political participation, representatives of the local units of political parties are invited to explain their programs and describe their concrete actions. This choice reflects the integrated structure of political parties noted in chapter 6, in which these units are the primary connecting link between the citizen and the political institutions. It also reflects the fact that, unlike elsewhere, such initiatives do not give rise to criticism of "politicizing" the classroom.[25] Both structurally and culturally, the consensual nature of Scandinavian institutions makes political parties legitimate constituents of community life.

Umeå as Case Study

Numbers of annual participants in study circles do not capture a crucial dimension of organizations affecting civic literacy, the fact that they are integrated into a dense network of the various organizations. The existence of such networks is conducive to civic engagement, attenuating geographical mobility by integrating individuals and families into the lives of their communities.[26] In Sweden, it is in the large northern hinterland (Norrland), with three-fifths of the territory but only one-eighth of the population, that people have been under the greatest economic pressure to move. The city of Umeå has best resisted these pressures and here serves as a case study of patterns of organized activities affecting civic literacy at the micro level in (nonmetropolitan) Sweden and Scandinavia. Umeå is not "average"—but it is also not unique—in manifesting the local features of policies and institutions that contribute to civic literacy.

Umeå is the administrative center of Västerbotten County. Its population of just over 100,000 places it among a number of midsize Swedish cities, but makes it the largest city in the north of Sweden. Of the five counties that make up Norrland, Västerbotten was traditionally one of the poorest, lacking a significant industrial base in mining, lumbering, and ironwork. Things began to change when far-sighted regional leaders were successful in making Umeå the site of the regional hospital and then university (see Lane 1983), and thus a magnet for a developing service economy as "smoke stack" industries elsewhere in Norrland entered a period of acute decline.

Study Circles

Västerbotten also stands out for its politics. Though the SAP became dominant elsewhere in Norrland in the 1920s, the Liberals remained the main party in Västerbotten until 1936 and a significant force until the 1970s. Liberal support was one expression of the deeply ingrained tradition of independent thought manifested most discernibly in the prohibition and—closely linked—free church movement in the nineteenth century.[27] The activities of these various movements gave rise to a powerful tradition of popular education, a tradition still very much alive. According to the 1997 report of the Royal Commission on Adult Education Services, Västerbotten, with roughly 45 percent of the population participating annually in a study circle in a given year, was highest in per capita participation, 55 percent above the national average.[28]

We have already said something about civics education in Umeå. Let us look more closely at adult education. The ABF is especially strong in Västerbotten, and plays a leading role in the association that coordinates the regional and local activities of the eleven adult-education associations. ABF's seven subregional units annually provide courses averaging thirty hours to a fourth of Västerbotten's quarter of a million people—in addition to organizing 1,600 separate cultural activities, led by almost 3,500 different people.[29] ABF's base in the region is tied to its historical role in the early Swedish labor and temperance movements, from which it drew inspiration for the principles guiding its program: the equal value of all people and the ability of every person to take responsibility for his or her own life and share in the responsibility for the common concerns of society.

A valuable insight into the role and guiding principles of adult education in Västerbotten's early labor and temperance movement, has been preserved in the work of social historian Ronny Ambjörnsson. His 1987 paper about the movement, titled "The Honest and Diligent Worker," evocatively re-creates the experiences in the coastal town of Holmsund (fifteen kilometers from Umeå) around the turn of the century. To do justice to this rich tradition, I can do no better than cite from this paper.[30] Based on minutes of discussion groups associated with the local temperance lodges and certain trade unions, and supplemented by interviews with people who had been active in these organizations in the 1920s, it vividly captures the spirit of a time and place.

> The discussions . . . form a pattern that can be formulated in the question: How shall the good life be lived? . . . At the meetings these sorts of existential questions are raised more and more often: What is it that makes life worth living? What is a good person? What is real happiness? . . . These discussions . . . once raised . . . take on their own life and insist upon authentic answers. The debates become successively more lively and the questions [extended]: What shall society that allows good people to live a good life look like?
>
> From reading aloud, the step is not long to a more regular, educational activity and already by the middle of the 1890s the ground has been laid for a library that not only comprises temperance literature but also books of a more general, culture-historical interest. . . . By 1900 it is the general opinion that "the people" need their own school because the existing school did not teach "anything of worth," only "long catechism and psalm verses.". . .

The diligence that the lodges cultivated finds its expression even in the early trade union movement. . . . Joint parties and trips were often arranged. . . . Enthusiasm for education is also high within the union. One reads aloud articles from the papers *Socialdemokraten* and *Västerbottenskurien* and also recommends the studying of different books. Ignorance is seen to be as great an enemy as drunkenness; one speaks sometimes of "the intoxication of ignorance." . . . Intoxication anesthetizes and makes the drunken man almost merge with his surroundings. Temperance gives distance. . . . The discussions . . . can be seen as exercises in looking at reality from different angles. . . . Reading has a similar function. . . .

The building of a study-circle [was] discussed . . . in the 1890s. The circle however does not start until 1912 and then mainly as an organisation for the acquiring of books for a library. . . . And one discusses within the circle how books shall be read, namely with "reflection and cogitation." . . . The study-circle is, firstly, itself a collective and one is very insistent that the circle-leader shall not come from the outside and that he—it is always a he—shall not dominate the group. It is collectively gathered knowledge one is out after and not, as in school, knowledge given from a teacher's desk. . . .

Within the study-circle, the lodge and the early trade union movements is developed . . . the idea that it is a person's duty as an individual to take part in the discussions that, alone, lead to a better world. By reading books the individual is given the separate perspectives which, when they are confronted with each other, create insight, which can in turn lead to a political action. . . . Parallel to the courses in . . . culture and literature, [are] courses . . . in local-government. . . . During the 1920s the discussions take on a more and more clearly defined political character. . . . Democracy must activate people. For those in the study circles the solution is obvious: Knowledge—or more correctly education—shall guarantee democracy."

While Umeå ABF's fall 1999 program offered the usual range of courses in languages, computers, art, music, and nature appreciation, most distinctive were the courses reflecting its objective of assisting people to take responsibility for their lives and the common concerns of society. These include courses in organizing groups and cooperatives, in public speaking, writing, and understanding media, as well as study circles on social and civil rights, the United Nations, war and peace, the future of democracy, feminism, various aspects of history, and important contemporary books.

Libraries and Newspapers

Ambjörnsson describes the organic link between the early study circles and libraries.[31] It was ABF's forerunner that opened the first library in Umeå.

In 1966 it became the interlibrary lending center for the northern region,[32] and in 1985 moved its large collection (in forty-eight languages in all) to a modern building at the center of Umeå, which is used each day by an average of four thousand people.[33] Large numbers are children, making use of its large children's library as well as taking part in book-related activities; five of the thirteen branch libraries also serve as school libraries. In Umeå, included with the information and guidance in proper feeding, exercise, and general care of the newborn given to all new mothers in Sweden by the district nurse is a gift from the library, *The Child's First Book*, a compilation of much-loved Swedish rhymes and stories for children. This is part of the library's community outreach program, and it is distributed by the nurse at the time of the first postnatal home visit in order to underscore that reading, just like proper nutrition and hygiene, is vital to the development of a healthy child.

The library also has a bookmobile providing service to two hundred towns and villages. Umeå's Stadsbiblioteket also has a specialized collection of books and other material about the northern region and the aboriginal Sami people, with its own database.[34] Reading is by no means limited to books. The Umeå Library subscribes to more than one thousand magazines and newspapers in forty different languages, with an online index of every periodical found in the system and ready access to links to the newspapers' and magazines' own websites. This reflects, and apparently has not dampened, the region's popular habit of reading newspapers. The local newspaper, the *Västerbottens Kurier*, is read by 75 percent of Umeå.[35] To this we need add the 25 percent who read the smaller local daily, the *Västerbottens Folkblad*, another 5–10 percent who read the national (Stockholm) morning papers, and at least twice that many who read one of the afternoon national tabloids.

Another important source of civic literacy is to be found in the services provided at the documentation center at Umeå's City Hall. The center is tailored especially to the needs of persons looking for written or electronic information about formal and adult education and training and employment. Easily accessible documentation can be found on every aspect, from compulsory school curricula and prerequisites to the programs offered annually in the *Folkhögskole* and *Komvox* to the subjects and dates of study circles, labor market training courses, and general interest courses and events offered at the university and by various organizations.[36]

Underlying the emphasis on making information readily available is a long-term regional strategy going back to the 1960s, when local leaders realized that their best long-term hopes lay in development tied to education.[37] Having consolidated the city library collection and services and built up the housing stock so that there was ample available at low cost for newcomers, local officials capitalized on the research opportunities resulting from the presence of the regional hospital to press home their case for locating the new northern university in Umeå (Lane 1983). Its arrival[38] added the final element to the city's legitimate claim to a position at the forefront of information technology (IT) development, which made it a force of attraction for several IT firms.[39]

The New Information Technology

What is especially interesting about the IT strategy of Umeå and similar regions in Scandinavia is its mass rather than elite character. Along with the library, the various city authorities are deeply involved in a concerted effort to spread and intensify computer access and usage. In all (the many) apartment-housing units administered by the municipality, Internet access is automatically provided, while incentive programs have led most of the private housing complexes to do the same. Even further ahead are several of the neighboring towns, which provide free high-speed Internet access to everyone with a telephone.[40] All of this is over and beyond the free Internet terminals at the library branches, at City Hall, and at other public buildings, and even at record and toy stores. By making use of voluntary organizations to serve individuals who might not have (or know how to make use of) computer access,[41] as well as taking advantage of appropriate government programs,[42] they hope to have everyone in the region to be in a position to use a computer and the Internet,[43] so that it will become possible to deliver all needed information to citizens via the Internet.

Umeå's efforts fit into a wider, coordinated regional initiative, "Västerbotten 2005," which seeks to place the region at the front line of informational technology (IT) infrastructure and application. The project is one of twenty-two European Commission–supported regional strategy and action plans known as RISI (Regional Information Society Initiatives) to integrate IT into regional development and employment policies. There is one other Swedish region—Blekinge, in the southeast—among the twenty-two Västerbotten 2005 draws deeply on the participation of organizations and people.[44] At the end of 1996, the County administration mandated CINS (the Center for IT in Northern Sweden) to prepare the groundwork. After its report was circulated among the region's municipalities, the County Council, and almost three hundred private and voluntary enterprises and organizations, in March 1999 the Strategy and Action Plan 1999–2006 was adopted by a board representing the county, the federation of municipalities, the federation of enterprises, the schools, the County Labor Board, CINS, Umeå University, and the Västerbotten Chamber of Commerce.[45]

Closing the Digital Divide

These networks—and the high level of functional literacy—place communities like Umeå in an enviable position to optimize the capacity of the new information technologies to enhance civic literacy. There can be little doubt of Scandinavia leading in this area. An indication comes from the Altavista system's (October 1998) breakdown by language of the 128 million web pages that it recognized. English came first with 87.5 million, followed by German with 5.5 and Japanese with 3.8 million.[46] If we combine the four Nordic languages, they place ahead of Japan, at 4.1 million for a combined population of only 25 million. This is very impressive, especially since we can assume—given the Nordic's legendary facility with foreign languages[47]—that the proportion of web pages originating from these countries in English and other major world languages is disproportionately high. By 2000, Sweden had surpassed the United States in use of personal computers and Internet connectivity and was, by all reports, the new mecca for "Internet entrepreneurs." According to International Data Corporation (IDC), Sweden has "become the world's dominant information economy. . . . All infrastructures—computer, Internet, information, and social—must be a strong interwoven body that works together to support the Information Society. Sweden understands this need for a balanced approach."[48]

The reference to a balanced approach reminds us why the term *literacy* was chosen. It is surely true in some other countries, especially the United States, that Internet use by the large wired minority is more intense than in Scandinavia, in the form of electronic commerce, chat rooms, games, and so on. But IT intensity is not the same as IT literacy: the proportion of people with both the resources and the competence to use IT effectively in their lives. We have no authoritative comparative measures of this, but we do have some fairly clear indications. Consider the case of Finland. While there are more personal computers in Norway, Denmark, and Sweden (UNDP 1998: 193), Finland, which is second only to Sweden in R-and-D investment per GDP,[49] may even be ahead of Sweden in IT literacy. Finland, like Sweden, is the site of two of the twenty-two European Commission–supported Regional Information Society Initiatives.[50]

Finland has been identified in the European Union's *Information Society Newsletter* as "Europe's Information Society," and its representative on the EU Commission, Erkki Liikanen, the commissioner for enterprises, in July 1999, won the coveted[51] post of commissioner for the information society.[52] According to the UNDP (1998: 193), in 1995 there were 70 Internet users in Scandinavia per 1,000 people, compared to 20 for the OECD countries as a whole; but the world leader was Finland with 139 (followed by Iceland with 112). Finland's score was more than twice that of third place Norway and four times the United States, which barely made the top ten.[53] Yet the United States is a close second to Switzerland in personal computers per capita (followed by Norway and Denmark). Finland actually has more Internet hosts per capita than (second place) America.[54]

Finns have apparently learned to make better use of their computers than people elsewhere, in part because full Internet service has been cheap, available at a monthly flat rate calculated to be about 50 percent below the U.S. standard rate. And Finland has first-class telecommunications service coverage throughout the country with costs lower than the OECD average.[55] But Finland stands out for more than providing the resources for access to information technology; it is proving especially adept at achieving the necessary degree of central coordination and monitoring to integrate the Internet into the web of information-related relationships at the local, regional, and national levels, relationships that link IT literacy to civic literacy. By 1997, 40 percent of the Finnish government's personnel had direct access to the Internet, over half had a publicly available e-mail address, and over 70 percent of government offices and agencies had a website (Turkka 1998); by 1998 about 80 percent of all Finnish schools were connected to the Internet. Another feature, a more ambitious application of the approach taken at the Umeå Library, merits mention. The "Link Library," based at the Helsinki City Library, and integrated into PULSE (Finnish Public Libraries Front Page) services, is a common Internet tool and user interface for information retrieval shared among public libraries. Its design facilitates easy information retrieval on the Internet, and it is constantly directly updated by librarians all over Finland.[56]

Through Nokia, Finland is at the forefront of technology facilitating Internet access through cellular telephones.[57] In the concluding chapter, we return to this discussion, asking if the relationship between IT and socioeconomic outcomes will take the form of a virtuous or vicious circle. From what we have seen in this chapter, if Finland succeeds in its ambitious program, it will be charting a path that other high-civic-literacy societies—especially Sweden—can take to realize the potential in the new information technologies to further enhance civic literacy. That is the virtuous circle, and it carries with it the potential of sustaining the welfare state outcomes of the late twentieth century into the twenty first.

But there is a vicious circle associated with the new information technologies for rich low-civic-literacy societies like the United States. This is the threat posed by the "digital divide," the possibility of the technical potential of IT being distributed unequally, with the vastly increased access to information going even more disproportionately to those already favored by the more traditional resources of information dissemination.[58] In such circumstances, the international differences in civic literacy we have seen thus far would be exacerbated. And the result would inevitably be even greater levels of inequality in the low-civic-literacy countries.

But it is unfair to compare small homogenous societies like Finland and Sweden with large pluralistic ones like the United States. We cannot possibly expect the latter to be able to match the former at coordinating the distribution and use of resources contributing to civic literacy. Before completing this part of the book, we provide a case study of New Zealand, a country that is comparable to the Nordic countries, but which has made some significantly different policy choices that may, over the long term, alter its level of civic literacy. (Chapter 10 adds unique insights from this intriguing story to the discussion in part three, especially that part of it concerned with the effects of TV dependency and electoral institutions. Nevertheless, chapter 10 stands alone. The reader wishing to proceed directly to the analysis of the outcomes associated with high civic literacy can proceed to part four without losing any threads of the argument being developed.)

10

The Case of New Zealand

In the size and homogeneity of its population, as well as its geography (if not climate), New Zealand is reminiscent of Scandinavia. Until the middle of the 1980s, moreover, the comparative welfare-state literature treated New Zealand—if at all—as a variant of the Scandinavian type.[1] Since that time, New Zealand has won much international attention as a kind of anti-Scandinavian model, its transformation a beacon for critics of the welfare state. This attention was welcomed, indeed sought, by the architects of the changes.[2]

If an analysis highlighting civic literacy sheds useful light on the Scandinavian countries, it should do likewise on this "counter" example. Doing so requires going beyond the rhetoric and identifying the actual changes that took place. As we shall see in part four, both the proponents and opponents of the "Swedish model" tended to overstate their cases; the same is true with regard to New Zealand's countermodel. Nevertheless, there has undeniably been a transformation; one need only look at changes in income distribution to see this. According to official data,[3] the Gini coefficient for the distribution of household equivalent disposable income in 1984 was .253; by 1991 it had risen to .307, and in 1996 it was .322.[4] In just a decade, New Zealand went from among the most to the least egalitarian OECD countries in income distribution.

There remains much controversy about the changes, and especially the way they were carried out. Lingering divisions color much that has been written about the entire issue. Does New Zealand's middling[5] economic performance since then justify the social costs paid? Only if one accepts that the situation would have been worse had the reforms not been adopted. And that we cannot fully know. We do know that in a matter of a few short years, this remote country of 3.5 million inhabitants went from among the most to the least protected, regulated, and statist of democratic regimes. Even if New Zealand's situation in the early 1980s was untenable, and some change in the direction of greater flexibility was inevitable, it is one thing to catch up to others; it is another to do so and surpass them in one fell swoop.

In summarizing here the main features of the transformation of New Zealand's institutions and policies, we are jumping the gun on part four's discussion of outcomes related to the sustainability of the welfare state. We do so because the dramatic changes were linked temporally and, in part, causally, to changes in institutions associated with civic literacy. First, economic changes were followed by, and to some extent gave rise to, a significant and rare change in political institutions, namely, the replacement of FPTP by a German form of proportional electoral system known as MMP (mixed-member proportional) for electing members of Parliament. Second, deregulation was extended to the media. Hence the transformation of New Zealand serves as a case study of the wider effects of changes in policies connected to civic literacy—anticipating the subject matter of the final part of this book.

The Economic Transformation of New Zealand

New Zealand's economy traditionally was based on productive agricultural exports, the earning of which sustained a manufacturing sector sheltered by licensing, tariffs, and other regulations. Highly progressive income taxes made possible a comprehensive welfare state. Government dominated, where it did not monopolize, telecommunications, banking, energy, forestry, tourism, and transportation. Its preferential access to the British market, rich natural resources, and highly literate population for many years gave New Zealand above-average per capita income and virtual full employment.[6]

This comfortable world, sheltered by price and export supports, marketing boards and tax concessions, was shaken in the 1970s by Britain's entry into the European Community and OPEC-induced oil shocks. Robert Muldoon's National Party government responded with a program of large state-funded investment: debt, especially foreign debt, mounted to a comparatively high level, growth slowed to an average of 0.2 percent between 1974 and 1984, and inflation persisted. In 1984, the new Labour government floated the overvalued Kiwi dollar, sold assets to reduce foreign debt, and embarked on a comprehensive economic reform program led by Minister of Finance Roger Douglas.

The breadth of changes ushered in during and after Douglas's period of office (he resigned in 1988 after a break with Prime Minster David Lange) is impressive by any yardstick. Controls on prices, wages, incomes, and most foreign investment, as well as regulations in transport and energy, were eliminated. Most subsidies to agriculture and industry were removed, and tariffs were reduced. The central bank was made independent and legally mandated to keep inflation below 2 percent. A GST (Goods and Services Tax or VAT) was introduced and the tax structure flattened (the top rate going down from 48 to 33 percent.[7] The public service underwent a series of changes following the principles of "new public management."[8] Public-sector reform and privatization (amounting to assets valued at around 3.5 percent of GNP—well above the figure for Britain during the Thatcher years) cut roughly 80,000 positions in the public service.[9]

In the early 1990s, the policies of Douglas's successor in the new National government, Ruth Richardson, added a large dose of social spending cutbacks and targeted more social programs.[10] Unions were significantly weakened by the 1991 Employment Contracts Act.[11] It was only when faced with the possibility of having to govern in coalition due to imminent changes in the electoral system after 1993 that Prime Minister James Bolger put on the brakes—and dismissed Ruth Richardson. Since that time, there have been no further radical reforms, but few significant efforts to turn back the clock. New Zealand remains among the most deregulated of states. At the end of the chapter, we shall return to the implications of the economic transformation.

Civic Literacy in New Zealand

Electoral reform added a pluralist element into what had been the most majoritarian of the majoritarian Westminster systems. Absent from New Zealand were any of the institutional constraints on government activity found in other Westminster systems, such as bicameralism, judicial review, federalism, and strong local governments. A party able to win a majority of MPs was effectively unstoppable. This institutional bias allowed Robert Muldoon to ignore pressures for needed changes, and Roger Douglas and Ruth Richardson to force through radical changes.[12]

Moreover, institutional arrangements differed from those of northern Europe and Australia in the absence of a system incorporating trade unions into policy making. The New Zealand welfare state was never rooted in corporatist institutions of this kind. The central government undertook the fundamental responsibilities of the modern welfare state effectively on its own. For, unlike Westminster, Wellington has never been the seat of a distant powerful elite. In this small homogenous and isolated country, government became a central institution in the lives of the people, closely integrated into civil society.[13] "The people . . . look upon the state quite healthily as being themselves under another form. When it acts they feel that they are acting. What it owns, they own."[14] Rather than distancing people from government, in a small, remote, and homogenous society, the

Westminster institutions acted more as integrative links, in which the local MP played a key integrating role.[15] With few voters per constituency, it was both useful and possible to personally know the MP. The salience and comprehensibility of government explains New Zealand's traditionally high turnout—averaging in the neighborhood of 90 percent of eligible voters well into the 1960s.[16]

Such turnout and political levels[17]—combined with a well-developed sense of civic duty[18]—suggest a high-civic-literacy society. The important role of Scots in developing this frontier outpost—given the emphasis on reading in the Church of Scotland—figured prominently in this. Evidence of high civic literacy is to be found in the figures for the indicators making up the United Nations' Human Development Index (HDI) compiled by Crafts (1997) for years going back to 1870. For New Zealand he provides data for 1913, 1950, and 1973. In 1913, New Zealand had the highest proportion of potential students actually enrolled, 59 percent;[19] in 1950, and again in 1973, New Zealand was in second place, behind the United States, with 68 and 72 percent enrolled.

High civic literacy was reflected in the local newspapers that abounded in New Zealand. According to the UNESCO *Statistical Yearbook* (1980: 1128), in 1970, total circulation was 376 daily newspapers per 1,000 New Zealanders, well above the 321 average for "developed countries." It was well above the average high human development countries when the United Nations' *Human Development Report* first began to report such figures in the mid-1980s. However, the economic transformation ushered in a perceptible decline in civic literacy. By 1995, as reported in the 1998 *Human Development Report*, daily newspaper circulation was below the high human development average to 239 per 1,000,[20] a decline over the decade greater than that experienced by any other developed country.[21]

The IALS figures are also quite revealing in this regard. Due to the increased number of years spent in school, the average functional literacy score on the three scales is from ten to forty points higher among respondents aged sixteen to thirty-five as compared to those aged forty-six to sixty-five in every participating country—except in New Zealand, where there is no difference (OECD 2000: 147–48). And in the IEA Reading Literacy Study of 1991 discussed in chapter 9, New Zealand's above-average mean was tarnished by its very high dispersion rate (Elley and Schleicher 1994: 59).

In chapter 7, figure 7–1 illustrated that when it comes to average hours of television watching, New Zealand is above the small European countries but still below the other English-speaking OECD countries.[22] Yet, on the TV dependency scale (figure 7–4), New Zealand is in the second highest group along with the U.K., Canada, Australia, and Ireland (the top category is occupied by the United States and Italy)—due largely to the commercialization of its television networks (Smith 1996).[23] This rating is the consequence of a seldom-noticed feature of the economic transformation of the latter 1980s. Like Norway and Sweden, New Zealand was slow to open its airwaves to the commercial sector. When it did, however, it made up for lost time, and, by the 1980s, New Zealand had gone to the other extreme, with only commercially driven television stations even though two of the four (TV1 and TV2) are—at last count—publicly owned.[24] The overall scene is not quite as bleak as in the United States, since public radio is still free of advertising and has a reasonably wide audience, and, as we saw in figure 9–1, New Zealanders placed high in the IALS's self-assessed measure of participation in adult education and training.[25] Overall, however, the trend toward the commercialization in the communication media is clear. We return to the implications of this at the end of the chapter.

Voter Turnout and Electoral Reform

On the civic side of civic literacy, as noted, a different phenomenon has occurred, one with a more positive effect on civic literacy. While still relatively high by international standards, turnout had been declining in recent decades. Of potential voters, the percentage of those casting a ballot dropped significantly after 1984 (when it was 85.6 percent) to the lowest ever, 76.8 percent, in 1990 (IDEA 1997: 72). Overall trends suggest that it would have continued to decline if electoral institutions had not been changed—that the factors discouraging turnout under FPTP (elaborated in chapter 6) would have increasingly come to take effect, reducing levels of civic literacy reflected in interest in politics, sense of civic duty, and high voter turnout. But the opposite occurred: turnout rose, starting in 1993, when New Zealand moved to adopt a new—proportional—electoral system.[26]

The change came about due to a number of sometimes unrelated events (see Aimer 1999). Underlying them was a profound discontent with the results of the FPTP system. In 1978, the Muldoon government was returned to power with a majority of seats, though only 39.8 percent of the vote. This was less than Labour, which had won 40.4 percent. Three years later National won another majority with only 38.8 percent, this time mainly at the expense of Social Credit, which garnered 21 percent but only two seats. Discontent with the government's policies increasingly focused on the system that got it elected. As Aimer puts it:

> Labour activists, largely as a result of the Prime Minister's devastatingly pugnacious style especially reviled the Muldoon National government. Labour,

naturally, was aggrieved by the two election results. Social Creditors felt similarly robbed. As a consequence, anti-National political antagonism began to focus on the electoral system, with a growing belief that the system was unjust and unfair. (Aimer 1999:147-48)

At the beginning of the 1980s, New Zealand's politically informed population was very dissatisfied. The government set up a commission to look at the question of electoral unrepresentativeness; but, instead of the expected minor changes, the New Zealand Royal Commission on the Electoral System in its 1986 report called for replacing FPTP by the German mixed-member proportional system (MMP). Despite the fact that this recommendation served the interests of neither major party, events forced a referendum, which endorsed MMP in 1993. Popular dissatisfaction with the radical economic policies being imposed without any explicit mandate led this very British country to trade in the classic Westminster electoral system for a continental import.[27]

In the October 1996 election, the first under MMP, New Zealand electors cast two votes, one for the party and one for the MP. Of the 120 parliamentary seats, 55 were filled from lists to compensate small parties that had surpassed the 5 percent vote threshold, so as to bring their overall share of seats to a number proportional to the party vote received. Six weeks later, National and New Zealand First (NZF) formed a coalition based on a detailed program of government.[28] The bumpy ride of the new government, and with it the new electoral system, provided ammunition to MMP's opponents.[29] Not surprisingly, surveys revealed MPP's critics to have been most successful among the part of the population with the lowest levels of civic literacy.[30]

Indeed, there is reason to believe that the changeover to MMP had a positive effect on civic literacy in New Zealand. Beyond the turnout boost, we see a corresponding change in attitudes when comparing the results of the New Zealand Election Surveys in 1990, 1993, and 1996. In 1993, an average of almost 80 percent, and in 1996, 84 percent (compared to the already high 75 percent in 1990) of those surveyed agreed that voting is important, that the citizen's vote counts, and that it is a citizen's duty to vote. In 1996, 21.1 percent stated they were very interested in the campaign compared to 14.6 in the two previous elections, while those who considered not voting went down from 14.2 percent in 1990 and 11.9 in 1993 to an incredibly low 7.6 percent in 1996. Between 1993 and 1996, more voters came to see that their votes really mattered, fewer though that their MPs were out of touch, and fewer thought that government was run by a few interests (Banducci, Donovan, and Karp 1997: 17).

These effects are, of course, not attributable only to MMP. We must take into consideration the fact that more attention was publicly focused on voting due to the novelty of the new system as well as the special efforts to inform voters.[31] On the other hand, opponents of electoral reform erroneously predicted that the complexity of the two-vote system under MMP would deter many voters. To counter the novelty effect, I surveyed political actors with long experience in New Zealand politics to ask them, in effect, to reflect on differences between the MMP election and previous ones. The study of the 1996 campaign and its effects as perceived by individuals who had been candidates in all three (1990, 1993, and 1996) elections is described in appendix IV. The respondents generally found voters in 1998 to be significantly more interested and more knowledgeable than in the earlier elections. They also reported a larger number of local candidates' debates, an observation supported by the New Zealand Election Study, which found a significant rise among respondents stating that they had attended political meetings—from 9.4 percent in 1993 to 12.7 percent in 1996.

It would seem, thus, that something was happening beyond the novelty of a new electoral system. There is good reason to suggest that, in contrast to the commercialization of television, the change in the electoral system had a positive effect on civic literacy. One indication of high civic literacy is to be found in the sophistication in voters' approach to their new voting system. The Electoral Commission's efforts to promote public awareness of the new electoral reality especially among those with low political information seem to have borne fruit. By the time of the 1996 election, over 70 percent of New Zealanders surveyed by the commission understood the crucial effect of their party (as opposed to constituency) vote in determining the composition of Parliament (Harris 1998).[32] And they appear to have made good use of that knowledge. A preelection survey by the New Zealand Politics Group at Victoria University found 38 percent planning to split their vote.[33]

New Zealand under MMP

Though it remained in office through its three-year term, it would be difficult to describe the first MMP government as stable, let alone consensual. The problem lay in large part in the role played by NZF, the pivotal member of the coalition. NZF was itself unstable, due both to its base being composed of two groups with little in common (Maori and pensioners) and to the mercurial personality of its leader, Winston Peters.[34] As a result, attitudes toward MMP shifted significantly, enabling its opponents at home and abroad to pronounce the experiment a failure.

Other factors contributed to the failure of MMP to live up to expectations.[35] Frequently commented on was the tendency of the main political actors in the two old parties to operate publicly as if the polarized two-party system were still in existence.[36] With scant media attention given to the small parties, there was thus little outward sign of a developing consensual political culture, something supporters of MMP had promised and electors welcomed during the referendum debate (Nagel 1999). In fact, rapid progress toward consensualism was unrealistic given that the formative process for most all the political actors had been under majoritarian institutions (74 of 120 MPs had previous parliamentary experience; many others had been active in the local political arena, which remained majoritarian). Indeed, the absence of the vertical dimension of consensual institutional arrangements (see chapter 6) makes it all the more difficult for MMP to live up to expectations. As a rule, the parliamentary parties do not take direct part in local contests.

In this environment, opponents of MMP in the business community and the two old parties met some success in their efforts to persuade people that the electoral system was to blame for New Zealand's ills.[37] A return to the majority system is unlikely, however, due both to the remaining antagonism to FPTP and to the vested interest of many legislators—especially from small parties needed to form coalitions—elected under MMP,[38] though there is still the prospect of a slow erosion of proportionality within MMP through a reduction in the number (and thus proportion) of the list seats.[39] In hindsight, the first MMP government begins not to look so bad.[40] Despite the fracturing of NZF, government policies did not stray very far from the National NZF agreement of December 1996, the content of which substantially reflected the prevailing consensus at the center of New Zealand politics.

While the first MMP Parliament failed to deliver greater consensualism, it may have contributed to the more profound positive effects on civic literacy associated with PR. Is there some reason to believe that, overall, New Zealanders entering the twenty-first century are more politically knowledgeable than they would have been if FPTP had been retained? Under MMP, the Parliament, which remains the unchallenged focus of political attention, better reflects New Zealand's social composition by the fair representation of Maoris[41] and the improved representation of women and Pacific Islanders (Arseneau 1999; Nagel 1999). Thus it makes it easier for members of these groups to find their place on the political map. In addition, MMP made parliamentary representation possible for groups bound by shared ideas—social democratic, libertarian and green—giving their supporters a greater stake in political decisions, bringing additional energies and efforts into the political arena.[42] For reasons elaborated in part two, there is good reason to believe that these developments enhance civic literacy.

It may be, therefore, that reform of the electoral system has, in a modest way, counteracted the effects of government policies in the 1980s and 1990s that tended toward reduced civic literacy. This would make abandonment or even erosion of MMP all the more regrettable. A high-civic-literacy society is a better society, one that gives a greater proportion of its citizens the capacity to make informed choices. But, as we shall argue in the next part of this book, it is also a better society because it is conducive to a fairer distribution of economic resources—an observation that brings us back to our discussion of the effects of New Zealand's radical economic transformation.

Conclusion

The electoral reform, by ending the days when a party with support of 40 percent of the people could impose its will with impunity, brought to a halt the ideologically driven radical transformation of New Zealand's economic and administrative structure. Although, after 1993, the Bolger government did increase spending on pensions, health, and education under pressure from NZF, the overall thrust of the changes was not reversed under the National-led coalitions, with the result that New Zealand entered the twenty-first century among the most unequal of modern democratic societies.

Has the "New Zealand model" taken root? Have marketization, deregulation, and privatization gone so far as to be irreversible? New Zealand's small size, homogeneity, and remoteness are guarantors of a certain social solidarity[43] that institutional reform cannot easily uproot. However, New Zealand lacks German-style corporatist institutions enabling encompassing business and labor organizations to engage in trade-offs potentially able to attain outcomes combining efficiency and equality. It has traditionally been the central state that has handled all the relevant aspects of redistributive trade-offs, as everyone took it for granted that it was there to serve the public interest. This is not apparent today: the state is smaller, and has far less discretion about how public money is spent. The favored method has been "outsourcing" services, that is, buying services on the market, including, especially, policy advice at the highest levels.[44] The locus and content of the policy advice have changed correspondingly. In the words of the main architects of the state-sector reforms, former Prime Minister (Sir) Geoffrey Palmer:

> What has developed in New Zealand is something of a disjunction between the policy-making process and the political process. The decision makers are a select few politicians who decide things, not on the basis of what the political process of representative democracy tells them, but on the basis of what some varieties of economic or policy theory tells them. (Quoted in Gregory 1998: 13)

Could such a "marketized" public sector arrive at and implement policies to enhance equality, or do its very structure and operational principles render it incapable of doing so? If the latter were the case, changing outcomes would necessitate "reinventing" government. The place to start, I contend, is with getting the political parties involved in revitalizing local government[45] to help fill the vacuum left by the state. Introducing PR to local politics would guarantee to the national parties sufficient return on resources invested at that level. On this, there has been an encouraging late-breaking development. The minister for local government in the new center-left coalition government, Sandra Lee, is a (left-wing) Alliance leader of Maori ancestry who has drawn attention to the relationship between the low level of Maori involvement in local government and the majoritarian system of elections, committing the government to allowing—indeed encouraging—municipalities to adopt a form of PR used in Ireland.

Moreover, if the argument advanced here is given credence, an important test for the new governing coalition[46] if it is seriously committed to responsibly reducing inequality—and thus ensuring that New Zealand not congeal into a "model" setting out the inegalitarian path to efficiency—will be its willingness to act to promote civic literacy. Is it prepared to reduce commercialism on the airwaves,[47] stimulate newspaper readership, and promote adult education—as well as reinforce rather than dilute the electoral reforms?

In a sense, the question is a wider one. It could be that New Zealand has set a course that cannot be fundamentally altered, a path that all nations in the globalizing world economy have no choice but to follow—which takes us to the questions posed in part four.

IV

Civic Literacy and Socioeconomic Outcomes

It is estimated that providing universal access to basic education and health, adequate food and safe water and sanitation for all, as well as reproductive health care for women is . . . less that 4% of the combined wealth of the 225 richest people in the world.

UNITED NATIONS, *Human Development Report, 1998*

11

Economic Outcomes:
Combining Growth and Fair Distribution

Compared to the argument advanced in the final part of this book, the task in the first three parts was rather straightforward. We have tried to establish what civic literacy is and how some societies attain higher levels. To the extent that we have gone beyond the descriptive to the normative, the high-civic-literacy society has been treated as an end in itself: I have assumed, to paraphrase Putnam's assertion about the high-social-capital community, that life is better in the high-civic-literacy society.

I do not retreat from this ethical position. Along with many others, I find myself content to accept a reduced income, and thus a lower material consumption level, in order to have the time and energy to be informed. This position rests not on some form of platonic essentialism but rather on a progressive utilitarianism, as formulated by John Stuart Mill, that individuals' happiness is maximized by their achieving their intellectual potential. Clearly, the high-civic-literacy society best meets Mill's standard. Mill believed that a society organized on appropriate utilitarian principles would also be materially prosperous. In broad terms, a positive relationship between intellectual and material progress makes intuitive sense: the society with the better-informed population should be the one able to make the best economic choices. The historical record can surely be read to give substance to such an intuition. Perhaps, were I writing this book in an earlier decade, I might have made this the concluding chapter—simply reminding the reader of the good economic performance of the high-civic-literacy societies.

But I write at the onset of the twenty-first century, with the low-civic-literacy United States entering its tenth year of economic expansion and its labor market such that its many educated young people can count on jobs with salaries that make them the envy of their European counterparts. Britain's New Labour government looks less to social-democratic continental Europe than to the United States for inspiration. Postunification Germany[1] in 1998 elected a left-of-center government, but one that draws inspiration most of all from Tony Blair's Britain, and thus—indirectly—the United States. Indeed, there seem no longer to be any alternative models to look to. The much-touted Japanese model is passé. Nor do we find Sweden being invoked as an alternative: scores, if not hundreds, of articles were published in the 1990s about the death of the Swedish model. And with some reason—though prematurely—as we shall see.

In this context, it is by no means obvious, as might have earlier been the case, that high civic literacy fosters economic success. We could simply draw our analysis to a temporary close, leaving the economic dimension to wait another day. But tempting though it may be, that will not do. This is, in the end, a work of political economy, not philosophy. The universe of political economy is one of practical policy choices. In a democratic society with the free passage of information—the only system of social organization that makes high civic literacy possible—policy choices with clearly suboptimal economic outcomes are doomed. Eventually, and likely sooner, people will vote with their hands and, if unheeded, their feet, against the policies and politicians deemed responsible for such outcomes.

We cannot, consequently, avoid the question of economic outcomes, not because material wealth is all that matters but because, over the long run, we cannot get other important things—like civic literacy—right if we do not get economic outcomes right. So we address a fundamental question in part four, one already previewed in chapter 10's discussion of the effect of New Zealand's single-minded pursuit of superior economic performance on civic literacy. But we reverse the relationship: is there reason to believe that, by virtue of civic literacy, societies are capable of the kind of economic performance required to attain and maintain relatively egalitarian outcomes, what we term the sustainable welfare state (SWS)?[2]

This latter question focuses our economic analysis not on economic growth per se but on the combination of economic growth and the redistributive outcomes that make the welfare state durable or sustainable. We assume that if total wealth is unchanged, welfare increases when more of it goes to those who have least. This assumption is based on the simple premise that, other things being equal, an additional dollar is more beneficial when all you have is five dollars than when you have fifty dollars. But, as events in the 1980s and 1990s taught anyone who needed to learn it, redistribution that undermines productive capacity is not viable: you cannot redistribute wealth you haven't created.

The Economic Performance of the Welfare State

It should come as no surprise (as we shall document in chapter 13) that the societies with the highest levels of civic literacy are generally the most redistributive. A simple indicator of this is that the Scandinavian and, following them, Benelux countries (see figure 11–3, page 153) continue to be leaders in the proportion of overall resources (GDP) that go to public expenditures generally, and on social programs in particular.[3] For that relationship to be sustainable, as noted above, redistributive societies must also hold their own in economic growth. Is this in fact the case? What do we know of the relationship between the two components of economic performance: wealth creation and distribution?

Blanket assertions about comparative economic performance based simply on national differences in per capita gross domestic product must be taken with a large grain of salt, given the inadequacies of GDP as a comparative indicator.[4] Using annual growth in per capita GDP to compare economic performance is less problematic, since it begins with a base measure specific to each nation. Using per capita growth over a long period to

TABLE 11–1

Income Distribution in OECD Countries

Country	Year (1980s)	GINI	Year (1990s)	GINI	Latest Year	GINI
Finland	87	.207	91	.227	95	.226
Sweden	87	.220	92	.229	95	.221
Austria	87	.227				
Norway	86	.234	91	.230	95	.238
Denmark	87	.254	92	.239		
Belgium	88	.235	91	.230	96	.260
Italy	86	.310	91	.290	95	.346
Germany	84	.249	94	.261		
Netherlands	87	.268	91	.268	94	.253
Canada	87	.289	91	.285	94	.285
Australia	85	.295	90	.309	94	.312
France	84	.296	94	.288		
UK	86	.304	91	.335	95	.344
Switzerland	82	.323	92	.307		
Ireland	87	.330				
US	86	.341	91	.350	97	.372
New Zealand	84	.253	91	.307	96	.322

Source: Luxembourg Income Survey; New Zealand's figures are from Robert Stephens (see chapter 10).

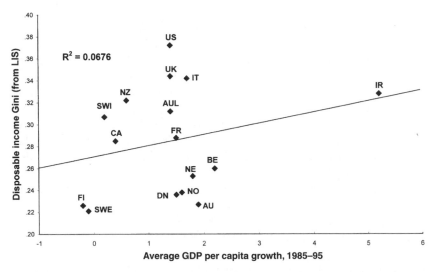

FIGURE II-I   Source: *Britannica World Data Yearbook* (1998:785–89).

avoid distortions due to cyclical effects can serve as a useful comparative economic performance indicator.

Equally complex is the selection of comparative measures of economic equality. For reasons elaborated in the discussion of figure 11–3 below, the Gini coefficient provided by the Luxembourg Income Study (LIS) serves as our primary indicator. Figure 11–1 sets out the relationship between the countries' per capita economic growth from 1985 to 1995[5] and the Gini level of disposable household-income distribution coinciding with the latter years of this period (from table 11–1).[6]

Figure 11–1 shows that there is effectively no relationship between the two. Some highly distributive countries do better than average, some worse. A similar exercise for a different period would produce a similar result. Looking at the world as we have known it in recent years, there is no reason to assume either a growth-retarding or growth-enhancing effect for redistributive outcomes among the rich industrial democracies.[7]

Figure 11–1 shows that, on average, the ten years between 1985 and 1995 were hard economic times for Finland and Sweden but relatively good ones for Norway and Denmark. Since then, the economic performance for the Nordic countries as a whole has improved. Table 11–2 provides the early 1998 data from the EU Commission's assessment of the readiness of member countries for European monetary union (EMU).

To this we can add 1998 figures for EU nonmember Norway (from the fall 1999 *Nordic Outlook*, published by SEB, the largest Swedish Bank), which show Norway with growth at 2.1 percent, unemployment at 3.2

TABLE 11-2

Macroeconomic Indicators, 1998

	Sweden	Denmark	Finland
Unemployment rate (%)	9.1	5.4	12.3
GDP growth rate (%)	2.6	2.7	4.6
Inflation (%)	1.5	2.1	2.0
Budget deficit/surplus (% of GDP)	0.5	1.1	0.3
Total public debt (% of GDP)	74.1	59.5	53.6

percent, and inflation at 2.3 percent, with a 5 percent budget surplus and public debt at a tiny 28.5 percent of GDP. While rich Norway's economy slowed somewhat in the next two years, and prosperous Denmark's stabilized, Sweden and Finland have shown signs of even further improvement as the century came to an end. According to the winter-spring 2000 *Nordic Outlook*, Sweden's economy grew by 3.8 percent in 1999, and the SEB predicted it would grow by 4.5 and 3.5 percent in 2000 and 2001, with unemployment down to 4.8 and 4 percent. For Finland, which grew 3.5 percent in 1999, growth was anticipated to be 4.5 and 4.0 percent for 2000 and 2001, with unemployment at 9.1 and 8.5 percent.

Overall, the macroeconomic position of the Scandinavian countries is quite solid—especially when seen within the context of economic difficulties undergone earlier in the decade. In Sweden, the state deficit reached 13 percent of GDP in 1992; replacement ratios for sick leave and unemployment insurance, which were close to 100 percent of wages, were reduced to 70 percent. Pensions were restructured toward a contribution-based system with public supplements. Though universality was not abandoned, market-type institutions were introduced in a number of sectors, and there was a tightening of access to care for the elderly and other groups (Malmberg and Sundström 1996). Only Norway, with its oil and gas wealth, was spared from having to cut social expenditure and reduce replacement rates and eligibility periods. Overall, Sweden faced more drastic reductions than Denmark, where needed changes had come earlier.[8] It was Finland, however, that confronted the most difficult challenge. Finland had to implement even deeper cuts to deal with a crisis exacerbated by the sudden loss of Soviet markets. Unemployment skyrocketed to 17 percent, though—as the Gini coefficients in table 11-1 show, and as Fritzell (1999) analyzes—there was a "striking lack of substantial increases in inequality" (Fritzell 1999: 182). While unemployment rates have been slow to come down to the low rates of the 1980s, Finland has made a remarkable recovery to become one of the most solid economies in the Euro zone.

Socioeconomic Outcomes

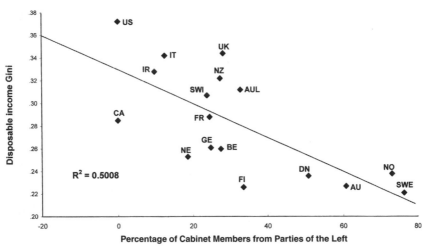

FIGURE 11-2   (Schmidt, 1996:10)

Many of the reforms introduced in the mid-1990s to cope with the situation were initiated by social-democrat-led governments. Indeed, the economic problems, if anything, strengthened the political position of the social-democratic parties. By the mid-1990s, they had been returned to power in all four states (though in Norway, after failing to win the targeted number of seats in the 1997 elections, Labor gave up power to a centrist coalition even though it had fewer seats combined than Labor). Overall, despite expectations to the contrary, Scandinavian social-democratic parties have not lost their traditionally dominant position, which, as illustrated in figure 11-2, distinguishes them (along with those of Austria) from parties of the left in other countries (Mair 1994; Schmidt 1996).

Critics on the right, such as eminent economist Assar Lindbeck (1995), have maintained that Scandinavian Social Democrats were incapable of the tough-mindedness needed to address the welfare state's underlying "hazardous dynamics." Conversely, some on the left (e.g., Bochert 1995) judged them to have undermined the Swedish/Scandinavian model through policies adopted in response to the economic situation. On balance, it would seem that neither has proven its case—so far. While Sweden has been the Scandinavian laggard in economic growth, there is disagreement over just how its performance compares to OECD countries as a whole. Lindbeck (1997: 32–33), using 1970 as base year, shows that Sweden fell well behind the OECD average in GDP per capita, going from fourth to sixteenth place,[9] but Korpi, by reinterpreting the figures in purchasing power parities, finds that, at least up until 1992, Sweden's growth placed it ahead of the OECD average (Korpi 1998: 57).[10] With Sweden's poor performance in the 1990s showing signs of being reversed in the next decade, we can safely conclude that, taken as a whole, the highly redistributive Scandinavian countries have more than held their own in economic performance.

Redistribution and Economic Performance

We can now look in more detail at our indicator of redistributiveness. Output indicators, such as social spending as a percentage of GDP, are the most common empirical indicators used to gauge the strength and extensiveness of welfare states. Despite the retrenchment we have seen in recent years, on these measures the Scandinavian countries maintain their leading position (see figure 11-3). Up-to-date output data of this kind are relatively easy to acquire and often used, but cannot compare to direct information of how citizens in the lower echelons actually fare. In using such indirect indicators, we assume that a society that spends more on social programs is one that makes life better for people below the mean in earned income. Generally speaking, this is a reasonable expectation, as we can see from the close correlation with Gini coefficients in figure 11-3.[11] Nevertheless, when it comes to output measures, differences between countries can vary significantly depending on how social spending is calculated.[12]

Hence, for our purposes, indicators getting at equality of outcomes are to be preferred. By their very nature, however, comparable outcome data are more difficult to come by. Fortunately, the Luxembourg Income Study (LIS) has adequately standardized the methodology for comparing incomes

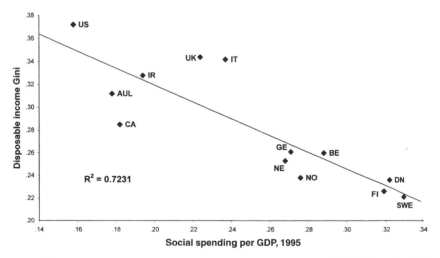

FIGURE 11-3   F = 28.726, sig F = 0.000

and applied it to a large number of OECD countries. And we know how closely low relative and absolute income correlates with higher infant mortality and lower life expectancy (Wilkinson 1996). Thus, here, as in many comparative studies, the LIS Gini coefficients for household disposable income[13] serve as the single best comparative indicator of welfare-state outcomes.[14] As we saw in table 11–1, the Scandinavian countries (though they, like other countries, became slightly less egalitarian in the late 1980s and early 1990s) have remained the most egalitarian, followed by Belgium[15] and Austria.[16]

Figure 11–3 also draws our attention to the Netherlands, whose economy has been performing especially well in recent years—so well in fact that if anything has replaced the Swedish model, it would be the "Dutch model." On the redistributive side, outputs and outcomes place the Netherlands somewhere between Scandinavia and Germany. Overall, the Netherlands resembles Scandinavia in social spending, while its income distribution and overall wage dispersion is continental.[17] Hence useful insights can be gleaned from a detailed comparison of welfare state outcomes in Germany, the Netherlands, and the United States (Goodin et al. 1999). The study is exceptional in that it makes use of large, comprehensive, and comparable sets of panel data over a ten-year period[18] on a number of indicators associated with different outcomes. The Dutch "social democratic welfare regime" ranks above the "corporatist" German and "liberal" American regimes in each of them, minimizing inequality and reducing poverty while promoting stability, social integration, and—even—individual autonomy.

> The crucial fact is simply that the social democratic welfare regime upon which we have focussed—the Netherlands—managed to sustain economic growth at a rate certainly on a par with (and in some ways higher than) the other countries under study. And both the social democratic and corporatist regimes passed on much more of that growth dividend to middle-income earners than did the liberal regime under study, at least over this period. . . . The social democratic welfare regime is at least as good as (and usually better than) either of the other welfare regimes in respect of all the social objectives we traditionally set for our welfare regimes. Furthermore, the social democratic welfare regime is at least as good as any other on economic objectives. (Goodin et al. 1999: 261–62)

These findings suggest that critics of the welfare state are unjustified in their claim that the poor in the more inegalitarian societies, though relatively worse off (in terms of their income share) are, in absolute terms, better off than those in the more egalitarian countries. This assertion is tested directly by Smeeding (1996) and Kenworthy (1998), who find this not to be the case. Using LIS data for the early 1990s, Smeeding (1996: 50) found

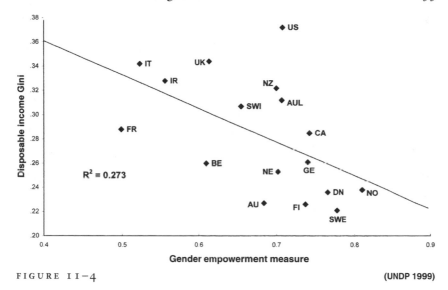

FIGURE II-4 (UNDP 1999)

American households with income at the tenth percentile earned less in absolute terms than comparable groups in other OECD countries.

This Gini coefficient for disposable income reflects both market income and net income from public sources. By using household income, it tells us nothing about differences linked to gender. On the whole, countries that redistribute among households also tend to be more sensitive to gender-based inequalities,[19] but there are important exceptions. We can see this in figure II-4, which shows the relationship between Gini levels and Gender Empowerment Measure (GEM) ratings from the 1999 United Nations *Human Development Report*. The GEM combines the percentage share of women in the legislature and in administrative, managerial, professional, and technical positions with the proportion of income earned by women. As we can see, the Anglo-American countries are more sensitive to gender than to household inequality, while for Austria and Belgium the reverse is true.[20]

Finally, if we combine the information in these figures with that pertaining to government composition (as depicted in figure II-2), we see, not unexpectedly, the greatest level of social equality in countries where Social Democrats have been most influential in setting government policies in the latter half of this century.

Rationality and Redistributive Outcomes

In the next chapter we shall have more to say about how the Scandinavian societies achieved "model" SWS outcomes. First, however, we need to return

to the question raised at the beginning of this chapter, of whether such outcomes are politically practicable: is it reasonable to expect a population with
free access to information and the capacity to vote with their hands and their
feet to make choices to reinforce the SWS? As we have seen, it is societies
that spend more—and therefore tax more—that achieve outcomes associated with the SWS. Is it possible, at a time when self-interest is a seemingly overwhelming factor in all economic decisions, to win popular support
for such policies? Does the SWS not rest on a larger measure of altruism
than can nowadays be counted on? I contend that this need not be the case.
In the context of an institutional framework favoring civic literacy, as set out
in parts two and three, the SWS need not rest on altruism, since it can rely
on informed rational individual choice. To conclude this chapter, I make
this argument in abstract form; flesh and bones will be added in the discussion of the development of the SWS in Scandinavia in the next chapter.

Figure 11–5 is a stylized representation of the relationship between
overall economic prosperity and fair distribution. The heavy black line (P)
represents the economic performance indicator being used, such as GDP
per capita, and the broken line (R) the level of income equality. A society's
overall welfare rating—its place on the thin line (the U curve)—is visual-
ized as a kind of sum of the values for it on P and R. Thus P is understood
to contribute to U disproportionately on the (left-hand) laissez-faire side
of the chart, while R does so on the (right-hand) welfare state side. The direction of P reflects trends in the democratic industrial world over the past
years: a kind of worst-case scenario of the relationship between redistribution and performance in which redistribution has a generally negative relationship with economic performance among societies with low levels of redistribution but has neither a positive or negative correlation among those
with medium and higher levels of redistribution.

To put it otherwise, in its stylized representation, figure 11–5 visualizes
output as decreasing with redistribution—that is, P slopes downward in a
trade-off between efficiency and equality: the more equally the pie is shared,
the smaller it gets—but only up to a point (here cast in the middle). Societies institutionally capable of a certain level of distribution, it is hypothe-
sized, tend to develop mechanisms to achieve a balance between output
losses from increased redistributiveness and output gains from increased
cooperation.[21] The mechanisms of gains from structured cooperation are
set out in the corporatist literature.[22]

> At the macro level, it helps foster more productive relationships among
> large-scale economic actors—among firms in different industries, among
> unions, and between government and interest groups. At the meso level . . . it
> can enhance ties between firms and their investors, between purchaser and

supplier firms, and among competing firms. Co-operation can also yield benefits at the micro level—within the firm—by improving relationships between labour and management, among workers, and among functional divisions within firms. (Kenworthy 1996: 53)

Kenworthy created an index of cooperation along nine dimensions from the macro to micro levels for the period beginning in the 1960s (see his scoring for the seventeen richest industrial democracies in figure 11–7 at the end of the chapter).[23] Kenworthy's comparative assessment of corporatist cooperation picks out Austria, Germany, the six small northern European countries (Norway, Sweden, Finland, Denmark, Belgium, and the Netherlands), and, especially, Japan as those that "feature a rather extensive amount of co-operation, especially at the macro level via their centralized labour and business associations" (1996: 55). Using a combination of unemployment, inflation, and productivity growth data for the period between 1960 and 1990, Kenworthy concludes that such cooperation is "a key to economic success" (1996: 55). In our terms, Kenworthy sees an upward-sloping P curve. In this, he goes further than most corporatist

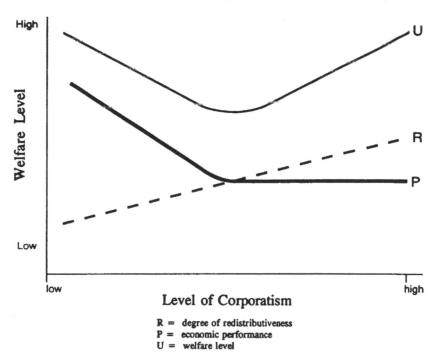

R = degree of redistributiveness
P = economic performance
U = welfare level

FIGURE 11–5

analysts, who tend to view P as a U-shaped curve.[24] (This is why I refer to the flattened P curve in figure 11–5 as a worst-case scenario, as it is more modest in its interpretation than even the corporatist U-shaped curve.)

There are thus two separate logics in operation. For people in the societies to the right of the point where the curve has flattened out in figure 11–5, any trade-off between equality and efficiency is sufficiently mitigated by SWS policies that the rational individual, given the choice, would reinforce them in his or her actions as voter, earner, organizational member, and consumer. This is not the case, however, for individuals in societies to the left of that point. In the concluding chapter we shall examine what happens when individuals operate within such a logic in the United States— probably the only country under consideration here unequivocally in this position[25] —as well as in the Westminster democracies, which tend to fall closer to the middle.

In the majority of the countries being considered here, a rational individual will prefer to live in a society further to the right-hand side of the U curve, that is, a society in which wealth is distributed more equally and poverty less extensive, over one with greater extremes between rich and poor. This applies to the majority of people, not just those below the mean in income and wealth. The exceptions are to be found in a minority with investments to guarantee their own and their heirs' security as well as an even smaller one that values risk for its own sake.[26] Thus, setting aside the often powerful factor of altruism for—or solidarity with—those of one's community who are worse off through no fault of their own, we can expect rational individuals to find good cause to support the institutions and policies of the SWS.[27]

Like any argument based on a rational choice model, this argument makes assumptions about individual behavior that are not necessarily borne out in the real world. It assumes, in fact, two things that are true only of high-civic-literacy societies: first, that individuals have ample information on which to make the relevant choices; second, that political institutions neither exclude a large underclass from meaningful political participation nor give preponderant political weight to those with money. In the absence of these conditions, societies on the right side of figure 11–5 may at a given point make policy choices that, over time, move them to the left side. For example, they may avoid difficult corporatist trade-offs, instead maintaining redistributive outcomes through inappropriate fiscal choices (e.g., incurring high levels of foreign debt) that undermine the capacity to maintain those outcomes. High civic literacy, we argue, serves to restrain such tendencies.

Well-functioning corporatist institutions also contribute to civic literacy. The traditional approach in the welfare state literature looks to the degree of corporatism in institutional relationships, especially the presence of strong centralized trade unions able and willing to enter trade-offs with business and (social-democratic–influenced) governments, to explain the success of the SWS in corporatist Scandinavia and Austria (e.g., Pekka-rinen, Pohjola, and Rowthorn 1992). Despite recent claims on both the right and left that national corporatist institutions have been undermined by globalization and European integration, we know that, as far as union density is concerned, for example, corporatist institutions in the Nordic countries have proven resilient. Not only are Scandinavian union density rates highest (see figure 11–6), but the gap is widening.[28] And, not surprisingly, as gauged by Iversen (1999: 56) and illustrated in figure 11–6, collective bargaining in these countries is most centralized.

In the next chapter we shall look at corporatist institutions in the context of the evolution of Scandinavian welfare states. In earlier chapters we have seen how transparency (in the requirement for tax-return information to be public and for public institutions to open their books to interested citizens) contributes to civic literacy. We have also traced the effects of the availability and quality of adult education, of reduced dependency on commercial television, and of consensual political institutions that simplify the political map. A similar effect can be attributed to the institutional arrangements

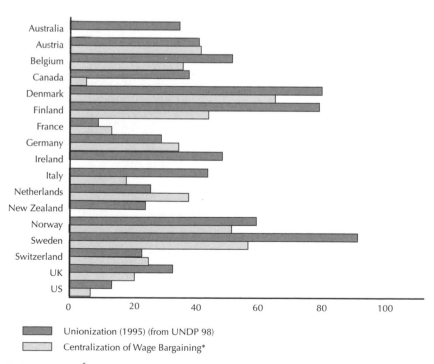

FIGURE 11–6

(Iversen 1999:7)

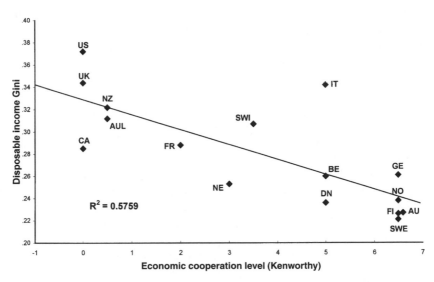

FIGURE II-7   F = 19.008, sig F = 0.000

promoting corporatist relationships on the labor market that reduce the
cost and increase the benefit of sharing information relating to technological research, human resource development, and so forth (Milner 1989:
31–45). The analysis provided so far suggests that it is this that helps explain the fact (as we can see in figure 11–7) that societies that encourage
corporatist cooperation are generally also better at fairly distributing resources among their citizens.

12

Civic Literacy and the Foundations of the Sustainable Welfare State in Sweden

So far in part four we have seen that the Scandinavian countries remain the most egalitarian, and more than hold their own in economic performance. In part two we learned that they are among the highest in civic literacy, and in part three we identified policies that account for this. It is time to combine these elements, to establish if there is, as suggested in the introduction, a relationship between the institutions and policies underlying Scandinavian civic literacy and the economic outcomes achieved by the sustainable welfare state. We address this question first longitudinally and then comparatively: in this chapter we focus on the place of civic literacy in the historical development of the SWS in Scandinavia; in the next, we place the relationship between the SWS and civic literacy in comparative perspective.

The subject matter of this chapter inescapably raises the question of Scandinavian exceptionalism. To what extent can we attribute outcomes to the often-heard contention that the Scandinavian welfare state succeeds at higher levels of redistribution because it has inherited a distinct culture, a culture uncomfortable with what it perceives to be unnecessary inequality? From the work of Svallfors (1995) among others, we know that even during the difficult days faced by the Swedish welfare state in the 1990s there was unwavering majority support for generous tax-financed social programs.[1] But, as Alesky (1998), citing data from the 1992 ISSP Survey on Social Equality, points out, there is nothing distinctive—even when compared to Americans on the value Scandinavians place on social equality. Indeed, neither Americans' nor Swedes' opinions stand out among the twelve ISSP industrial democracies on whether income differences are too large, or whether the differences are necessary to secure the county's prosperity. The distinction between the two countries comes out only on the question of whether the government has a responsibility to reduce income disparity.

Those Swedes who support social equality also support state intervention; this is not true in the United States.

Consequently, we are not likely to make much progress toward explaining differences in policies and outcomes by focusing on cultural predispositions toward altruism. Moreover, there is little evidence of any such cultural predisposition toward the welfare state in traditional Scandinavian policies. By most of the indicators we use today, only at the end of the 1950s did the Scandinavian SWS begin to distinguish itself. In the 1930s, "Swedish social legislation was limited and in some ways inferior to what the New Deal introduced" (Swenson 1998: 10).

To attribute the achievements of the Scandinavian welfare state to cultural exceptionalism is, in effect, to reverse the causality process. We have already noted predispositions toward civic literacy in the inherited traditions,[2] which, as we shall see, found their way into the ideas of the founders of the modern welfare state. But the success of the Social Democrats and their allies in building on these predispositions to develop and institute SWS policies was not founded on an appeal to some exceptional cultural value placed on social equality. They won and maintained support for their policies because these policies proved effective, thereby reinforcing awareness that appropriate state initiatives can effectively mitigate social inequalities created by the market. This is a matter of historical record, one of undoubted success for the Swedish or Scandinavian "model" from its emergence in the 1930s to at least the latter 1960s.[3] Missing from the story of the model as usually recounted is what we have called civic literacy, that is, the capacity of the citizens to understand what policies and institutions underlay that success and choose accordingly. It is this capacity—and not a cultural empathy for state-fostered equality—that is crucial.

It is only recently that Scandinavian traditions found their way into policy choices. In 1870, the literacy rate in Sweden was 75 percent. This placed it even with the United States, and behind Switzerland, Denmark, Germany, the Netherlands, Canada, and the U.K., and well ahead of Norway, at 55 percent, and Finland, at only 10 percent (Crafts 1997: 306). Since then, Scandinavia has stood out in its propensity to incorporate the knowledge dimension into a wide range of the programs of the developing SWS. With a little imagination, we can visualize a third dimension to the relationship between policies, institutions, and outcomes in figure 0–1 from the introduction. Rather than constituting separate policy choices, civic literacy enhancement constitutes an additional dimension to key policy choices (going from the center to the right in figure 0–1) affecting SWS outcomes.

As conceived here, in the context of institutions through which informational as well as material resources are fairly and effectively distributed, citizens of the Scandinavian SWS gain an adequate understanding of the relationship between their own choices and the outcomes they favor. We cannot here tell the story of how the knowledge dimension was incorporated into the various policies of the Scandinavian SWS, but we can bring out what, in hindsight, turn out to be highlights in that development. In this way, to put it simply, we can better understand the place of civic literacy in the "Swedish model."

Civic Literacy and the Emergence of the Swedish Welfare State

In part three we looked at the networks of local organizations closely associated with civic literacy in Swedish communities. We noted their origins in the free church movement and temperance societies and, later, the trade unions of the latter nineteenth century. In the twentieth century, popular education became an important element in the policy priorities of the Social Democratic Labour Party, the SAP, which entered government in the 1920s and 1930s. The dominant image of this period was articulated in the favorite metaphor of Per-Albin Hansson, Social Democratic prime minister in the 1930s and 1940s, of Sweden as (building) the "People's Home," in which one acts toward others as toward family members, the weakest to be helped, not exploited. Such help, it was clearly understood, was designed to foster intellectual as much as material advancement.

Earlier, I cited Gunner Myrdal's stress on public access to tax information as a manifestation of the principle that people must have the knowledge to make sense of economic decisions that affect them. Myrdal, with his wife Alva Myrdal, had an important influence on the Swedish welfare state in its formative years, especially in those policies which addressed the acute needs of children. Often disparaged by contemporary observers as "social engineering," the Myrdals' approach seems manipulative by today's standards, but their position is often exaggerated because of a tendency by critics to treat programs designed to protect children[4] as if they were meant to be applied to adults (see Milner 1997a). This misses a fundamental distinction: unlike children, adults can, when provided access to the requisite institutions, become what Gunnar Myrdal termed "propaganda safe."

> Progress has to rely on education. The individual must be made to know the social facts more accurately, including his own true interests and the ideals he holds on a deeper level of his sphere of valuations. . . . I am quite aware that this prescription is nothing less and nothing more than the age-old liberal faith that "knowledge will make us free." (Myrdal 1958: 80–81)

In somewhat unfortunately chosen words, Myrdal is calling for fostering civic literacy. Politically engaged intellectuals had a key role to play.

Myrdal described his own work as that of an "economic technician . . . grouping problems even before they reach actuality and formulating them in a way that is intelligible to the general public . . . [to] lead public opinion and by his initiative give a realistic setting and a rational shape to political questions as they arise" (cited in Olsson 1994: 48–49). Myrdal's direct political involvement ended abruptly after the war, shortened by his failure as a member of the government to see that the Keynesian policies he had successfully promoted in the 1930s would not suffice in the postwar boom of high profits and little unemployment. The major thrust of his work was henceforth to be international in scope. Alva Myrdal, in contrast, returned in the latter 1960s to chair an SAP working group on equality, and her report, *Towards Equality* (see below), became a powerful statement of Swedish social-democratic policy goals for the next decade.

The policy priorities of what came to be known as the "Swedish model" were articulated by the new generation of social-democratic economists, the most influential of which was Gösta Rehn, economic adviser to the Swedish Labour Confederation (LO). Rehn saw that Keynesian nonselective macroeconomic stimulation, because it depended on the union's restraining wage demands, was a long-term prescription for job-destroying inflation. Only under conditions corresponding to what came to be known as the "Rehn model" could trade unionists be expected to take the principle of wage solidarity—equal pay for equal work—into contract negotiations, and thus promote efficient industries and enterprises. Apart from centralized collective bargaining, the key element of the model was "active" labor market policies, most important of which were retraining programs that enabled workers to move from declining to expanding industries.

These programs constituted the core element of a wide network of activities oriented toward adult education and training (see chapter 9), one objective of which was to promote optimal labor market choices. A wider goal was noninflationary growth, through a combination of active labor market programs with tight fiscal and monetary policies, thus enhancing the demand for, and supply of, appropriately trained workers, their mobility underpinned by solid welfare-state guarantees. In this way, policies associated with the Rehn, or Rehn-Meidner, model put into place an institutional framework in the context of which well-informed workers and employers acting on their interests could share in the fruits of noninflationary growth.[5]

According to the model, the welfare state guarantees were to be tied to one's status as citizen rather than employee. This universalistic principle was introduced primarily as a means to an end, the end being to foster the mobility fundamental to the workings of the model under the circumstances of the 1950s and 1960s. Ultimately, Rehn took a flexible approach to social and labor market policies, an approach reflected in a number of innovative policy contributions later in his career, including tax-supported wage subsidies and voluntary early retirement schemes. For Rehn, it was outcomes that mattered, and different means of achieving those outcomes could be envisaged for different circumstances. As Eklund (2001) put it:

> If Gösta Rehn had been here today, to attack unemployment, injustice and inflation, he would not have started by looking for available theories, blue-prints or "models" to follow. He would have asked: What are the problems? What do we want to achieve? Had the available theories shown inadequate, he would gladly have thrown them out the window, only to proceed to kill off a number of sacred cows and happily propose any sacrilegious idea he could think of! Why? Because, to quote Gösta himself, "intelligent people are superior to the theory they happen to have available."

The sine qua non of optimal adaptation—especially under the constraints that globalization places on the available policy choices—is an informed citizenry. Myrdal, Hansson, Rehn, and the other founders of the Swedish welfare state, building on the base set by the early popular movements, left a valuable legacy to contemporary decision makers. Central is civic literacy, policies built on the assumption that, as the opening section of the Social Democratic Party's official position paper on EU membership put it, "everybody is both desirous and capable of playing a part in the running of society . . . of acquiring knowledge and insights which will enable him to play a part in the life of the community" (SAP 1993: 6).[6] Beyond transparency, an informed citizenry must have assured access to continuing education. A concrete expression of this principle came in the publication of the Myrdal report, which recommended allowing older Swedes to return to school to catch up on opportunities missed and thus enter the "educational society for all" (Myrdal et al. 1971). In following this recommendation, a new Education Act explicitly established "recurrent education" as a core objective of the education system, and placed increased emphasis on such education as an alternative to the traditional youth-based system. Another aspect of civic literacy already noted, an appreciation of the potentially adverse effects of commercialism, also found its way into legislation in this period. This was in the comprehensive bill on cultural policy (adopted with the support of all Swedish political parties) in 1974,[7] which affirmed one of the four objectives of cultural policy to be counteracting the negative effects of commercialization.

The "Model" Undermined

During the early 1970s, the Swedish labor movement was in its most radical phase, out of which emerged a series of policies based on an approach that fit rather poorly with the traditional model's emphasis on informed individual choice. Ironically, this approach came to be associated with Rudolf Meidner, Rehn's close collaborator at the LO in the 1950s and early 1960s.[8] Meidner headed a task force named by the LO to rethink the relationship between labor and management within enterprises. Influenced by New Left ideas, a new generation of labor intellectuals had come to question the old corporatist "historical compromise" written into the 1938 Salsjöbaden agreement between labor and business. In 1972, the Meidner Commission issued its report, calling for union-dominated wage-earner funds that would eventually—at least as claimed in certain public statements at the time[9]—rupture the historical compromise. Rehn, at the time in Paris at the OECD, acquiesced to the wage-earner funds only in a watered-down form (see Milner 1989: 131–37) as a trade-off for workers' accepting wage restraint when Swedish manufacturers were reaping high profits.[10]

The Meidner Plan in effect sought to put into action the call of the "power-resource" theorists for a class coalition around the public control of capital investment as the next stage in the struggle of "politics against markets" (Korpi 1978). For Esping-Andersen (1985), "decommodification of labour," as indicated by the level, accessibility, and duration of income replacement for work, was the unalterable criterion of the social-democratic welfare state. Decommodification was an end in itself, and not a means—as under the Rehn model.

The transformative pressure central to the Rehn model, which forced business and labor alike to move to productive industries, fits poorly with decommodification as an end in itself (see Milner 1997a). With LO's adoption of the Meidner Plan, key actors became less disposed to policy adaptation. The result was a reduction in the flexibility of labor-market institutions critical to the effectiveness of the Scandinavian welfare state. The Swedish labor movement, stronger both organizationally and politically than its counterpart in the other Nordic countries, was thus comparatively slow to make the required adjustments during this period. Swedish sick-leave and long-term disability replacement rates were raised to 90 and even 100 percent of pay, measures to monitor employees' actions were minimized, and financial incentives for employers doing so removed.[11] In the tight Swedish labor market of the latter 1980s, this drove absenteeism and the relative cost of labor up to worrisome levels. And, as we saw in chapter 11, the Swedish economy paid dearly for these policy choices during the 1990s.

The decommodification policies of this period diminished the Swedish economy's capacity to adapt to external shocks through corporatist compromises, just as the international economy slowed and globalization and

European economic integration made capital more mobile. As Jochem points out: "In Denmark, Norway, and—not until the mid 90s—Finland, the wage bargaining systems could be remodelled, but not so in Sweden. . . . [a situation exacerbated by] the reluctance of Swedish governments to release the employers from the financial burden of the welfare state" (Jochem 1998: 1). The effects of these decisions on the traditional "Swedish model" have been well summarized by Rothstein.

> The Swedish Model rested on a limited role for government. It left the parties in the labour market to sort out their problems by themselves. This limited role for the political sphere in the labour market was abandoned during the 1970s. The LO and the Social Democratic party gave the electorate the impression that the political system would be able to increase social equality through the expansion of the welfare state, introduce economic democracy through the wage-earner funds, establish industrial democracy through the new system of labour laws, secure full employment through an active labour market policy and Keynesian economics, and so forth. The result in every one of these areas has been retreat or outright defeat. . . .The SAF abandoned the central wage negotiations, began a vigorous and rather successful campaign supporting neo-liberal economic principles and withdrew from all corporatist boards and agencies. The situation between the parties today can best be described as endemic distrust. (Rothstein 1998: 60)

This situation has more or less prevailed since the late 1980s. Though the trade unions, on the whole, continue to favor a return to central negotiations, SAF, the Swedish employers' organization, remains opposed. Yet it was, in fact, SAF that took the initiative in the 1950s to establish centralized bargaining—and thus wage solidarity. LO overcame its reluctance only when the central agreements came to be used not only to attain equal pay for equal work but to reduce wage disparities. The situation changed in the 1980s. In the context of labor's seeming rejection of the "spirit of Salsjöbaden," SAF members were less willing to accept the leveling inherent in wage solidarity as the price for control of aggregate wage increases, since high wage drift[12] increasingly weakened the impact of such control. Instead, they sought to have the process of wage formation decentralized to the industry level following the example of the first industry-level agreement signed in 1983 by the Swedish Engineering Employers' Association and the unions representing its employees.

Still, these setbacks have not meant the end of Swedish corporatism. In the 1990s there were somewhat successful efforts to contain inflation through pattern bargaining, though agreement on adapting labor laws to the globalizing economy proved elusive. Nevertheless, progress was made following the 1998 election in the form of an "Alliance for Growth" agreement between labor and management (see Pestoff 1999). Moreover, the overall picture changes somewhat once we look at concrete developments rather than organizational rhetoric. Just as LO's rhetoric on the wage-earner funds went beyond the views of members in the 1970s, the same appears true of SAF tirades against corporatist cooperation a decade later. For example, Agell and Lundborg (1993: 18) conclude from their research[13] that Swedish "firms are much less convinced about the advantages of decentralized bargaining than the organization that speaks in their name." Indeed, beginning in 1997, the Swedish Engineering Employers' Association "shifted away from the dramatic decentralization of bargaining it had pioneered" (Sheldon and Thornthwaite 1999: 514). Still, compared to the previous twenty-five years, and to the experience of its Nordic neighbors, Swedish corporatism has cut a poor figure in the last quarter of the twentieth century. Corporatism in Denmark is on relatively solid footing (Jochem 2001), while the same is true of Norway[14]—but, if there is still a social-democratic corporatist "model," it would probably be Finland.[15]

> The striking feature of the data we have collected on changes in collective bargaining institutions in the post-war period in the four Nordic countries is the diversity of national experiences and the absence of strong evidence of a common trend. Only the Swedish case offers clear support to scholars who see a general movement toward greater discretion over wages at the industry or plant level. The new Danish system of five large bargaining cartels . . . is hardly evidence of a move toward industry level bargaining. . . . Bargaining in Norway has been recentralized. Finally, events in Finland reveal no significant change in the level of centralization. (Wallerstein and Golden 1997: 724–25)[16]

On this note we can bring this chapter to a conclusion. The corporatist underpinnings of the Scandinavian SWS are not what they were in the heyday of the Rehn model. But, so far, they have proven robust enough to allow Sweden to hold its own in economic performance and maintain the requisite level of civic literacy. A good illustration of this is provided by one result of the International Adult Literacy Survey's test of functional literacy. In chapter 9 we noted the success of Sweden's long-term efforts to fairly distribute intellectual resources as being reflected in the exceptional functional literacy level of Swedes who have not finished high school. A related IALS question asked subjects about their parents' educational attainment, income, and occupation. For each of these categories, differentials in IALS scores were smaller for the Nordic participant, Sweden, than for all other countries. It is figures like these, set in the context of the relatively favorable economic performance of the Nordic region, that suggest that

Sweden's economic upsurge of the latter 1990s will continue, that it has found the means of surmounting the economic difficulties brought on by its own failure to adhere to underlying principles of the "Swedish model."

A more profound question is whether the institutions underlying civic literacy and the SWS can stay intact in the context of globalization and, especially, continental integration. I take up this question in the concluding chapter. But before doing so, the time has come to tie together the main threads of our analysis so far, to see if the virtuous circle we have identified in the relationship between civic literacy and SWS outcomes attained in the Nordic countries holds for the industrial democracies as a whole. To do this we return in chapter 13 to the macro level of analysis and the aggregate comparative data to probe the overall relationship between civic literacy and economic outcomes.

13

Civic Literacy and the Sustainable Welfare State

We have explored how the capacity of the Scandinavian sustainable welfare state (SWS) to adapt policy to achieve relatively egalitarian outcomes reflects the quality of the information that enters the decision process. This relationship, we have argued, holds not just at the elite level but also at the level of "ordinary" citizen, since informed individuals are better able to identify the appropriate policies—and the actors to implement those policies—in order to achieve desired welfare outcomes. In the context of appropriate institutions—the "supply side" of civic literacy—citizens are also more knowledgeable about the effect their individual choices will have on the institutional arrangements themselves.

Economic Ideas and Civic Literacy

In this chapter we return to our analysis at the macro level. If informed individuals can better identify the effects that alternative policy options have on their own interests and those of others, there is reason to expect, according to the logic set out in chapter 11, that societies with a larger proportion of informed citizens will be more egalitarian in their outcomes. Information is a resource like any other: those at the bottom of the social ladder tend to have less. Institutional choices and policies designed to reduce information costs, even when not directed specifically at them, affect the disadvantaged disproportionately, since a dollar's worth of information is more expensive for someone with five dollars than with five hundred. This asymmetry itself has another side: for, as Mancur Olson (1990: 58) puts it, the costs of redistribution to the poor are lower, but—unlike their needs—more conspicuous than the costs of the combination of tariffs, quotas, subsidies, favorable regulations, and similar "implicit" redistributions to powerful interests. While these narrow special-interest organizations could be outvoted since, he points out, they represent only a tiny minority of the population, the problem is that wider interests are poorly understood. "A special-interest organization can get its way [when] most of the society doesn't notice or understand what is happening" (Olson 1996: 78).

Such understanding, he continues, depends "on the quality of economic thought and the extent of economic literacy." Applying this insight in a little-known monograph about Sweden, Olson looked more carefully at that country's economic performance from the 1950s to the 1980s. An important factor in explaining Sweden's ability to resist implicit redistributions, he finds, is its policy makers' unusual capacity to see through such distortions, and the high level of influence of its—extremely competent—professional economists.[1] But he has nothing to say about how that knowledge entered the political process. Had he pursued the matter, he might have discovered policies and institutional arrangements such as those discussed in earlier chapters that make the economists' and other appropriate knowledge widely available at low cost.[2] He might have noticed the efforts, in Olof Palme's words (referring to disabled citizens), "to organize institutions . . . so that their demands and needs be as self-evident for social planning as the needs and interests of other more established citizens" (cited in Tilton 1994: 218).

Civic-literacy-enhancing policies related especially to media consumption described in part three countervail the capacity of these powerful interests to, as Olson (1990: 58) puts it, conceal the cost of implicit redistributions in a "thirty-second commercial," that is, countervail the detrimental effects on civic literacy of the combination of money, commercial television, and politics (described in chapter 8). Under such circumstances, the cost of low civic literacy is borne especially by the economically disadvantaged, while its economic benefits go mainly to the privileged. To counter this, the Scandinavian approach has been to level the playing field by enhancing civic literacy. High-civic-literacy societies are those which equip ordinary citizens with (access to) the knowledge to make appropriate (individual, policy, and institutional) choices, including those which make the welfare state sustainable. As we have noted, the difficulty is not that these choices run counter to self-interest and thus must be underpinned by altruism; it is rather that in a complex, economically interdependent world, it is by no means self-evident just what the effects of particular choices will be. To make choices that reinforce the SWS's capacity to redistribute without undermining its capacity to adapt requires appropriate information linking actors, policies, institutions, and outcomes.[3]

An example of the effects of institutions on civic literacy emerges from Bridges's analysis of the "Big-city Reform" systems in the American Southwest discussed in chapter 5. Bridges found that such systems, which discourage voting by the poor and racial minorities, not only reduced over-all redistributive spending but also skewed spending on service provision in the direction of the needs of the reformers' relatively wealthy constituency. One example, close to our concerns about civic literacy, was public library location: branch libraries were located to best serve the incumbent local government's strongest supporters. "Of the seven branch libraries in Austin, five were located in communities that provided large margins for [mayor] Armstrong in 1961. . . . In Albuquerque, where the median income was $6,626 in 1960, neighbourhood branches were in very affluent neighbourhoods in the Heights" (Bridges 1997: 112).

An example of institutional choices adopted by high-civic-literacy societies to reinforce the SWS is found in the distinctive Scandinavian approach to immigration and foreign aid, which, as in other countries, combines altruism and self-interest. The general principle has been to accept refugees in need, but to accept immigrant applicants based on labor market requirements. Both refugees and immigrants receive comprehensive training in language and other programs designed to foster adaptation to unfamiliar customs and norms. At the same time, a great deal is invested in targeted foreign aid.[4] This combination of targeting aid where it is needed together with making sure that newcomers are given the information needed to integrate is a particular illustration of civic-literacy-related programs that complement the outcomes of the SWS. A manifestation of the results of such policies is to be found in levels of trust. Based on statistical analysis of the foundations of interpersonal trust, Uslaner (2000: 21) suggests that equality leads to trust, but not vice versa.

> In the democratic nations the single biggest barrier to interpersonal trust is economic inequality. Both over time in the United States and across 33 countries without a legacy of Communism, trust goes down as inequality goes up. . . . While there is no direct connection from trust to economic equality, trusting societies in democratic regimes pursue programs that indirectly will boost faith in others. Trusting nations spend more of their total income on governmental programs in general and on education in particular. They also have a larger share of their total population employed by the government. In particular, trusting societies are more likely to devote a higher share of their national wealth to transfer programs that assist the poor.

This relationship between equality and trust described by Uslaner is real, but misses the crucial civic literacy link between them. One example noted in part three is the principle of public access to tax information. To pay for redistribution without undermining trust in public institutions, citizens must have confidence that the money finds its way to the needed individuals and services, and that all contribute fairly.[5] It is civic literacy that, over time,

sustains trust in redistributive public institutions. We have seen this relationship at work in our discussion of historical developments in Scandinavia. We are now in a position to see if the expected relationship between
civic literacy and economic outcomes emerges at the aggregate level. Are
more civically literate nations more socially just?

Civic Literacy and Equality

Together, the three charts that follow clearly and dramatically illustrate the
aggregate relationship between indicators of civic literacy and sustainable
welfare state outcomes. On the x-axis, we plot each country's combined
civic literacy score, as set out at the end of chapter seven in figure 7–7.
This score combines the composite TV dependency scale rating with average turnout in municipal elections—except that it is set over a base of 100.
As we can see, there is a remarkably high correlation with redistributiveness as measured by the disposable income Gini coefficients. (Note that
high civic literacy, like greater redistributiveness, is indicated by a low
score.) Indeed, figure 13–1 provides perhaps the best single snapshot of the
aggregate relationship that lies at the heart of the analysis presented.
Though, as before, we must be careful not to give undue numerical weight
to this statistical relationship, given the high level of abstraction of such an
argument and the small number of cases, the figures make the connection
between civic literacy and the sustainable welfare state undeniable.

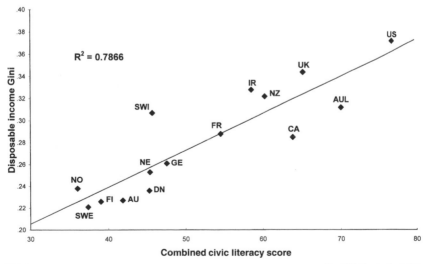

FIGURE 13–1   F = 47.910, sig F = 0.000

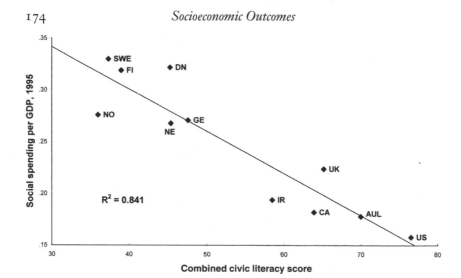

FIGURE I 3–2   F = 47.619, sig F = 0.000

Figure 13–2 plots the equally robust relationship between civic literacy and social spending. The general rule is clear: the more egalitarian the outcome and the greater the role of government in achieving it, the higher the level of civic literacy.[6]

The next chart plots the parallel relationship between corporatist cooperation and redistributiveness. Given what we have seen so far, we naturally expect corporatist societies to be high in civic literacy. Nevertheless, the very high correlation between indicators of the two, in this case using Kenworthy's index of economic cooperation (figure 13–3) is quite remarkable. Clearly there is a connection between policy choices favoring civic literacy and corporatist institutional arrangements. In strengthening those institutions that reinforce the capacity of citizens to understand the policy choices affecting them and their community, the founders of the SWS in Sweden and elsewhere were building on solid ground. The result is the kind of virtuous circle schematically depicted in figure 0–1 (in the introduction). An informed population chooses institutions and policies that reinforce egalitarian (SWS) outputs and outcomes, and also—indirectly— contribute to keeping the population informed. The SWS enhances civic literacy directly by encouraging newspaper readership and adult education, discouraging reliance on commercial television, limiting the influence of money in political communication, and making its laws and regulations transparent. It enhances civic literacy indirectly by reinforcing consensual institutions, which in turn enhance political participation at different levels and thus civic literacy. The SWS thus arrives at economic, social, labor market, and related policies that enhance sustainable welfare

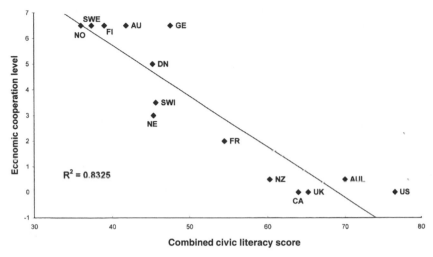

FIGURE 13-3   F = 59.769, sig F = 0.000

state outcomes. Finally, the attainment of these outcomes reinforces support for the various policy measures—including those contributing directly to civic literacy.

The Two Dimensions of Civic Literacy

We have some idea how civic literacy is built up and maintained and of its
effects on societal outcomes, and we can see the connections that, potentially, bring policies and outcomes into a virtuous circle. Let us delve a little more deeply into the underpinnings of the virtuous circle. We can do
this by distinguishing two dimensions that comprise civic literacy: one
quantitative, the other qualitative. The latter concerns how interests are
understood, the former concerns which interests enter the decision-
making process.[7]

The quantitative dimension is associated primarily with the civic side of
civic literacy. It brings into the equation just whose interests find their way
into the policy choices. As we have seen in part one, those excluded
through lack of civic competence are not "average citizens." This applies to
both the civic and the literacy side of civic literacy. On the civic side, as the
data on who votes clearly show,[8] if turnout averages 50 percent in country
or period A, and 80 percent in country or period B, then we can reasonably expect that different interests will be aggregated in A than in B: policy choices in A will be skewed more closely to the interests of people at
higher levels of income and wealth. As Franzese (2000: 37–38) concludes

a sophisticated analysis of OECD countries: "Effective political pressure emanating from some degree of income disparity in the economy depends on the relative political participation of different income groups . . . because the relatively well-off vote and otherwise participate effectively everywhere while the less well-off participate much more effectively only where they turnout to vote." Similarly, according to a study of the relationship between the degree of mobilization of lower-class voters at election time and the generosity of welfare benefits provided by the U.S. state governments,

> Even after adjusting for other factors that might predict state welfare policy—the degree of public liberalism in the state, the federal government's welfare cost-matching rate for individual states, the state unemployment rate and median income, and state taxes—robust relationships were found between the extent of political participation by lower-class voters and the generosity of state welfare payments. In other words, who participates matters for political outcomes, and the resulting policies have an important impact on the opportunities for the poor to lead a healthy life. (Daniels, Kennedy, and Kawachi 2000: 9)

Hence it makes a great difference in terms of outcomes just whose interests find their way into policy. Other things being equal, a society with 40 percent of its citizens excluded from active, informed citizenship (due to a lack of the basic resources needed for civic competence) would choose policies significantly different from, and reinforce the institutions underlying these policies differently than, a society with only 15 percent excluded.

But quantity is not a substitute for quality. The qualitative dimension is associated primarily with the literacy side of civic literacy. On this side, a similar (and closely connected) relationship holds. Like political participation, TV dependency is linked to class. Information resources available to people in the upper and middle classes, as a rule, extend well beyond commercial television. If daily newspaper circulation is around one for every four people, as it is in our high-TV-dependency countries, it is a good indication that those occupying the lower half of the socioeconomic ladder are by and large dependent on commercial television. Where it is around one for every two people, as it is in our low-TV-dependency countries, that dependence is greatly reduced. It is only in the latter rather than in the former case that the quantitative dimension can be expected to lead to the sustainable outcomes emphasized here: uninformed political participation at 90 percent turnout levels cannot be expected to produce results as good as informed participation at 80 percent.

A useful illustration of this is to be found in a comparison of the Scandinavian countries with Belgium and Italy, both of which have as high or higher levels of turnout—but through compulsory voting. If we look again at table 11-1, we note that while the Scandinavian Gini coefficients remained stable (and low) during the recession of the early 1990s, Belgium's rose from low to average and Italy's from above average to very high during this period. From Italy and Belgium's notoriously high debt levels, we infer that high-social-spending policies aimed at reducing income inequality are more fragile in low-civic-literacy countries, where the high turnout leads governments to raise public debt to pay for the social programs. Unlike the Scandinavian countries, they do not have recourse to the kinds of sophisticated corporatist trade-offs possible in the high-civic-literacy countries.

To summarize: in making policy choices that reinforce both the qualitative and quantitative dimensions of civic literacy, a society is also promoting SWS outcomes. These are, in turn, conducive to high civic literacy, since key policies affect the distribution of not only material but also intellectual resources, that is, fostering or impeding civic literacy. It is possible to speak of high-and low-civic-literacy societies as being distinguished by their different—virtuous or vicious—circles of policies, institutions, and outcomes, a difference exacerbated by the new information technology and its potential "digital divide."

Policies enhancing civic literacy and reinforcing the institutions underlying it make possible the adoption of policies that sustain the welfare state. Of course, making it possible is not the same thing as making it happen. Not all labor movements emulated Sweden's by taking advantage of historical opportunities to implement programs enhancing the civic literacy of their members. Some were business unions, interested only in their piece of the pie; others were caught up in historical materialism, which dismissed individual interest—and therefore the knowledge to act upon it—as "false consciousness." As noted in chapter 12, fallible human beings can make inappropriate choices that break the virtuous circle—especially in the context of unexpected external challenges. On this thought we turn to the concluding chapter and some speculation about future prospects.

14

Conclusion: The Future of the Sustainable Welfare State

We have come a long way in these pages. Rather than retracing the steps that have taken us from the causes to the consequences of civic literacy, I shall use this concluding chapter to address the prospects for maintaining in the twenty-first century the prime social development of the twentieth, namely, the combination of social equality and economic efficiency—what we term the sustainable welfare state (SWS for short). In this final part, I have tried to show that it is through the institutions and policies that enhance civic literacy as set out in the earlier parts that contemporary welfare states have achieved sustainability. If that is so, the term *high-civic-literacy welfare state* is redundant (as well as awkward): the *sustainable welfare state*, by definition, combines relatively egalitarian outcomes in the distribution of both material and intellectual (i.e., civic literacy) resources.

Concluding discussions of future prospects often take the form of carefully hedged exercises in wishful thinking, with recommendations for action limited to vague generalizations coupled with calls for further research. I shall try to go further by addressing the concrete situation faced by policy makers in both a high- and low-civic-literacy society, drawing on firsthand knowledge. I begin with Sweden, where I spend a good part of my time these days.

The Prospects of the High-Civic-Literacy Scandinavian Welfare State

The last two chapters outlined the current situation in the Nordic welfare states, suggesting that they remain sustainable, that they have not lost the capacity to adapt to change while preserving what is fundamental.

Sweden's impressive recovery at the end of the 1990s, though not restoring the "model" to its glory, shows that despite the mistakes of the

1970s and 1980s it has not lost its capacity to adjust and adapt. Like its sister Scandinavian states,[1] it remains a remarkably good place to live, especially for those with lower than average incomes.[2] It appears, then, that as long as it can count on an informed population, the SWS should be able to find appropriate means of adjusting to the exigencies of economic globalization while keeping in sight traditional outcome objectives, and thus to equitably distribute both the benefits and the costs of globalization.[3] If this analysis is correct, then the crucial question will come down to the capacity of the Scandinavian SWS to maintain informed participation. The answer to that question lies, in the end, in institutions. Will there continue to be a strong enough popular desire to resist the forces that have been chipping away at the consensual political institutions and corporatist labor-market institutions that complement civic literacy?

One source of concern is decreasing voter turnout. A significant reduction in voter turnout could transform the virtuous circle described in the last chapter into a vicious circle of declining civic literacy and mounting economic inequality. In Sweden, turnout has been declining since the mid-1980s, though the sharpest drop still resulted in a turnout of 81 percent of eligible voters in 1998. More clear-cut is the drop in party membership (Widfeldt 1997), linked to the rise of "postmaterial and self-expression values."[4] Some Swedes have indeed traded their party membership cards for those of single-issue groups;[5] but this cannot account for the decline in voter turnout (Holmberg 1999).

If in fact a lasting drop in mass political participation is in the cards, it would reflect a corresponding decline in civic literacy. On the civic side, perhaps the best reassurance that Sweden is not likely to enter the vicious circle of declining civic literacy and a less sustainable welfare state is the fact that public opinion and public authorities are not complacent. Toward the end of the 1990s, a high-profile investigatory commission, chaired by a former education minister, held public hearings with experts and interested citizens, and published a series of readily accessible analyses concerning democratic participation based on work carried out by 116 researchers.[6] As I write, responses to the commission's recently published report are being discussed in various settings as part of the "remiss" process.

Let us turn to the literacy side. In part three, we noted a decline in daily newspaper consumption that paralleled the economic recession of the 1990s. The economic upturn seems at least to have ended this: according to the 1999 *Mediebarometer*, average daily newspaper readership actually rose at the end of the decade, including among young people, the solid majority of which—compared to 21 percent in the United States[7]—still read the newspaper every day. In addition, the proportion of Swedish young people—like Swedes as a whole—watching at least one of the public television news broadcasts has remained steady.[8] A study conducted at Gothenburg

University[9] shows further that even with the increase in private station viewership, the feared "race to the bottom" has not materialized. Programming trends since 1993 (when commercial TV became readily available in Sweden) show SVT1 and SVT2—and (terrestrial, commercial) TV4—to have actually increased the proportion of information (as opposed to entertainment) programs.

What about education? In 1971, only 75 percent of students continued beyond compulsory school. Today, practically all students (98 percent) continue beyond compulsory school at age sixteen, and 80 percent graduate from upper secondary schools within four years (Skolverket 1998). Such developments are taking place in the context of educational reforms designed to maintain high levels of educational performance in a period of rapid change. Despite a traditionally weak private educational sector, Sweden is in fact among the countries that have gone furthest in the direction of school choice, permitting parents to select any public or independent— usually church-based—school in their locality.[10] Nevertheless, the law requires independent schools to be approved and inspected by the National Board of Education[11] and to provide the same services as the public schools, and it does not permit them to charge fees, or to be selective in their admissions policies (Lidström, forthcoming).[12]

An especially instructive example of SWS adaptation is provided by a new independent secondary school in Stockholm to teach the entrepreneurial skills needed in the new industrial environment, founded by a local People's House association. The organization, which is closely connected to the labor and adult education movement described in chapter 9, maintains that the initiative is in keeping with the traditions of the movement's pioneers, who were themselves entrepreneurs (Schartau 2000). In the context of Stockholm's becoming a mecca for Internet entrepreneurs, such measures should be seen as part of the process of narrowing the digital divide.[13] A special Eurobarometer study (50.1)[14] suggests fair prospects for success in this endeavor. It found that while 30.8 percent of Europeans stated that they used a PC in their own home, the proportion was over 50 percent in Sweden (59.8), the Netherlands (58.8), and Denmark (56.7). Finland at 38.6 percent followed (after Luxembourg with 42.5).[15] With respect to home connection to the Internet, where the European average is 8.3 percent, Sweden led with 39.6 percent, followed by Denmark, 24.6 percent, the Netherlands, 19.6 percent, and Finland, 17.2 percent.[16]

On the subjective side, the highest levels of interest in—and willingness to pay for—on-line/interactive training was among Swedes, 52.9 percent, followed by Finns, 47.3 percent, Danes, 44.5 percent, and Netherlanders, 44 percent.[17] Similarly, on interest in and willingness to pay for electronic access to local or national government information about local or national policy initiatives and decisions, local services, and so on, the three Nordic

EU members were among the seven member states above average in both. In sum, there is good reason to believe that in adjusting to the world of the Internet, Scandinavians are capable of and willing to provide the resources to ensure that the process enhances civic literacy rather than curtailing it by allowing the digital divide to grow.

The Challenge of European Integration

EU figures such as those cited above serve to underscore the fact that the more fundamental challenge to the (high-civic-literacy) SWS lies in external developments, specifically continental integration. Critics of globalization (e.g., Mishra 1999) argue that integrated labor and capital markets push the more advanced welfare states toward the lowest common denominator. Similarly, closer integration with societies characterized by a deeper digital divide could place an added strain on the institutions underpinning civic literacy. Historically, Scandinavian institutions have enabled their societies to meet the challenges posed by change in the external environment. The question at this point is whether the current challenge is to institutions themselves, and thus ultimately to the capacity of the SWS to adapt without undermining its underlying principles. While I can only touch on the question here, I suggest that if there is an imminent threat to the Scandinavian SWS at this time, it lies in the possible effect of EU political union on the civic side of civic literacy.

Scandinavians are generally ambivalent about the European Union: Norway remains outside; Finland, Denmark, and Sweden are members; but only Finland has accepted monetary union. The Eurobarometer (e.g., in #46, autumn 1995) has regularly found Scandinavians lower in support for European integration (along with the U.K. and Austria). It was these same nations who most identified with their nation rather than with the European Union in Eurobarometer #50 (autumn 1998).[18] Yet, Scandinavians are not uninformed[19] and the various Eurobarometers generally find Scandinavian respondents fairly knowledgeable about the European Union.[20] And they rank high in "Europeanness":[21] in their attitudes toward people from other European countries, fluency in European languages, and propensity, when young, to travel and live outside their national boundaries.

This combination reflects, I suggest, an informed appreciation of the possible advantages but also dangers presented by EU integration to the way of life they have created. The underlying opposition to political union is a perception that political institutions are intricately tied to national identity.[22] Though many Swedes and Danes would simply like to turn back the clock on integration, most favor the current situation of economic integration in an intranational structure but reject the supranational project of European political union.[23] For small states especially, membership in multinational confederations can readily be justified by the benefits of economic integration, a means by which people of the member communities can attain common objectives.[24]

However, political union along federalist lines is more than a convenient or necessary complement to economic integration. The European Union as an economic confederation leaves more or less intact the role and relationships of national political institutions, even if it increases constraints on their capacity to generate expected outcomes. Hence, though economic confederation adds new dead ends to the political roadmap, it need not reduce the capacity to democratically weigh the costs and benefits of alternate routes—and thus make appropriate choices. Citizens in the Scandinavian countries, with a long history of making such adjustments consensually, could thus choose to maintain desired outcomes and act on them through policy adjustments via existing political (and corporatist labor-market) institutions.[25]

Under existing confederal arrangements, institutions—like the EU Council—are constituted on an interstate basis. There is no profound ambiguity about where the primary locus of political deliberation, identity, and accountability is located: at the level of the governments of the member states. In contrast, federalism or political union entails a central institutional apparatus with significant powers and responsibilities accountable not to the member states but, if democratic principle is observed, to the people as a whole. The primary relationship is between the "European citizen" and the institutions of Europe, a relationship to which the states are, ultimately, interlopers.[26] Under such circumstances, to remain informed, citizens must understand, not merely the relationship between the institutions of their own state and those of the supranational bodies, but also the cultural-ideological-institutional contexts in which representatives of other member states act.[27] The political map of one's own state turns out to be a poor guide; in fact it could lead one astray. The value of experience, skills, and knowledge gained in engagement in the local and national political arena in member states shrinks compared to that acquired from affiliation in multinational networks open only to elites.[28]

The positions of Scandinavian representatives to the European Union reflect this concern. The Danes continue to insist that "member states retain full sovereignty and the right of veto" (Worre 1994: 2), a position reflected in the views of the new Nordic members, for example in the official statements presented to the EU Intergovernmental Commission that drafted the Amsterdam declaration.[29] Real democratization, they insist, is rather a matter of public access to EU operations and documentation.[30] Both new entrants insisted that this aspect of transparency be included in the EU treaty—a reflection of their own constitutional guarantees of citizen access to all documents, unless specifically excepted for reasons of security.[31]

At the onset of the twenty-first century, the possibility of political union, though still real, seems to have receded. This is largely due to the authority of the commission declining at exactly the time when its hands became full with the daunting task of negotiating the conditions of membership for up to a dozen new applicants. As a result, it appears that the external threat presented by initiatives to "deepen" the European Union in the direction of Euro-federalism can be kept at bay—as long as Nordic participants continue to defend the position of the people they represent.

The Low-Civic-Literacy Society

The July 2000 *OECD Observer* compared countries as to the proportion of the total labor force employed in R & D in 1997. The top three were Finland, Sweden, and Iceland. Denmark was seventh and Norway tenth, with Canada thirteenth and the United States fifteenth. All in all, the outlook remains moderately hopeful for the high-civic-literacy SWS in Sweden and its Nordic cousins. What of the low-civic-literacy society? While we often read about the widening income gap in the United States in the 1980s and 1990s,[32] we hear less about the widening knowledge gap. Yet it is impossible not to conclude from what we have seen in parts one and two that the majority of Americans—at least young Americans—lack basic political, geographical, and historical information.[33] Yet America is as wealthy as the wealthiest high-civic literacy society. The challenge is immense. In his analysis of Internet use in the United States, Miller (2000: 14) concludes: "Political knowledge and participation have long been stratified, mainly along class lines. These are deep structural aspects of socioeconomic life that the Internet cannot be expected to ameliorate." If Americans prove unable to find ways to use their impressively accumulating wealth to close the widening gap in civic knowledge, then the gap will grow as the digital divide widens. As reported by the United States Department of Commerce (1999: 6), between 1997 and 1998, "the digital divide has widened substantially when comparing households of different incomes. . . . The divide for Internet access between the highest and lowest income groups grew 29 percent."[34]

Yet the economic conditions of many Americans improved during the period of sustained growth in the 1990s, opening financial possibilities of increased private and public investment into civic-knowledge-enhancing activities. Unfortunately, however, this does not appear to have been the case: the Internet has turned out to be "utilitarian, entertainment-oriented and related to social communication" (Miller 2000: 14). Additional income has simply fueled more feverish material consumption in a complex pattern of consumer behavior that is especially well portrayed by economist Robert Frank (1999). Frank's analysis of housing-related expenditures is illustrative. Eighteen percent of new homes built in the United States in 1986 were 2,400 square feet or larger; in 1996 it was 30 percent. These expenditures (and thus working hours), he insists, are driven more by the need to keep pace with others than by the pleasure derived from the product itself. An insidious aspect of this concerns the future career prospects of one's children, as better schools are usually those in communities with the more expensive homes. And, of course, to acquire the income to purchase, furnish, and landscape these houses, Americans have to work longer.[35] Indeed, the United States is the only industrial democracy where average annual working hours have increased since 1980 (by 4 percent to 1,996 hours per year in 1997).[36] Larger homes necessitate more distant residential suburbs, more cars, and more time spent commuting, and entail the sacrifice of various forms of what Frank terms "inconspicuous consumption," including reading.

As a remedy against the perverse incentives through which conspicuous consumption forces out inconspicuous consumption (thus reducing civic literacy), Frank proposes a progressive consumption tax. But no such change in the tax structure is in the cards; indeed, the most likely—though still improbable—reform would be to a flat tax, which would invite even more conspicuous consumption. As described in chapter 8, American political institutions are stacked against policy reforms in the common interest, and American institutions are virtually immutable, since even modest reform entails curbing the baleful influence of money in American politics—something that has so far proved unfeasible, despite a near consensus in its favor. And entirely outside the realm of practical possibility are the more fundamental institutional reforms—adoption of a system of responsible (parliamentary) government complemented by proportional electoral institutions that leave place on the political map for third parties—needed to make long-term policy choices that would enhance civic literacy. Instead, we have the reinforcement of the vicious cycle of low civic literacy and high inequality.

Hence, as with the Nordic welfare states, so with the United States; institutions matter. Within existing institutions, Americans face the stark prospect that political participation will be restricted to a materially and informationally privileged minority of the population comprised of a sufficiently large and organizationally capable proportion of active citizens so as to keep it that way.[37] Hence, the path toward changing overall American institutions is a cul-de-sac, the avenue of escape from which can lie only at the periphery, in states and regions where it is possible to mobilize a majority of politically active citizens behind a different agenda. Despite fading geographical diversity due to McDonaldization, there remain regional differences pertinent to civic literacy and the SWS. We know, for example, that Minnesota (which elected a third-party candidate as governor in 1998) consistently leads in presidential voting turnout with a very respectable 69 percent of potential voters (in the 1990s), and that the average North Dakotan claims membership in three voluntary associations (Weinstein 1999: 10), highest in the United States.

This may have something to do with Scandinavian ancestry; it also has to do with location. Minnesota's voter turnout is similar to that in neighboring Canada. All the border states except New York are high or very high on Putnam's (2000: 293) Social Capital Index; North Dakota's associational density is reminiscent of its Canadian neighboring province, Saskatchewan, which has the highest level in Canada (Caldwell and Reed 1999). Minnesota and North Dakota are the two states where children watch the least TV (Putnam 2000: 303) and are joined by Wisconsin as the three states where the proportion of people covered by health insurance comes closest to Canada's total coverage.[38] New Hampshire and Vermont are the states with the lowest income inequality (Kawachi, Kennedy, and Lochner 1997: 58).

Canadians are apprehensive about being swamped by American culture; but there may be a parallel phenomenon in the opposite direction in American border regions with access to Canadian public radio and TV. If so, the prospects for civic literacy in Canada take on an added importance. And, in some ways, Canada looks far more like Europe than the United States, especially in the fact that Canadians see themselves as different from Americans in relation to exactly those policies and institutions identified with the SWS. The question is whether they have the will and the capacity to live up to that identity in concrete institutional and policy choices. In addressing the options facing Canadians we raise the wider question of how comparable societies could avoid the low-civic-literacy, high-inequality, vicious circle.

The Canadian Case

I thus end by addressing the situation in my own country, the policy choices confronting Canadians concerned about civic literacy and the sustainable welfare state. Conditions in Canada are not untypical of most industrial democracies that find themselves at a fork in the road: one leads down the well-paved low-civic-literacy highway the United States has laid out, the other the more difficult high-civic-literacy path of the Scandinavian SWS. Informed opinion in continental European states is still, on balance, oriented toward the latter, while among the English-speaking democracies, in contrast, the American road appears increasingly enticing. We have seen how erstwhile social democrats in New Zealand led the way in the 1980s, with similar views expressed—if less acted on—by their counterparts across the Tasman Sea. And the debate taking place in Britain around Thatcherite influences on the policies of the "New Labour" government[39] echoes some of these same concerns.

Only Canada's social-democratic party (the NDP) has remained un-moved. Though politically marginal, its attitude reflects something pro-found in Canadian consciousness. Perhaps it is its long "undefended" bor-der with the United States, or the presence of Quebec with its cultural links to the Continent, that makes Canada wary of the model of its power-ful neighbor, and more jealous of its social programs—especially universal medicare. The 1992 ISSP Survey showed Canadians to be closer to Swedes than to Americans in their views about whether the government has a re-sponsibility to reduce income disparity. In that survey—of eleven industrial democracies, including Sweden—Canadians were the least likely to agree that income differences are needed for the country's prosperity (Pammett and Frizell 1996: 174, 176). Such figures are especially impressive when we note that Canada's proportion of resident foreigners (17.4 percent) is quite a bit higher than that of the United States (9.7 percent—which is not much higher than that of a number of European countries, including Germany at 9.0 percent).[40]

It is not only about attitudes but also about conditions that people who lump Canada and the United States together are mistaken. Average work-ing hours are declining in Canada, as in Europe but not in the United States. And, as table 11-1 in chapter 11 reveals, almost alone among OECD countries, Canada's disposable income was as equally distributed in the mid-1990s as a decade earlier, which resulted in Canada going from being closer to the United States to being closer to Scandinavia and north-ern Europe.[41] A tax gap between Canada and the United States appeared for the first time in the 1960s, stabilizing at around 10 percent of GDP in the early 1980s—similar to that between Denmark and Germany.[42]

Such figures should provide some grounds for optimism, especially as no threat to political institutions comparable to the extension of European integration appears on the horizon in North America. But such optimism is ill advised: continental integration does threaten the cultural dimension of the Canadian SWS. The inability to counteract the effects of external cultural influences compounds the fragility of the welfare state in Canada. Let us refer back to the charts in previous chapters. We note first that Can-ada is very much an outlier in the figures in chapter 13; that is, its level of income inequality is discernibly lower than predicted by its level of civic literacy. On the civic side, we find Canadian voter turnout only a little higher than those of the United States, Switzerland and Japan. And on the key indicator on the literacy side, newspaper reading, Canada is below the United States and above only Ireland and Italy.[43]

Educational performance indicators as set out in part two present a more mixed picture. For those aged 16 to 25, Canada's average places it fifth in the prose scale, eighth in the document scale, and ninth in the quantitative scale among the fifteen relevant countries in the latest adult literacy study (OECD 2000: 145–47), well above the United States in each case. In the 1998 TIMSS international test of proficiency in science and mathematics, of students in the thirteen countries, compared in this book that took the test, Canadian sixteen-year-olds placed seventh in mathematics and eighth in physics. And, as seen in figure 4–3, page 62, Canada looks even better (tied for fifth place) when comparing the mean scores of those at the bottom (5 percent level) in combined math and physics literacy. Yet this result is misleading, since high Canadian dropout figures[44] (in stark contrast with the above-noted figure of only 2 percent who do not continue in upper secondary school in Sweden) suggest that an abnormally large number of potential low scorers were not included in these averages. There is no little irony, thus, in the fact that Canada owes its consistently top rating in the United Nations' Human Development Index to its high education score.[45]

There is good reason to believe that civic literacy in Canada is low, and going lower (Howe, 2001):

> In a 1990 survey carried out for the Royal Commission on Electoral Reform and Party Financing, 5 percent of Canadians could not name the Prime Minister. In a similar survey commissioned by IRPP in March 2000, this had grown to 11 percent. In that same survey, only 46 percent of respondents could name the federal Minister of Finance, and just over one-third (35 percent) could identify the official opposition in the House of Commons. . . . In 1990, 56 percent of 18 to 29 year olds were able to answer at most one of three political knowledge questions correctly (Who is the PM? Who is the Liberal leader? Who is the NDP leader?). For the survey sample as a whole, the figure was 16 points lower at 40 percent. By 2000, the younger group was lagging further still: when asked to identify the PM, finance minister and official opposition, fully 67 percent of 18 to 29 year olds scored no more than one out of three compared to 46 percent for the sample as a whole.

It would therefore be foolish in the extreme for Canada to rest on these laurels. Raising civic literacy[46]—and thus reinforcing the shaky underpinnings of its welfare state—is a matter of urgency, beginning with identifying and counteracting societal developments that lead young men especially to drop out of school and face a life of functional illiteracy. This requires more attention to habits of literacy (see chapter 9) throughout the system of formal education but also in the priority placed on adult education. Closely related is the urgent need to raise the level of newspaper readership. This means serious consideration of programs such as those used in the Nordic countries described in chapters 7 and 8—including subtitling in films, videos, and television shows.[47] It entails also intensified efforts to keep cultural products out of North American and international free trade agreements while reinforcing public broadcasting against competition from specialized cable channels as well as American commercial networks. The signs are not encouraging: a comparative study of support for public broadcasting between 1995 and 1998 found that Canada was losing ground, with money for public television dropping 28.8 percent—the largest decline for all OECD countries.[48]

On the civic side of civic literacy there are actions to reduce the effects of money in politics that would prove salutary (see Kent 1999).[49] The most fundamental change called for is on the "supply side:" institutional reforms to render the political map more comprehensible by following New Zealand's example and introducing proportional representation, the potential beneficial effects of which are set out in chapter 6. Apart from the more profound but long-term enhancement of informed political participation,[50] PR would allow for a more consistent social-democratic input into policy debate and, potentially, government formation. This would free the NDP from the ever present threat of electoral annihilation and thus place it in a position to systematically reassess its policies and the potential allies for realizing them.

Any such effort at transforming Canadian institutions is bound to come up against the "national question."[51] As in many other ways, Quebec differs from English-speaking (regions of) Canada in the relative strength of its underpinnings of civic literacy and the SWS. Quebec is more corporatist in its labor-business-government relationship (Haddow 2000); Quebec came close to adopting PR for provincial elections in 1983. Overall, Quebec is higher in civic aspects of civic literacy,[52] such as turnout, interest in politics, and party membership, but lower on the literacy aspect. Quebeckers read fewer newspapers and watch more television[53] than Canadians in the other provinces: in the IALS prose comprehension test, a very high 28 percent of Quebeckers were functionally illiterate (level 1) compared to 20 percent for the rest of the country (Statistics Canada 1999).[54]

Placing the Canadian SWS on a firmer base of civic literacy would entail accepting the demands of at least moderate Quebec nationalists for greater institutional autonomy. This would make it possible for Quebeckers to build on their strengths and, as a community, adapt institutions to address their weaknesses. The same would be true for (the regions of) English-speaking Canada. Much more could be said about strengthening the SWS in Canada, but this is not the place. For Canada, as well as Quebec, the Pacific Northwest, and New England, as it was for New Zealand in chapter 10, it is a matter of identifying civic-literacy-enhancing choices that reflect a region's particular composition and circumstances.

To Conclude

The lessons to be learned from the high-civic-literacy countries as set out in part three can thus be put to use only in the context of a strategy that allows a relatively low-civic-literacy country or community to build on its strengths and adapt institutions to address its weaknesses. Economic globalization and the danger of a widening digital divide add an element of urgency to the choice confronting democratic societies. All face the prospect of mirroring a globalized world economy with its minority of "winners" and majority of "losers"—losers not only due to economic deprivation but, increasingly, to their inability to take informed action to make their society better for themselves and others. Only high-civic-literacy societies institutionally arranged so that a substantial majority of their citizens have meaningful maps to guide them through the complexity of decisions that their community will face in the coming years will, potentially, be equipped to meet the challenge. Only those communities can hope to distribute fairly the costs of globalization and new information technology so as to draw optimal advantage from their benefits. As we enter the twentieth century, this is what sustaining the welfare state—the great achievement of the twentieth century—will be all about.

APPENDIX I

The CSES Questions on Political Knowledge

At the time of this writing, the countries below had completed national electoral surveys as part of the Comparative Study of Electoral Systems (CSES). These surveys, which polled a minimum of two hundred respondents, cover roughly the period 1996 to 1999. The CSES participants were instructed to ask three political information items of their choosing, with possible response codings of correct, incorrect, and don't know. The three items were expected to include one question that about two-thirds of respondents could correctly answer, one that about one-third could correctly answer, and one that about half could correctly answer. Below are found the questions asked (and the percentages of correct responses among all respondents) in the CSES countries discussed in this book.

Australia

- "Australia became a federation in 1901." *(true)* (65%)
- "The Senate election is based on proportional representation." *(true)* (45%)
- "No one may stand for Federal parliament unless they pay a deposit." *(true)* (31%)

Britain

- "MPs from different parties are on parliamentary committees." *(true)* (71%)
- "Britain's electoral system is based on proportional representation." *(false)* (57%)
- "The longest time allowed between general elections is four years." *(false)* (64%)

(There was no question in the British battery so difficult that only one-third got it right.)

Canada

Respondents were asked to identify:
- their provincial premier (78%)
- the federal minister of finance *(Paul Martin)* (37%)
- the only woman prime minister *(Kim Campbell)* (40%).

Denmark

"Do you remember any of the candidates who ran for the election in your county?"
- 3 or more candidates correct (41.7%)
- 2 candidates correct (15.9%)
- 1 candidate correct (19.8%)

Germany

- "Who is Germany's Foreign Minister?" *(Klaus Kinkel)* (67 %)
- "How many *Laender* are there?" *(16)* (45%)
- "What is the number of EU members?" *(15)* (11%)

The Netherlands

- Photo of Thom de Graaf (one of the leading politicians of Democrats 66 (fourth largest party) shown, followed by a question asking respondents to identify the person. (33.5%)
- Is Norway a member of the EU? *(no)* (47.5%)
- Is CDA (the Christian Democrats) a member of present coalition? *(no)* (70.5%)

New Zealand

- "There are 99 members of Parliament." *(false)* (64%)
- "Cabinet Ministers must be MPs." *(true)* (69.3%)
- "The NZ Parliament has never had an Upper House." *(false)* (32.3%) (The Legislative Council was abolished in 1951.)

Norway

- To which party does the President of the *Storting* during the last four years belong? *(Labor Party)* (77.5 %)
- Do you remember who has been the Minister of Local Government and Labor the year before the election? *(Kjell Opseth)* (28.8%)
- How many representatives are selected at the *Storting*? *(165)* (36%)

United States

Respondents were asked to identify the office held by:
- Al Gore *(Vice President)* (87.8%)
- William Rehnquist *(Chief Justice of the Supreme Court)* (9.3%)
- Newt Gingrich *(Speaker of the House of Representatives)* (57.8%)

APPENDIX II

The International Adult Literacy Survey (OECD 1997)

TABLE 4–1A

Percentage Who Reported Participating in Community or Volunteer Activities at Least Once a Month

	Literacy Level	Literacy Category		
		Prose	Document	Quantitative
Canada	I	10.6	9.0	7.0
	2	15.9	19.7	18.2
	3	24.1	30.5	27.8
	4/5	39.6	28.0	34.7
Germany	I	17.7	19.7	22.4
	2	25.8	23.5	23.7
	3	28.5	27.6	27.6
	4/5	25.2	27.5	24.9
Netherlands	I	24.1	22.3	18.3
	2	28.9	30.9	30.2
	3	33.1	31.1	31.4
	4/5	37.1	38.0	40.3
Sweden	I	34.1	28.3	30.3
	2	42.1	43.5	40.7
	3	46.7	46.9	47.6
	4/5	54.3	52.9	53.4
Switzerland (French)	I	10.3	9.4	3.8
	2	21.0	20.6	18.5
	3	22.2	22.3	22.8
	4/5	24.2	23.5	24.8
Switzerland (German)	I	11.6	9.8	6.1
	2	21.9	19.7	20.6
	3	25.9	25.3	24.7
	4/5	36.8	36.1	32.5

(Table 4-1A continued)

	Literacy Level	Literacy Category		
		Prose	Document	Quantitative
United States	1	18.5	20.1	17.2
	2	29.9	27.3	27.6
	3	37.7	42.2	40.1
	4/5	44.4	42.8	44.6

Source: OECD 1994a: 190.

The International Adult Literacy Survey (IALS) assessed three categories of literacy:

1. Prose literacy: the ability to understand and use information from texts such as editorials, news stories, poems, and fiction
2. Document literacy: the ability to locate and use information from documents such as job applications, payroll forms, transportation schedules, maps, tables, and graphs
3. Quantitative literacy: the ability to perform arithmetic functions such as balancing a checkbook, calculating a tip, or completing an order form

The specific literacy tasks designed for IALS were scaled by difficulty from 0 to 500 points. This range was subsequently divided into five broad literacy levels.

- Level 1 indicates very low literacy skills, where the individual may, for example, have difficulty identifying the correct amount of medicine to give to a child from the information found on the package.
- Level 2 respondents can deal only with material that is simple, clearly laid out, and in which the tasks involved are not too complex. This is a significant category, because it identifies people who may have adapted their lower literacy skills to everyday life but would have difficulty learning new job skills requiring a higher level of literacy.
- Level 3 is considered to be the minimum desirable threshold in many countries, but some occupations require higher skills.
- Levels 4 and 5 show increasingly higher literacy skills requiring the ability to integrate several sources of information or solve more complex problems. It appears to be a necessary requirement for some jobs.

Literacy Levels by Category

1. Prose

Level 1: 0–225. Most of the tasks at this level require the reader to locate one piece of information in the text that is identical or synonymous to the information given in the directive. If a plausible incorrect answer is present in the text, it tends not to be near the correct information.

Level 2: 226–275. Tasks at this level tend to require the reader to locate one or more pieces of information in the text, but several distractions may be present, or low-level inferences may be required. Tasks at this level also begin to ask readers to integrate two or more pieces of information, or to compare and contrast information.

Level 3: 276–325. Tasks at this level tend to direct readers to search texts to match information that requires low-level inferences or that meets specified conditions. Sometimes the reader is required to identify several pieces of information that are located in different sentences or paragraphs rather than in a single sentence. Readers may also be asked to integrate or to compare and contrast information across paragraphs or sections of text.

Level 4: 326–375. These tasks require readers to perform multiple-feature matching or to provide several responses where the requested information must be identified through text-based inferences. Tasks at this level may also require the reader to integrate or contrast pieces of information, sometimes presented in relatively lengthy texts. Typically, these texts contain more distracting information, and the information that is requested is more abstract.

Level 5: 376–500, Some tasks at this level require the reader to search for information in dense text that contains a number of plausible distractions. Some require readers to make high-level inferences or use specialized knowledge.

2. Document

Level 1: 0–225. Most of the tasks at this level require the reader to locate a piece of information based on a literal match. Distracting information, if present, is typically located away from the correct answer. Some tasks may direct the reader to enter personal information onto a form.

Level 2: 226–75. Document tasks at this level are a bit more varied. While some still require the reader to match a single feature, more distracting information may be present or the match may require a low-level inference. Some tasks at this level may require the reader to enter information onto a form or to cycle through information in a document.

Level 3: 276–325. Tasks at this level appear to be most varied. Some require the reader to make literal or synonymous matches, but usually the matches require the reader to take conditional information into account or to match multiple features of information. Some tasks at this level require the reader to integrate information from one or more displays of information. Other tasks ask the reader to cycle through a document to provide multiple responses.

Level 4: 326–375. Tasks at this level, like those in the previous levels, ask the reader to match multiple features of information, to cycle through documents, and to integrate information; frequently, however, these tasks require the reader to make higher-order inferences to arrive at the correct answer. Sometimes, conditional information is present in the document, which must be taken into account by the reader.

Level 5: 376–500. Tasks at this level require the reader to search through complex displays of information that contain multiple distractions, to make high-level inferences, process conditional information, or use specialized knowledge.

3. Quantitative

Level 1: 0–225. Although no quantitative tasks used in the IALS fall below the score value of 225, experience suggests that such tasks would require the reader to perform a single, relatively simple operation (usually addition) for which either the numbers are already entered onto the given document and the operation is stipulated or the numbers are provided and the operation does not require the reader to borrow.

Level 2: 226–275. Tasks in this level typically require readers to perform a single arithmetic operation (frequently addition or subtraction) using numbers that are easily located in the text or document. The operation to be performed may be easily inferred from the wording of the question or the format of the material (for example, a bank deposit form or an order form).

Level 3: 276–325. Tasks found in this level typically require the reader to perform a single operation. However, the operations become more varied—some multiplication and division tasks are found in this level. Sometimes two or more numbers are needed to solve the problem, and the numbers are frequently embedded in more complex displays. While semantic relation terms such as "how many" or "calculate the difference" are often used, some of the tasks require the reader to make higher-order inferences to determine the appropriate operation.

Level 4: 326–375. With one exception, the tasks at this level require the reader to perform a single arithmetic operation where typically either the quantities or the operation are not easily determined. That is, for most of the tasks at this level, the question or directive does not provide a semantic relation term such as "how many" or "calculate the difference" to help the reader.

Level 5: 376–500. These tasks require readers to perform multiple operations sequentially, and they must dissemble the features of the problem from the material provided or rely on background knowledge to determine the quantities or operations needed.

Sample

Between 2,000 and 3,000 adults (5,660 in Canada) in each of the twelve countries in the first two rounds—Australia, Belgium, Canada, Ireland, Germany, the Netherlands, New Zealand, Poland, Sweden, Switzerland, the United Kingdom, and the United States—took part. All the respondents were tested in their national language(s) and in their own homes. The prose and document literacy scales were each based on 34 tasks, and the quantitative literacy scale was derived from performance on 33 tasks. All the tasks were of varying difficulty. Below is one of the sample questions for level 1 in each category.

Sample Questions

Prose Scale

Typically the match between the task and the text is literal, although sometimes a low-level inference may be necessary. The text is usually brief or has organizational aids such as paragraph headings or italics that suggest where the reader can find the specified information. Generally, the target word or phrase appears only once in the text.

The easiest task in level 1 (difficulty value of 188) directs respondents to look at a medicine label to determine the "maximum number of days you should take this medicine." The label contains only one reference to number of days, and this information is located under the heading "DOSAGE." The reader must go to this part of the label and locate the phrase "not longer than 7 days."

Document Scale

A task involves a chart from a newspaper showing the expected amounts of radioactive waste by country. This task, which has a difficulty value of 218, directs the reader to identify the country that is projected to have the smallest amount of waste by the year 2000. Again, there is only one percentage associated with each country; however, the reader must first identify the percentage associated with the smallest amount of waste, and then match it to the country.

Quantitative Scale

The easiest quantitative task (225) directs the reader to complete an order form. The last line on this form says "Total with Handling." The line above it says "Handling Charge $2.00." The reader simply has to add the $2.00 to the $50.00 entered on a previous line to indicate the cost of the tickets. In this task, one of the numbers is stipulated; the operation is easily identified from the word "total"; and the operation does not require the reader to perform the "borrow" or "carry-over" function of addition. Moreover, the form itself features a simple column format, further facilitating the task for the reader.

APPENDIX III

The TV Dependency Scale: Data and Sources

Countries Ranked According to Average Weekly Viewing Time per Capita, 1993

Rank	Country	Hours:minutes	Rank	Country	Hours:minutes
1	United States	28:20 *	12	Switzerland (It.)	17:51
2	Japan	27:39 **	13	Denmark	17:09
3	United Kingdom	25:40	14	Finland	16:55 *
4	Italy	24:08	15	Switzerland (Fr.)	16:48
5	Canada	22:48	16	Netherlands	16:41
6	Australia	22:45 **	17/18	Austria	15:31
7	Ireland	22:17	17/18	Belgium (Fl.)	15:31
8/9	Germany	21:49	19	Norway	15:21
8/9	Belgium (Fr.)	21:49	20/21	Switzerland (Ge.)	14:35
10	France	20:39	20/21	Sweden	14:35
11	New Zealand	18:45 *			

These figures are not standardized as to age. Typically they include children (starting from anywhere between 3 and 12 years of age) as well as adults.

Sources

For European countries: *Statistical Yearbook, 1994–95: Cinema, Television, Video and New Media in Europe* (Strasbourg, France: European Audiovisual Observatory [Council of Europe].

For Canada: *1996 International Television and Video Almanac* (New York: Quigley Publishing Company, 1996, p. 681).

For the United States: *1996 International Television and Video Almanac* (New York: Quigley Publishing Company, 1996, p. 14a) and "The Public Perspective: A Roper Center Review of Public Opinion and Polling," August/September 1995, p. 47.

For Australia: "Oz Increases Time at Tube" (A. C. Neilsen company reports average viewing in Australia), *Variety* (New York), 27 April 1992.

For New Zealand: "Country at a Glance," *Variety* (New York), 9–15 October 1995, p. 52.

For Japan: "Country at a Glance," *Variety* (New York), 21 September 1992, p. 44.

* 1994 statistics; ** 1992 statistics

Expenditure on Television Advertising Per Capita, 1993

Rank	Country	TV Adspend (1993 US$ millions; current prices)	Population (1993; millions)	Adspend per capita (US$; current prices)
1	United States	26,732	257.59	103.77
2	Japan	12,496	124.34*	100.50
3	New Zealand**	273	3.50	78.11
4	Australia	1,238	17.66	70.10
5	United Kingdom	3,347	58.23	57.48
6	Italy	2,855	57.25*	49.87
7	Canada	1,322	28.08	47.08
8	France	2,562	57.8	44.32
9	Austria	284	7.91	35.90
10	Belgium	356	10.01	35.56
11	Denmark	181	5.18	34.94
12	Germany	2,671	80.97	32.99
13	Netherlands	501	15.34	32.66
14	Ireland	102	3.57	28.57
15	Finland	128	5.1	25.10
16	Sweden	205	8.75	23.53
17	Switzerland	162	6.97	23.24
18	Norway	100	4.32	23.15

Adspend sources:

For Europe, United States, and Japan: *Statistical Yearbook, 1994–95: Cinema, Television, Video and New Media in Europe* (Strasbourg, France: European Audiovisual Observatory [Council of Europe], 1994, tables 7.5 and 1.4).

For New Zealand: "New Zealand at a Glance," *Variety* (New York), 9–15 October 1995, p. 52.

For Australia: TV adspend figure (AU$ thousands 1,761,177) from "Advertising Expenditure in Main Media, 1986–1995" (Australia Bureau of Statistics, Canberra, 1996). Exchange rate to 1993 US$ from *Year Book Australia 1996.*

For Canada: Television Bureau of Canada, *TVB Television Basics 96/97* (Toronto, 1997).

Population sources:

For Europe, United States, and Japan: *Statistical Yearbook, 1994–95: Cinema, Television, Video and New Media in Europe* (Strasbourg, France: (European Audiovisual Observatory [Council of Europe], 1994, table 1.1).

For New Zealand: "New Zealand at a Glance," *Variety* (New York), 9–15 October 1995, p. 52.

For Australia: *OECD Economic Surveys 1994–1995 Australia* (Paris: OECD, 1995).

For Canada: Television Bureau of Canada, *TVB Television Basics 96/97* (Toronto, 1997).

*1992 population; **1994 statistics

TV Advertising Expenditure as a Percentage of GDP, 1993

Rank	Country	Total Display Adspend as % of GDP	TV Adspend as % of Total Ad Expenditure	TV Adspend as % of GDP
1	New Zealand*	1.87	33	0.61
2	Australia**	?	?	0.43
3	United States	1.01	42	0.42
4	United Kingdom	0.84	42	0.35
5	Japan	0.63	47	0.30
6	Italy	0.55	52	0.29
7	Canada	0.96	25	0.24
8	Ireland	0.76	30	0.23
9	France	0.64	34	0.22
10	Germany	0.86	23	0.20
11	Belgium	0.51	33	0.17
12	Netherlands	0.82	19	0.16
13	Austria	0.66	23	0.15
14	Denmark	0.53	26	0.14
15	Finland	0.64	19	0.12
16	Sweden	0.56	19	0.11
17	Norway	0.52	19	0.10
18	Switzerland	0.75	10	0.08

Sources:

For Europe, United States, and Japan: *Statistical Yearbook, 1994–95: Cinema, Television, Video and New Media in Europe* (Strasbourg, France: European Audiovisual Observatory [Council of Europe], 1994, table 7.3).

For New Zealand: "New Zealand at a Glance," *Variety* (New York), 9–15 October 1995, p. 52; A. C. Neilsen website: http://www.nielsen.com/home/trends/octworlt.htm.

For Australia: GDP figure (AU$ millions 413,832) from *OECD Economic Surveys 1994–1995, Australia* (Paris: OECD, 1995); TV adspend figure (AU$ thousands 1,761,177) from "Advertising Expenditure in Main Media, 1986–1995" (Commercial Economic Advisory Service of Australia, St. Leonards, NSW Australia), 1996, p.12.

For Canada: GDP figures from Abel, Bernanke, and Smith, *Macroeconomics* (Don Mills, Ontario: Addison-Wesley Publishers, 1995); advertising figures from Television Bureau of Canada, *TVB Television Basics 96/97* (Toronto, 1997).

*1994 statistics; **1993 TV adspend = AU$ 1,761,177,000

A Survey of New Zealand Candidates

This survey[1] was conducted to get another perspective on the effects of the new (MMP) electoral system on the campaign and the behavior of the voters. It is very hard to distinguish changes perceived by the voters themselves, due to the novelty of the new system, from the effects of the system itself. This is not likely to be quite as true of political actors with long experience in New Zealand politics. These individuals were especially well placed to reflect on differences between the MMP election and previous ones.

My presence in New Zealand in the fall of 1996 in the three months before, after, and during the election campaign made it possible to gain firsthand data about the evolution and practice of the new system. Initially I contemplated interviews with all candidates, but this proved impossible because of time and geographical constraints. However, I was able, together with Frances Boylston, to conduct a study of the 1996 campaign and its effects as perceived by such political actors. The opportunity took the form of collaboration with Professor Peter Aimer, codirector of the New Zealand Electoral Study, who, immediately after the vote, sent out a modified version of the University of Auckland–University of Waikato questionnaire to all the candidates, as he had in 1993. A one-page supplementary questionnaire (found at the end of this appendix) was sent out to a subset of the candidates, namely, the sixty-three identified as having run in constituencies (electorates) in 1990, 1993, and 1996 for one of the six parties with a chance of winning a seat in the legislature in 1996. We received forty-eight valid responses, a very impressive rate of response from a group that included many of the country's leading politicians.[2] In addition to our questionnaire, we made use of responses from the forty-eight respondents to eight of Aimer's questions relevant to our analysis.[3]

The overall objective was to compare the three elections on their use of different campaign techniques, the level of information and interest among citizens, and the effect of the campaign. We chose candidates from, and asked questions in relation to, all three elections to ensure that our respondents would have longer experience as participants and close observers, and would draw from that experience in answering the questions. (It also allowed us to base our comparisons to 1996 on the 1990 instead of 1993 data, if the latter proved aberrant due to the effect of the referendum having been held simultaneously. This proved not to be necessary, as the main changes were in almost every case seen to have taken place between 1993 and 1996, with relatively consistent results between 1990 and 1993.)

Results of Our Survey

In general, the respondents noted heightened activity and interest in the 1996 campaign. In response to question 2, local candidates' debates were reported to have gone up in number. Table IV-A compares responses for 1993 and 1996.

These results correspond to the responses to the New Zealand Election Study for the two elections, which saw a significant rise among respondents who stated that they attended political meetings during the campaign—from 9.4 percent in 1993 to 12.7 percent in 1996.

The key questions for the purposes here are 3, 4, and 5, which asked the respondents to assess, respectively, the voters' interest and knowledgeability, and the informativeness of the campaign in each election. Interest (question 3), which we know to correlate fairly closely to knowledge, was included in part to round out the questionnaire and also not to draw undue attention to questions 4 and 5. In the charts that follow, the score is based on the difference between the assessments for 1993 and for 1996.[4] Figures IV-1 and IV-2 are highly skewed on the positive side; thus we can see that the candidates found voters in 1996 to be significantly more interested and more knowledgeable than in 1993. Figure IV-1 indicates that our respondents on average also rated the 1996 campaign better at helping voters make informed decisions than the 1993 one, though the difference between the two elections is smaller than for questions 3 and 4.

TABLE IV-A

Number of Candidates' Debates in Electorate by Number of Respondents

	0 Debates	1–5 Debates	6–10 Debates	11+ Debates
1993	2	21	18	3
1996	0	17	10	17

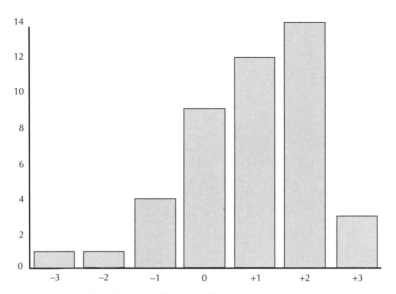

FIGURE IV–I 1996 Voter Interest Compared to 1993

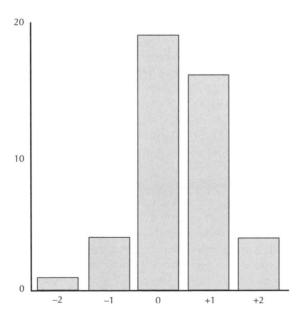

FIGURE IV–2 1996 Voter Interest Compared to 1993

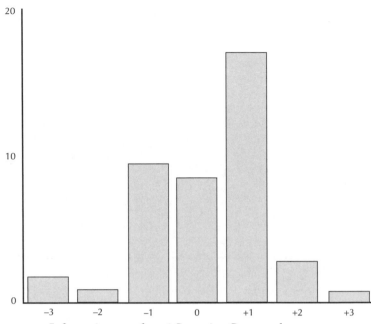

FIGURE IV-3 Informativeness of 1996 Campaign Compared to 1993

Despite the small number of respondents, we should not underplay the significance of those perceived differences. Indeed, if anything, the unambiguity of the results are unexpected, since this is not a group we would expect to be favorably disposed toward MMP, given that most established politicians were known to oppose MMP.[5] This lack of sympathy for MMP, I suspect, helps explain the less positive comparative assessment of the 1996 campaign in response to question 5 in figure IV-3 than in the assessment of the interest and knowledge of voters in response to questions 3 and 4. Clearly a number of the candidates who found the voters more knowledgeable and interested in 1996 were unwilling to give credit to the new electoral system for this.

Were there any specific characteristics associated with the favorableness of the respondents' judgments? We tested for factors that correlate with a positive versus negative comparative assessment of the knowledge of the voters and the informativeness of the 1996 campaign. Most proved insignificant, including the density and concentration of elderly persons and children in the electorate and whether the candidate won or lost in 1996. Only three showed any significant correlation: women candidates rated more positively both the knowledge of the electorate and the informativeness of the campaign in 1996 compared to 1993; National and New Zealand

First candidates were comparatively less positive, especially about the comparative informativeness of the 1996 election, than candidates of Labour and the other parties.[6] Clearly, something was happening beyond the novelty of a new electoral system.

The Questionnaire

Please circle the answer closest to your assessment.

1. Campaigns use various tools to reach voters. How much in the way of resources (time, money, volunteer efforts, etc.) did your campaign invest in each of the following?

a. neighbourhood meet-the-candidate meetings

	a great deal						very little
1990:	1	2	3	4	5	6	7
1993:	1	2	3	4	5	6	7
1996:	1	2	3	4	5	6	7

b. local media coverage

	a great deal						very little
1990:	1	2	3	4	5	6	7
1993:	1	2	3	4	5	6	7
1996:	1	2	3	4	5	6	7

c. household mailings

	a great deal						very little
1990:	1	2	3	4	5	6	7
1993:	1	2	3	4	5	6	7
1996:	1	2	3	4	5	6	7

d. door-to-door campaigning (by the candidate)

	a great deal						very little
1990:	1	2	3	4	5	6	7
1993:	1	2	3	4	5	6	7
1996:	1	2	3	4	5	6	7

e. telephone canvassing

	a great deal						very little
1990:	1	2	3	4	5	6	7
1993:	1	2	3	4	5	6	7
1996:	1	2	3	4	5	6	7

2. Approximately how many all-candidates debates took place in your electorate?

1990:	none	1 to 5	6 to 10	11 to 15	16 to 20	more than 20
1993:	none	1 to 5	6 to 10	11 to 15	16 to 20	more than 20
1996:	none	1 to 5	6 to 10	11 to 15	16 to 20	more than 20

3. Based on your experience, evaluate the voters' interest in the election.

	very interested					not at all interested	
1990:	1	2	3	4	5	6	7
1993:	1	2	3	4	5	6	7
1996:	1	2	3	4	5	6	7

4. Based on your experience, evaluate the voters' knowledge of election issues.

	very knowledgeable					not at all knowledgeable	
1990:	1	2	3	4	5	6	7
1993:	1	2	3	4	5	6	7
1996:	1	2	3	4	5	6	7

5. Overall, how would you rate each campaign as far as helping voters make informed decisions at the polls?

	excellent						poor
1990:	1	2	3	4	5	6	7
1993:	1	2	3	4	5	6	7
1996:	1	2	3	4	5	6	7

Notes

Preface

1. I was thus able to take advantage of an opportunities to do something that has been well described by senior European political scientist Jean Blondel in the fall 1996 *Bulletin* of the European Consortium on Political Research (ECPR). "I sometimes go so far as believing, perhaps exaggeratedly, that it is not truly possible to undertake comparative government research without having 'belonged', so to speak, to different countries, because this 'belonging' is what provides, not just knowledge about the countries concerned, but more generally, a sense that political life is both different and similar, relative and universal. . . . What living in another country forces you to do . . . is to reflect about this relativity and this universality."

2. Such research can be very useful, as historical and constitutional differences can be controlled when comparing subunits of the same country. (Given Switzerland's uniqueness as a member of no supranational organizations, it is, I suspect, no coincidence that the single most comprehensive contemporary intrastate research relevant to this book is the Swiss study discussed in detail in chapter 5.)

Introduction

1. This is a fundamental element in John Stuart Mill's approach to political participation (Mill 1910).

Chapter 1. The Uses and Abuses of Social Capital

1. Note that, since simple rather than multiple regressions are used, there is no claim that even highly significant statistical relationships such as these prove causality. Here I differ with some social scientists who make claims of causality based on multiple regressions with aggregate data of this kind, since I contend that it is impossible to include all the relevant possible explanatory factors into such regressions.

2. As the reader will note, the number of countries graphically displayed can be as low as eleven and as high as sixteen. Countries used for aggregate comparisons are the industrial democracies of North America, Australasia, and Europe. This means that Japan is excluded—a result also of the author's failure to assemble the necessary data on turnout in local elections. (In addition, as we shall see in chapter 2, Italy and Belgium are excluded from certain chapters due to their use of compulsory voting in elections at all levels.) Among European countries, Iceland, Luxembourg,

and Malta are excluded as too small; Spain, Portugal, and Greece, as well as the new democracies of eastern Europe, are excluded because they tend to be lower in GDP per capita and also have a relatively short experience of uninterrupted parliamentary democracy. Moreover, since we rely in large part on secondary data, several charts and tables are limited to the subset of countries considered in the studies from which the data are drawn.

3. Putnam modestly notes that he was, until the publication of this article "in a respected but little known periodical, the *Journal of Democracy* . . . an obscure academic" (Putnam 2000: 506).

4. Putnam shifted toward comparative political analysis the heretofore sociological concept of social capital. Coleman had widened Glen Loury's conceptualization of social capital as "the set of resources that inhere in family relations and in community social organizations and that are useful for the cognitive or social development of a child," applying it, in particular, to the relationship between the family and the social structure (Coleman 1990: 300). In comparing the time and energy parents invest in helping their children, he found in the low dropout rates in Catholic schools a manifestation of the potential social-capital generating capacity inherent in the relationship between religious structure and educational structure.

5. Social capital is affected by the trustworthiness of structures, by informational channels and norms, by effectiveness of sanctions. Related to it are the closure of social networks (so that all actors interact, one with another) and multiplex relationships (so that resources of one relationship can be appropriated for use in a second relationship" (Coleman 1990: 98).

6. "Because political scientists, in their work on social capital, rely so heavily on survey research, the variable is usually conceived of as something that inheres in individuals (norms and attitudes such as trust) . . . the value of which does not fluctuate as the individual moves in and out of numerous social contexts. [As a result] the central argument of Coleman's treatment, that the presence of such attitudes and behaviors will provide resources for others who depend upon them, is never directly engaged" (Foley and Edwards 1998: 4–5; see also Jackman and Miller 1998 and 1996).

7. Fishkin, cites Tocqueville, arguing that voluntary associations are "the great free school" of American democracy. What Americans learn from politics they take to all the associations of civic life. . . . They 'acquire a general taste for associations. . . . Large numbers see, speak, listen and stimulate each other to carry out all sorts of undertakings in common. They then carry these conceptions with them into the affairs of civic life . . . '" (Fishkin 1995: 144).

8. For example, Newton (1997a) noted that modern society is characterized by relatively amorphous, multiple, and overlapping groups creating crosscutting ties that bind society together by its own internal divisions and produce pluralist competition between different interests. These are quite different from small, face-to-face communities, generated by intense contact between people of the same background found in tribal societies; small, homogenous, and isolated communities; and total institutions such as sects, churches, and ghettos. This raises the question of the circumstances under which voluntary organizations are essential for social capital, as opposed to the kind of organic (endogenous) ties of participation in school, family, work, and community stressed in Coleman's approach. We might

note in this context a Danish study that distinguishes between the "classical" formal organizations of the Tocqueville type and "network associations." The latter are looser, more informal, and more personal forms of association, and have a stronger impact on the attitudes and behavior of those who participate" (Gundelach and Torpe 1996: 31).

9. The Bank notes that common to approaches to social capital is the assumption that reliable and stable social relationships influence markets and, more generally, the effectiveness of human action, and that social capital can be strengthened (Kajanoja 2000).

10. "Organized religion, at least in Catholic Italy, is an alternative to civic community, not part of it" (Putnam 1993: 107).

11. This is another criticism that Putnam appears to have taken to heart. In *Bowling Alone*, he places much emphasis on the social-capital-building role of religion. "Faith-based communities remain . . . a crucial reservoir of social capital," calling upon Americans to become "more deeply engaged . . . in one or another spiritual community of meaning (2000: 409).

12. "Thus 47 [percent] of Americans and 30 of West Germans volunteer; but if American religious attendance and religious membership rates are reduced to the level of West German rates, the proportion volunteering is not significantly different between the two" (Greeley 1997: 590; see also Gabriel 1995).

13. Almost half the American respondents to the WVS stated that they participated in religious organizations, compared to 10 to 20 percent among the Scandinavians.

14. The surveys cover the following types of organizations: labor unions, religious organizations, sports/recreation organizations, educational/cultural organizations, political parties, professional associations, social welfare organizations, youth groups, environmental organizations, health-volunteer groups, community action groups, women's organizations, third world development groups, animal rights groups, and peace movements.

15. Carried out for the New Zealand electoral commission by the Colmar-Brunton polling firm in the mid and latter 1990s.

16. A useful recent comparative study breaks down WVS (1991) associational participation in western Europe and North America down into socially oriented groups (including religious ones) and politically oriented ones. Looking at responses to the question of volunteering as well as membership, two contrasting profiles emerge: Americans and Canadians clearly lead in volunteering in socially oriented groups, while the Scandinavians and Dutch do so for membership in politically oriented ones (Herreros and Morales 2000: 18).

17. In an effort to overcome this limitation, I recalculated the data from the 1990 WVS to identify that part of the population that responds positively *only* to questions of participation in religious organization. For example, of the 953 (of 2,010) Americans who stated that they participated in religious organizations, 30 percent (288) did not participate in any other type of organization. I thus isolated those who fail to conform to the expectations of Greeley and Uslaner since their church involvement fails to foster participation in other social-capital- generating activity. To this group, I added those stating that they belong to no organizations at all. I thus arrive for each country at a rate of what might be termed organizational exclusion. Comparing the two indicators, the major shift is that, on the latter

measure, the United States is relegated further down toward the middle of the pack, behind the Scandinavians and Dutch.

18. In Putman's terms, these are "bonding" rather than "bridging" organizations. Bonding associations are "inward looking and tend to reinforce exclusive identities and homogeneous groups." Bridging ones "are outward looking and encompass people across diverse social cleavages. . . . However, "I have found no reliable, comprehensive, nationwide measures of social capital that neatly distinguish 'bridgingness' and 'bondingness'" (Putnam 2000: 22–23).

19. This is the conclusion of a 1998 study titled "Political Diversity, Public Administration, Participation" by the Dutch Social and Cultural Planning Office (SCP). It finds a larger percentage of people taking part in pressure groups, joining a demonstration or signing a petition than ever before. Memberships in voluntary organizations with apolitical objectives have increased by 5 percent since 1980. Fast-growing organizations support international solidarity (+176 percent) and nature preservation (+510 percent), and are involved in moral questions such as abortion and euthanasia (+662 percent). Contributions to idealistic organizations and causes grew more than fourfold from 1974 to 1996.

20. This point was raised in a personal discussion by Uwe Becker of the University of Amsterdam.

21. A number of contemporary studies have tested the relationship between these two indicators. For example, in their analysis of responses to the American General Social Survey, Brehm and Rahn did identify a causal relationship from trust to participation but found it to be secondary, concluding that "the effect of civic engagement on interpersonal trust was much stronger than the reverse" (1997: 1017).

22. Influential here is the analysis of Fukuyama, for whom trust is crucial in reducing transaction costs—that is, "costs of negotiation, enforcement, and the like." According to Fukuyama, Germany, Japan and the United States have healthy endowments of social capital compared to low-trust countries like Taiwan, Hong Kong, Italy, or France (Fukuyama 1995: 103).

23. A good example is the work of Canadian economist John Helliwell, who has collaborated with Putnam and who, without any effort to justify the decision, equates the level of social capital in a given region with the sample average of positive answers to a question of this kind (e.g. Helliwell 1996).

24. Newton argues that trust is fostered in a number of quite different ways depending on the institutional context. The voluntary sector is just one source of social capital, and probably a less important source than family, work, education, and neighborhood. Moreover there are also "imaginary," "empathetic," or "reflexive" communities that are built on abstract trust. . . . "Abstract trust is not built on the personal relations of primordial society, nor on secondary relations in formal organizations. In contemporary society, abstract trust may be generated by the all-important institutions of education and the media. Education provides us with a common knowledge of a set of dates, places, names, events, concepts, references, and quotations that help the social interaction of otherwise disparate individuals. Schools also set out to teach the art of cooperation by means of collective learning tasks, team games, school plays and bands, and joint activities of many kinds. They also develop an understanding of abstract ideas such as citizenship, trust, fairness,

equality, universalism, the common good, and the golden rule" (Newton 1997a: 580–81).

25. Foley and Edwards 1998: 19–20. The article reviewed over thirty recent scholarly articles reporting empirical research.

26. The Eurobarometer asked: "Generally speaking would you say that most people can be trusted or that you can't be too careful in dealing with people?" with responses broken down into four categories: those expressing a lot of trust, some trust, not very much trust, and no trust at all.

27. "Generally speaking, would you say that most people can be trusted or that you can't be too careful in dealing with people?" allowing for only two categories of responses.

28. The data are to be found in Newton 1999a.

29. While the fairly strong aggregate relationship between WVS ratings in associational density and trust tends to be reproduced in individual-level research, causality remains elusive. In a recent paper, Stolle (2000) looks at individual-level data and finds, against her expectations, that long-term members of these groups are no more trusting than newcomers, suggesting self-selection rather than a Tocquevillian promotion of civic virtue to underlie the relationship. A similar inference can be drawn from data gathered by Smith (2000) showing that the American tenth-grade students surveyed expressed lower levels of trust after nine months of extracurricular activities.

30. There is a very low correlation between WVS figures for social trust with trust in parliament and the civil service. Only for trust in the police force does it approach significance.

31. In contrast, Putnam, who concludes from his study of Italy that citizens in high-social-capital communities (have good reason to) look to local government to provide efficient services, draws a link between declining horizontal and vertical trust.

32. Indeed, as reported by Listhaug, Aardal, and Ellis (2000), among the sixteen old and new democracies in the CSES data, "satisfaction in the democratic process is highest in Norway (90%)." Other differences are worth noting: while political trust appears to be declining in Britain and Japan, this has not been the case in the Netherlands (Listhaug 1995).

33. We know this, for example, from the 1997 SNS "Democratic Audit" (Petersson et al. 1997).

34. This emerges from Holmberg's detailed analysis of voters in the 1994 Swedish national election, which showed that the higher the political knowledge the higher the trust in political leaders and institutions (Holmberg 1999). Note that the direction of the effect is not all that clear or consistent. Ginsberg (1982) reports on a study that shows both that trust in government varies widely and that it can very much be affected by political participation. In the study, a sample of adults was asked before and again after the 1968 and 1972 American presidential elections whether "People like me don't have any say about what the government does." Before the 1968 election, most people agreed with the statement: 71 percent of those who voted in that election, and 83 percent of those who ended up not voting. The numbers went down remarkably: after the election, only 37 percent of those who had voted still felt this way, for a drop of 34 percentage points, and among those

who did not vote (but nevertheless experienced the campaign), the figure dropped by 25 percentage points. In 1972, in contrast, only 34 percent of those who would vote and 58 percent of those who abstained took the cynical view of government, a number reduced only 5 and 4 percent respectively by the election.

Chapter 2. Civic Engagement and Political Participation

1. Putnam at times appears to regard social capital as the same thing as civic engagement, at others as its cause.

2. Turnout is also one of the components of his index used to distinguish high- from low-social-capital regions in Italy, and one of the fourteen indicators in his Social Capital Index, which ranks American states.

3. Indeed, in the closing chapter of *Bowling Alone*, his effort at "an agenda for social capitalists," Putnam turns to politics only after education, work, urban design, religion, the media, and culture. His (italicized) exhortation testifies to the relative importance of voting turnout: "*Let us find ways to ensure that by 2010 many more Americans will participate in the public life of our communities—running for office, attending public meetings, serving on committees, campaigning in elections, and even voting*" (Putnam 2000: 412).

4. For example, McCann (1998) finds that not only are more informed voters likely to vote—as expected—but American voters are significantly more socially and politically engaged than nonvoters, even when we control for age, education, etc.

5. A similar distinction is made by Mancur Olson with regard to human capital. Olson points to "knowledge of the real consequences of different public policies" as a second, nonmarketable, form of human capital. Unlike the acquisition of the first kind of human capital (marketable skills), such knowledge is a public good but cannot improve the individual's relative position (Olson 1996a: 16).

6. Green and Shapiro (1994) are thus off the mark when they state: "Starting with Anthony Downs, rational choice theorists have characterized voter turnout as a collective action problem in which individuals are asked to sacrifice time and transportation costs on behalf of a public good, the election of a particular candidate or party" (47). Of course some political scientists have taken this tack and, in so doing, "shift the collective good from 'being well-informed' into the act of voting itself, but for Downs, voting is a private good, analogous to a producer producing and a consumer consuming, which economists see no need to explain, rather than the act of informing oneself, which is a public good" (Pellikan 1998: 3–4).

7. Of course, this is not to suggest that voter turnout will not be increased by making it compulsory or extending the hours or allowing postal ballots—all of which are discussed below. But, while relevant, such matters are not interesting from the perspective of economic analysis; they are matters of fact comparable to the effect of the hours the stock exchange is open on the behavior of traders.

8. It should not surprise us that such judgments have not been confined to Americans. For example, a leading Canadian journalist commented as follows on the results of a 1997 citizenship survey: "a large segment of Canadian society lacks much of the civic knowledge required to understand and effectively participate in the country's political life . . . cut off from media stories, political debates and

community discussions . . . lacking the shared . . . context to interpret the aspirations of their fellow citizens" (Gwyn 1997: 21–22).

9. "There are plenty of reasons for people to procure information; it is just that none of these reasons has anything to do with enhancing people's prospects of gain from casting an informed vote in a mass election. Well-informed voters have not gathered information in order to cast an informed vote; rather, they are able to cast an informed vote because they have accumulated information for other unrelated purposes" (Fiorina 1990: 336–41).

10. It is well known, for example, that there is an average discrepancy of 10 percent between respondents to the American national election survey who claim to have voted in the previous presidential election and the actual turnout figures.

11. The overall mean tells us very little about the specific effect of the compulsory vote. More useful are longitudinal studies applying to more than one jurisdiction in the same country. A rare detailed analysis of this kind, comparing the turnout in Australian states and for the commonwealth in the election before and after the introduction of compulsory voting, found an increase averaging 23 percent, varying from a low of 12.4 to a high of 37.8 (McAllister and Mackerras 1998: 2). Goldsmith and Newton (1986: 146) estimate the difference in local election turnout levels between Australian states where voting is compulsory and those where it is not at 50 percent. The difference in Australia is significantly higher than in the Netherlands, which changed in the opposite direction, eliminating compulsory voting. The average difference in Dutch elections before and after the change was 10 percent. This latter number corresponds rather closely to the additional difference in presidential turnout between those Austrian provinces which maintained compulsory voting and those which removed it during the 1980s (Hlrczy 1994).

12. For example, in Australia, the law allows for exemption from paying a fine for nonvoting when a legitimate reason is provided. The rules as to what constitutes a legitimate excuse and how the excuse must be presented vary, with the apparent result that effectively any excuse is legitimate for failing to vote in the "compulsory" local elections.

13. VAP is acronym for voting age population (the more accurate term would be voting age citizenry).

14. This, as noted in chapter 1, also appears to be true of vertical trust; distrust in politicians and political institutions does not, at least in the United States, lead to nonvoting (Popkin and Dimock 1999).

15. Verba, Schlozman, and Brady (1995: 338–39) find that only organizations in which members acquire "civic skills" affect political participation.

16. For a contemporary expression of this argument, see Barber 1984 and 1998.

17. American political scientists have tried to measure the extent of evocation of emotional reactions to candidates in U.S. presidential elections. One study of the 1996 campaign finds that "the campaign stimulated voters to forge emotional bonds with the candidates and that these emotional ties heavily influence candidate evaluation and the vote. . . . In 1996 as the campaign drew to a close, individuals relied more heavily on their emotions than their party identification in evaluating challengers" (Belt, Crigler, and Just 1998: 1).

18. This is the most recent period for which I have been able to get data. There have been subsequent elections in many countries, and the general trend is one of

declining turnout. Among the high-turnout countries, Finland and Norway appear to have declined most sharply, though not enough to affect the comparative positions of the countries over the entire period. In European countries, an additional factor has entered and helps explain the decline. In recent years, the franchise for local elections has been extended to citizens of other EU countries as well as landed immigrants, groups with low-turnout tendencies.

19. The pros and cons of compulsory voting are beyond the scope of this book. Lijphart (1997) endorses compulsory voting, arguing that as voters participate they also develop habits of citizenship. The main drawback of compulsory voting is that it reduces the incentive on political parties to get voters to the polls (a major part of which consists of informing them of the issues and stakes) and thus, as has been suggested by some observers on Australian political parties, atrophies the local political party organization.

20. Other rules that could be relevant concern the selection of the mayor— elected directly, indirectly elected, or appointed (as a town manager). While the mayor is now directly elected in all German municipalities, this is not the case in Austria, where only mayors are directly elected in only five of the *Länder*. Relevant also could be whether, as in France, the mayors and councillors are eligible to hold higher-level office.

21. I could have simply used the actual numbers, which are 2 percent lower on the local than national ballots, but this underestimates the phenomenon. Norway, Denmark, and Finland hold local elections two years after holding national elections. Norway's electoral system and party composition is very much like Sweden's. Denmark's electoral system is similar, but the electoral threshold for party representation is lower, which means a larger number of parties win representation. Finland's electoral system is quite different, and Finnish institutions differ in that the president (who has real powers) is elected separately, which makes national (legislative) elections less important than in Sweden. According to my calculations, during the 1980s, Norway averaged a 10 percent difference in turnout for national elections and local ones, Denmark a 12 percent difference, and Finland a difference of 5 percent. I simply apply the difference from the median and most similar case, that of Norway, so that the Swedish total of 84 percent is reduced by 10 to arrive at a figure of 74 percent. This is in fact a conservative estimate, since Swedish local governments are somewhat more powerful than Norwegian ones. A less conservative alternative would have been to use the 6.5 percent difference between the turnout in the last year in which local elections were held separately (1966: 83 percent), and the 1968 national turnout figure of 89 percent (SCB 1974: 10).

22. The three together account for more than 80 percent of the population; I was unable to acquire data for the third largest, British Columbia.

23. Municipal elections take place on a staggered basis on the same day every fall. In 1997, 35 percent of 782 elections saw the position of mayor contested with an average turnout of 52.2 percent (Quesnel 1998). My own calculations for 1998 arrived at an average of 59 percent for the 94 mayoral elections (104 were acclaimed). (These numbers are not all that different from the 51 percent average for the 8 large cities that elected mayors in 1997 and 1998, nor the 54 percent for the 28 of the 53 Quebec municipalities with over 20,000 population that had a contested election for mayor in 1993 or 1994.)

24. The data were gathered by the Committee of the Regions of the European Union and published by the European Union under the title *Voter Turnout at Regional and Local Elections in the European Union, 1990–1999*. The European Union was apparently unable to find the relevant information for France, but I have been able to find a published source—Bréchon 1998.

25. Given the newness of the experience, I have chosen to exclude the former DDR Länder from the figures. I have also adjusted the Austria figures downward by 4 percent to give appropriate weight to Vienna, where turnout is roughly 15 percent lower than for the rest of the country.

26. Similar results for 1991 and 1995 are found in Rallings and Thrasher (1998), and for earlier elections in Goldsmith and Newton (1986: 146). The 1999 result, averaging England, Scotland, and Wales, is also very close but conceals the fact that the English vote went down to the mid thirties while the Scottish vote (due to devolution, no doubt) shot up to 58 percent.

27. New Zealand data are for 1992 and 1995 and taken from the *Local Authority Election Statistics* of the Department of Internal Affairs.

28. The twenty-one cities with more than 100,000 averaged approximately 10 percent less than Ontario municipalities as a whole.

29. It is also to some extent unfair not to take into account the fact that U.S. voters are, on average, called on to vote more frequently, just as they still, though less than before (Highton and Wolfinger 1998), face obstacles to registration not faced by voters elsewhere. According to Wattenberg (1998). voters in the United States and Switzerland face unusually high information costs, being called on to vote for numerous office holders as well as participate in frequent referenda.

30. Lijphart (1997) cites Teixeira (1992:7), and Ansolabehere and Iyengar (1995: 145–46) to the effect that turnout in local U.S. elections has been about 25 percent in recent years.

31. Indeed, it is greater, though we should note that the discrepancy is in good part due to different bases being used: in the case of national elections, it is potential voters; in local elections, it is registered voters.

32. The relationship remains weak when we exclude from associational participation those who participated only in religious organizations.

Chapter 3. Political Participation and Political Knowledge

1. An indicator that the distance between expressed good intentions and concrete actions can be a long one is to be found in the responses to a question asked in Eurobarometer #50 in October–November 1998. More than seven in ten EU citizens stated their intention to vote in the June 1999 European Parliament elections; when it came time to vote, only 43 percent bothered to do so. (The same question was posed in Eurobarometer #51, in March and April. It found that those planning to vote had declined by 4 percent, to 67 percent.)

2. Van Deth (1998) finds little use in the standard measures of political interest since they, in effect, give a negative rating to people who are well informed about politics but do not see politics as salient to them as are their work, family, or leisure activities.

3. Helliwell (2000: 39) asserts that "almost all studies of social capital find that individuals who have more education are more likely to be trusting."

4. As Warren (1996: 23) puts it, "What maintains a background of trust is my knowledge that I could monitor and challenge authorities and trusted others, as well as the others' knowledge that I can do so."

5. "Informed survey respondents tend to give what seem to be better quality opinions. . . . People knowledgeable about politics tend to express policy preferences that are more consistent with their political values than people who are poorly informed about politics . . . ideology is a better predictor of vote choice for people with higher levels of political knowledge than it is for people who are relatively less informed. . . . Knowledgeable people who identify themselves as Democrats are more likely to express typically Democratic policy preferences than people who call themselves Democrats but have lower levels of political knowledge. . . . When changes in information about policies occur, the more knowledgeable respondents are likely to update their preferences so that they remain consistent with their predispositions" (Althaus 1998a). A detailed study by Delli Carpini and Keeter (1995) showed that the quartile of their sample who were most ignorant of political actors, institutions, and procedures were only very slightly more likely than not to voice support for a candidate consistent with their expressed views on a given issue.

6. The authors add a reflection pertinent to findings in a later chapter: "If campaigns are geared at a higher level in Sweden and aimed more at the involved and knowledgeable non-partisans, this could be part of the reason why."

7. Reported in the SNS 1998 Democratic Audit (Petersson et al. 1998: 115). In June 1997, International IDEA published a report titled *Youth Voter Participation— Involving Today's Young in Tomorrow's Democracy*, which provided a comparative analysis on the political activity of young people in fifteen western European countries. While the average turnout level for voters between eighteen and twenty-nine years old was 8 percent below the overall participation rate, in Sweden it was only 4.3 percent.

8. We need to be careful in choosing and defining our terms. A rather insidious use of the term *competent voter* is to be found in a recent paper in which the authors define a voter as competent if seen to have made the same choice that would have been made if fully informed. In other words, being competent need not be a matter of being informed (Lupia and Johnston 1999). This goes too far. It is like suggesting that a person who learns where the door marked "exit" is by watching other people leave can be deemed literate.

9. They placed respondents on a scale based on their responses to four political knowledge questions as well as their responses on three questions getting at whether they follow and read about politics (Strate et al. 1989: 450).

10. The authors maintain that civil rights for blacks in the United States resulted from efforts to mobilize black voters. "The more passionate efforts of political parties to get people to the polls are an important reason why class equality in American voter turnout was greater a century ago than it is today. . . . The most dramatic example of how political mobilization can undo the class biases of political participation, however, comes from the era of the civil rights movement in America. During the 1950s when the political parties mobilized whites more than

blacks and registration laws systematically excluded blacks (particularly in the South), the racial disparities in citizen participation were immense. During the 1960s and into the 1970s, in contrast . . . , the political parties reached out to blacks, and the racial inequalities in political participation narrowed. During the 1980s, finally, political mobilization declined, and progress toward equal representation in the political community stalled" (Rosenstone and Hansen 1993: 244).

11. "Most electoral outcomes are not determined in any meaningful sense by turnout" (Teixeira 1992: 96–97).

12. There is good reason to be skeptical about such claims. Consider the following: The Republican congressmen and women all voted to bring Clinton before an impeachment process a month before the November 1998 midterm elections despite the fact that polls (conducted for the *New York Times* and CBS and published in the *International Herald Tribune*, 26 September 1998) were showing that two-thirds of Americans opposed the idea. Commentators explained the apparent political suicides as based on the Republican congressmen's fears that they would be denied renomination by the religious right of their party. A simpler explanation arises, however, in keeping with our discussion of the unrepresentativeness of the politically active population. There was no political suicide involved, since fewer than 40 percent of potential voters turn out to vote in these elections; and the same polls found that when the opinions of only those who said unequivocally that they planned to vote in the election were counted, one-half favored impeachment.

13. For example, Bartels (1996) and Delli Carpini and Keeter (1996). Althaus (1998) finds that the low levels and uneven social distribution of political knowledge in the United States results in opinion surveys often misrepresenting the mix of voices in a society. First, those who are poorly informed about politics tend to give "don't know" and "no opinion" responses at much higher rates than more knowledgeable people, thus overrepresenting advantaged groups. In addition, information asymmetries affect the "quality of opinions." The well informed are more likely to express policy preferences consistent with their political interests, which are then more accurately reflected in measures of collective opinion. Overall, "one in five policy questions might have a different collective preference if everyone were equally well informed about politics" (555).

14. As Kuklinski et al. (1998: 144–46) put it, it is less that people are uninformed than that they are systematically misinformed. Thus their policy preferences are distorted, and they resist accepting the correct facts even if these are made available. Their study of a sample of Illinois residents "found that many people had systematically inaccurate factual beliefs (for example, they grossly overestimated the payments received by a typical family) [with an] overall bias toward beliefs that one would expect to be associated with negative views about welfare. . . . People held their beliefs confidently, . . .[and] these beliefs are strongly linked to policy preferences in the expected ways." The authors relate their conclusions to the strategy of deliberative polls sponsored by James Fishkin (Luskin and Fishkin 1998). "Both in several days of briefings and discussion and through written materials provided in advance, Fishkin exposes a representative sample of citizens to a massive amount of competing advocacy. At the end, he asks them whether the presentations and discussions were informative and fair, and obtains consistently favorable responses.

There is evidence that deliberative polls improve people's judgments. At least, they often alter people's opinions."

15. In part four we investigate the connection between outcomes and higher turnout in countries that institutionally, to use Rosenstone and Hansen's term, "counteract biases due to socioeconomic status."

16. The commission asked if they expected to vote in the next election. Of those having little knowledge, 13.5 percent did not expect to vote or were uncertain, which declined to 6.5 percent and 3.5 percent for those having some and much knowledge.

17. A similar study cited by Archer et al. (1995) found being informed about politics a much better predictor of likelihood to vote than any aspect of the individuals' social background.

18. For example, Vromen (1995) interviewed an Australian sample of mainly seventeen-year olds, finding that those who responded affirmatively to the statement "I am looking forward to voting when I am 18" knew significantly more about Australian politics. A similar finding emerges from a study of 1,500 Dutch students from thirteen to seventeen years of age summarized by Dekker (1999: 456–58).

19. Compulsory voting makes it impossible to use turnout data for Australia.

20. The study was conducted on behalf of the Civic Experts Group set up in 1994 "to prepare a strategic plan for a non-partisan program of public education on civic issues" (Civics Expert Group 1994: 3). It found widespread ignorance and misconceptions about Australia's system of government despite a reasonable level of familiarity with voting and elections. The overall low levels of political knowledge were largely confirmed by the 1996 Australian Election Study survey (McAllister 1998).

21. Ward (1988) carried on in-depth interviews with thirty individuals. These, she found, divided clearly into two distinct and equal groups: one saw democracy as consisting simply of what he or she understood to be the way things are done in America; the other articulated certain concepts against which experience could be judged. Of the eleven who said they did not vote, only two could reason about democracy.

22. An analysis of turnout in twenty countries found an average decline of 5 percent, from 83 percent in the 1950s to 78 percent in the 1990s (Dalton 1996: 44–45), half that of the United States.

23. (1) Names of respondent's U.S. senators; (2) Name of district's congressman; (3) Did the federal government in the past few years spend more on NASA or social security? (4) Is the Fifth Amendment mainly a protection against forced confessions, or does it mainly guarantee freedom of speech? (5) Who mainly favored primaries, party bosses . . . or reformers . . . ? (6) Civil liberties as the right to vote and run for office, or to freedom of speech, press, assembly; (7) Is the main difference between democracy and dictatorship: private property or the right to freely choose representatives? (8) How old do you have to be to vote for president? (9) Which party has more members in the U.S. House of Representatives—the Democrats or the Republicans? (554–55).

24. The three questions in category 1 tested knowledge of the Fifth Amendment, democracy versus dictatorship, the meaning of civil liberties; the five in category 2: names of both senators, congressman, state representative, and head of

the local school board; the four in category 3 asked about the majority party in Congress, whether more was spent on NASA or social security; the official voting age; and the increased use of primaries.

25. The correct answer is the Democrats. It is, of course, possible that a few respondents were in fact giving a highly sophisticated critique of the absence of significant ideological difference between the parties in selecting the answer "no difference."

26. Entman created a "leadership knowledge index" based on knowledge of the stand taken by candidates in the previous presidential election. He found that less than 15 percent fit his category of knowledgeable voters (i.e., those who were right on more than half the candidate placements), a finding that corresponds to other findings he cites that show a majority of voters unable to classify even Ronald Reagan as conservative rather than liberal (Entman 1989: 25). A number of other studies portray an American electorate incapable of identifying "the ideological postures and policy positions of political leaders" (Baker et al. 1996: 47) locating liberals and conservatives on policy dimensions. Luskin and Fishkin (1998: 2) describe Americans' ability to draw such policy-ideology relationships as "barely different from chance"—a description also true, as we saw, of Americans' ability to name the party of their member of the legislature.

27. Compared to 8 percent for Europe in the IDEA report cited in note 1 above.

28. Conducted by the National Constitution Center in Philadelphia (reported in *USA Today*, 3 September 1998: 8).

29. For example, Nie, Junn, and Stehl-Barry (1996: 40–44, 67) include the well-validated measure of verbal cognitive proficiency in the form of a vocabulary test from the general social survey, finding a fairly strong correlation between verbal cognitive proficiency and voting.

30. The contrast is starkest with the Netherlands, Switzerland, and the U.K.; but it is also found, though to a lesser extent, with Australia and Canada.

Chapter 4. Civic Literacy in Comparative Context

1. His index is composed of fourteen indicators, of which six of the nine indicators of participation and membership in various kinds of associations as well as "average number of times entertained at home in the last year" are "stockable," while only four (e.g., "served as officer of some club. . . .") require either-or type responses (Putnam 2000: 291).

2. *Knowledge* is not the only term encountered in the literature. Others, some of which we have already encountered, include *political sophistication, civic competence, political awareness,* and *cognitive engagement* (see Zaller 1992). None serves our purposes as well as *literacy*.

3. The cutoff points are nevertheless more useful than the mean scores for each country. The latter treats identically a society with a large and equal number in the top and bottom categories and one where the scores converge around the mean, even though the latter has a smaller proportion below any reasonable cutoff point.

4. This is not due to the term itself, which they usefully define as "the basic concepts and facts that constitute a necessary condition for understanding the contents

of public debate" (179), but rather reflects the constraints on its meaning due to the pejorative connotations associated with politics and politicians.

5. An alternative sometimes used here is *public-affairs knowledge*, which does not have the same pejorative connotations as *political knowledge* but is cumbersome.

6. For example, the noted American educational historian R. Freeman Butts describes civics education in American schools as seeking to enable students to play their roles as "effective, responsible, committed and effective members of the modern democratic political system" by encompassing "political values, political knowledge, and the skills of political participation needed for making deliberate choices among real alternatives" (Butts 1980: 123).

7. To judge by a number of high-profile activities, the term is gaining currency. For example, the wide program funded by George Soros offering Western-trained scholars to teach in postcommunist societies is called the "Civic Education Project" while a major theme of the World Democracy Movement, headed by Nobel laureate Amartya Sen, emerging at its founding conference with delegates from eighty countries in February 1999, was a concern with "civic education." The American Political Science Association, for its part, has a blue-ribbon task force on civic education.

8. I have recently come across use of the term *civic literacy* to identify the objectives and content of a course designed—and taught—by members of the Wayne State University Department of Political Science for high school and continuing education students in the Detroit area.

9. A small country, though, may still be high in institutional complexity due to membership in supranational institutions such as the European Union. Moreover, political institutions are not set in cement: the size of a country can be changed quite rapidly, as events in Germany and Czechoslovakia illustrate.

10. See Dalton (1998) for a survey of the use of questions of these types in the National Election Studies or similar surveys in twelve industrial democracies.

11. In response to my query on whether the ongoing pilot studies would be seeking out that information, the coordinator at the time, Steven Rosenstone of Michigan, sent me the following communication: "The political information items were not asked on the pilot studies. The planning committee thought that those items should be moved to the 'background' section, meaning that each nation will ask an appropriate set of political information items so as to produce a 5-point political information scale within their polity. *It is a hopeless task to come up with items that will work in a comparable fashion across polities.* Instead, the hope is to have a scale in each polity that divides the population into quintiles of information" (my emphasis).

12. The result, of course, is that it becomes impossible to compare countries on the basis of an acceptable indicator of aggregate or average political knowledge. Note that the CSES is not atypical and, thus, hardly alone responsible for the absence of the needed data. A major comparative European study of six hundred pages (Van Deth and Scarborough 1995), part of the five-volume Belief in Government series, compared the impact of values on such things as political interest, participation, behavior, trust, efficacy, involvement, and socialization—but not knowledge. In the entire project, apparently, no political knowledge questions were asked.

13. Greenwood Press publishes a biennial *Index to International Public Opinion* prepared by E. H. Hastings and P. K. Hastings. I consulted the reports, which do

not include the United States, from 1985 to 1994 and identified the political information questions listed. Use of such questions was fairly frequent in Great Britain and, though less so, in Switzerland, Canada, and Japan. I could not find any questions that were similar enough to allow useful comparison, since each country tended to approach the matter differently. Britain, for example, favored asking respondents to identify political leaders from their picture. The Japanese questions tended to get at the functioning of political institutions.

14. The reliability of these tests would improve with repeated use. Incumbency effects would be reduced in this way, as each country's score would consist of an average over the time series. The test is not perfect, of course: for example the diffuseness of power under Switzerland's Constitution would likely make it look unjustifiably low in civic literacy. Nevertheless, given that the Swiss federal presidency rotates every year, it is quite impressive that the name of the president, according to annual polls compiled in the *Index to International Public Opinion*, is typically known to 65 to 70 percent of respondents.

15. By using more than one question of each type, it is possible to compensate for national bias in any given question.

16. In September and October 1997. (See *Europinion* no.13.)

17. In contrast, British first-year university students scored significantly higher than their American and Canadian counterparts in a test that asked them to identify past and present society leaders and rank foreign countries on the basis of population and GDP. The scores on the former were United States 25.5 percent, Canada 25.6 percent, Britain 42.4 percent; on the latter, 43 percent, 45.3 percent, and 75.2 percent respectively (Holloway 1995).

18. Respondents were asked to identify: (1) the president of Russia (Boris Yeltsin); (2) the country threatening withdrawal from the nuclear nonproliferation treaty (North Korea); (3) Boutros Boutros-Ghali's position (UN secretary-general); (4) the ethnic group that had captured much of Bosnia and surrounded Sarajevo (the Serbs); and (5) the group with which Israel had just reached an accord (Palestinians, or PLO).

19. Where possible I have calculated and provide an overall average of the score on the prose, document and quantitative scales. In some cases, the IALS provides only one, usually the score on the document scale. This is not a major drawback, since there is fairly close correspondence between the three, with the score on the document scale generally falling in between the other two.

20. The UN Development Program has four components in its Human Poverty Index for developed countries, one of which is "deprivation in knowledge by functional illiteracy" (UNDP 1999: 130), and the indicator is the proportion in category one in the IALS.

21. In the combined average on the two tests, the Netherlands had a mean score of 559, with 498 at the 25th and 407 at the 5th percentile. (The comparable figures were 555, 490, and 413 for Sweden; 528, 470, and 399 for Denmark; and 536, 474, and 403 for Norway.) In comparison, the United States fared poorly overall but especially at the bottom percentiles (with scores of 471, 407 and 334 respectively). Australia, New Zealand, and Canada scored quite respectably at the mean (526, 525, and 525), but the former two especially attained relatively lower scores at the lower percentiles (468 at the 25th and 395 at the 5th percentile for Canada, 464 and 370 for New Zealand, and 462 and 366 for Australia).

Chapter 5. Political Participation and Political Institutions

1. It appears strange, at first glance, that the large body of work by political scientists concerned with political participation has, relatively speaking, neglected the information dimension at the center of this book. But, in fact, there is a reason for this. A case in point: Blais (2000: 143) concludes his comprehensive analysis of voter turnout by introspectively testing the relevance of rational choice explanations: he himself usually votes because he believes in democracy and it would be inconsistent to abstain. Moreover, Blais would make more of an effort to vote if the outcome is in doubt. But, he adds, he would not vote if it made no difference to him who won. He does not note that he is in fact raising the question of information. This is because political scientists take it for granted that they are sufficiently informed to know that candidates or parties are alike. But that is an assumption. It may be that Blais is unaware of differences, which, were he aware of them, would make the outcome matter enough for him to vote. In reality, every voter is in this position. For the voter with insufficient information to distinguish between the parties and candidates, it does not, by definition, make a difference as to who wins.

2. The effect of such factors on civic literacy is neither clear nor consistent. Lijphart's (1997) assertion that as voters participate they also develop habits of citizenship applies to civic literacy within a given institutional context. Can we expect an uninterested voter to inform herself when voting by the post if the vote is undertaken to avoid being fined for not doing so?

3. Highton and Wolfinger (1998: 79) compared the effect of easier registration by comparing turnout before and after the adoption of "motor voter" provisions in certain American states, finding turnout increases between 4.7 and 8.7 percent.

4. This finding is supported by Martinez and Hill (1999).

5. See, e.g., Lijphart 1997. It has also been suggested that the fact that the outcome of the presidential elections is often known before many voters in the western time zones cast their ballots may also have an effect (which is why Canada prevents television and radio election coverage until the polls have closed).

6. Phoenix, Albuquerque, and Dallas averaged less than 20 percent—compared to New York with 43.6 percent, Chicago 54.3 percent, New Haven, 57.3 percent—in votes cast in municipal elections from 1946.

7. For example, the Center for Voting and Democracy's statistical analysis of the 1994 elections for the House of Representatives found a clear correlation between margin of victory and voter participation: the more competitive an election, the higher the turnout:

Margin of Victory	Turnout	Number of Races
0.0–9.9%	42.7%	87
10.0–19.9%	39.7%	72
20.0–39.9%	39.7%	132
40.0–59.9%	38.5%	84
60.0–100.0%	29.7%	54
(plus 6 uncontested)		

8. "The *National Journal,* in a special issue on the Electoral College that includes a photo of CVD's web site, reports that states without a single campaign visit from the presidential candidates between April 1 and the election included Idaho, Utah, Montana, North Dakota, South Dakota, Nebraska, Kansas, Oklahoma, Mississippi, South Carolina, Hawaii, Delaware, and Vermont. In addition, four of the nation's top eight media markets—Boston, Dallas, New York City, and Washington, DC—had a grand total of six presidential ads aired, while eight media markets in battleground states each aired more than 6,500 presidential ads" (22 November 2000, electronic report of the Center for Voting and Democracy—www.fairvote.org).

9. To his surprise Eagles (1991) found no such association in 1988 and speculated that the effects of the local campaigns that year "might have been nullified by the combined effects of the multi-million dollar campaigns of the national parties and the estimated $10 million advertising campaign mounted by proponents and opponents of free trade in that election."

10. Differences in the extent of "second orderness" are generally being reduced among OECD countries due to convergence in the degree of financial and political autonomy of local governments resulting from consolidation of small municipalities and replacement of earmarked allocations by bloc grants.

11. Both factors probably account for the meager (41.6 percent) turnout of the normally high-voting Swedes in their first EP elections in 1995 (Widfeldt 1996).

12. For a detailed analysis based on Canada's experience in international context, see Milner 1999.

13. Germany is another country where variation is to be found, but it seems to be essentially linked to the openness of the ballot. Bavaria and Baden-Württemberg have followed several other states in recent years in allowing voters in local elections to alter the order of candidates.

14. The effect of proportionality is moderated by the low number of councillors (four) per district, which is even lower than the seven used for state electoral districts, and constrains the effects of proportionality.

15. The improvement in 1997 is due especially to the introduction of postal ballots in eight municipalities, which, according to the report of the Western Australia Municipal Association, averaged turnouts of 45.33 percent compared to 19.84 percent for those that did not.

16. The ballot is not identical in each of these cases, but it typically allows voters to choose the party slate or to specify individual preferences. Proportionality is weakened because the number of seats distributed is typically fairly small—for example, six in Senate elections and seven in the Tasmanian lower house—which effectively sets a very high threshold on smaller parties.

17. We are uncertain as to the effect of the introduction of postal ballots. One study of turnout in local elections in the state of Victoria—where failing to vote makes one potentially (though rarely in practice) subject to a fine—compared councils with postal ballots to those not using them. It found an increase averaging less than five percent, one which the author suggests might simply be attributable to the "Hawthorne effect," that is, greater media and public attention to something new (Kiss 1999).

18. Note that there could be a nonparty form of politicization if we think in terms of the state political culture. Only Tasmania uses PR to elect members to the

state lower house, which makes it possible for smaller parties to win seats. Does this additional politicization at the state level contribute to higher local voting turnout? Probably, but unfortunately, since compulsory voting is used at the state level, we cannot separate these two elements by comparing the differences in turnout in local and in state elections.

19. Research projects at the Institute of Sociology at the University of Zurich and the Institute of Political Science at the University of Bern on three occasions (1988, 1994, and 1998) surveyed the communal secretaries of all Swiss municipalities.

20. Under the majority system, the voter casts up to as many votes as there are seats.

21. To allocate the seats the majority system takes two different forms: if the candidates winning a plurality of the votes are elected, it is called a "relative majority" or single-ballot system, because it always produces winners. In the second form, the "absolute majority" system, a candidate needs a minimum percentage of the votes, equivalent to 50 percent plus one of the votes cast per seat, to be elected. If the first ballot does not fill all the seats, a second ballot based on a relative majority takes place for the remaining ones. In proportional elections the votes go not to candidates but to political groups (parties).

22. This difficulty is not insurmountable, as demonstrated by the canton of Tessin, where even the very small communities use PR.

23. This is not to say that there is not an indirect relationship, since the very existence of a few of the smaller parties is due to the use of PR at higher levels. Were a majority system used, it is fair to assume that there would be fewer parties over time and, thus, fewer to contest communal elections whatever the system of elections.

Chapter 6. Civic Literacy and Political Institutions

1. The results of these polls were published in *Dagens Nyheter*, whose editor, Hans Bergström, kindly made them available to this writer.

2. We should remember that the high turnout (over 80 percent) means that included in the nine thousand voters were more people with a lower level of education than would be included in low-turnout countries.

3. Marsh paraphrases Alfred Deakin, founding father of the Commonwealth of Australia, as stating bluntly that the value of political institutions lies in their capacity to make citizens.

4. Beginning here we use the term FPTP as a kind of shorthand for nonproportional electoral systems, since this is the way majoritarian systems are most frequently identified in the literature. Most typical of them are single-member districts using either majority or—more frequently—plurality (winner-take-all) systems. (It is also used here to include the rare systems that use multimember districts in which the voter supports individual candidates by casting as many votes as there are seats.)

5. A Similar finding for the United States is reported in Anderson and LoTempio 1999.

6. In his original formulation, comparing and contrasting fifteen Western European countries, plus the US, Canada, Japan, Israel, Australia, and New Zealand,

Lijphart identified two basic models of democracy—majoritarian and consensus, with two dimensions to the differences in the political institutions in the two models. The first, the "executives-parties dimension," was based on five characteristics related to the party and electoral systems; the second, on three variables linked to the contrast between federal and unitary government.

7. As indicator of the proportionality of electoral systems, Lijphart (1994 and 1995) develops the notion of the "effective electoral threshold" to a party's winning a legislative seat. (Under it, the FPTP legislatures, as well as Australia's lower house, are given an effective threshold of 35 percent, France 32 percent, and Ireland 17 percent. The PR systems are given their legal thresholds, except in the case of countries that use regional lists without correction, which are given their effective thresholds: Norway 8.9 percent, Switzerland 8.5, Finland 5.4, Belgium 4.8, Denmark 1.6, Netherlands 0.7, Italy 2.3. . . .

8. In a later article, Lijphart and Crepaz (1991) attempted to incorporate the type of interest group system—corporatist versus pluralist—into the analysis, arguing that the correspondence is so close that corporatism can be included among the indicators of consensus democracy. This variable was found to correlate highly with the five variables of the executives-parties dimension, corporatism fitting as expected into the consensus model—but not much at all with those of the second dimension, federalism. The authors go on to suggest not only that is there significant conceptual affinity between consensual systems and corporatism but that the correspondence is close enough for corporatism to be included among the indicators of consensus democracy. This finding is corroborated by a recent study that found the electoral-party dimension of consensualism to be strongly associated with more active governments and lower income inequality, but the opposite to be true of the federal-unitary dimension (Vergunst 1998). We take up this relationship in our discussion of the link between the institutional arrangements underlying civic literacy and economic outcomes in part 4.

9. In comparing the rules regulating legislative committees in different countries, Powell (1996) found those with proportional systems to be more consensual in that they featured powerful committees with opposition parties sharing chairing duties, while others typically had weak committees dominated by the governing parties.

10. I thus duck the debate over classification. Evidently not all electoral systems can fit into these two simple categories, while those that do, especially PR systems, break down into numerous variations. Moreover, there can be variation between the system used for national elections and that used locally, as in France. Since we are here interested in something nontechnical, namely, the overall logic related to the electoral system, it is possible to speak of two such logics, majoritarian or FPTP, and consensual or PR. The latter includes all countries using electoral systems that allow people to choose the members of their main legislative body from party lists and where the result is close enough to proportionality to, as a rule, not shut out any serious minor party. (The STV system used in Ireland fits, though admittedly uncomfortably.) All the rest (including Australia and France) are classified as majoritarian (see Milner 1999).

11. In another paper (1999) Karp and Banducci show that compared to supporters of large parties, supporters of small parties are more satisfied with the political process under PR. And the IDEA report cited in chapter 3, note 7, reported that

countries in which the electoral system facilitates parliamentary representation for small parties have a youth turnout rate almost 12 percentage points higher than countries that do not.

12. Britain has been experimenting with PR in recent European elections and for its new Welsh and Scottish assemblies. Moreover, the close-to-proportional electoral system used for the Scottish Holyrood Assembly produced a Labour minority, which entered coalition talks with the Liberal Democrats. According to reports of the May 1999 negotiations, the Liberal Democrats made the introduction of proportional representation in local government one of their top bargaining positions, arguing, among other things, that it would stimulate voting turnout.

13. The autonomy of Swiss communes and the relative weakness of the central state—as well as the fact that the national voting turnout percentage is calculated based on potential voters, while for local elections it is registered voters—explain Switzerland's exceptional negative score in figure 6–1.

14. Here, I suspect, salience does enter the picture, in combination with FPTP's tendency to "waste votes." Given developments accelerated under Margaret Thatcher, which reduced the already limited powers of local government, it is hard to imagine any good reason for party supporters to bother to vote in one of the great majority of seats that are "safe" in the hands of one or another party.

15. See Lijphart 1995; Jankowski 1993; and Quirk 1989.

16. While parties are more stable under PR, empirical studies do not show any less turnover among legislators under PR than majoritarian systems (Karvonen 2000).

17. Crepaz (1999: 75) notes that under the two-party system "incentives to obstruct legislation are high" compared to multiparty systems in which governmental responsibility is shared.

18. Rogowski summarizes the arguments of British industrialists who favor electoral reform as fostering a business climate favorable to long-term investment. He goes on to argue that there is a relationship between reliance on international trade and PR since states that can provide the required continuity and stability of policy are better able to engage effectively in international trade. One measure of this comparative instability and stability is the extent to which governing parties (irresponsibly) use their macroeconomic powers to strengthen their position with voters at the end of their mandates (see Rogowski 1987). This "political business cycle" is characteristic of countries using PR (see Tufte 1978).

19. In fact, the mandate is no more solid under FPTP than it is under PR. Despite expectations to the contrary, the "manifesto group" found, in its detailed study of party programs and government policies in ten Western countries, that PR-based parties are at least as good at turning their programmatic commitments into government policy as those in FPTP-based systems, that the Westminster system proved "unremarkable" (Hofferberg 1994). It turns out that the "clear mandate" under FPTP is not really clear; the outcome under FPTP is clear only in being numerically decisive at the cost of distorting the voters' wishes.

20. A parallel argument has been recently developed by Australian political scientist Ian Marsh, who writes that the two-party system (a result of FPTP) has inherent "disabilities" when it comes to policy making due to its "political learning capacities." The two-party regime [is] "structurally incapable of building a broadly

based, public, bipartisan consensus about major strategic national issues. . . . The structure of incentives inhibits bipartisanship when the logic of policy making and the logic of electoral competition conflict. Further, the focus on electoral competition and the ritual nature of parliamentary opposition combine to exacerbate policy conflict and to exaggerate and distort partisan rhetoric. This impedes strategic policy making and distorts political learning in the wider community and amongst its component interests. The realities of policy making are deliberately distanced from electoral group awareness" (Marsh 1995a: 53).

21. Irvine (1979) cites figures showing only 10 percent of defeated Canadian party candidates standing in the subsequent elections.

22. Carty (1991) found that in the latter 1980s local organizations of Canada's national mass party, the NDP, averaged six times more members in districts where they had incumbents.

23. Swedish data collected by SNS in its 1997 "Democracy Audit" (Petersson et al. 1997: 117) show that fully 93 percent of Swedish MPs (and 90 percent of county (regional) councillors, and 89 percent of members of the European Parliament) have been and/or are still municipal councillors, while 53 percent of MPs have been and/or are still county councillors. Sundberg (1991) argues that as the members of local branches of social democratic parties have increasingly taken up elected office at the local level, they have become more like those of other parties, "deradicalized" by the constraints of local politics.

24. Related to this is the finding of a comparative study edited by Clark (1998), which compared the redistributive preferences of mayors in seventeen countries at the end of the 1980s and beginning of the 1990s. Parties drive policy (preferences), it was found, in western Europe but not in the United States and Canada.

25. Mancur Olson (1989) applies public-choice logic differently, in favor of the Westminster majoritarian model linked to FPTP. He argues that only a party with a chance of having more than half the seats has an "encompassing" interest in the society, similar to large centralized trade unions in a corporatist system, while small parties will be "opportunistic." The evidence does not support his contention, however, as effective policies, it would seem, are at least as likely to emanate from a coalition under PR as from a majority government in a Westminster system (see Crepaz 1996; Jankowski 1993).

26. In this instance, France is placed in the consensual camp since, unlike in the case of national elections, its complex mixed system of local elections is, on balance, more proportional than majoritarian (Hoffmann-Martinot, Rallings, and Thrasher 1996). Note that the difference in the averages does not change appreciably if Ireland and France, the two cases with "mixed" electoral systems, are placed in the FPTP category, since their average turnouts fall in between the two at 58.6 and 64.1 respectively.

Chapter 7. Civic Literacy and the Media

1. As is often the case, he is here following in the footsteps of Tocqueville, who observed that "of all countries on earth, it is in America that one finds both the most associations and the most newspapers. . . . Only a newspaper can put the same

thought at the same time before a thousand readers. . . . Without newspapers, there would be hardly any common action at all." A newspaper "talks to you briefly each day about the commonweal . . ." (Cited in Fishkin 1995: 154–56). Note that newspaper reading is not included among the fourteen indicators used to rank American states (Putnam 2000: 291).

2. *Public Attitudes toward Television and other Media in a Time of Change* (New York: Television Information Office, 1985); and *America's Watching: Public Attitudes toward Television* (New York: Television Information Office, 1987).

3. Even among the university-educated, television has a 10 percent lead.

4. Radio use has not been included in our quantitative comparisons because it has been superseded by television as a medium of information and entertainment. Moreover, a glance at what we know does not show significant differences overall in the public/private mix in the two electronic media. This means that were we to use radio consumption as a separate indicator, it would not significantly change the pattern from what we observe using television and newspapers. In addition, since so much of the data in this chapter are American, the choice of media must reflect this. Hence, even if it were possible to obtain the relevant comparative data on radio, I would still not use them in the analysis of the relationship between media use and civic literacy. The reality is that for the United States in particular, radio plays little meaningful political-information role: private radio has effectively abandoned this role and public radio is insignificant and usually careful to avoid news stories that put its fragile financial base at risk. Of course, in other countries (e.g., Sweden), this is not the case. Of Swedish Public Radio's (SR) 120,000 broadcasting hours on three national (P1, P2, and P3) and sixteen local channels, current-affairs and arts programs make up 46 percent of the hours while music accounts for 44 percent. Of those aged 9–79, P1, which provides in-depth news and current affairs, dramas, documentaries, and other programs about the arts, science, and social and philosophical issues, has an estimated 13 percent of the listening audience; P2, which broadcasts classical, contemporary, jazz, and folk music, as well as educational and minority-language programs, has 12 percent; and P3, which broadcasts pop music, news, and cultural programs, as well as programs dealing with social issues aimed at young people, has 19 percent. (Fifty-three percent of those over 35 tune in daily to P4, Local Radio, which combines news, and information, sports, and popular music programs—information from SR website.)

5. From the November 1997 PEW Center's Values Update.

6. According to *Harper's Index* (November 1991:19), 13 percent of Americans describe themselves as addicted to television.

7. Sowing distrust is a narrow expression of a wider accusation launched at television. For example, in his wide-ranging critique of the effects of U.S. television, Gans (1993) argues that television has atomized American society by eroding the critical faculties of the citizens and undermining the credibility of political institutions and the very civility underlying democratic politics. (At one point, he even refers to the process as undermining "civic literacy.") This analysis draws on data showing a cultural bias in American programs toward—and thus a tendency to foster—individualism (Gerbner et al. 1986; McBride 1998).

8. *Harper's Index* (October 1990) reports that the average number of words in the written vocabulary of an American child declined from 25,000 in 1945 to 10,000 in

1990. According to neuropsychologist Jane Healy (in a study titled "Endangered Minds: Why Our Children Don't Think," reviewed in the *Montreal Gazette*, 24 April 1991), "the child's brain up to age 7 is plastic, restructurable." TV, she concludes, brings an estimated 20 percent decline in creativity, in effect structuring the brain against learning. Twenty years ago writer Jerzy Koszinski spent a great deal of time with adolescents. His conclusion: "On television the world is exciting, single-faceted, never complex. In comparison, their own lives appear slow, uneventful, bewildering. They find it easier to watch televised portrayals of human experience . . . than to gain the experience for themselves" (cited in Newcomb 1976).

9. Fukuyama, for example, argues that America's inherited stores of social capital are eroding primarily due to the "'rights revolution' in the second half of the twentieth century which has promoted individualistic behaviour" (1995a: 284–85).

10. Brehm and Rahn's analysis of responses to the General Social Survey found TV viewing to be "a serious drain upon the civic participation side of social capital" (Brehm and Rahn 1997: 1017).

11. While the differences were reduced somewhat when controlled for education, they remained significant. Only age proved a meaningful independent factor: those who had been children before television was pervasive were less influenced.

12. For example, a study of a large sample of residents of Illinois found a significant correlation between the amount of television watched and the likelihood of overestimating, among other things, the frequency of drug use, hospital visits, use of prostitutes, and participation in satanic cults (O'Guinn and Shrum 1991).

13. By the 1980s, American children watched an average of 20,000 television commercials annually (OECD 1982: 13). In 1986, there were sixty-two children's programs in which the key character was based on a toy they could buy in a store (Lapham, Pollan, and Etheridge 1987: 53).

14. See, for example, Defleur et al. 1992; Facorro and Defleur 1993; Gunter, Furnham, and Gietson 1984. The result has been, as an analysis of public attentiveness to more than five hundred news stories over the last ten years confirms, that the American public pays relatively little attention to many of the serious news stories of the day (Parker and Deane 1997).

15. For detailed information about sources of data about television consumption, see appendix III.

16. I have calculated the correlation between levels of interpersonal trust and the two measures of associational participation and average TV-watching hours for the sixteen OECD countries (discussed below). The R^2 calculations are, respectively, .093 and .208.

17. Norris examined the responses to the eight questions in the American Citizen Participation Study relating to political knowledge (set out in chapter 3); see also Delli Carpini 1993; Lambert et al. 1988.

18. Some observers point to another phenomenon that affects the relationship between newspapers and knowledge: newspapers, in order to compete with television, are in fact coming to resemble it. Entman argues that American media do not provide the information needed to exercise informed citizenship. There is a vicious circle: "With limited demand for first-rate journalism, most news organizations cannot afford to supply it and because they do not supply it, most Americans have no practical source of the information necessary to become politically sophisticated.

Yet it would take an informed and interested citizenry to create enough demand to support top-flight journalism" Entman 1989:17. A case in point: Jamieson found that in 1996 the amount of broadcast and print coverage devoted to the election plummeted. From September 1 through November 1, the number of words in broadcast reports dealing with the presidential campaign dropped 55 percent from the corresponding total in 1992. The print media followed the same pattern, with front-page campaign coverage dropping 40 percent.

19. Television campaign advertising does not qualify as news. It is also inaccurate. "The percentage of ads containing misleading claims skyrocketed in 1996; 52 percent of all the ads broadcast by the Republican and Democratic presidential candidates from the first day of the political conventions until the campaign ads went off the air at midnight on election eve contained misleading information, up from 14 percent of the ads in 1992" (Jamieson 1996: 28).

20. High TV watchers with little overall political knowledge, they note, are especially vulnerable to distortion. Local newscasts are also especially vulnerable to ratings, and the programs reflect it: violent, dramatic stories—even when not local—crowd out others; or news is eliminated entirely. The following was reported by Tim Cuprisin in the *Milwaukee Journal Sentinel* on 12 November 1998: "Channel 4's decision to cancel its Monday night news may have been one of screwiest TV moves in memory, coming as it does from the station that considers itself the big dog in local broadcast news. . . . We're in the middle of the November 'sweeps,' one of the four annual four-week periods designed by Nielsen Media Research to measure what we're watching on TV—and, ultimately, to determine advertising rates. . . . Channel 4 figured the bulk of viewers Monday night would stay tuned to the Packers-Steelers game on Channel 12. In a controversial decision, it took what was sure to be a low-rated 10 p.m. newscast out. . . ."

21. The authors' research design allowed them to test the direction of the relationship between knowledge and media consumption. They dismiss the suggestion sometimes made that causality is reversed: "We find no evidence that having higher levels of campaign knowledge led voters to read newspapers . . . or watch television news more frequently" (Hartley and Dautrich 1998: 3).

22. The AP news service reported on February 11, 1999, that viewership of CNN, the principal cable news source, had not recovered from its mid-1990s slump.

23. The Pew Research Center 1998 survey found while almost three-quarters of eighteen- to twenty-four-year-olds channel surf during the news, fewer than half of those aged 65 and over do.

24. One measure of the extent to which commercialism has penetrated television-watching habits may be found in differing attitudes toward TV commercials. On the whole, it appears, Europe has not as yet welcomed commercial television. According to a survey carried out in ten European countries by Universal Media Gmbh at the end of 1997, less than 10 percent of Germans, one-third of the British and one-quarter of the Italians, were favorably disposed to TV commercials.

25. While we have no systematic comparisons of public- and private-network news reports, specific studies do point at significant differences. For example, Brant and Neijens (1998) compared the content (issues versus personalities), format (straightforward presentation versus use of music, audience participation, etc.), and style (seriousness versus the lightheartedness of the presentation) of Dutch

television newscasts, finding that the private stations were higher in entertainment and the public stations higher in information.

26. Public radio, in contrast, is still very much alive in New Zealand.

27. "The assumption is that the technology and the delivery of content might change, but public service broadcasting is still a standards setter and a guarantor of impartial news and diverse programming" (Steemers 1999: 6).

28. Between 1990 and 1995, commercial television expanded rapidly. Swedes can now choose three private networks, two on cable, one terrestrial—not to mention various news programs in other languages on cable; nevertheless, the data indicate that a steady 60 percent of adults watch one or both of the public news broadcasts.

29. While there was a certain knowledge gain during the campaign due to media use, it did not much alter the relative position: those who knew more continued to know more. One interesting finding is that among the youngest group of voters, media use affected the knowledge of the males but not the females. As expected, age was an overall factor in news watching, with usage increasing with age. (Eighty percent of those over 65 said they watched the news every day. To get the same percentage of those 15–24, one had to go down to once per week. Of the total population, 45 percent watched the news daily, a percentage that has remained quite steady.)

30. Inaba (1997) compared the effects of watching the public (NHK) versus the private channel. NHK viewers learned more about issues, while private-broadcast viewers learned more about the personal lives of politicians.

31. Another study focused on the 1998 Dutch national election campaign. It found that "public television news and current affairs viewing has by far the strongest and most consistently positive influence on   political . . . knowledge, and this when controlling for interest, age and level of education, whereas viewing news or light entertainment on the commercial channels has a consistently negative influence" (Aarts and Semetko 2000: 11–12).

32. In 1990, the public-service share in the four Nordic countries ranged from 58 percent in Finland to 83 percent in Sweden (Carlsson and Harrie 1997: 230).

33. For this reason, advertisers insist on ratings based on boxes that meter the actual programs watched and not what people say they watch. Hence they make use of highly sophisticated techniques that test underlying consumer desires. "People meters" report which member of the household is watching what TV program when; advertising and program content is "people tested." Messages are first reduced to momentary visual and aural images to which sample viewers' immediate reactions are registered through their pressing (+) and (–) buttons. The minuses are extracted and the pluses are then turned into an ad by the best writers, directors, designers, composers, and actors money can buy.

34. He employed a technique, used in other commercial marketing studies, of identifying the claims the ad was making, determining externally which claims were false, and then measuring the perceptions of a representative sample of consumers exposed to the ad.

35. For example, one was the notorious ad for Bush in 1988 that "attacked the Massachusetts furlough program, showing an apparently endless stream of convicts passing in and out of prison through a revolving door, from captivity back to the commonwealth. At one point in the ad, the narrator speaks of first-degree

murderers escaping from the program. This is followed immediately by a caption reading '268 escaped.'"

36. They were presented with a set of seven names of contemporary U.S. political figures and instructed to identify their political office. A plurality of the sample (twenty-four in all) correctly identified one or none of the seven political figures. Nineteen percent (ten subjects) correctly identified a majority of the figures.

37. The emphasis here would be on study circles and other types of associations directly concerned with information dissemination.

38. In a comprehensive study of Norwegians, Wolleback and Selle (2000: 36) find that those who are members of no associations are roughly 10 percent less likely to report that they read the news daily.

39. Newton (1999: 589–90) found that British readers of daily broadsheets—but not tabloids—were far more politically knowledgeable than readers of tabloids, who differed little from nonreaders. See also Norris and Curtice 1998.

40. It is not possible to set hard and fast rules. There are good national tabloids in Norway, for example, while some local daily broadsheets in a number of countries provide absolutely no news content outside of local gossip.

41. Similarly, another Eurobarometer poll (#50, March 1999: 94) asked people in EU-member states if they read the news in the paper every day. The Swedes and Finns led with 74 and 68 percent, respectively, responding affirmatively. The middle group went from the Netherlands (61 percent) to Germany, Denmark, Austria, the U.K., and Ireland (47 percent). Italy, Belgium, and France were at 28 and 29 percent.

42. From data for book titles published annually (from UNESCO), I calculate that the U.K. and Switzerland join the Nordic countries with around two titles per capita; all other OECD countries are below one per capita.

43. In Denmark, between 1980 and 1995, daily newspaper readership dropped by 12 percent, but it increased by 209 percent on Sundays in that same period (Carlsson and Harrie 1997: 23).

44. The data for all European countries are provided in Pilati (1993: table 1). Danes say they read magazines 25 minutes per day, and Germans 22, compared to the European average of 13. If magazine reading were somehow to be included, it would marginally affect the TV dependency rating, lowering it for Denmark and Germany, raising it for the U.K. (with 7 minutes' magazine reading) and Norway (8 minutes).

45. The main source of information for these data was the European Audiovisual Observatory, *Statistical Yearbook 1994–1995: Cinema, Television, and New Media in Europe*. To standardize the material internationally, the year 1993 served as base year. I have verified in the latest available (1998) European Audiovisual Observatory *Statistical Yearbook* (table 7.6, page 165) that no significant changes have taken place in the relative position on this scale.

46. I first tried to break down TV watching in each country into entertainment versus information, but this proved unmanageable because countries break their programming down in different ways, and because the existing information tends to be on programs offered rather than time spent watching them.

47. As above, the main source of information for these data was the European Audiovisual Observatory, *Statistical Yearbook 1994–1995: Cinema, Television, and New Media in Europe*. And, as above, I verified in the latest available (1998) European

Audiovisual Observatory *Statistical Yearbook* (table 10.5, page 393) that no signifi-cant changes have taken place in the relative position on this scale.

48. In a large survey of adult literacy in America conducted in 1993 by the Na-tional Center for Education Statistics (NCES), it was found that 53 percent of American adults do not read a daily newspaper. For the Nordic countries, the share of nonreaders has been estimated at less than 20 percent.

49. To make the score meaningful, the newspaper-reading score was recom-puted to bring the maximum to around 100, and the sign then changed by subtract-ing each score from 100.

50. An analysis of the American IALS data (NCES 1993: 55–59) found that of those saying they never read a newspaper, about three-quarters scored in the lowest level on the three tests. And only print-media usage (as primary source of informa-tion about current events) correlated positively with functional literacy scores.

51. While we must be wary applying individual-level logic to aggregates, the ex-traordinary high correlation allows a bit of leeway. We should not be surprised that someone who watches a large amount of mainly commercial television and seldom reads newspapers knows far less about the United Nations than someone who reg-ularly reads newspapers and watches little commercial TV.

52. Indeed, had we included magazine reading in our method of calculation as suggested above, thus raising the TV dependency rating for Norway and the U.K. and lowering it for Denmark and Germany, we would see that the correlation in figures 7–5 and 7–6 would be even higher.

53. We do not see Italy in figure 7–6 because it is excluded due to its use of com-pulsory voting. However, the low turnout in Italy's referenda—the most recent was in April 1999, which failed even to get the 50 percent needed to validate the majority's choice to back electoral reform—suggest that it would fit neatly on the upper left of the chart. France is a more complex case. My guess is that France looks better on both scales than it deserves to look due to incomplete information. (France withdrew from the IALS, apparently displeased with the poor results. Available and partial figures on local turnout seem high when compared to turnout of age-eligible voters in parliamentary elections—which according to IDEA [1997: 23] averaged an unimpressive 67.9 percent between 1945 and 1997.)

Chapter 8. Promoting Civic Literacy through Political Institutions and the Media

1. Among the high-civic-literacy Nordic countries, Sweden will receive the lion's share of attention – since the author knows it best.

2. It was the pastor's responsibility to see to it that every man and woman in his parish acquired basic reading skills. Hence, astoundingly, Sweden approached 100 percent reading literacy in the seventeenth century (Fägerlind and Saha 1983: 146).

3. Putnam's interpretation of civic engagement in Italian regions can be read as deterministic, his analysis suggesting that current conditions are based on century-old traditions.

4. In 1990 there were roughly 275 daily newspapers in the three countries plus Denmark (Hoest 1991), which have a combined population slightly lower than that

of Canada—where, by way of comparison, there were 106 dailies in 1995. There are also a comparatively large number of weekly newspapers and magazines in these countries. For example, in the early 1990s there were 85 Swedish weekly newspapers and 46 magazines.

5. Outside Scandinavia, the European VAT rates for newspapers are Britain and Belgium, exempt; France 2.1 percent; Italy 4 percent; the Netherlands 6 percent; Germany 7 percent; Austria 10 percent; and Ireland 12.5 percent (De Bens and Østbye 1998: 13).

6. Austrian direct press subsidies in 1995 totalled ECU 18 million, of which 28 percent was divided among all newspapers and the rest, following the Scandinavian system, went to those not in first place in their market (Grisold 1998).

7. See figure 7–2. I have written on the importance of such policies in earlier books on the development of the contemporary welfare in the Nordic countries (Milner 1989 and 1994), and the reader is referred to them for general background information.

8. The total subsidy was drastically reduced from a high of FIM 478 million in 1991 to FIM 150 million in 1993, and since reduced even further, and overall circulation declined almost 15 percent between 1989 and 1996 (Salokangas 1999: 100).

9. Not included in these figures are the free tabloids, including the fairly serious tabloid *Metro*, launched in the early 1990s and distributed by the hundreds of thousands in Stockholm (and now Gothenburg).

10. Later, in 1998, the subsidy declined to NRK 188 million. In summer 1999, one U.S. dollar equaled 8.5 SEK, 7.9 NRK, and 5.8 FIM.

11. Those not reading at least one morning or (less weighty) afternoon paper in Sweden make up 19 percent of those aged 9–79 (*Mediebarometer* 1997: 52). In 1995, for Norway it was 16 percent, for Finland it was 3 percent (aged 12+), and for Denmark (aged 13+) 28 percent (Carlsson and Harrie 1997: 156).

12. In 1993, only 78 percent of all Danes, and 71 percent of women, read daily newspapers (Søllinge 1999).

13. Overall, a daily morning paper is read by 72 percent of Swedes (aged 9–79) but only 60 percent of those aged 15–24 (*Mediebarometer* 1997: 54). There are also substantial efforts by newspaper associations to promote newspaper consumption especially among young people in a number of European and especially Nordic countries. The latter are noted for their interactive media centers at which visitors get a hands-on sense of the world of newspapers (ENPA 1997: 33–34; ENPA 1996).

14. A survey asking Finns to identify the essentials of life that state welfare programs had to meet found that 55.3 percent of respondents regarded a daily paper as a necessity of life, a proportion placing it above twenty-five of thirty-seven consumption items including television, stereo, video, cinema, and new clothes. The daily paper was described by 53.7 percent as something they both had and could not do without, and by 29.4 percent as something they had but could do without. Only 7.1 percent said they neither received it nor wanted it, while 9.7 percent said they wanted but couldn't afford it (Kangas and Ritakallio 1995: table 1).

15. This strategy would have payoffs for countries that dub English-language programs, such as Germany, France, Italy, and Spain. There is, however, insufficient interest in English-speaking countries for foreign-language material for such material in subtitled form to have much impact—as the experience of Australia's SBS suggests.

16. As we shall see in chapter 11, two of New Zealand's four television channels are still publicly owned but are commercial rather than public-service enterprises.

17. PBS in the United States, with only 3 percent of audience share, also receives some revenues from the discrete messages of its corporate sponsors.

18. The information comes from an early 1999 McKinsey report on the world's public broadcasters commissioned by the BBC and reported on by the *Globe and Mail*, 10 June 1999.

19. Schaffner and Streb (2000: 16) show that, of those already casting a ballot in California, roughly 16 percent abstained from voting in nonpartisan races (i.e., those where party affiliation was not included on the ballot), and that these were "disproportionately less educated than those who did vote in the contest."

20. Television contributes to informing voters through debates and interviews. In Sweden, there are two televised TV debates (one on a public-service channel, one on a commercial one) in which the leaders of all parties with parliamentary representation take part.

21. A contrasting American example is to be found in Craig and Kane's (1999) finding that the least politically informed among Floridians tended to be those most in favor of direct democracy.

22. Krouwel developed a seven-point openness scale (most centralized and closed to most decentralized and open) and applied it to eighty-three political parties in twelve western European countries. From these figures, he established comparative ratings for each country, broken down into separate five-year periods between 1945 and 1990.

23. The Nordic countries have the most open systems, and, as a rule, those with comparatively closed systems, notably Belgium, Italy, and France, are among the lowest in organizational participation and – with the exception of France – in level of local turnout. Anomalies such as these add weight to the suggestion made at the end of chapter 7 that France looks better on these scales than it deserves to, due to incomplete information.

24. Given the lower costs of campaigns in the Nordic countries, the state grants cover a majority of party campaign expenses without being lavish. In Finland, for example, in 1987, FIM 165 million in grants covered 82 percent of party campaign spending (Wiberg 1991: 62). The three others contribute slightly less but in each case cover at least half the money spent by parties in their electoral campaigns (Gidlund 1991: 44; Wiberg 1991: 92; Pederson and Bille 1991: 160–61).

25. To again take Finland as case study, press support is distributed to parties according to their number of parliamentary members. In the budget proposition for 1998, the total support was for FIM 75 million, of which FIM 40 million is for the selective support and FIM 35 million for the parliamentary support.

26. The United States does provide public money to candidates for president in the form of matching grants. Candidates become eligible for such funds by raising at least $5,000 in twenty different states from individuals contributing less than $250. Given the high costs of television campaigns, these funds do not, as we see below, counter the dependency on privately raised money in American politics—especially unregulated "soft money."

27. Personal communication from Professor Erik Åsard of Uppsala University, 22 November 2000.

28. This amounts to around thirty dollars per vote. The center also found that in nine of ten cases, the higher spender was successful in getting elected.

29. A good example of how appropriate institutions affecting the dissemination of political information can contribute to civic literacy is provided by the Netherlands. The Dutch Central Planning bureau is politically independent and is widely respected for its statistical analysis. Governing parties are forced to be realistic in their forecasting in fear of being made to look bad by the bureau. Beginning with the spring 1998 election, the bureau tested the electoral program commitments of the parties on unemployment, growth, and the tax burden against its economic forecast for the life of the next parliament.

30. See Gronbech-Jensen (1999) for a description of the transparency rights of Danish and Swedish citizens.

31. In advance of important issues coming before the EU Council of Ministers, the Danish minister involved briefs the all-party parliamentary Market Committee, answers questions, and receives advice. Though the process is usually informal, the minister is expected to follow the wishes of the committee; the same, though less formally, applies to the prime minister's meetings with the committee before meetings of the European Council. In addition, the Market committee receives a list of all proposals sent to the Council of Ministers as well as other pertinent documents, which are studied in detail by subcommittees and working groups reporting to the committee (Nehring 1992).

32. The principle is that paying taxes is a public and not a private act. Private matters having to do with all aspects of personal life are sheltered from public view. However, since tax revenues make social services possible, keeping their sources secret contributes to public ignorance over policy alternatives and arouses suspicions that others are not paying their share. The public thus knows, for example, how much of the king's income goes toward taxes. Such information is rarely the stuff of exposés. It is simply part of the background of everyday information. For example, when journalists write about public (or even not so public) figures, they almost always include annual income in the profile (along with age, marital status . . .).

33. The facts and figures on spending by governments and public institutions, and the results of comprehensive and detailed research into the effects of those expenditures, are widely disseminated. The result is that you don't need an accounting degree and the resources of an investigative reporter to understand public finance.

34. Denmark and Sweden, supported by Finland, have been the most vociferous exponents of transparency in the operations of the EU Council and Commission, often to the discomfiture of other members, who prefer keeping discussions behind closed doors. Indeed, commentators suggested that it was the new climate of (relative) transparency with the arrival of Sweden and Finland that lay behind the revelations of corruption and mismanagement that led to the resignation of the commission in early 1999.

35. In addition to the principle of transparency, this assumption is built into the prevailing attitude toward cultural policy. The comprehensive bill on cultural policy (adopted with the support of all Swedish political parties in 1974) affirmed as one of its four goals to counteract the negative effects of commercialization on cultural awareness.

36. Information about Swedish programs in these areas is to be found in Milner 1989; for information about the even more generous programs in Norway, see Dägre 1989.

Chapter 9. Promoting Civic Literacy through Adult Education

1. Compulsory education, in contrast, is intended to help form the citizens of the future. I argue elsewhere (Milner 1997a) that our understanding of the early Swedish welfare state has been distorted by a tendency to take the logic applied to policies affecting children as if it applied to adults, yet children cannot be expected to inform themselves to act as competent citizens—the opposite of what we expect for adults.

2. The OECD and UNESCO assemble such data on primary, secondary, and tertiary schooling; but not adult education.

3. For example, the average scores of Canadian francophones were substantially (about 10 percent) lower than anglophones in the International Adult Literacy Survey (IALS). More important in their effect on literacy than the lower level of formal education of—especially older—francophones were indicators of the "literacy habit." On these (weekly) indicators, anglophones consistently outscored francophones: 66 to 54 percent on reading daily newspapers, 56 to 40 percent on reading books, 28 to 18 percent on visiting a library, 41 to 26 percent on writing letters. (The data come from a detailed analysis of the Canadian results reported on in the *Globe and Mail* on 11 January 1999.)

4. This effect is most apparent when the courses are taken in the final years of high school (Niemi and Junn 1998; Westholm, Lindquist, and Niemi 1989).

5. Both American and Dutch researchers have found students who have taken civics courses to be more politically knowledgeable. However, the fact that in the Dutch case there was a correlation only for the less than 10 percent of students (Hahn 1998: 15) who took the civics course (called "society") as a part of their formal program leading to the final examination (Dekker 1999) suggests that its effects are likely to prove short-lived. This corresponds to the suggestion that the effects of civics courses taken one hour per week from grade 7 or 8 by practically all German students (Händle, Oesterreich, and Luitgard 1999) seem to have little effect on the adolescents.

6. Because of the complexity of the Australian electoral system, the Australian Electoral Commission employs a number of people throughout the country whose job is to explain the voting system in the schools. In private conversation in May 1999, two individuals responsible for this program in northern Australia explained that they concentrate their efforts on primary school students (using games to simulate the voting situation) because younger children see mastering the system as a challenge. In contrast, adolescents typically remain aloof, to show that they are above such things. As Australian researcher Hugh MacKay concluded, "Typically, teenagers find little to interest or inspire them in the political process, and they often report that politics is the most boring subject discussed at home" (quoted in Civics Expert Group 1994:182).

7. The commission identified "educating individuals . . . capable of . . . the exercise of their responsibility as citizens" as the second of the major functions of education.

8. "To shape a national identity and a sense of active citizenship . . . in the US, civics education currently forms part of a social studies course extending through elementary and high school. . . . linked with programs in American history and geography, government, economic systems and research skills. . . . France has a discrete *éducation civique* curriculum with its own specification and timetable. . . . [dealing with] the history of French institutions, . . . current political processes . . . [and] a community project. . . . Civics education in the UK . . . is not encapsulated in a particular subject, such as social studies, nor is it a topic in its own right. Rather, civics education is an emphasis that . . . is embedded in the core subjects of the curriculum. . . . as one of five cross-curricular themes: . . . economic and industrial understanding, careers education and guidance, health education, citizenship and environmental education" (Civics Expert Group 1994: 32–34).

9. One indirect confirmation of the limited effects of such knowledge when acquired in adolescence is to be found in the results of the "Youth and History" research project conducted among teenagers in twenty-seven European countries in the mid-1990s (Angvik and von Borries 1997). The project surveyed almost 32,000 teenagers using a standardized questionnaire. Ten of the questions are relevant here: respondents were given ten pairs of five events in modern political history (the Russian Revolution, the Great Depression, the decolonization of Africa, the foundation of the United Nations, and World War II) and asked to put them in chronological order. There is no correlation of any kind between the comparative results and our (adult) functional literacy indicators. For example, Britain and France do better than the Netherlands, Germany and Sweden, quite the opposite of the IALS.

10. What young people are expected or likely to learn about by age fourteen or fifteen: (1) how leaders are selected, laws and regulations established, and individuals and groups participate in political processes; (2) the right to form or join political parties, unions, and other organizations, and to a minimal standard of living or to employment, medical care, and education; (3) obligations, including voting, military/national service, and to work, pay taxes, and obey laws. Are they expected or likely to believe that the government is or should be responsive to citizens' views, and to feel confident about being able to make their opinions heard?

11. Are young people expected or likely to have acquired as a sense of national identity or national loyalty by age fourteen or fifteen? Through what documents, historical events, national stories, and ideals, heroes and role models? How much and what kinds of criticism about national leaders are thought to be appropriate? Are students encouraged to ignore events of which many people are not proud? What supranational structures or international organizations and subnational (e.g., ethnic or religious) groups are thought to be important enough to have a place in the young person's awareness, identity, or loyalty?

12. What are young people expected or likely to have learned about those belonging to groups which are seen as set apart or disenfranchised (as defined, for example, by ethnicity, race, immigrant status, mother tongue, social class, religon or gender)? Is there tension between perceptions of the need for social cohesion and the need to recognize the cultural, social, political, and economic situation of these groups? How is conflict between these groups or between them and the broader society dealt with in education?

13. It may confirm the results of an earlier study in which Denmark stood out among the five countries surveyed in its young people's interest in politics and declared involvement in political activities. "Danish students . . . live in a wider political culture, and . . . construct a view of the political realm that both reflects and supports participatory democracy to a greater extent than is evident in the other countries in this study" (Hahn 1998: 101–2). The others are England, Germany, the Netherlands, and the United States.

14. A visit to a typical Swedish elementary school in Umeå (see below) found each classroom equipped with up-to-date pull-down Swedish, European, and world maps, which ten-year-olds would routinely consult.

15. Another development taking place in the schools may have an impact on civic literacy comparable to that of commercialism on TV watching. Many large corporations, from McDonald's to Microsoft, are present through brand advertising through curricular involvement, and trading off donations for a monopoly for sale of their product (see Richards et al. 1998). A recent disturbing example recounted in *The American Prospect* (July 99: 14) concerns hundreds of schoolchildren who, in exchange for a computer donation to their schools, filled out market research booklets and participated in focus groups over a six-month period to help firms target their products. Ironically, commercialism has also penetrated the classroom via news programs. Companies like Zap Me, which is based in San Ramon, Calif., offer schools free computers with screens that include continuously flashing ads. Zap Me also collects information that students provide and makes it available to its advertisers—including Microsoft and Toshiba, which also supply the computers" (*New York Times*, 14 September 2000). *The New York Times* article, based on a report from the General Accounting Office, notes also that 25 percent of middle schools and high schools present Channel One television programs during school hours, composed of news, features, and compulsory commercials directed at the teenagers.

16. New Zealand tied Norway at 48 percent. Except for Ireland and Belgium, which trailed with levels in the 20s, the remaining countries clustered between 44 and 37 percent. Switzerland is placed in this intermediate category by combining the German-speaking Swiss, who were quite high, at 45 percent, with the French-speaking, who were low at 34 percent. See OECD 1997: 93.

17. The figures cited here are from an English-language summary of the Swedish Royal Commission investigation into adult education services (Statistika Meddelanden, 1998).

18. Outside the major urban centers, the majority of citizens take part. Rubensson (1994) estimated that, overall, 43 percent of Swedish adults participate in at least one such program in a given year.

19. Further evidence of the effectiveness of such study circles can be found in the fact that Sweden, in November 1998, was the first country to reduce smoking below the 20 percent barrier. Other leaders in reducing smoking are Finland, Norway, and Denmark.

20. More recently, study circles considered the pros and cons of the plan to change the European Union framework at the Intergovernmental Conference (IGC), which later came to be known as the Amsterdam Treaty. As part of their preparatory work in the latter half of 1995, Finland, Denmark, and Sweden set up

all-party parliamentary commissions. The Swedish commission's task included a specific mandate to inform the population by stimulating discussion so that, by the date the conference began, at least 50 percent of the population had adequate knowledge about it.

21. In 1999, more than 200,000 adults took such *komvux* courses at the upper secondary level (*Swedish Budget Statement* 1999: 18).

22. Westholm, Lindquist, and Niemi (1989) found that upper secondary students taking civics courses were more likely to retain knowledge about international organizations (11 percent more) and international events (6 percent more) when retested two years later than those in a control group.

23. As with public radio and television, educational institutions are bound by the laws of transparency. This means that any citizen has the right to evidence that a given educational institution does in fact meet the objectives set out in its statements of goals and principles.

24. The Swedish approach was positively singled out by the Civics Expert Group (1994: 177) of Australia in its investigation as a mix of three basic approaches that characterized current practice in OECD countries.

25. Walker (2000: 647) quotes from the newsletter of the Corporation for National Service, major funder of national service and service learning. "National service has to be non-partisan. . . . Strikes, demonstrations and political activities . . . divide and polarize."

26. In the United States, according to the U.S. Census Bureau, the median time people lived at one residence was 5.2 years (cited by Randolph E. Schmid in the Associated Press, 29 November 1998). In the Nordic countries, in contrast, young people are highly mobile in their postadolescent years, but, once ready to settle down, they make great efforts to settle in the community in which they grew up; and once they settle down, they are not very mobile, and are supported in those efforts: Norway in particular is famous for the vast resources invested in the infrastructure and institutions in its vast northern hinterland. Overall such outcomes favor civic literacy, since too much, as well as too little, mobility will inhibit civic engagement.

27. A similar tradition is also found in Småland in the south.

28. The Stockholm region was lowest, with only half the rate of Västerbotten.

29. Of the 3,500, only 500 are employed on a full-time basis; the rest, typically members of constitutent organizations, have undergone training provided by the ABF.

30. The paper is described as "seminal" by translator Donald Broady.

31. When the municipality took over responsibility for this book collection in 1937 it founded what became the city of Umeå's public library, which became the central library for Västerbotten County in 1946. Its collection grew rapidly after 1950, when it was named one of five libraries that, by law, received a copy of each book published in Sweden.

32. At these centers, rare Swedish books are received from libraries throughout the country; the books are entered into the National Union Catalogue (LIBRIS) and are available for interlibrary loans.

33. Talking books as well as cassettes of daily newspapers are available for loan to the visually impaired, mentally handicapped, aphasics, physically disabled,

chronically ill, and dyslexic individuals. Books in braille are borrowed from the Swedish Institute for Talking Books and Braille. The Talking Book Department also produces materials for individuals and groups. Over one hundred videotapes subtitled in sign language are available for the deaf, and children´s books in sign language are available. There is a large selection of Easy Readers and a special newspaper, *8 Sidor*, written in Easy Swedish for those with learning difficulties and for those new to the Swedish language.

34. It makes genealogical data from the archives of all the churches in Västerbotten available throughout Sweden. (English-language versions of the municipality's and library's web pages can be found at http://www.umea.se/ eng/ index.html.)

35. This number was arrived at in an analysis conducted by the paper, and constitutes a decline from the 80 percent level attained before the recession of the early 1990s.

36. Students and graduates can also find help in the form of exercises for preparing for university entrance exams, as well as leads to jobs in foreign countries.

37. Umeå is some eight hundred kilometers north of Stockholm, too far away and too cold to become a prime tourist destination despite clean air, untouched forests, and northern lights in the sky.

38. In the university's thirty-five years of existence (since 1965), there developed none of the usual antipathy between "town and gown." Local officials know that the university's strength is the town's strength. Indeed, the city takes responsibility to ensure there is housing for all, and sends out detailed information packages to all new students.

39. These included Ericsson's Software Division and Astra's Product Development Division. The effort is made all the harder not only by Umeå's distance from Sweden's population center but also by the centrifugal forces pulling southward stemming from EU integration.

40. When the telephone/utility lines were installed a few years ago they had the foresight to lay an extra cable just for that eventuality.

41. Senior citizens receive needed information in this manner through their own organizations that are plugged into the Net.

42. For example, employees in private firms at all levels can lease or buy computers at a very low cost and tax free from their companies.

43. In the fall 1999 budget statement, the Swedish government promised to do its part by laying a nationwide (200,000-kilometer-long) cable network of broadband fiber-optic cable within five years. This would allow every Swede to connect to the Net at very high speed without tying up telephone lines. The decision followed up a report of the IT commission set up in 1998. Comparing the project to the construction of the national railway system one hundred years earlier, industry minister Björn Rösengren estimated the cost at potentially as high as US $10 billion, and called on the private sector to contribute.

44. The easy-to-follow links—in Swedish—to the various regional organizations, services, and enterprises can be found on the Umeå home page.

45. The strategy adopted in 1999 was "within five years . . . to offer at 95 percent of all County residents the opportunity to obtain a 5M bit per second Internet connection from their homes for the cost of a present monthly bus ticket" (AC Direct 1999: 125).

46. Swedish placed seventh, while Finnish, Danish, and Norwegian placed twelfth, thirteenth, and fourteenth.

47. The Eurobarometer (#50, March 1999: 108) asked respondents about their ability to take part in a conversation in another langauge. The leaders were the Luxembourgers with 98 percent, followed by the Dutch with 86, the Danes 83, and the Swedes 81. A distant fifth were the Belgians at 62 percent.

48. The IDC "tracks data from 55 countries that collectively account for 97% of the global GDP and 99% of IT expenditure. . . . drawn from highly reliable sources including IDC, UNESCO, ITU, World Bank, and Freedom House" (IDC.Com/Global Research, 14 February 2000).

49. In 1997, according to *The Economist* (28 August 1999: 85).

50. Finland's population is only five million, compared to Sweden's nine million. One of Finland's RISI initiatives is coordinated by the West Finland Alliance, a consortium of the 137 municipalities, the universities, and major businesses of the region of Ostrobothnia, just across the Bay of Bothnia from Västerbotten.

51. It was no secret that the Swedes were disappointed to lose the position to their Baltic cousins and rivals.

52. In January 1999, Finland was the site of the second Politics and Internet Conference sponsored by the European Commission. Presentations to the conference at simultaneous events in a number of electronically linked locations gave Finnish policy makers all over the country an opportunity to describe their information society programs. Overall, the facts cited there herald a decade of impressive achievement in the construction of an information society based on "humane and sustainable development, user-friendly and safe electronic services to help people in their work, leisure pursuits and learning environments." To find the information from these and other reports, the reader is referred to the summary, titled "On the Road to the Finnish Information Society" on its website: http://www.stat.fi/tk/yr/tttietoti_en.html.

53. These numbers need to be taken merely as indicative, since the method by which they are calculated does not seem to be standardized. Moreover, they are changing very rapidly all the time. For example, according to the *Mediebarometer* (1998: 13), 20 percent of Swedes aged nine to seventy-nine use the Internet for private purposes on a daily basis.

54. The data are for 1998 and are from the *2000 World Development Indicators*, published by the World Bank. This is an extraordinary fact given the incentive for multinational corporations to host Internet sites in the dominant economic power.

55. Finland was the first country where mobile phone penetration exceeded 50 percent; by 1999, penetration had surpassed 60 percent.

56. PULSE thus turns the web into an active medium of cooperative effort. (The English-language Internet site is to be found at http://www.lib.hel.fi:7001/english/projects/linklibrary.htm.)

57. One manifestation is the "virtual Helsinki" system linking every single resident through the computers, televisions, or cell phones (see article in *L'Expansion*, 16 March 2000: 98–99).

58. It is possible that the Internet informs those who do not get information by the traditional media. Unfortunately the evidence suggests otherwise. For example, a study of 529 American undergraduate students found that the Internet is

used mainly as a source of entertainment, with use of the web as a news source confined essentially to those who get news from newspapers (Althaus and Tewksbury 1998).

Chapter 10. The Case of New Zealand

1. The classic comparative analysis of modern welfare state policies depicts New Zealand welfare programs as "exemplary" (Heidenheimer, Heclo, and Adams 1990: 370).

2. By the early 1980s, the leading figures in the Treasury and the Reserve Bank had come to a shared perspective. The shakiness of the New Zealand dollar and the general vulnerability of the economy in 1984 provided an opportunity to place their agenda before the politicians and the informed public and have it adopted. For most of them, the situation provided an opportunity to put into play their belief that markets were better than (and thus should replace) state-provided services.

3. I am indebted to Robert Stephens of Victoria University in Wellington, New Zealand, for these data.

4. The data are drawn from the regular Statistics New Zealand publications titled "Incomes." Since the methods used are not identical to those of the Luxembourg Income Study, Stephens recalculates them using the LIS criteria with very similar results for the years in question: .264, .316, and .331. (The possible minimum Gini is 0.0, i.e., all income equally distributed; the possible maximum is 1.0, i.e., all income going to the 10 percent of households receiving the most income.)

5. Rapid growth in the mid-1980s slowed considerably between 1988 and 1992, when the economy again took off. According to *The Economist* (15 May 1999: 114), by 1996, growth had again descended to the OECD average, and, in 1998, hit by the Asian crisis, to well below it. Unemployment averaged just under 7 percent in this period. Inflation has been brought under control, but New Zealand has not managed to overcome its traditional current account imbalance.

6. "With the further advantages of a mild climate, marvellous scenic beauty, low population density, and a lifestyle centred around outdoor recreation, the inhabitants of 'God's Own Country' understandably believed that they enjoyed the best quality of life on the globe" (Nagel 1998: 227).

7. It had been as high as 66 percent under the Muldoon government.

8. Administrators were hired and fired based on performance, and under detailed fixed-term contracts. A radically different system of financial management and accountability was instituted, requiring audited annual departmental financial statements and reports under parliamentary scrutiny.

9. A good summary of changes in the public service is in Gregory 1998.

10. A means test was applied to the universal government pension, reducing social security spending by 1 percent of GDP. The governance of schools was transferred to parent-elected boards and funding based on a per capita formula. Healthcare user fees for the wealthiest third supplemented public financing.

11. The act guaranteed employees "the freedom to choose with whom, and within what structures, they associate."

12. A useful comparison can be drawn with their equally determined Australian confrere during the same period, Paul Keating, who was inhibited by the federal structure, and the PR-elected Senate elected under a quasi-proportional system, from instituting key aspects of similar radical transformations he sought (see Easton and Gerritsen 1995). For example, Keating tried to introduce a New Zealand–style GST but was unsuccessful. It was only in June 1999 that the center-right coalition succeeded in doing so, but only through a compromise with the center-left Democrats, who held the balance of power in the Senate.

13. "What we have is a picture of dedicated long-service employees with ordinary social backgrounds . . . [an] unlikely . . . remote and superior power-seeking cabal" (Gregory 1998: 17).

14. From a 1948 publication by Leslie Lipson, New Zealand's first professor of political science, cited by Gregory (1998: 12).

15. We saw evidence of this fact in chapter 5 in the comparatively high proportion of New Zealanders surveyed who could name their MPs and identify their parties.

16. New Zealand averages 85.2 percent in the IDEA tables of turnout of age-eligible voters between 1945 and 1997, well ahead of the major Westminster countries, the U.K. (75.3), Canada (69.2), and even Australia with its compulsory voting (84.4 percent). Only tiny Iceland has a higher average among democratic countries with no compulsory voting (IDEA 1997: 22–23).

17. Note that New Zealand's relative ranking in the charts using voting turnout based on municipal elections is slightly lower than it would be on national turnout. Yet despite the relative weakness of local government in New Zealand, local turnout level in recent elections is quite respectable at 52 percent, above the other Westminster countries.

18. And it is the latter two characteristics that are most significant in explaining the former (Vowles et al. 1995: 141–47).

19. The United States and Canada followed at 56 percent. Combining this score with its literacy, longevity, and GDP per capita, Crafts places New Zealand first in its HDI level that year—above second place Australia.

20. Of the five metropolitan dailies, with over half the total circulation between them, only one is owned by New Zealanders; three are owned by Rupert Murdoch (McGregor, Fountaine, and Comrie 2000).

21. In contrast, the percentage of New Zealanders who say that they regularly read a newspaper climbed to over 90 percent in 1990, having dropped to 85 in the 1980s (Levine and Roberts 1998). This suggests that economic changes had led some people to replace buying newspapers with reading them in libraries and elsewhere. The high self-reported figure also reflects the traditional cultural expectations placed on being politically informed while the changes in circulation, unfortunately, likely signal a more profound change in media consumption patterns.

22. I suspect this has something to do with New Zealanders' lifestyle, with its stress on long walks through unspoiled natural environments.

23. As we can see in appendix III, New Zealand, at US$78 in 1993, follows only the United States and Japan in television advertising spending per capita—a reality easily perceptible to the viewer, with commercial interruptions that frequently exceed fifteen minutes per hour. "I now leave for England with a new set of desires: to watch a 90 minute film on TV in one and a half hours instead of two . . ." (Smith 1996: 152).

24. There is limited government funding available to support the production of public-interest programs, or programs reflecting the needs of minorities, the Maori in particular. But such programs are limited in their impact. Overall, New Zealand television is a showcase for the neoconservative principle that markets should dictate production and distribution of all commodities and services. The assumption that media information should be treated as any other commodity is in stark opposition to the views of the mainly conservative founders of broadcasting systems in Britain, New Zealand, Australia, and Canada.

25. I have not been able to find information about possible changes in adult civics or other aspects of education that may have affected civic literacy. However, the IALS figures comparing those over and under thirty-five suggest something did change.

26. Turnout went up 3 percent in 1993 (when the election coincided with a referendum on MMP) to 79.6 percent (of VAP), and again (to 82.9 percent) in the first MMP election in 1996.

27. "Electoral reform would never have captured public attention if not for the anger that followed the radical economic reforms of the Lange-Palmer Labour government of 1984–90 and their acceleration under, combined with the broken promises of, the Bolger-led National government of 1990–93" (Aimer 1999: 148).

28. The coalition program agreed on in 1996 by National and New Zealand First illustrates the potential consensual effects of MMP. Though there were clear limits on government intervention due to fiscal constraints, the coalition was prepared to use the state to address the specific needs of groups, and no rhetoric about the best thing being for government to move out of the way.

29. These unmet expectations were effectively exploited by opponents of MMP. See, for example, Graeme Hunt's (1999) no-holds-barred-attack on MMP, which he terms "the electoral disaster of the century."

30. In the polls commissioned by the Electoral Commission of New Zealand, the sample was broken down into two groups: the "politically versed," both knowledgeable and interested in politics, and the "politically uninterested," who are neither. The politically versed were significantly more likely to agree that under MMP sensible decisions will be made, and to reject the idea that it hardly matters which party is in power. Furthermore, they did not share the views of the politically uninterested that, under MMP, the economy will often be unstable, that politicians won't be interested in the average person, and that one person's vote won't make much difference.

31. In 1993 the election was held simultaneously with the referendum on electoral system reform, while 1996 witnessed an effective campaign to inform voters about the changes entailed by MMP.

32. This seems to be the case in comparison to Germany, where a substantial number of voters appear to continue to misunderstand the complexities of MMP (Jesse 1998).

33. The survey was conducted by the New Zealand Politics Group at Victoria University (Levine and Roberts 1998: 186). McRobie identified sixteen (of the sixty-five) electorates where the winning candidate ran more than 30 percentage points ahead of his or her party, concluding it to be a "clear indication that large numbers of voters took the opportunity to cast their constituency vote for a preferred

candidate regardless of party, and to cast their party vote for their preferred party" (1998: 175). The votes cast for the two parties for which polls showed support to be close to the 5 percent threshold are also indicative of strategic voting. The Christian Coalition received 1.55 percent of constituency votes and 4.33 percent of party votes, and ACT 3.75 and 6.1 percent respectively. (In fact, over one-fifth of the 3.75 percent of constituency votes won by ACT were highly strategic. They went to leader Richard Prebble, enabling him to win Wellington Centre, thereby guaranteeing ACT its overall share of the seats—even if its party vote had fallen under the threshold, which polls showed to be a distinct possibility.)

34. NZF split in 1998 when Peters was fired for opposing government policy and took more than half of NZF's caucus out of the coalition, leaving National to rule as a minority government, relying on minor parties and independent solo MPs to stay in power (see Nagel 1999).

35. Nagel (1999) argues persuasively that, in fact, the dissatisfaction stemmed not from MMP's not having delivered on the claims made for it by its advocates but from its not having lived up to inappropriate expectations.

36. Miller (1999: 25) cites the cases of two women MPs who resigned during the term having been worn down by the "brutalizing nature of the business of politics." Ironically, though not surprisingly given the prevailing media ethos, doing the commenting were typically the same journalists who, out of habit as well as commercial imperative, played up and—thus—encouraged traditional rivalry and partisanship.

37. Perhaps as much overseas as at home: in the debate over British electoral reforms proposed by the Jenkins Commission report late in 1998, the "failure" of PR in New Zealand was trumpeted by the Conservatives and others opposed to changing the Westminster system.

38. Richard Prebble, leader of the neoconservative ACT Party, wrote in his 1999 book *I've Been Writing*, that "voters have made a good job of MMP, 'it's the politicians that have made a hash of it. . . . People are not prepared to go back to a Parliament dominated by middle-class white males'" (from a review in the *Christchurch News*, 21 July 1999).

39. The law adopting MMP stipulated that it would be used for at least two elections followed by parliamentary review. Among changes proposed in advance of that review is the reduction of the number of MPs from 120 to 99 (Miller 1999).

40. The 1999 election saw a reduction in the opposition to MMP (Vowles 2000). One factor is the reduced role for Winston Peters and the NZF, which made it into the second MMP Parliament only because Peters won his own seat. More recently, the directors of the NZES, Jack Vowles and Peter Aimer, in an article in the *New Zealand Herald* (29 December 2000), agreed that "opinions about "MMP are still divided, with a solid core of New Zealanders opposed, and many others uncertain." They noted further that "although support for MMP has softened since 1996, strong opposition to it has also declined . . . respondents who agreed that we should 'get rid of' MMP fell from 40 per cent in July 1998 . . . to 29 per cent immediately after the [1999] election. . . . By far the largest body of electors—from 49 to 51 per cent since July 1998—agree that 'it is too soon to tell' whether MMP has been 'a disaster' or 'a success.' . . . The NZES data thus depict a public in which a preference for outcomes consistent with the proportional representation of MMP continues to have an edge over those consistent with FPP."

41. Beyond quantitative representation there is a qualitative dimension apparent to this Canadian observer. In Canada, most native leaders insist that Canada is not their country. When they participate in political institutions, it is mainly to redress historical grievances and win self-government. In contrast, in New Zealand, the predominant position expressed by Maori leaders was to welcome their opportunity to contribute to making decisions for the good of all New Zealanders, and whatever else one can say about the first MMP Parliament, it was one in which Maori legislators were very much present.

42. We know that voters to the left of Labour turned out in significantly greater numbers (Karp and Banducci 1998).

43. The 1992 ISSP Survey, which compared the views of people in eleven industrial democracies on aspects of social equality, found only 17 percent of New Zealanders agree that large income differences are needed for the country's prosperity. This was the second lowest, behind Canada (16 percent) and tied with Norway. Moreover, when it came to the question of whether the government has a responsibility to reduce income disparity, 53 percent of New Zealanders agreed, above not only Americans (at 39 percent) but also Australians and Canadians (Pammett and Frizell 1996, 174, 176). This may be reflected in figures provided by *The Economist* (8 May 1999, Survey: 14): New Zealand chief executives are still underpaid by the standards of other Western countries including Australia. Kiwi CEOs come in last —after Germany and Sweden— in a 1997 survey of ten countries.

44. "Whereas in 1987/88 the Treasury's expenditure on consultants was 5.8 percent of its total expenditure. . . . The average for the years 1989/90 to 1996/97 was 39.1%. Contractualised outsourcing of a wide range of goods and services, including policy advice, has rapidly blurred the state's institutional shape. . . . Chief executives are free to play the labour market in controlling staff appointments in their agencies, under the terms of the Employment Contracts Act 1991, which effectively removed collective bargaining and introduced individual contracts negotiated between the employer and employee, in both the public and private sectors. . . . What may now be emerging in new Zealand is a group of top public servants who inhabit rather remote policy ministries that are increasingly divorced from the real experiences of the communities they are meant to serve" (Gregory 1998: 13).

45. The administrative relationship between central and sublevels of government I have in mind would be like that in Scandinavia. A good analysis of that relationship and why it avoids the "joint-decision trap" inherent in federal systems is to be found in Blom-Hansen 1999.

46. The 1999 election strengthened the position of MMP (Vowles 2000). The new government, which was formed only a week after the election, is composed of a coalition between Labour and the Alliance (and supported by the Greens), based on a short and clear agreement that was made public well before the election. One of its first acts was to make it impossible for list-elected candidates to change parties, a practice the abuse of which in the previous Parliament subjected MMP to much criticism.

47. The 1996 MMP election essentially ignored the question of commercialization of the airwaves. Labor favored a slight reduction in the dependency of the major publicly owned channel (Channel One) on advertising. National's program said nothing, though it was known that some leading figures supported the neoconservative ACT Party's demand for privatization of Channels One and Two.

The left-wing Alliance program called for eliminating all commercials from TV1. It was the commitment of NZF to get the time allocated per hour to TV commercials reduced slightly that found its way into the policies of the new government. The issue seems also to have been neglected in the 1999 campaign.

Chapter 11. Economic Outcomes: Combining Growth and Fair Distribution

1. This is not to assert that such attitudes are necessarily justified. *The Economist* (10 April 1999: 17), which is editorially highly sympathetic to the American economic model, notes that growth per capita from 1989 to 1998 in the United States was no faster than in Japan, and actually slightly slower than in Germany – once the effects of unification are taken into account.

2. The term *welfare state* is used here in its Anglo-American and not continental European sense, that is, it has to do with outcomes rather than the fact that such outcomes are attained through state programs. The term *sustainable welfare state* owes its origins to environmentalists who stress that economic growth must be in harmony with the ecosystem to be durable. Similarly, to be sustainable, the redistributive outcomes of the welfare state must be in harmony with the institutional structures of the society.

3. We use the latter measure below, but the pattern is similar. Just as figure 11–3 shows with relation to social spending (OECD 1999: 252), overall state spending figures for the 1980s and 1990s indicate Sweden and Denmark were highest, followed by the rest of northern Europe, France, and Italy, while the United States was lowest, preceded by the other English-speaking countries and Japan.

4. These include a tendency to overvalue military and weapons production, underestimate environmental costs, and ignore the state of national assets and infrastructures (Henderson 1996). GDP measures, for example, tell us nothing about the efforts that go into waste recycling. According to the UN *Human Development Report* UNDP (1999: 209), the recycling rate for paper, cardboard, and glass between 1992 and 1995 was over 70 percent for the German-speaking countries and the Netherlands, roughly 60 percent for the Nordic countries, and approximately 30 percent for the Anglo-American countries.

5. We should note that this is a decade during which the generous welfare states were especially vulnerable – compared to what came before and after.

6. The exceptions are low-Gini Austria and high-Gini Ireland, for which the most recent data are from 1987. There is no reason whatsoever to believe that mid-1990s data for these two countries would in any meaningful way affect the comparative rankings.

7. In 1998, *Challenge* magazine published an excerpt from the 1997 report of the UN Conference on Trade and Development, which examines the effects of income distribution on capital accumulation and growth. The excerpt—which concentrates on various channels through which personal and functional income distributions influence savings, investment, and growth—concludes that a more equal distribution of income can enhance growth ("Income Distribution, Capital Accumulation, and Growth," Challenge 41: 61–80).

8. Danish policy makers were especially innovative in their approach, winning support from the trade unions in efforts to make labor markets more flexible. Eschewing American terms like "workfare" as loaded, they developed their own terminology. For example, welfare state policies were referred to as providing a trampoline rather than a safety net (Torfing 1999).

9. This relative decline in labor productivity, he argues, is due to the overly large dependence in Sweden on the state both for employment and for transfers. According to his calculations (Lindbeck 1997: 23), the ratio of tax-financed to market-financed individuals in Sweden went from 0.382 in 1960 to 1.51 in 1990 and rose (due to increased unemployment) to 1.83 in 1995.

10. An earlier version of the Korpi article (1996) provoked a debate among economists. Australian economist Steve Dorwick (1996: 1778–79) concluded the debate with the suggestion that "there is a stiff challenge for the proponents of the 'lagging behind' thesis . . . to explain why Swedish GDP performance was consistently reasonable for forty years and only shows a marked decline after 1990."

11. Note that the lower the Gini, the greater the redistributiveness. This means that scattergrams in this chapter that link Gini scores with other measures related to redistributiveness will have the appearance of inverse relationships.

12. Figure 11–3 uses gross total social expenditure data, taken directly from the OECD's standard measure of public spending on or related to pensions, unemployment insurance, and disability and sickness benefits as well as to public health and social services (Adema 1999). Yet, if an effort is made to calculate "net" social expenditure taking into account the taxes governments place on these benefits as well as the fact that some governments require private companies to provide sick pay and workers' compensation and offer tax incentives for privately provided pensions, the picture changes considerably. In "The Growing Role of Private Social Benefits," an OECD working paper summarized in *The Economist* (24 October 1998: S8), Adema and Einerhand compare the relative positions of countries on gross versus net public expenditures. They note that Sweden's 19 percent lead over the United States (36 versus 17 percent of GDP—as in figure 11–3) in gross public expenditures shrinks to 2.5 percent when using net current public expenditure and adjusting net public benefits for the net value of these government-fostered private benefits. On the other hand, if we were to include public spending on education, child care, and so forth under social spending, it would again bring up Sweden's lead.

13. Household income is a total in which different weights are assigned to the income of the first adult and the remaining members of the family.

14. While the Gini figures are the best such data available to us, they are not perfect, and sometimes, as in the case of France, Germany, and Italy, have to be recalculated. Note that Austrian data are not really comparable, since they exclude income from self-employment (see Smeeding 1996). More generally, like any one measure used for aggregate comparisons, Gini figures tend to make some countries look better than if other measures were used. For example, under the formula used, which ignores noncash benefits, expenditures on consumption taxes, and employers' contributions to social security while treating redistributive expenditures across the life cycle as if they were transfers from the rich to the poor, Australia looks more unequal than is justified (Whiteford 1998). Nevertheless, observers

who make this point tend to agree that, overall, these are minimized in the method used by the LIS (see Atkinson, Rainwater, and Smeeding 1995).

15. Given Belgium's notoriously high level of public debt (116 percent of GDP in 1998, second only to Italy among OECD countries—OECD 1999: 258), it might not be unfair to suggest that its high Gini rests in part on involuntary redistribution from future generations.

16. Ginis provide only snapshot figures that ignore the effect of economic mobility. However, recent studies show that low inequality need not mean low mobility, as is often assumed. Björklund and Jantti (1997), using comparable samples of fathers and sons, show Sweden's level of intergenerational mobility is probably higher than that of the United States (see also Björklund and Jantti 2000). And, using different methodology, Åberge et al. (1998) find that even when the accounting period for income is extended up to eleven years (1980–90), when compared with the four Scandinavian countries, the United States remains "by far the most unequal." And an intriguing recent study finds a significantly lower correlation in the earnings of brothers in Scandinavia than in the United States (Björklund et al. 2000).

17. New Gini figures from the LIS for the Netherlands (released after the charts went to print) show that the Gini has risen to Canadian levels.

18. The American data are from the Panel Study of Income Dynamics (PSID), based on panel surveys from 1983 to 1992 for about 32,000 respondents. The German Socio-Economic Panel (GSOEP) goes from 1985 to 1994, with about 26,000 respondents on file. The Dutch Socio-Economic Panel (SEP) uses results of the panel surveys from 1983 to 1994, with a similar number of respondents.

19. And clearly to those inequalities affecting children. A UNESCO study of child poverty in rich countries (reported in the *Toronto Globe and Mail*, 13 June 2000: 1) on the proportion of children in families with income at less than 50 percent of the median placed the four Nordic nations lowest followed by the Netherlands, France, and Germany. The English-speaking countries and Italy had the highest proportions.

20. If one limits gender-based inequalities to the public sector, the gap between the Scandinavian and English-speaking countries widens. In Sweden, for example, in 1997, 46 percent of members of the boards of agencies in the national government and 40 percent in the regional governments were women (Furst 1999: 66).

21. We are not discussing extreme forms of inegalitarianism and egalitarianism, both of which are impediments to efficiency. We know, for example, that income inequality, as measured by the multiple of the incomes of the richest to the poorest 20 percent of households, was lowest in the fastest-growing industrializing economies of the 1980s and highest in the slowest growing ones (*The Economist*, 16 November 1991: Survey 17–19).

22. See Milner 1994: 114–30. For an analysis of the relationship between consensualism in political institutions and corporatism, see Lijphart and Crepaz 1991 and Vergunst 1999.

23. There are no data available for Ireland. The U.K., Canada, and United States are included; but Kenworthy gives each a score of zero. (Note that in order to make the bars in figure 11–7 comparable, I have multiplied Kenworthy's score—of 0 to 9 for each country—by 10.)

24. The logic of the U-shaped curve is that societies at middle levels of corporatism, with labor markets dominated by medium-size institutions with sufficient market power to win concessions but small enough to pass most of the cost of added inflation onto others, end up with the worst performance (Rowthorn 1992; Calmförs and Drifill 1988; Freeman 1988).

25. Switzerland might be a candidate for this category but constitutes a special case for many reasons having to do with the effects of unique institutions, such as relatively autonomous local governments and direct democracy.

26. This latter group is small since individuals who are risk takers for themselves can nonetheless generally be expected to seek to reduce risk once the well-being of dependents and descendents is at stake. (Hence immense sums of money are "wasted" on insurance policies.)

27. For a discussion of the relevance of rational choice theory to comparative politics, see Milner 1996a.

28. The most recent figures (to 1993) show that only the Nordic countries (and, to a lesser extent, Belgium) are increasing in union density (Lange and Scruggs 1997: table 5).

Chapter 12. Civic Literacy and the Foundations of the Sustainable Welfare State in Sweden

1. Support for the welfare state is not uncritical, however. For example, Ervasti concludes from Finnish data that there is significant criticism of the welfare state not only in the middle but even among the lower class. But he concludes that even for the former, most criticism is "constructive rather than disruptive: people would like to see the welfare state improved where they see problems in it" (Ervasti 1998: 297).

2. See the discussion of the discussion groups in the nineteenth century temperance movement in Västerbotten in chapter 9. I attempted, in an earlier work, to summarize key inherited values (Milner 1989: 46–57).

3. That success was, of course, due to more than good policies. Sweden no doubt benefited from its neutrality during World War Two. Yet historical context is not an ample explanation. The Finnish SWS, which started from significantly lower levels of literacy, schooling, and GDP per capita (Crafts 1997: 306–7), took much longer to develop than the Swedish one due in large part to Finland's harsh wartime and post-war experience. Nonetheless, it did develop (See Milner 1994: 171–81), attaining—as we have seen—perhaps the highest levels of civic literacy and economic equality.

4. As active SAP intellectuals, they addressed the plight of children in many of their writings in the 1930s and 1940s, as well as on prominent government commissions, seeing their ideas put into effect in such reforms as maternity allowances and rent and mortgage-interest subsidies for families with children. Their proposals proved especially influential as they drew on prevailing fears that the declining birthrate threatened the survival of the Swedish nation. They opposed cash transfers, fearing that ignorant parents might divert resources from meeting the real needs of their children. Incentives had to be carefully structured

through in-kind transfers reinforced by regulations such as those that restricted rent subsidies to lodgings deemed large enough for the recipient family (Tilton 1994: 156).

5. A study comparing the attitudes of workers in the same industries in Canada in the early 1990s bears out Rehn's expectation that well-informed people would place their interests in the context of policies that favor long-term, wider economic improvement. Half the Canadian respondents but only 39 percent of the Swedes expressed sympathy for the idea of resisting technological change, while 53 percent of Canadians and only 44 percent Swedes favoured policies that attempt to protect home markets (van den Berg, Furåker, and Johanssen 1997: 176–78.)

6. Because of this, the sine qua non of EU membership for the labor movement was maintaining the transparency guarantees of Swedish institutions and, as we shall see in the concluding chapter, winning greater transparency within EU institutions themselves.

7. Culture in this context is not just "high culture," the arts and so forth, but also popular culture, including communications-related policies.

8. So close was their relationship that Rehn preferred that the model bearing his name be referred to as the Rehn-Meidner model.

9. For example, according to the LO newspaper Fack in 1975, the funds "deprive capital owners of their ownership," without which "we can never fundamentally alter society and carry through economic democracy" (cited in Heclo and Madsen 1987: 298).

10. Though he never criticized his old comrade publicly. Privately—to the author among others—Rehn disassociated himself from the funds and lamented that the entire episode had played into the hands of anticorporatist forces among the employers.

11. These are policies that, in Esping-Andersen's terms, decommodified workers, constituting a further victory over markets.

12. In the 1970s, the average annual wage drift (local wage rises above the centrally set levels) in manufacturing was over 40 percent of the total wage increases for blue-collar workers, and about 20 percent for white-collar workers; in the 1980s, it rose to nearly 50 percent for both categories (Elvander and Holmlund 1998).

13. The research consisted of a survey of personnel directors of 180 Swedish manufacturing firms, employing 40 percent of the sector's employees.

14. "The high degree of integration and close ties between central, industrial and local levels characteristic of the Norwegian model have enabled it to display considerable adaptability. . . . The most likely scenario seems to be a process of cautious adjustment and decentralization, closely controlled by the central actors" (Dolvik and Støkke 1998: 141–42).

15. In Finland, "continuity is still the strongest feature. . . . Contacts and implicit understandings . . . can be used as the social 'infrastructure' for consensual policy making at the national level" (Lilya 1998: 187; see also Bobacka 1999).

16. Useful comparisons can also be drawn with Austria, the Netherlands, Germany, Ireland, and Belgium (see relevant articles in Ferner and Hyman 1998; also Wood 1997).

Chapter 13. Civic Literacy and the Sustainable Welfare State

1. See Olson 1990. In particular, Olson attributes Sweden's performance to its embracing free trade and thus inhibiting implicit redistributions to powerful interest groups through tariffs and other forms of protectionism. The economic gain to be realized from trade liberalization is probably the most important shared conviction of professional economists.

2. One trivial example is the "op-ed" page of the national newspaper in societies like Sweden, where it is read by "everyone." Sweden's internationally acclaimed economists, Knut Wicksell, Gustav Cassell, Eli Heckscher, Gunnar Mydal, and Bertil Ohlin, regularly wrote such columns. It has been calculated that Cassel published 1,500 such pieces and Ohlin 2,100 (Carlsson, Orrje, and Wadensjö 2000).

3. An interesting study of Illinois residents suggests that, in the United States at least, there is a relationship between ignorance and attitudes toward redistributive policies. Kuklinski et al. (1998: 144–45) "found that many people had systematically inaccurate factual beliefs (for example, they grossly overestimated the payments received by a typical family) . . . with an overall bias toward beliefs that one would expect to be associated with negative views about welfare. . . . People held their beliefs confidently . . .[and] these beliefs are strongly linked to policy preferences in the expected ways." A clear inference was to be drawn: "to the extent that factual beliefs shape policy preferences, misinformation biases aggregate preferences against welfare."

4. In 1998, once again, the leaders in per capita foreign aid were Denmark, Norway and Sweden (*The Economist*, 3 June 1999: 93). When only aid to the poorest countries is considered, those three countries are even further above the OECD average (UNDP 1998).

5. In his comparative study of tax evasion, Lewis (1982: 153–54) concludes: "Tax ethics are negatively and significantly correlated with a general distrust of other people and the suspicion that others cheat; educational level, knowledge of fiscal matters and belief in perceived fairness of the tax burden are all positively correlated with tax ethics."

6. A parallel finding, using social capital based on American data, merits citing here. In a study testing for a relationship between income distribution, mortality, and social capital (distrust and participation in civic associations) in different American states, Kawachi and his colleagues found a strong relationship between income equality and per capita group membership and social trust. They found also that states with high social mistrust and low group membership had higher age-adjusted rates of mortality. . . . The coefficients for social trust remained highly statistically significant for total mortality, malignant neoplasms, infant mortality, and stroke. Per capita group membership was strongly inversely correlated with all-cause mortality. They conclude: "Social capital tends to be underproduced if left to the market. A major finding of this study (which needs to be confirmed in longitudinal studies) is that the size of the gap between the rich and the poor is powerfully and negatively related to level of investment in social capital. In other words, disinvestment in social capital appears to be one of the path-

ways through which growing income inequality exerts its effects on population-level mortality" (Kawachi et al. 1997: 1498).

7. In proceeding in this manner, I am not reducing human preferences to self-interest. Values matter, but the values of adults are not in themselves amenable to deliberate policy choices in democratic societies. What is amenable, apart from the incentives framing those interests, is the information actors bring to bear in making choices.

8. A recent American study found that "the voting rate of persons below the poverty line was 25% in 1992 . . . and of persons above the poverty line . . . was 65%" (Leighley and Nagler 2000: 1).

Chapter 14. Conclusion: The Future of the Sustainable Welfare State

1. Probably the most instructive case is Finland's rapid and remarkable economic recovery during the 1990s. If Finland could so well overcome a potentially crippling market dislocation without sacrificing distributiveness, there is good reason to expect the Nordic SWS to prove resilient in the face of the forces of globalization.

2. As Björklund tentatively concludes in his (1998: 75–76) study on income distribution in Sweden: "Sweden has been able to retain its position . . . as one of the four or five countries with the most equal distributions of annual income . . . [with no less] long run equality and . . . equality of opportunity."

3. Streeck (2000: 1) usefully describes the process of globalization as one under which "higher competitiveness forces firms to eliminate slack with the result that the distribution of primary incomes is increasingly determined by market forces, and the capacity of governments to tax their economies declines; yet, at the same time, the responsibility for protecting social cohesion is more than ever turned over from the sphere of production to the political sphere, so that modern welfare states [must become] . . . both leaner and more redistributive." According to an exhaustive survey of what is known on the subject, "at least as of the mid-1990s, the data simply do not support the argument that globalization is producing policy convergence" (Hoberg, Banting, and Simeon 1999: 44). A similar conclusion is reached in a comprehensive analysis of the Nordic countries (Swank 1999; see also Kuhnle 2000).

4. Using responses to the most recent wave (1995–1998) of the World Values Survey, Inglehart (1999) finds Sweden to be highest among sixty-five countries in such self-expression (as opposed to "survival") values, followed by the Netherlands (Inglehart 1999).

5. The phenomenon is far less acute than in the Netherlands (De Hart and Dekker 1999).

6. In contrast to other countries, all Swedish elections take place on the same day every four years. After the 1998 election the government named a "minister for democracy" mandated to propose reforms to foster enhanced democratic participation. In February 2000 the commission published its thirteen-volume report, which analyzes every aspect of the situation, calling, notably, for local elections being held on separate days from national ones. One of the arguments heard by the commission was that the greater difficulties apparently experienced by parties in attracting

local volunteers in 1998 (and thus, perhaps, voter support) is a manifestation of the long-term effect on local party organizations of moving back to four-year terms without having local elections halfway through. Sweden moved from three- to four-year terms only in 1990 but did not at that point adopt its neighbors' (and its own, before 1970) system of staggering state and local elections.

7. In the United States only 21 percent of those aged eighteen to twenty-nine (down from 49 percent in the early 1970s) say they read a daily newspaper (Putnam 2000: 219).

8. Budget-cutting efforts by network administrators, which would reduce resources and thus the impressive depth of television news coverage, have so far been successfully resisted. (This information comes from personal communications from Hans Bergström, editor of *Dagens Nyheter,* and Bengt Nordström, who is responsible for monitoring audience magnitude for SVT.)

9. Dramatic differences were found between the public (SV1 and SV2) and private channels in the proportion of information versus entertainment-oriented programs, and in the variety of sources. Though, as a rule, the private (cable) channels offered largely "top ten" music shows and American sitcoms and films, the most popular (and terrestrial) channel, TV4, fell halfway between them and the high-variety, high-information public channels. (The study was reported on in an article by Kent Asp in *Dagens Nyheter* on 13 October 1999: A4.)

10. As a result, during the 1990s, many public and independent schools assumed quite distinctive characters, for example, stressing music, languages, or environmental studies. A number of municipalities encourage parents to take advantage of this right by issuing vouchers. The number of independent schools rose from 63 in 1990 to 238 in 1996. They are concentrated in the three major cities, and (in 1997) attracted 2.7 percent of primary-level students and 3.1 percent of secondary-level students (Lidström, forthcoming).

11. In Sweden as a whole 4.6 percent of all educational institutions were run by nonstate bodies in 1998; in that year, the Board of Education received 272 applications for such schools (Schartau 2000).

12. New Zealand's libertarian-oriented ACT, in its 1996 program, cited the Swedish example as the one to follow. Its spokespersons seemed to be unaware, however (and horrified when so informed by the author), that independent schools cannot charge fees to supplement the vouchers.

13. Sweden appears to be taking the lead with a government plan to extend broadband networks to rural areas so that, by 2005, 95 percent of Swedes would have access.

14. It is titled "Measuring Information Society" and was prepared by INRA Europe in March 1999.

15. From what we know of Finland from chapter 10, Finland's low level (by Nordic standards) of home use is compensated for by access through employment or institutional membership. The Eurobarometer study does not provide a breakdown by country, but overall, 40 percent of Europeans have PCs and 13.3 percent have Internet access at work, compared to 30 percent and 8.3 percent at home.

16. Finland places more emphasis on access to Internet connection outside the home. This has proven to be a successful strategy. We know that, for example, Finland led all other countries with Internet connections (in January 1999), with

107 per thousand inhabitants (this is calculated mechanically on the basis of the country code shown in the network address, an approach that entails a number of uncertainty factors—source: http://www.tieke.fi, Network Wizards), despite the fact that it placed third (fourth if one includes Iceland) in Internet users per capita after Sweden and the United States (GlobeNews, winter 2000: Globenews@kahl.net). (A similar ranking placed Norway just after Sweden, and Australia before Finland—Norris 2000: 10).

17. Another question asked about interest in and willingness to pay for access to electronic information on products such as videos, music, CDs, books, computer software, or computer hardware. Again, countries of the northern European states had the highest levels of interest in this subject: Sweden (49.5%), the Netherlands (48.2), Finland (44.7), and Denmark (39.2)—as well as Ireland (41.9).

18. The Swedes were second highest (60 percent compared to 62 percent for Britain), followed fairly closely by the Danes and Finns (with 53 and 52 percent) to identify only with their country. Finland is an especially interesting case. It is a member of the European Monetary Union, and, from all reports, its representatives in Brussels are more effective than the more ambivalent Swedes and Danes. This is because, I suggest, European integration holds the least danger to Finnish identity, and hence institutions and outcomes. Only 1 percent of Finns identified themselves as exclusively Europeans in Eurobarometer #50, below even Sweden, Denmark and the U.K., with 2, 3, and 5 percent respectively.

19. See, for example, figure 4–1 in chapter 4.

20. For example, to the question posed in Eurobarometer #50 as to whether respondents were for or against European Monetary Union, in Sweden, Denmark, and Finland 90 to 94 percent expressed an opinion, compared to only 84 percent in Britain. An analysis of the high level of Nordic EU knowledge is to be found in Schemeil 1997.

21. Eurobarometer #51 (B12) found 31 percent of both Swedish and Danish respondents to be "very attached" to Europe (second only to the Luxembourgers).

22. Sten Johansson, who led the "NO-to-EU" campaign among Swedish Social Democrats in 1994, represented more than just no voters when he stressed that something quite intangible was threatened by EU membership, "a common language, culture and media as being prerequisites for 'living democracy'" (cited in Aylott 1995).

23. The project is embodied in efforts to turn the European Parliament into a powerful legislative body with the commission responsible to it. They would agree with eminent democratic theorist Robert Dahl's characterization as "fanciful" expectations that the European Parliament could be as responsive to citizens as national parliaments (Dahl 1994: 32–33).

24. Furthermore, membership can alter incentives so as to promote optimal policy decisions. In an economic confederation there is a potential payoff for informing the electorate of existing constraints and for fostering institutional arrangements that do so. An economic confederation can be a means by which the parties impose rules on each other that change the nature of the game. The existence of these rules and the establishment of institutions to apply and enforce them—the commission and court in the case of the European Union—result in a net benefit for each party. With the source of external constraints clearly identified, national leaders

have less political incentive for advancing unrealistic policies. They can instead credibly identify constraints imposed at the level of the union as reflections of the facts of global economic life, facts that can therefore not be altered by "throwing the bums out" at the ballot box. Rather than supporting candidates promising to protect existing jobs and industries with tariffs and subsidies, voters may thus, if given the alternative, turn to parties proposing compensating measures the effect of which would be to move labor and investment toward advancing sectors.

25. They are also working toward integration into a "social-democratic Europe." This however is to imagine that rhetorical solidarity emanating from a Brussels-based "wide and well co-ordinated brotherly network" (Klausen 1991: 12–13) translates into policy outputs.

26. In its "warning to governments" of June 8, 1996, the new, pretentiously named *Forum permanent de la société civile*, a coalition of eighty Euro-federalist groups, denounced their governments who "keep putting forward the archaic conception of 'national interests'" and called for "intensifying . . . the legislative role of the European Parliament, the only institution elected by direct universal suffrage, [as] . . . the first step towards a real democracy."

27. In the European Post-1989 Election Survey in Eurobarometer #31A, only 16 percent of respondents credited the campaign with bringing out differences between the parties on European matters.

28. Such concerns are understandably less salient in the larger, more elitist and consociational societies of Europe than in Scandinavia. But they are not limited to Scandinavia. One concrete manifestation of the elite-mass distinction is in the very poor fit between the highly pro-European Monetary Union views of EP members and the distinctly mixed views of citizens (Schmitt 1999).

29. "The Finnish government's . . . point of departure is that the Union's character as an association of states should be preserved" (Government of Finland 1996: 24): 24; "The Swedish government's starting point is that the EU would continue to develop a community of independent states to which some decision-making power may be transferred, so that common goals may be more easily achieved" (Government of Sweden 1996: 13).

30. Sweden waited only three months after entering the European Union to join in the Danish-led push for removing the veil of secrecy from European Union institutions. The Finns took a similar position, stressing access to documents. The attitude toward transparency is a good illustration of the above-noted difference between the political culture prevailing in the European Union and in Scandinavia. As Gronbech-Jensen (1999) puts it, transparency in the European Union does not mean what it means in Scandinavia, that is, the citizen's right of access to the same documents seen by the politicians. In the EU, it is taken as an obligation to communicate with the public and facilitate access to politicians by organized interests.

31. As far as the Danes are concerned, it was only when transparency in council activities was guaranteed that they were willing to reconsider the Maastricht treaty they had previously rejected by referendum. Such transparency makes it possible to ensure Danish representatives on council are answerable to the Danish Parliament, and, in particular, the all-party parliamentary Market Committee discussed in chapter 8.

32. See, for example, the *International Herald-Tribune* (6 September 1999). The latest estimate cited by *The Economist* (30 September 2000: 142) is that the CEOs of the largest firms earned 475 times the income of the average employee, compared to 11–24 times for European bosses. "Between the late 1970s and the mid 1990s . . . on average, incomes of the richest fifth of families increased by 30 percent . . . in sharp contrast, incomes of the poorest fifth of families with children decreased in 44 states in this period. . . . In the late 1970s, there was no state where the richest families had average incomes ten or more times larger than those of the poorest families. By the mid-1990s, 30 states had "top-to-bottom" ratios of 10 or greater. . . ." ("Pulling Apart: A State-by-State Analysis of Income Trends by the Center on Budget and Policy Priorities. 16 December 1997: http://chpp.org/pa-rel.htm).

33. The 1990 *National Geographic* survey found that proportionately more Swedes than Americans had a roughly accurate picture of the U.S. population. Benjamin J. Stein, a man who conducts focus groups in Los Angeles, told E. D. Hirsch (1988: 6) that he had "not yet found one single student . . . in either college or high school, who [knew] when World War II was fought . . . when World War I was fought . . . when the American Civil War was fought. . . . Only two could tell me where Chicago is, even in the vaguest terms."

34. This was from a 42.0 to a 52.2 percentage point difference. Bucy (2000) investigated 1998 Internet use poll data for South Carolina and Indiana. As expected, income, education, age, and family structure proved important determinants of Internet access and use, portending an information gap between those with access and those without.

35. "American workers received one day of paid vacation time for each 23.9 days of work in 1996, as compared to one for every 22.4 days of work in 1987. . . . [At] 10 days of annual paid vacation received by the average entry-level worker, . . . the United States ranked dead last among a sample of 13 industrial nations" (Frank 1999: 51). These numbers suggest that the pressures of extra work compound the effects of income inequality to explain why Americans live two to three years less than people in other wealthy countries (UNDP 1999: 168).

36. In Canada, average annual working hours declined from 1,784 to 1,732 and in the U.K. from 1,775 to 1,731. Larger drops were recorded on the Continent, bringing France to 1,656, Germany 1,559, Sweden 1,552, and Norway, lowest, to 1,399 (*Key Indicators of the Labour Market: 1999 Trends*, ILO, September 1999).

37. A study comparing voters and nonvoters in the 1996 U.S. presidential elections found that 33 percent of those with incomes under thirty thousand dollars voted, compared to 60 percent for those with incomes above that amount (Dopplet and Shearer 1999: 18).

38. The data are for 1995. The percentages not covered are: Wisconsin 7.3, Minnesota 8.0, Northand North Dakota 8.3. Source: U.S. Bureau of the Census, *State and Metropolitan Area Data Book*, 1997–98, table A-11.

39. See, for example, Shaw 1999.

40. The data are for 1997 and are from the *2000 World Development Indicators* (354), published by the World Bank.

41. In their analysis of levels and cycles of poverty, Kangas and Palme (1998) find that unlike the U.K. and Australia, Canada's welfare state has moved further from the American "liberal" model and closer to the Nordic one in recent decades, especially

in its approach to pensions. One reflection of this difference is in a study by Phipps (1999), who compared very specific measures of social distress in children. She found that, when it came to infant mortality, and low birth weights, but not levels of anxiety or accident proneness, Canada was closer to Norway than to the United States.

42. "The record of the 1980s and early 1990s offers only limited support for the proposition that closer economic integration of Canada and the United States necessitates social policy convergence. . . . Change was not driving both societies more firmly towards a single model of the welfare state. The most prominent pattern in many sectors is divergence, and it is arguable that the Canadian and American welfare states were more different in the early 1990s than they were in the late 1970s" (Banting 1996: VII 46–47).

43. But, as we can see in appendix III, Canada is fifth in TV viewing and seventh in TV-advertising spending per capita.

44. An October 1999 report of the Quebec Superior Council of Education revealed that 42 percent of boys and 29 percent of girls left school without completing their secondary education (though roughly half of these do return to school later on). The Quebec figures appear to be only slightly worse than the Canadian average. (Education being a matter of provincial jurisdiction, available statistics are provincial.)

45. I argue (Milner 2000) that this is misleading, essentially because it places far too much weight on the average number of years spent in university education.

46. One indicator of Canada's low level is to be found in a 1988 Gallup poll that reported that only 31 percent of respondents could name a *single* cabinet minister four years after the Mulroney government had come to power. Only 5 percent could identify Don Mazankowski, deputy prime minister, perhaps the most powerful member of the cabinet (Savoie 2000).

47. The subtitling would be used mainly in French-language Quebec, where the low IALS score indicates it is most needed.

48. The United States reduced its public television funding by 4.7 percent, while it went up slightly in France, Japan, Germany, and Britain. This leaves Canadian public television with 16 percent of revenues from state funds compared to 32 percent for Germany, 34 for Italy, 25 for France, 23 for Japan, and 21 for the U.K. The information comes from a study for the OECD by the Centre d'études sur les médias at Laval University, reported in *Le Devoir* (10 August 1999).

49. With its openness to corporate donations and its loopholes on disclosing their sources, Canada's restrictions place it halfway between the wide-open United States and the highly regulated Scandinavia portrayed in chapter 8.

50. The effect of FPTP on parties and politics following the results of recent Canadian elections are discussed in Milner 1999.

51. Canada's failure to make certain obvious institutional changes, such as eliminating or democratizing its Upper House (whose members are appointed by the prime minister), is largely due to the fact that such changes—at least symbolically—threaten the relative positions of linguistic and regional communities.

52. Using data from the 1991 World Values Survey, Johnston and Soroka (1999) found Quebeckers lower in organizational memberships and interpersonal trust but higher in political trust than the rest of Canada.

53. I have calculated from 1999 circulation figures provided by the Canadian Newspaper Association on its website that there are roughly 13 daily newspapers

circulated for every hundred Quebeckers. This compares with 16.6 for Canada as a whole (in 1995, from figure 7.2). Francophone Quebeckers on average (in 1993) watched 26 weekly hours of television, compared to 22 for Anglo-Quebeckers, the same number as for Canadians as a whole (*International Television and Video Almanac*, Quigley Publishing Company, New York, 1996: 681). It should be added that a much greater proportion of French-language television is locally produced, suggesting that these often high-quality, popular programs contribute more to civic literacy than the American programming that dominates English-language television viewing.

54. Contemporary Quebec schools more than hold their own—except that we must keep in mind the high dropout rate. The IALS disparity more than disappears if we look only at the products of the current educational system, that is, those sixteen to twenty-five years old. And Quebec students do better than students in Canada as a whole in the TIMMS math and science tests (see Statistics Canada 1999).

Appendix IV. A Survey of New Zealand Candidates

1. For a more detailed discussion, see Milner 1998b.

2. The high rate of response from a group that included many of the country's leading politicians reflected New Zealand political culture. There proved to be no obvious overrepresentation by party or region among the respondents. Of the sixty-five electorates (constituencies) in the 1996 election, only four had two candidates among the forty-eight. The forty-eight were reasonably representative of the candidates by gender, by party, by winners and losers, and by the relative wealth and density of the electorates in which they ran.

3. Additional data were drawn from published documents providing detailed information on the sixty-five electorates (constituencies).

4. The scoring is based on the distance between the two responses, with maxima of plus and minus six: a respondent who categorized the voters as extremely interested in 1993 and not at all interested in 1996 would have a 1993 interest score of −6, while a respondent who categorized the voters as extremely knowledgeable in 1996 and not at all knowledgeable in 1990 would have a 1990 knowledge score of +6. A score of zero indicates no change.

5. This was confirmed by responses to the question in Aimer's study asking how they voted in the 1993 electoral-system referendum. Of the forty-eight respondents, twenty-six stated favoring FPTP, and only fourteen MMP.

6. The most statistically significant factor, not unexpectedly, turned out to be the candidates' feelings about MMP: of the fourteen who stated having voted for MMP in the 1993 referendum, none saw a deterioration in the knowledgeability of the voters since that time. It would have been interesting to pose a similar set of questions to these actors two or three years later, when the shine on MMP had—deservedly or not—faded, to see if their retrospective judgments would have been different as well.

References

Aarts, Kees, and Holli Semetko. 2000. "The Divided Electorate: Effects of the Campaign and Media Use on Political Involvement." Presented at the ECPR joint sessions, Copenhagen, April.

Åberge, Rolf, et al. 1998. *Income Inequality and Income Mobility in the Scandinavian Countries Compared to the United States*. Stockholm: SOFI.

Abrial, Stéphanie, and Fabienne Greffet. 1997. "La Satisfaction à l'égard de la Démocratie," in Pierre Bréchon and Bruno Cautrés, eds., *Les Enquêtes Eurobaromètriques: Analyse Comparée des données socio-politiques*. Paris: L'Harmattan.

AC Direct. 1999. *Västerbotten County in the Information Society: Strategy and Action Plan, 1999–2006*. Umeå.: Västerbotten County Council.

Adema, Willem. 1999. "Net Social Expenditure." OECD Directorate for Education, Employment, and Social Affairs, Occasional Paper #39, Paris.

Agell, Jonas, and Per Lundborg. 1993. *"Theories of Unemployment: Survey Evidence from Swedish Manufacturing Firms."* Stockholm: IUI.

Aimer, Peter. 1999. "From Westminster Plurality to Continental Proportionality: Electoral System Change in New Zealand," in Henry Milner, ed., *Making Every Vote Count: Reappraising Canada's Electoral System*. Peterborough: Broadview.

Aldrich, John. 1993. "Rational Choice and Turnout." *American Journal of Political Science* 37:246–78.

Alesky, Pamela D. 1998. "Public Opinion and Social Welfare Policy: A Comparison of the Role of Structural Determinants of Attitudes toward Social Inequality in Sweden and the United States." Presented at the American Political Science Association annual meeting, Boston, September.

Alford, R., and E. Lee. 1968. "Voting Turnout in American Cities." *American Political Science Review* 62:796–813.

Almond, Gabriel, and Sydney Verba. 1963. *The Civic Culture*. Princeton, N.J.: Princeton University Press.

Althaus, Scott L. 1998. "Information Effects in Collective Preferences." *American Political Science Review* 92:545–58.

———. 1998a. "Toward a Theory of Information Effects in Collective preferences." Presented at the American Political Science Association annual meeting, Boston, September.

Althaus, Scott L., and David Tewksbury. 1998. "Patterns of Internet and Traditional News Media Use in a Networked Community." Presented at the Midwest Political Science Association, Chicago, April.

Ambjörnsson, Ronny. 1987. *The Honest and Diligent Worker*, trans. by Donald Broady. Stockholm: HLS Förlag.

Amy, Douglas J. 1989. *Real Choices/New Voices*. New York: Columbia University Press.

Anderson, Christopher J. 1998. "When in Doubt, Use Proxies: Attitudes toward Domestic Politics and Support for European Integration." *Comparative Political Studies* 31:569–601.

Anderson, Christopher J., and C. A. Guillory. 1997. "Political Institutions and Satisfaction with Democracy: A Cross-National Analysis of Consensus and Majoritarian Systems." *American Political Science Review* 9:66–81.

Anderson, Christopher J., and Andrew LoTempio. 1999. "Winning, Losing, and Political Trust in America." Presented at the American Political Science Association annual meeting, Atlanta, September.

Angvik, Magne, and Bodo von Borries, eds. 1997. *Youth and History: A Comparative European Survey on Historical Consciousness and Political Attitudes among Adolescents.* Hamburg: Körber-Stiftung.

Ansolabehere, Stephen, and Shanto Iyengar. 1995. *Going Negative: How Attack Ads Shrink and Polarize the Electorate.* New York: Free Press.

Archer, K., R. Gibbins, R. Knopff, and L. Pal. 1995. *Parameters of Power, Canada's Political Institutions.* Toronto: Nelson.

Arseneau, Therese. 1999. "Electing Representative Legislatures: Lessons from New Zealand," in Henry Milner, ed., *Making Every Vote Count: Reappraising Canada's Electoral System.* Peterborough: Broadview.

Atkinson, A., L. Rainwater, and T. Smeeding 1995. *Income Distribution in OECD Countries: Evidence from the Luxembourg Income Study.* Paris: OECD.

Axberger, H-G. 1996. "Public Access to Official Documents." Current Sweden #414, Swedish Institute, Stockholm.

Aylott, Nicholas. 1995. "Why National Sovereignty Matters: Swedish Social Democrats and European Integration." Contemporary Political Studies, London: PSA.

Baker, John R., L. M. Bennett, S. E. Bennett, and R. S. Flickiger. 1996. "Citizens' Knowledge and Perceptions of Legislatures in Canada, Britain and the United States." *Journal of Legislative Studies* 2:44–62.

Banducci, Susan, Todd Donnovan, and Jeffrey Karp. 1997. "Citizen's Attitudes about Democracy after Electoral Reforms: Institutional Change in New Zealand." Presented at the 1997 Congress of the American Political Science Association, Washington, D.C.

Banting, Keith. 1996. "The Social Policy Divide: The Liberal Welfare State in Canada and the United States," in Keith Banting, George Hoberg, and Richard Simeon, eds., *Canada and the United States in a Changing Context.* Montreal: McGill-Queen's.

Barber, B. 1984. *Strong Democracy.* Berkeley: University of California Press.

———. 1993. "America Skips School: Why We Talk So Much about Education and Do So Little." *Harper's* 1722:39–47.

———. 1998. *A Place for Us: How to Make Society Civil and Democracy Strong.* New York: Farrar, Strauss.

Bartels, Larry M. 1996. "Uninformed Votes: Informational Effects in Presidential Elections." *American Journal of Political Science* 40:194–230.

Bean, Clive. 1989. "Orthodox Political Participation in Australia." *Australia and New Zealand Journal of Sociology* 25:451–79.

Belt, Todd, Ann Crigler, and Marion Just. 1998. "Campaign Effects and Candidate Appraisals: The Role of Emotions and Civic Attitudes." Presented at the American Political Science Association annual meeting, Boston, September.

Bennett, Stephen E. 1998. "Young People's Indifference to Media Coverage of Public Affairs." *PS* 31:539–42.

Bennett, Stephen E., et al. 1995. "The Impact of Mass Media Exposure on Citizens' Knowledge of Foreign Affairs: A Five Nation Study." Presented at the Annual Meeting of the American Political Science Association, Chicago, August.

Björklund, Anders. 1998. "Income Distribution in Sweden: What Is the Achievement of the Welfare State?" *Swedish Economic Policy Review* 5:39–80.

Björklund, Anders, and Marcus Jantti. 1997. "Intergenerational Mobility in Sweden Compared to the United States." *American Economic Review* 87: 5.

———. 2000. "Intergenerational Mobility of Socio-Economic Status in Comparative Perspective." *Nordic Journal of Political Economy* 26: 3–32.

Björklund, Anders, Marcus Jantti, Tor Eriksson, Raaum, Oddbjörn Raaum, and Eva Österbacka. 2000. "Brother Correlations in Earnings in Denmark, Finland, Norway and Sweden Compared to the United States." IZA Discussion Paper #158, Bonn.

Björklund, Tor. 1998. "The Norwegian Local Elections: A Protest Election with a Swing to the Right." *Scandinavian Political Studies* 13:211–34.

Black, J. H. 1991. "Reforming the Context of the Voting Process in Canada: Lessons from Other Democracies," in Herman Bakvis, ed., *Voter Turnout in Canada*. Research Study of the Canadian Royal Commission on Electoral Reform and Party Financing. Toronto: Dundurn Press.

Blais, André. 2000. *To vote or not to vote: The merits and limits of rational choice theory*. Pittsburgh, Pa.: University of Pittsburgh Press.

Blais, André, and R .K. Carty. 1990. "Does Proportional Representation Foster Voter Turnout?" *European Journal of Political Research* 18:179.

Blömgren, R. and A-M. Blömgren. 1999. "Broadcasting Policy in the Nordic Countries: Policy Networks, Institutions and Policy Design." Presented at the ECPR joint sessions. Mannheim, April.

Blom-Hansen, Jens. 1999. "Avoiding the Joint-Decision Trap: Lessons from Intergovernmental Relations in Scandinavia." *European Journal of Political Research* 25:1–18.

Blondel, J., R. Sinnott, and P. Svensson. 1997. "Representation and Voter Participation." *European Journal of Political Research* 32:243–72.

Bobacka, Roger. 1999. The Development of Working Hours Legislation in Finland in the 1990s—Concertation as Principle vs. Concertation in Practice." Presented at the ECPR joint sessions, Mannheim, April.

Bochert, Jens. 1995. "Of Everlasting Dreams and Distinctive Eras: The End of Social Democracy (as we know it)." Presented at the American Political Science Association annual meeting, Chicago, August.

Boiney, John. 1993. "You can fool all of the people . . . Evidence on the Capacity of Political Advertising to Mislead." Presented at the Congress of the American Political Science Association, Washington, D.C.

Bordasson, Throbjörn. 1996. *Television in Time: Research Images and Empirical Findings*. Lund, Sweden: Lund University Press.

Bowler, Shaun, Elisabeth Carter, and David M. Farrell. 2000. "Studying Electoral Institutions and Their Consequences: Electoral Systems and Electoral Laws." Presented at the International Political Science Association (IPSA) Conference, Québec, Canada, August.

Brant, Kees, and Peter Neijens. 1998. "The Infotainment of Politics." *Political Communication* 15:149–64.

Bréchon, Pierre. 1998. *La France aux Urnes: Cinquante Ans d'historie électorale*. Grenoble: Les Etudes de la documention Francaise.

Brehm, John, and Wendy Rahn. 1997. "Individual Level Evidence for the Causes and Consequences of Social Capital." *American Journal of Political Science* 41:888–1023.

Bridges, Amy. 1997. "Textbook Municipal Reform." *Urban Affairs Review* 33:97–119.

Bucy, E. Page. 2000. "Social Access to the Internet." *Harvard International Journal of Press/Politics* 5:1.

Butts, R. Freeman. 1980. "The Revival of Civic Learning: A Rationale for Citizenship Education in American Schools." Bloomington: Phi Delta Kappan Educational Foundation.

Calmförs, L., and E. J. Drifill. 1988. "Bargaining Structure, Corporatism and Macroeconomic Performance." *Economic Policy* 6:13–47.

Caldwell, Gary, and Paul Reed. 1999. "Civic Participation in Canada: Is Quebec Different?" *Inroads*, 8:215–22.

Carlsson, Benny, Helena Orrje, and Eskil Wadensjö. 2000. "Ohlins artikler: Register över Bertil Ohlins artiklar i Skandinaviska tidningar och tidskrifter 1919–1979." Stockholm: SOFI.

Carlsson, Ulla, and E. Harrie. 1997. *MedieSverige: Statistik och analys.* Göteborg: Nordicom.

Carty, R. K. 1991. *Political Parties in the Constituencies.* Research Study of the Canadian Royal Commission on Electoral Reform and Party Financing. Toronto: Dundurn Press.

Cassel, Carol, and Celia C. Lo. 1997. "Theories of Political Literacy." *Political Behavior* 19:317–35.

Civics Expert Group. 1994. *Whereas the People: Report of the Australian Commission on Civics and Citizenship.* Canberra: Australian Government Publishing Service.

Clark, Terry N. 1998. The International Mayor. Text attached to *FAUI* (Fiscal Austerity and Innovation Project) *Newsletter,* March 19.

Clark, Terry N. and Michael Rempel 1997. *Citizen Politics in Post-Industrial Society.* Boulder Colo. Westview.

Clayton, Richard, and Jonas Pontusson. 1998. "The New Politics of Welfare Revisited: Welfare Reforms, Public-Sector Restructuring and Inegalitarian Trends in Advanced Capitalist Societies." EUI Working Paper, Florence.

Cohen, Stephen S. 1993. "Geo-Economics: Lessons from America's Mistakes," in Martin Carnoy et. al., eds. *The New Global Economy in the Information Age.* University Park: Pennsylvania State University Press.

Coleman, James S. 1990. *Foundations of Social Theory.* Cambridge: Harvard University Press.

Converse, Philip E. 1964. "The Nature of Belief Systems in Mass Publics," in David Apter, ed., *Ideology and Discontent.* New York: Free Press.

Coulson, Tony. 1999. "Voter Turnout in Canada: Findings from the 1997 Canadian Election Study." *Electoral Insight* 1:18–22.

Crafts, N. F. R. 1997. "The Human Development Index and Changes in Standards of Living: Some Historical Conditions." *European Review of Economic History* 1:299–322.

Craig, S. C., and J. G. Kane. 1999. "Public Opinion and Direct Democracy." Presented at the Conference on Referendums in Liberal-Democratic Societies, Queens University, Kingston, Canada, May.

Crepaz, Markus. 1996. "Constitutional Structures and Regime Performance in 18 Industrialized Democracies: A Test of Olson's Hypothesis Engineering." *European Journal of Political Research* 29:87–104.

———. (1999). "Inclusion versus Exclusion: Political Institutions and Welfare Expenditures." *Comparative Politics* 31:61–80.

Curtice, John, and W. Phillips Shiveley. 2000. "Who Represents Us Best? One Member or Many?" presented at the 2000 International Political Science Association (IPSA) Conference, Québec, Canada, August.

Cusack, Thomas R. 1997. "Social Capital, Institutional Structures, and Democratic Performance: A Comparative Study of German Local Communities." WZB (Social Science Research Center), Berlin.

Dägre, Tor. 1989. "Norwegian Culture under International Pressure." Norwegian Information Service, Oslo.

Dahl, Robert, A. 1994. "A Democratic Dilemma: System Effectiveness versus Citizen Participation. *Political Science Quarterly*" 109:1.

Dalton, Russell. 1996. "Political Cleavages, Issues and Electoral Cleavages," in Leduc Lawrence, Richard Niemi, and Pippa Norris, eds. *Comparing Democracies: Elections and Voting in Global Perspective*. Thousand Oaks: Sage.

———. 1998. "Political Support in Advanced Industrial Democracies." Research Paper, Center for the Study of Democracy, University of California, Irvine.

Daniels, Norman, Bruce Kennedy, and Ichiro Kawachi. 2000. "Justice Is Good for Our Health." *Boston Review* 25, 1:4–10.

Darmofal, David. 1999. "Socioeconomic Bias in Turnout Decline: Do the Voters Remain the Same?" Presented at the American Political Science Association annual meeting, Atlanta, September.

De Bens, E., and H. Østbye. 1998. "The European Newspaper Market," in McQuail Denis and Karen Siune, eds., *Media Policy: Convergence, Concentration and Commerce*. London: Sage.

Defleur, M. L., L. Davenport, M. Cronin, and M. Defleur. 1992 "Audience Recall of News Stories Presented by Newspaper, Computer, Television, and Radio." *Journalism Quarterly* 69:1010–22.

De Hart, Joep, and Paul Dekker. 1999. "Civic Engagement and Volunteering in the Netherlands: a 'Putnamian' Analysis," in J. W. Van Deth, M. Maraffi, K. Newton, and P. Whiteley, eds. *Social Capital and European Democracy*. London: Routledge.

Dekker, Hank. 1999. "Citizenship Conceptions and Competencies in the Subject Matter 'Society' in Dutch Schools," in J. Torney-Purta, J. Schwille, and J-A. Amadeo, eds., *Civic Education across Countries: Twenty-four National Case Studies from the IEA Civic Education Project*. Amsterdam: Eburon-IEA.

Delli Carpini, Michael. 1993. "Measuring Political Knowledge: Putting First Things First." *Public Opinion Quarterly* 55:583–612.

———. 1996. *What Americans Know about Politics and Why It Matters*. New Haven, Conn. Yale University Press.

Delli Carpini, Michael, and Scott Keeter. 1995. "Political Knowledge and Enlightened Group Interests." Presented at the 1995 Congress of the American Political Science Association, Chicago.

Denver, David, and Gordon Hands. 1990. "Does Studying Politics Make a Difference? The Political Knowledge, Attitudes and Perceptions of School Students." *British Journal of Political Science* 20:263–78.

Dimock, Michael A. 1998. "Political Knowledge and the Political Environment: Reassessing Trends in Partisanship, 1960–1996." Presented at the American Political Science Association annual meeting, Boston, September.

Dolvik, J-E, and T. A. Støkke. 1998. "Norway: The Revival of Centralized Concertation," in Anthony Ferner and Richard Hyman, eds., *Changing Industrial Relations in Europe*. Malden, Mass. Blackwell.

Dopplet, Jack, and Ellen Shearer. 1999. *Nonvoters: America's No-Shows*. Thousand Oaks: Sage.

Douglas, Roger. 1993. *Unfinished Business*. Auckland: Random House.

Downs, Anthony J. 1957. *An Economic Theory of Democracy*. New York: Harper.

Dowrick, Steve. 1996. "Swedish Economic Performance and Swedish Economic Debate: A View from the Outside." *The Economic Journal* 106:1772–79.

Eagles, Monroe. 1991. "Voting and Non-voting in Canadian Federal Elections: An Ecological Analysis," in Herman, Bakvis, ed., *Voter Turnout in Canada*. Research Study of the Canadian Royal Commission on Electoral Reform and Party Financing. Toronto: Dundurn Press.

Easterlin, Richard A., and Eileen M. Crimmins. 1991. "Private Materialism, Personal Self-Fulfillment, Family Life, and Public Interest." *Public Opinion Quarterly* 55:499–533.

Easton, Brian, and Rolf Gerritsen. 1995. "Economic Reform: Parallels and Divergences," in Frances Castles, Rolf Gerritsen, and Jack Vowles, eds., *The Great Experiment: Labour Parties and Public Policy Transformation in Australia and New Zealand*. Auckland: Auckland University Press.

Edlund, Jonas. 1999. "Trust in Government and Welfare Regimes: Attitudes to Redistribution and Financial Cheating in the United States and Norway. *European Journal of Political Research* 35:341–70.

Eklund, Klas. 2001. "Gösta Rehn and the Swedish Model: Did We Follow the Rehn-Meidner Model Too Little Rather Than Too Much?" in H. Milner and E. Wadensjö, eds., *Gösta Rehn and the Swedish Model at Home and Abroad*. Aldershot, U.K.: Ashgate.

Eldersveld, S. J., L. Strömberg, and W. Derksen. 1995. *Local Elites in Western Democracies*. Boulder, Colo.: Westview.

Elley, W.B., and A. Schleicher. 1994. "International Differences in Achievement Levels," in W. B. Elley, ed., *The IEA Study of Reading Literacy: Achievement and Instruction in Thirty-two School Systems*. Wheaton, Exeter, U.K.: Pergamon.

Elvander, Nils, and Bertil Holmlund. 1998. *The Swedish Bargaining System in the Melting Pot: Institution, Norms and Outcomes*. Stockholm: Arbetslivsinstitutet.

ENPA (European Newspaper Publishers' Association). 1996. *Europa Liest Zeitung*. Brussels: ENPA.

———. 1997. *From Child to Citizen*. Brussels: ENPA.

Entman, Robert. 1989. *Democracy without Citizens: Media and the Decay of American Politics*. Oxford: Oxford University Press.

Ervasti, Heikki. 1998. "Civil Criticism and the Welfare State." *Scandinavian Journal of Social Welfare* 7:288–99.

Esping-Andersen, Gösta. 1985. *Politics against Markets*. Princeton: Princeton University Press.

Euromedia Research Group. 1997. *The Media in Western Europe: The Euromedia Handbook*. London: Sage.

Facorro, L. B., and M. L. Defleur. 1993. "A Cross-Cultural Experiment on How Well Audiences Remember News Stories from Newspaper, Computer, Television and Radio." *Journalism Quarterly* 70:585–601.

Fägerlind, Ingemar, and Lawrence Saha. 1983. *Education and National Development*. London: Pergamon.

Farell, David M. 1997. *Comparing Electoral Systems*. London: Harvester Wheatsheaf.

Ferner, Anthony, and Richard Hyman. 1998. *Changing industrial relations in Europe*. Malden, Mass. Blackwell.

Findahl, Olle. 1991. *Begreppet 'public service' i meiedebatten. Medianotiser #4*. Göteberg: Nordicom.

———. 1993. *Sverige elfte TV-val*. Umeå: Medier & Communication, University of Umeå.

Fiorina, Morris P. 1999. "Information and Rationality in Elections," in John A.

Ferejohn and J. A. Kuklinski, *Information and Democratic Processes*. Urbana: University of Illinois Press.

Fishkin, James. 1995. *The Voice of the People: Public Opinion and Democracy*, New Haven, Conn. Yale University Press.

Foley, Michael W., and Bob Edwards. 1998. "Is It Time to Disinvest in Social Capital?" Presented at the American Political Science Association annual meeting, Boston, September.

Frank, Robert. 1999. *Luxury Fever: Why Money Fails to Satisfy in an Era of Excess*. New York: Free Press.

Franklin, Mark N., 1996. "Electoral Participation," in Leduc Lawrence, Richard Niemi, and Pippa Norris, eds., *Comparing Democracies: Elections and Voting in Global Perspective*. Thousand Oaks: Sage.

Franklin, Mark N., C. Van der Eijk, and E. Oppenhuis. 1995. "The Motivational Basis of Electoral Participation: European Elections Provide a Crucial Test." Presented at the European Consortium for Political Research joint sessions, Bordeaux.

Franzese, Robert J., Jr. 2000. "Political Participation, Income Distribution, and Public Transfers in Developed Democracies." Presented at the American Political Science Association annual meeting, Washington, D.C., September.

Freeman, Richard. 1988. "Labor Market Institutions and Economic Performance." *Economic Policy*, no. 6:64–80.

Freeman, Richard, Birgitta Swedenborg, and Robert Topel. 1995. "Economic Troubles in Sweden's Welfare State," SNS Occasional Paper, Stockholm.

———. 1995. "The Limits of Wage Flexibility to Curing Unemployment." *Oxford Review of Economic Policy* 11:63–72.

Fritzell, Johan. 1999. "Changes in the Social Patterning of Living Conditions," in M. Kauto, M. Heikkilä, B. Hvinden, S. Marklund, and N. Ploug eds., *Nordic Social Policy: Changing Welfare States*. London: Routledge.

Fukuyama, Francis. 1995. "Social Capital and the Global Economy," *Foreign Affairs*, September/October 89–103.

———. 1995a. *Trust: The Social Virtues and the Creation of Prosperity*. New York: Free Press.

Furst, Gunilla. 1999. *Sweden: The Equal Way*. Stockholm: Swedish Institute.

Gabriel, Oscar W. 1995. Political Efficacy and Trust," in J. W. Van Deth and E. Scarborough, eds., *The Impact of Values*. Oxford: Oxford University Press.

Galston, William. 1991. *Liberal Purposes: Goods, Virtues, and Diversity in the Liberal State*. New York: Cambridge University Press.

Gans, Curtis. 1993. "Television: Political Participation's Enemy #1," *Spectrum: The Journal of State Government* Lexington 66:2.

Garrett, Geoffrey, and Christopher Way. 1994. "The Sectoral Composition of Trade Unions, Corporatism, and Economic Performance," Los Angeles: Center for German and European Studies, University of California.

Gerbner, G., and L. Gross. 1976. "The Scary World of TV's Heavy Watcher." *Psychology Today*, April.

Gerbner, G., L. Gross, M. Morgan, and N. Signorelli. 1986. "Living with Television: The Dynamics of the Cultivation Process," in J. Bryant and D. Zillman, eds., *Perspectives on Media Effects*, Hillsdale, N.J.: Laurence Erlbaum Assoc.

Gidlund, Gullan. 1991. "Public Investment in Swedish Democracy," in M.Wiberg, ed. *The Public Purse and Political Parties: Public Financing of Political Parties in Nordic Countries*. Helsinki: Finnish Political Science Association.

Gilliam, Franklin D., and Shanto Iyengar. 2000. "Prime Suspects: The Influence of Local Television News on the Viewing Public." *American Journal of Political Science* 44:3.

Gillyam, Mikael, and Sören Holmberg. 1995. *Väljarnas val.* Stockholm: Fritzes.

Ginsberg, Benjamin. 1982. *The Consequences of Consent: Election, Citizen Control, and Popular Acquiescence.* Reading, Mass.: Addison-Wesley.

Goldsmith, M. 1992. *Options for the Future—Local Democracy Abroad.* London: LGMB (Local Government Management Board).

Goldsmith, M. and K. Newton. 1986. "Aspects of Local Democracy," in *Report of Committee of Inquiry into the Conduct of Local Authority Business,* vol. 4. London: HMSO.

Goodin, Robert E., Bruce Headey, Ruud Muffels, and Henk-Jan Dirven. 1999. *The Real Worlds of Welfare Capitalism.* Cambridge: Cambridge University Press.

Gordon, Stacy B., and Gary M. Segura. 1997. "Cross-National Variation in the Political Sophistication of Individuals: Capability or Choice?" *Journal of Politics* 59:126–47.

Gottschalk, Peter, and Timothy Smeeding. 1996. "The International Evidence on Income Distribution in Modern Economies: Where Do We Stand?" in Michael Bruno and Yuset Mundlab, eds., *Contemporary Economic Development Reviewed.* London: MacMillan.

Government of Finland. 1996. "Finland's Points of Departure and Objectives at the 1996 Intergovernmental Conference." Report to the Parliament by the Council of State, 27.2.1996.

Government of Sweden. 1996. "The EU Intergovernmental Conference 1996." Government Report to the Parliament, 1995/96.

Granberg, Donald, and Sören Holmberg. 1986. "Political Perception Among Voters in Sweden and the U.S.: Analysis of Issues with Explicit Alternatives." *The Western Political Quarterly,* vol. 39.

———. 1988. *The Political System Matters: Social Psychology and Voting Behavior in Sweden and the United States.* Cambridge: Cambridge University Press.

Greeley, Andrew. 1997. "Coleman Revisited: Religious Structures as a Source of Social Capital." *American Behavioral Scientist* 40:587–94.

Green, Donald P., and Ian Shapiro. 1994. *Pathologies of Rational Choice Theory: A Critique of Applications in Political Science.* New Haven, Conn.: Yale University Press.

Gregory, Robert. 1998. "The Changing Face of the State in New Zealand: Rolling Back the Public Service?" Presented at the American Political Science Association annual meeting, Boston, September.

Grisold, Andrea. 1998. "Regulatory Reforms in the Media Sector: Small Countries and the Legend of the Free Market." Presented at the 10th SASE conference, Vienna.

Gronbech-Jensen. 1999. "The Scandinavian Tradition of Open Government and the European Union: Problems of Compatibility?" *Journal of European Public Policy* 5:185–99.

Gundelach, P., and L. Torpe. 1996. "Voluntary Associations: New Types of Involvement and Democracy." Paper presented to the ECPR joint sessions of workshops, Oslo, Norway.

Gunter, B., A. Furnham, and G. Gietson. 1984. "Memory for the News as a Function of the Channel of Communication." *Human Learning* 3:265–71.

Gwyn, Richard. 1997. "Rediscovering Our Citizenship." Toronto: Dominion Institute.

Haddow, Rodney. 2000. "The Variable Prospects for Corporatism in Canada." Presented at the meeting of the Canadian Political Science Association, Quebec City, July.

Hadenius, Stig, and Lennart Weibull. 1999. "The Swedish Newspaper System in the Late 1990s: Tradition and Transition." *Nordicom Review*, vol. 1.

Hahn, Carole L., ed. 1998. *Becoming Political: Comparative Perspectives on Citizenship Education*. Albany, N.Y.: SUNY Press.

———. 1999. "Challenges to Civic Education in the United States," in J. Torney-Purta, J. Schwille, and J-A. Amadeo. eds., *Civic Education across Countries: Twenty-four National Case Studies from the IEA Civic Education Project*. Amsterdam: Eburon-IEA.

Händle, Christa, Oesterreich Detlef, and Trommer Luitgard. 1999. "Concepts of Civic Education in Germany Based on a Survey of expert Opinion," in J. Torney-Purta, J. Schwille, and J-A. Amadeo. eds., *Civic Education across Countries: Twenty-four National Case Studies from the IEA Civic Education Project*. Amsterdam: Eburon-IEA.

Hao, Xiaoming. 1994. "Television Viewing among American Adults in the 1990s." Journal of Broadcasting and Electronic Media, 353–60.

Harris, Paul. 1998. "Changing New Zealand's Electoral System: Continuity or Crisis?" in Jonathan Boston, Stephen Levine, Elizabeth McLeay, and Nigel Roberts, eds., *Campaign to Coalition: the 1996 MMP Election*. Wellington: Dunsmore Press.

Hartley, Thomas, and Kenneth Dautrich. 1998. "Do Voters Learn More from the News Media, or Do Knowledgeable People Use News More?" Presented at the American Political Science Association annual meeting, Boston, September.

Heclo, Hugh, and Henrik Madsen. 1987. *Policy and Politics in Sweden: Principled Pragmatism*. Philadelphia. Temple University Press.

Heidenheimer, Arnold J., Hugh Heclo, and Carolyn Teich Adams. 1990. *Comparative Public Policy*. New York: St. Martin's Press.

Helliwell, J. F. 1996. "Do Borders Matter for Social Capital? Economic Growth and Civic Culture in US States and Canadian Provinces." Presented at the Canadian Economics Association, St. Catherines, Ontario, June.

———. 2000. "Globalization: Myths, Facts, and Consequences," Toronto: C. D. Howe Institute.

Henderson, Hazel. 1996. "What's Next in the Great Debate about Measuring Wealth and Progress?" *Challenge* 50, November–December.

Hepburn, Mary A. 1990. "Americans Glued to the Tube: Mass Media, Information, and Social Studies." *Social Education* April/May.

Herreros, Francisco, and Laura Morales. 2000. "Is It about Trust? A Reappraisal of Associational Participation and Social Capital." Presented at the ECPR joint sessions, Copenhagen, April.

Highton B., and R. E. Wolfinger. 1998. "Estimating the Effects of the National Voter Registration Act of 1993." *Political Behavior* 20:79–104.

Hirczy, Wolfgang. 1994. "The Impact of Mandatory Voting Laws on Turnout: A Quasi-Experimental Approach." *Electoral Studies* 13:64–76.

Hirsch, E. D. 1988. *Cultural Literacy*. New York: Vintage.

Hjellum, Torstein. 1967. The Politicization of Local Government: Rates of Change, Conditioning Factors, Effects on Political Culture. *Scandinavian Political Studies* 2:67–93.

Hoberg, George, Keith Banting, and Richard Simeon. 1999. "North American Integration and the Scope for Domestic Choice: Canada and Policy Sovereignty in a Globalized World." Presented at the meeting of the Association for Canadian Studies in the United States, Pittsburgh, Pa., November.

Hoefer, Richard. 1996. "Swedish Corporatism in Social Welfare Policy, 1986–1994: An Empirical Examination." *Scandinavian Political Studies*, vol. 19, no. 1.

Hoest, Sigurd. 1991. "The Norwegian Newspaper System, Structure and Development," in H. Roenning and K. Knulby eds., *Media and Communication*. Oslo: ISAF.

Hofferberg, R. I. 1994. "Parties, Policies, and Democracy: An Overview," in H. D. Klingemann, R. I. Hofferberg, and I. Budge, eds., *Parties, Policies, and Democracy*. Boulder, Colo.: Westview.

Hoffmann-Martinot, V., C. Rallings, and M. Thrasher. 1996. "Comparing Local Electoral Turnout in Great Britain and France: More Similarities than Differences?" *European Journal of Political Research* 30:241–57.

Hofrichter, Jurgen, and Michael Klein. 1993. *The European Parliament in the Eyes of EC Citizens*. Report on behalf of the European Parliament. Brussels: Directorate General III, Information and Public Relations.

Holloway, Steven. 1995. "Through a Glass Darkly: Documenting Assymetries in Neighbourly Knowledge," in the *Bulletin* of the Canadian Political Science Association, spring: 51–56.

Holmberg, Sören. 1999. "Down and Down We Go: Political Trust in Sweden," in Pippa Norris, ed., *Critical Citizens: Global Support for Democratic Governance*. Oxford: Oxford University Press.

Holtz-Bacha, Christina, and Lynda L. Kaid. 1995. "A Comparative Perspective on Political Advertising," in Christina Holtz-Bacha and Lynda L. Kaid, eds., *Political Advertising in Western Democracies*. Thousand Oaks: Sage.

Holtz-Bacha, Christina, and Pippa Norris. 2001. "To Entertain, Inform and Educate: Still the Role of Public Television?" *Political Communication* 19:123–40.

Hooghe, Marc, and Anton Derks. 1997. "Voluntary Associations and the Creation of Social Capital." Presented at the joint workshops of the ECPR, Bern, Switzerland.

Høst, Sigurd. 1999. "Newspaper Growth in the Television Era: The Norwegian Experience." *Nordicom Review*, vol. 1.

Howe, Paul. 2001. "The Sources of Campaign Intemperance." *Policy Options* January–February.

Hoynes, William. 1994. *Public Television for Sale*. Boulder, Colo.: Westview.

Hunt, Graeme. 1998. *Why MMP Must GO: The Case for Ditching the Electoral Disaster of the Century*. Auckland: Waddington Press.

Hunter, Susan, and Richard Brisbin. 2000. "The Impact of Service Learning on Democratic and Civic Values." *PS* 33:623–27.

IDEA (Institute for Democracy and Electoral Assistance). 1997. *Voter Turnout from 1945 to 1997: A Global Report on Political Participation*. Stockholm: International IDEA.

Inaba, Tetsuro. 1997. "How Japanese Get Political Information." Presented at the American Political Science Association annual meeting, Washington, D.C., September.

Inglehart, Ronald. 1990. *Culture Shift in Advanced Industrial Society*. Princeton: Princeton University Press.

———. 1997. *Modernization and Postmodernization: Cultural, Economic and Political Change in 43 Societies*. Princeton: Princeton University Press.

———. 1999. "Changing Values in the New Millenium: Challenges to Representative Democracy." Presented at the Conference on the Future of Representative Democracy, University of Umeå, Sweden, October.

Irvine, William. 1999. *Does Canada Need a New Electoral System?* Kingston: Institute of Intergovernmental Relations, Queen's University.

Iversen, Torben. 1999. *Contested Economic Institutions: The Politics of Macroeconomics and Wage Bargaining in Advanced Democracies.* Cambridge: Cambridge University Press.

Jackman, Robert W., and R. A. Miller. 1995. "Voter Turnout in Industrial Democracies during the 1980s." *Comparative Political Studies* 27:467–92.

———. 1996. "A Renaissance of Political Culture?" *American Journal of Political Science,* 40:632–59.

———. 1998. "Social Capital and Politics." *Annual Review of Politics* 1: 47–73.

Jahn, Detlef, and Anders Widfeldt. 1996. "European Union and its Aftermath in Sweden: Are the Swedes Fed Up with European Union Membership?" Contemporary Political Studies. London: PSA.

Jamieson, Kathleen Hall. 1996. "Scholarship and the Discourse of Election Campaigns." *Chronicle of Higher Education,* 22 November.

Jankowski, Richard. 1993. "Responsible, Irresponsible and Westminster Parties: A Theoretical and Empirical Evaluation." *British Journal of Political Science* 23:107–29.

Jenssen, A. T., and O. Listhaug. 1999. "Voters' Decisions in the Nordic EU Referendums of 1994." Presented at the Conference on Referendums in Liberal-Democratic Societies, Queens University, Kingston, Canada, May.

Jesse, E. 1988. "Split Voting in the Federal Republic of Germany: An Analysis of the Federal Elections from 1953 to 1987." *Electoral Studies* 7:109–24.

Jochem, Sven. 1998. "The Social-Democratic Full-Employment Model in Transition: The Scandinavian Experiences in the 80s and 90s." Presented at the 1998 joint workshops of the ECPR, Warwick UK.

———. 2001. Equality, Solidarity and the Welfare State: The Nordic Performance in Comparative Perspective," in H. Milner and E. Wadensjö, eds, *Gösta Rehn and the Swedish Model at Home and Abroad.* Aldershot, U.K.: Ashgate.

Johnston, Richard, and Stuart Soroka. 1999. "Social Capital in a Multicultural Society: The Case of Canada." Presented at the Canadian Political Science Association, Sherbrooke, Quebec, June.

Junn, Jane. 1991. "Participation and Political Knowledge," in *Political Participation and American Democracy.* New York: Greenwood.

———. 1995. "Participation in Liberal Democracy, What Citizens Learn from Political Activity." Presented at the American Political Science Association annual meeting, New York, N.Y.

Kaase, Max. 1999. "Interpersonal Trust, Political Trust and Non-institutionalised Political Participation." *West European Politics* 22:1–21.

Kajanoja, Jouko. 2000. "Social Capital—New Arguments for the Welfare State." Presented at the meeting of the Society for the Advancement of Socio-Economics (SASE), London, July.

Kangas, O., and V-M Ritakallio. 1995. "Different Methods, Different Results: Approaches to Multi-dimensional Poverty." Presented at the ISA Research Committee 19th Conference on Comparative Research on Welfare State Reforms, Pavia, Italy, April.

Kangas, O., and J. Palme. 1998. "Does Social Policy Matter? Poverty Cycles in OECD Countries." *Working Papers* #187, LIS.

Kaplan, Robert D. 1999. *An Empire Wilderness: Travels into America's Future.* New York: Vintage.

Karp, Jeffrey, and Susan Banducci. 1998. "The Impact of Proportional Representation on Turnout: Evidence from New Zealand." Presented at the Meeting of the Australasian Political Science Association, Christchurch, N.Z.

———. 1999. "The Impact of Proportional Representation on Turnout: Evidence from New Zealand." Presented at the meeting of the American Political Science Association, Atlanta, Georgia, September.

Karvonen, Lauri. 2000. "Preferential Voting: Does It Make a Difference?" Presented at the International Political Science Association (IPSA) conference, Québec, Canada, August.

Katz, R. S. 1980. *A Theory of Parties and Electoral Systems*. Baltimore: Johns Hopkins University Press.

Kawachi, Ichiro, Bruce P. Kennedy, and Kimberly Lochner. 1997. "Long Live Community: Social Capital as Public Health." *The American Prospect* 35:56–59.

Kawachi, Ichiro, Bruce P. Kennedy, Kimberly Lochner, and Deborah Prothrow-Stith. 1997. "Social Capital, Income Inequality, and Mortality." *American Journal of Public Health* 87:1491–98.

Kenworthy, Lane. 1995. "Equality and Efficiency: The Illusory Tradeoff." *European Journal of Political Research* 27:225–54.

———. 1996. *In Search of National Economic Success: Balancing Competition and Cooperation:* Thousand Oaks: Sage.

———. 1998. "Do Social-Welfare Policies Reduce Poverty? A Cross-national Assessment." Luxembourg. Working Paper #188, LIS.

Kinder, Donald R., and Donald O. Sears. 1985. "Public Opinion and Political Action," in G. Lindzey and E. Aronson, eds., *Handbook of Social Psychology*, Vol. 3. New York: Random House.

Kiss, Rosemary. 1999. "It's in the Mail: A VLGA Discussion Paper on Postal Voting," Victoria Local Governance Association, Melbourne.

Klausen, Jytte. 1991. "After Keynesianism: The Political Challenge of European Economic Integration to Social Democratic Labor Coalitions." Presented at the American Political Science Association annual meeting, Washington, D.C.

Korpi, Walter. 1978. *The Working Class in Welfare Capitalism*. London: Routledge and Kegan Paul.

———. 1996. "Eurosclerosis and the Sclerosis of Objectivity: On the Role of Values among Economic Policy Experts." *Economic Journal* 106:1727–46.

———. 1998. "Tro och vetande I debatten om Sveriges ekonomiska tillväxt: Samhällsvetenskapens objektivitetsproblem I åskådlig form. *Sociologisk Forskning* 2:41–72.

Koruda, Y., K. Zhou, and N. Yoshikawa. 1998. "Japanese Communitarianism and the Elimination of Poverty." Presented at the American Political Science Association annual meeting, Boston, Mass., September.

Krouwel, A. 1999. "The Selection of Parliamentary Candidates in Western Europe: The Paradox of Democracy." Presented at the ECPR joint sessions, Mannheim, April.

Kubey, Robert, and Mihaly Csikszentmihaly. 1990. *Television and the Quality of Life*. Hillsdale, N.J.: Lawrence Erlbaum.

Kuhnle, Stein. 2000. "The Scandinavian Welfare State in the 1990s: Challenged but Viable," *West European Politics* 23:209–28.

Kuklinski, James H., Paul J. Quirk, David W. Schwieder, and Robert F. Rich. 1998. "'Just the facts, ma'am': Political facts and public opinion." *Annals of the American Academy of Political and Social Science* 560:143–54.

Kushner, J., D. Seigel, and H. Stanwick. 1997. "Ontario Municipal Elections: Voting Trends and Determinants of Electoral Success in a Canadian Province." *Canadian Journal of Political Science*, vol. 20, no. 3.

Ladd, Everett. 1996. "A Vast Empirical Record Refutes the Idea of Civic Decline." *Public Perspective* 7:4.

Ladner, Andreas. 1991. "Direkte Demokratie auf kommunaler Ebene—die Beteiligung an Gemeindeversammlungen," in *Schweizerisches Jahrbuch für politische Wissenschaft* 31:63–86.

Ladner, Andreas, and Henry Milner. 1999. "Politicization, Electoral Institutions, and Voting Turnout: The Evidence from Swiss Communal Elections in Comparative Context." *Electoral Studies* 18:235–50.

Lambert, R. D., J. E. Curtis, B. J. Kay, and S. D. Brown. 1988. "The Social Sources of Political Knowledge." *Canadian Journal of Political Science* 21:359–75.

Lane, Jan-Erik. 1983. *Creating the University of Norrland: Goals, Structures and Outcomes.* Umeå: CWK Gleerup.

———. 1995. "The Decline of the Swedish Model." *Governance,* 8:579–90.

Lane, Jan-Erik, and Ersson, Svante. 1997. *Comparative Political Economy: A Developmental Approach.* London: Pinter.

Lange, Peter, and Lyle Scruggs. 1997. "Where Have All the Members Gone? Union Density in the Era of Globalization." Presented at the American Political Science Association annual meeting, Washington, D.C.

Lapham, L., M. Pollan, and E. Etheridge. 1987. *The Harper's Index Book.* New York: Henry Holt.

Leighley, Jan, and Jonathan Nagler. 2000. "Socioeconomic Class Bias in Turnout: Evidence from Aggregate Data." Presented at the American Political Science Association annual meeting, Washington, D.C., September.

Levine, Stephen, and Nigel Roberts. 1998. "Surveying the Snark: Voting Behavior in the 1996 New Zealand General Election," in Jonathan Boston, Stephen Levine, Elizabeth McLeay, and Nigel Roberts, eds., *Campaign to Coalition: The 1996 Election MMP Election.* Wellington: Dunsmore Press.

Lewis, Alan. 1982. *The Psychology of Taxation.* New York: St. Martin's.

Lidström, Anders. Forthcoming. "Swedish Education in Transition," in J. Richardson, ed., *Sweden: Consensual Governance under Pressure.* London: Edward Elgar.

Lijphart, Arend. 1984. *Democracies: Patterns of Majoritarian and Consensus Government in Twenty-one Countries.* New Haven, Conn.: Yale University Press.

———. 1994. *Electoral Systems and Party Systems: A Study of Twenty-seven Democracies, 1945–1990.* Oxford: Oxford University Press.

———. 1995. "Democracies: Forms, Performances, and Constitutional Engineering." *European Journal of Political Research* 25 1–18.

———. 1997. "Unequal Participation: Democracy's Unresolved Dilemma." *American Political Science Review* 91:1–14.

———. 1997a. "Dimensions of Democracy." *European Journal of Political Research* 31:195–203.

———. 1999. *Patterns of Democracy: Government Forms and Performances in Thirty-six countries.* New Haven, Conn. Yale University Press.

Lijphart, Arend, and M. Crepaz. 1991. "Cooperation and Consensus Democracy in Eighteen Countries: Conceptual and Empirical Linkages," *British Journal of Political Science* 21:235–46.

Lilya, Kari. 1998. "Finland: Continuity and Modest Moves toward Company Level Corporatism," in Anthony Ferner, and Richard Hyman, eds., *Changing Industrial Relations in Europe.* Malden, Mass.: Blackwell.

Lindbeck, Assar. 1995. "Hazardous Welfare State Dynamics." *American Economic Review* 85:9–15.

———. 1997. *The Swedish Experiment.* Stockholm: SNS Förlag.

Listhaug, O. 1995. "The Dynamics of Trust in Politicians," in H. D. Klingemann and D. Fuchs, eds., *Citizens and the State*. Oxford: Oxford University Press.

Listhaug, Ola, Bernt Aardal, and Ingunn O. Ellis. 2000. "Institutional Variation and Political Support: An Analysis of CSES Data from 16 Countries." Presented at the International Political Science Association (IPSA) conference, Québec, Canada, August.

LO (Swedish Trade-Union Confederation). 1995. "Swedish Economic Prospects." Stockholm.

Lundström, Tommy, and Filip Wijkström. 1998. *The Nonprofit Sector in Sweden*. Baltimore: Johns Hopkins University Press.

Lupia, Arthur. 1994. Shortcuts versus Encyclopedias: Information and Voting Behavior in California Insurance Reform Elections. *American Political Science Review* 88:63–76.

Lupia, Arthur, and Richard Johnston. 1999. "Voter Competence and Elite Manoeuvers in Public Referendums." Presented at the Conference on Referendums in Liberal-Democratic Societies, Queens University, Kingston, Canada, May.

Luskin, Robert C., and James S. Fishkin. 1998. "Deliberative Polling, Public Opinion and Democracy: The Case of the National Issues Convention." Presented at the American Political Science Association annual meeting, Boston, September.

Malmberg, Bo and Gerdt Sundstrom. 1996. "Age Care Crisis in Sweden." *Current Sweden #412*. Swedish Institute.

Mair, Peter. 1994. "Britain: Labour and Electoral Reform," in P. Anderson and P. Camiller eds., *Mapping the European Left*. London: Verso.

Marsh, Ian. 1995. *Beyond the Two Party System: Political Representation, Economic Competitiveness and Australian Politics*. Cambridge: Cambridge University Press.

———. 1995a. "Political Learning Disabilities of the Two-Party System (a Result of FFP) Has Inherent 'Disabilities' When It Comes to Policy Making Democratic Failure of Single-Party Government: the New Zealand Experience." *Australian Journal of Political Science* 30:40–60.

Martinez, Michael D., and David Hill. 1999. "Assessing the Impact of the National Voter Registration Act on Midterm Elections." Presented at the American Political Science Association annual meeting, Atlanta, September.

McAllister, Ian. 1998. "Civic Education and Political Knowledge in Australia." *Australian Journal of Political Science*. 33:7–24.

McAllister, Ian, and Malcolm Mackerras. 1998. "Compulsory Voting, Party Stability and Electoral Bias in Australia. Presented at the ECPR joint sessions,. Warwick, U.K., March.

McBride, Allan. 1998. "Television, Individualism, and Social Capital." *PS* 31: 542–52.

McCann, James A. 1998. "Electoral Participation and Local Community Activism: Spillover Effects, 1992–1996." Presented at the American Political Science Association annual meeting, Boston, September.

McGregor, Judy, Susan Fountaine, and Margie Comrie. 2000. "From Contest to Content: The Impact of Public Journalism on New Zealand Election Campaign Coverage." *Political Communication* 17:2.

McLeod, Douglas M., and Elizabeth M. Perse. 1994. "Direct and Indirect Effects of Socioeconomic Status on Public Affairs Knowledge." *Journalism Quarterly* 71:433–42.

McRobie, Alan. 1998. "Raw Statistics and Raw Facts: An Aggregate Analysis of the Results," in Jonathan Boston, Stephen Levine, Elizabeth McLeay, and Nigel Roberts, eds., *Campaign to Coalition: The 1996 Election MMP Election* Wellington: Dunsmore Press.

Mediebarometer. 1997. *Medienotiser*. Gothenburg: Nordicom.

Mediebarometer. 1998. *Medienotiser*. Gothenburg: Nordicom.

Mill, J. S. 1910. *Representative Government*. London: Dent and Sons.

Millard, William J. 1993. "International Public Opinion of the United Nations." *International Journal of Public Opinion* 5:92–99.

Miller, Arthur H., and Kent Asp. 1985. "Learning about Politics from the Media: A Comparative Study of Sweden and the United States," in Sidney Kraus and Richard M. Perloff. eds.,. *Mass Media and Political Thought on Information-Processing Approach*. Beverly Hills: Sage.

Miller, James. 2000. "An Unlikely Public Sphere: Constraints on Politics on the Internet." Presented at the International Political Science Association (IPSA) conference, Québec, Canada, August.

Miller, Raymond. 1999. "New Zealand and Scotland: Candidate Selection and the Impact of Electoral System Choice." Presented at the ECPR joint sessions, Mannheim, April.

Milner, Henry. 1989. *Sweden: Social Democracy in Practice*. Oxford: Oxford University Press.

———. 1994. *Social Democracy and Rational Choice: The Scandinavian Experience and Beyond*. London: Routledge.

———. 1994a. "Obstacles to Electoral Reform in Canada." *American Review of Canadian Studies* 24:39–55.

———. 1996. "The Welfare State as Rational Choice: Social Democracy in a Postsocialist World." *Scandinavian Political Studies*, vol. 19, no. 2.

———. 1996a. "Methodological Individualism and the U-Shaped Curve: Some Theoretical Guidelines for the Comparative Analysis of Public Policy," in L. M. Imbeau and R. D. McKinley, eds., *The Comparative Observation of Government Activity*. London: Macmillan.

———. 1997. "Electoral Systems, Integrated Institutions, and Turnout In Local and National Elections: Canada In Comparative Perspective." *Canadian Journal of Political Science* 30:89–106.

———. 1997a. "Institutions, Information and Values: Collective versus Individual Interest in the Swedish Welfare State," in Pauli Kettunen and Hanna Eskola, eds., *Models, Modernity and the Myrdals*. Helsinki:Renvall Institute, University of Helsinki.

———. 1998. "The Case for Proportional Representation in Canada." *Inroads* 7:39–51.

———. 1998a. "Politicization, Electoral Institutions, and Voting Turnout: The Evidence from Swiss Communal Elections in Comparative Context." Presented to the New Urban Politics: How Urban Politics are Changing workshop at the World Conference of the International Sociology Association, Montreal, July.

———. 1998b. "Political Institutions and Information: A Preliminary Analysis of the First New Zealand MMP Campaign," in Jonathan Boston, Stephen Levine, Elizabeth McLeay, and Nigel Roberts, eds., *Campaign to Coalition: the 1996 MMP Election*. Wellington: Dunsmore Press.

———. 2000. "Is Canada Really Number One? Civic Literacy and the Shaky Foundations of Canada's Welfare State." Presented at the Canadian Political Science Association annual meeting, Québec, July.

———, ed. 1999. *Making Every Vote Count: Reappraising Canada's Electoral System*. Peterborough: Broadview.

Mishra, Ramesh. 1999. *Globalization and the Welfare State*. London: Edward Elgar.

Morin, Richard. 1996. Tuned out, Turned off: Millions of Americans Know Little about How Their Goverment Works." *Washington Post National Weekly Edition*, February 5–11.

Morlan, Robert L. "Municipal vs. National Election Voter Turnout: Europe and the United States." *Political Science Quarterly* 99:457–70.

Myrdal, Alva, et al. 1971. *Towards Equality: The Alva Myrdal Report to the Swedish Social Democratic Party*. Stockholm: Prisma.

Myrdal, Gunnar. 1958. *Beyond the Welfare State*. London: Duckworth.

Nagel, Jack H. 1998. "Social Choice in a Pluralitarian Democracy: The Politics of Market Liberalization in New Zealand." *British Journal of Political Science* 28:223–67.

———. 1999. "The Defects of Its Virtues: New Zealand's Experience with MMP," in Henry Milner, ed., *Making Every Vote Count: Reappraising Canada's Electoral System*. Peterborough: Broadview.

NCES (National Center for Education Statistics). 1993. *Adult Literacy in America: A First Look at the Results of the National Adult Literacy Survey*. Washington: GPO.

Nehring, Neils Jurgen. 1992. "Parliamentary Control of the Executive," in Lise Lyck, ed., *Denmark and EC Membership Evaluated*. London: Pinter.

Newcomb, Horace. 1976. *Television: The Critical View*. New York: Oxford University Press.

Newton, Kenneth. 1997. "Social and Political Trust." Presented at the Conference on Confidence in Democratic Institutions, Washington, D.C. August 25–27.

———. 1997a. "Social Capital and Democracy." *American Behavioral Scientist* 40:575–86.

———. 1999. "Mass Media Effects: Mobilization or Media Malaise." *British Journal of Political Science* 29:577–99.

———. 1999a. "Social and Political Trust in Established Democracies," in Pippa Norris, ed., *Critical Citizens*. Oxford: Oxford University Press.

New Zealand Electoral Commission. 1994, 1995, 1996. *Quantitative Monitor*. Wellington, N.Z.: New Zealand Electoral Commission.

Nie, Norman H., Jane Junn, and Kenneth Stehl-Barry. 1996. *Education and Democratic Citizenship in America*. Chicago: University of Chicago Press.

Niemi, Richard, and Jane Junn. 1998. *Civic Education*. New Haven, Conn.: Yale University Press.

Nordberg, Karin. 1998. *Folkhemmets röst: Radion som folkbildare 1925–50*. Stockholm: Brutus Östlings Bokförlag Symposium.

Norris, Pippa. 1996. "Does Television Erode Social Capital?" *PS*, September, 474–80.

———. 2000. "The Worldwide Digital Divide." Presented at the PSA Annual Conference, London, April.

Norris, Pippa, J. Curtice, D. Sanders, M. Scammell, and H. Semetko. 1999. *On Message: Communicating the Campaign*. London: Sage.

OECD. 1982. *Advertising Aimed at Children*. Paris: OECD.

———. 1993. *Education at a Glance: OECD Indicators*. Paris: OECD.

———. 1994. "New Orientations in Social Policy." Social Policy Studies, no. 12. OECD, Paris.

———. 1994a. *Literacy, Economy and Society: Results from the International Adult Literacy Survey*. Paris: OECD.

———. 1996. *Lifelong Learning for All: Meeting of the Education Committee at Ministerial Level, 16–17 January 1996*. Paris: OECD.

———. 1997. *Literacy Skills for the Knowledge Society: Further Results from the International Adult Literacy Survey*. Paris: OECD.

———. 1997a. *Education at a Glance:* OECD Indicators. Paris: OECD.

———. 1998. *Human Capital Investment: An International Comparison*. Paris: OECD.

———. 1999. OECD Economic Outlook. Paris: OECD, June.

———. 2000. *Literacy in the Information Age: Final Report of the International Adult Literacy Survey*. Paris: OECD.

O'Guinn, Thomas C., and L. J. Shrum. 1991. "Mass-Mediated Social Reality: The Social Cognition and Ecology of Economic Norms." Presented at the SASE/IAREP conference, Stockholm, June.

Oliver, Leonard P. 1987. *Study Circles: Coming Together for Personal Growth and Social Change*. Washington, D.C.: Seven Locks.

Olson, Mancur. 1982. *Rise and Decline of Nations*. New Haven, Conn.: Yale University Press.

———. 1989. "Is Britain the Wave of the Future? How Ideas Affect Society." *LS. Quarterly* 3:279–304.

———. 1996. "The Varieties of Eurosclerosis: "The Rise and Decline of Nations since 1982," in N. Craft and G. Toniolo, eds., *Economic Growth in Europe*. Cambridge: Cambridge University Press.

———. 1996a. "Big Bills Left on the Sidewalk: Why Some Nations Are Rich, and Others Poor?" *Journal of Economic Perspectives* 10:3–24.

———. 1990. *How Bright Are the Northern Lights? Some Questions about Sweden*. Lund: Lund University Press.

Olsson, Ulf. 1994. "Planning in the Swedish Welfare State," in W. Clement and R. Mahon, eds., *Swedish Social Democracy: A Model in Transition*. Toronto: Scholar's Press.

Pacek, Alexander, and Benjamin Radcliff. 1995. "Turnout and the Vote for Left-of-Centre Parties: A Cross-national Analysis." *British Journal of Political Science* 25:137–43.

Pammett, John H., and Alan Frizell, eds. 1996. *Social Inequality in Canada*. Ottawa: Carleton University Press.

Parker, Kimberly, and Claudia Deane. 1997. "Ten Years of the Pew News Interest Index." Presented at the meeting of the American Association for Public Opinion Research.

Pederson, M. N. and L. Billie. 1991. "Public Financing and Public Control of Parties in Denmark," in M. Wiberg, ed., *The Public Purse and Political Parties: Public Financing of Political Parties in Nordic Countries*. Helsinki: Finnish Political Science Association.

Pekkarinen, J., M. Pohjola, B. Rowthorn, eds. 1992. *Social Corporatism: A Superior Economic System?* Oxford: Clarendon Press.

Pellikaan, Huib. 1998. "Rationality of Voter Turnout." Presented at the Society for the Advancement of Socioeconomics (SASE) annual meeting, Vienna, July.

Pestoff, Victor. 1999. "The Disappearance and Reappearance of Social Partnership in Sweden during the 1990s and Its Sudden Reappearance in late 1998." Presented at the ECPR joint sessions. Mannheim, April.

Petersson, Olof, et al. 1997. *Democracy across Borders*. Stockholm: SNS.

———. 1998. *Democrati och Medborgarskap*. Stockholm: SNS.

Pierre, Jon, Lars Svåsand, and Anders Widfeldt. 2000. "State Subsidies to Political Parties: Confronting Rhetoric with Reality." *West European Politics* 23:1–24.

Phipps, Shelley. 1999. The Well-Being of Young Canadian Children in International Perspective," LIS Working Paper #197, Luxembourg.

Pilati, Antonio. 1993. *Mind: Media Industry in Europe*. Milan: Mind Institute of Media Economics.

Popkin, Samuel, and Michael Dimock. 1999. "Political Knowledge and Citizen Competence," in S. Elkin and K. Soltan, eds., *Citizen Competence and Democratic Institutions*. University Park: University of Pennsylvania Press.

Postman, Neil, and Steve Powers. 1992. *How to Watch the TV News*. New York: Penguin.

Powell, G. Bingham, Jr. 1982. *Contemporary Democracies: Participation, Stability, and Violence*. Cambridge: Harvard University Press.

———. 1989. "Constitutional Design and Electoral System Control." *Journal of Theoretical Politics* 1:107–30.

———. 1996. "Political Responsiveness and Constitutional Design." Presented at the American Political Science Association, San Francisco.

Powell, G. Bingham, Jr., and George Vanberg. 1998. "Election Laws, Disproportionality and the Left-Right Dimension: Implications for Two Visions of Democracy." Presented at the Congress of the American Political Science Association, Boston.

Puro, Steven. 1998. "Gated Communities: A New kind of Community?" Presented at the Congress of the American Political Science Association, Boston.

Putnam, Robert. 1993. *Making Democracy Work*. Princeton: Princeton University Press.

———. 1994. "Bowling Alone: Democracy in America at the End of the Twentieth Century." Presented at the 1994 Nobel Symposium, Uppsala, Sweden.

———. 1995. "Tuning In, Tuning Out: The Strange Disappearance of Civic America." *PS*, December: 664–83.

———. 1995a. "Bowling Alone: America's Declining Social Capital." *Journal of Democracy* 6:65–78.

———. 1996. "The Strange Disappearance of Civic America," *Policy* 12:3–13 (first published in *American Prospect*, winter:34–48.

———. 2000. *Bowling Alone: The Collapse and Revival of American Community*. New York: Simon and Schuster.

Quesnel, Louise. 1998. "Le local dans la glace," in R. Boily, ed., *L'Année politique au Québec*. Montreal: Les Presses de l'Université de Montréal.

Quirk, Paul J. 1989. "The Cooperative Resolution of Policy Conflict." *American Political Science Review*, 83:905–21.

Rallings, Colin, and Michael Thrasher. 1998. "The Slow Death of a Governing Party: The Conservatives in Local Government 1979–97. Presented at the ECPR joint sessions, Warwick, U.K., March.

Reich, Robert. 1997. *Locked in the Cabinet*. New York: Knopf.

Reif, Karlheinz, and Hermann Schmitt. 1980. "Nine Second-Order National Elections: A Conceptual Framework for the Analysis of European Election Results." *European Journal of Political Research* 8: 3–44.

Richards, J. I. et al. 1998. "The Growing Commercialization of Schools," *Annals of the American Academy* 557:148–63.

Roberts, Nigel, and Stephen Levine. 1996. "Political Perceptions of the New Zealand News Media," in Judy McGregor, ed., *Dangerous Democracy? News Media Politics in New Zealand*. Auckland: The Dumore Press.

Rogowski, Ronald. 1987. "Trade and the Variety of Democratic Institutions." *International Organization* 41:203–04.

Rokkan, Stein, et. al. 1970. *Citizens, Elections, Parties*. New York: David McKay, 1970.

Rosenberg, Shawn. 1988. *Reason, Ideology, and Politics*. Cambridge: Polity.

Rosenstone, Steven. 1995. "Electoral Institutions and Democratic Choice." Presented at the workshops of the European Consortium on Political Research, Bordeaux, April.

Rosenstone, Stephen, and John M. Hansen. 1993. *Mobilization, Participation and Democracy in America*. New York: Macmillan.

Rothstein, Bo. 1998. "Social Capital in the Social Democratic State: The Swedish Model and Civil Society." Presented at the Conference of Europeanists, Baltimore, March.

Rowthorn, B. 1992. "Corporatism and Labor Market Performance," in J. Pekkarinen, M. Pohjola, and B. Rowthorn, eds., *Social Corporatism: A Superior Economic System?* Oxford: Clarendon Press.

Rubensson, Daniel. 2000. "Participation and Politics: Social Capital, Civic Voluntarism, and Institutional Context." Presented at the PSA annual conference, London, April.

Rubensson, Kjell. 1994. "Adult Education Policy in Sweden, 1967–1991." *Policy Studies Review* 13:367–90.

Salokangas, Raimo. 1999. "From Political to National, Regional and Local: The Newspaper Structure in Finland." *Nordicom Review*, 1.

Sanchez-Tabernero, A. 1993. *Media Concentration in Europe*. Manchester: European Institute for the Media.

Sanders, Arthur. 1998. "How Watching Television Affects Our Views of Politics." Presented at the American Political Science Association annual meeting: Boston, September.

SAP (Swedish Social Democratic Party). 1993. "Social Democracy on the Eve of the EC Membership Negotiations." Official translation of position adopted by the Parliamentary Group, January 19.

Savoie, Donald. 2000. "The Canadian Prime Minister: Primus in All Things." *Inroads*, no. 9.

SCB, Statistika Centralbyrån (Statistics Sweden). 1974. *Allemänna valen, 1973*. Stockholm:SCB.

Schaffner, Brian, and Matthew Streb. 2000. "Voters without Cheat Sheets: The Education Bias of the Non-partisan Ballot." Presented at the American Political Science Association annual meeting, Washington, D.C., September.

Schartau, Mai-Brith. 2000. "Privatisation in Sweden." Presented at the Society for the Advancement of Socio-Economics (SASE) meeting, London, July.

Schemeil, Yves. 1997. "Compétences et Implication Politiques en Europe: Balade dans la Forêt Magique des Eurobaromètres," in Pierre Bréchon and Bruno Cautrés, eds., *Les Enquêtes Eurobaromètriques: Analyse Comparée des données sociopolitiques*. Paris: L'Harmattan.

Scheuer, Jeffrey. 1999. *The Sound Bite Society: Television and the American Mind*. New York: Four Walls Eight Windows.

Schmidt, Manfred. 1996. "When Parties Matter: A Review of the Possibilities and Limits of Partisan Influence on Public Policy." *European Journal of Political Research* 30: 155–83.

Schmitt, Hermann. 1999. "The Architecture of EU Institutions and Citizen Participation." Presented at Conference on Citizen Participation in European Politics by the Commission on Democracy in Sweden, October.

Schuckman, Harvey P. 1998. "What Motivates Civic Engagement in Local Politics: Deconstructing the Role of Local Political Institutions: An Examination of Mayoral Electoral Turnout." Presented at the American Political Science Associations annual meeting: Boston, September.

Schwarz, Norbert, and Howard Schuman. 1997. "Political Knowledge, Attribution, and Inferred Interest in Politics: The operation of Buffer Items." *International Journal of Public Opinion Research*. P:vol. 2:191–95.

Semetko, Holli A. 1996. "The Importance of Issues in Election Campaigns: A Comparison of TV News in Germany, Spain, Britain and the US." Presented at the Meetings of the European Consortium for Political Research, Oslo.

Semetko, Holli A., and Patti M.Valkenburg. 1996. "Political Efficacy and Media Use in the New Germany: Evidence from a Three-Year Panel Study." Presented at the American Political Science Association, San Francisco.

Shaw, Eric. 1999. "New Labour's Third Way." *Inroads*, no. 8: 215–22.

Sheldon, Peter, and Louise Thornthwaite. 1999. "Swedish Engineering Employers: The Search for Industrial Peace in the Absence of Centralised Collective Bargaining." *Industrial Relations Journal* 30:5.

Silverman, Brian, Alan Bollard, and Ralph Lattimore. 1996. *A Study of Economic Reform: The Case of New Zealand*. Amsterdam: Elsevier.

Skolverket. 1998. "*Gymnasieskola för alla — andra. En studie om marginalisering och utslagning i gymnasieskolan.*" Stockholm: Skolverket.

———. 1996. "America's Income Inequality: Where Do We Stand?" *Challenge*, September–October.

———. 1996a. "American Income Inequality in a Cross-national Perspective: Why Are We So Different?" LIS Working Paper #157, Luxembourg.

Smeeding, Timothy. 1991. "Cross-national Comparisons of Inequality and Poverty Position," in Lars Osberg, ed., *Economic Inequality and Poverty*. Armonk, N.Y.: M. E. Sharpe.

Smith, Elizabeth. 2000. "Youth Voluntary Association Participation and Political Attitudes: A Quasi-experimental Causal Analysis." Presented at the International Political Science Association (IPSA) conference, Québec, Canada, August.

Smith, Julie. 1995. "The 1994 European Elections: Twelve into One Won't Go." *West European Politics* 18:199–217.

Smith, Paul. 1996. *Revolution in the Air*. Auckland: Addison-Wesley.

Sniderman, Paul M., Richard A. Brody, and Philip E. Tetlock. 1991. *Reasoning and Choice*. New York: Cambridge University Press.

Søllinge, Jette. 1999. "Danish Newspapers. Structure and Developments." *Nordicom Review*, Issue 1.

Statistics Canada. 1999. *Education Indicators in Canada: Report of the Pan-Canadian Education Indicators Program*. Ottawa: Statistics Canada.

Statistika meddelanden. 1998. "*Studie Förbund 1997: Studiecirklar och Kulturprogram*" (Adult Education Associations 1997: Study Circles and Activities). KU 10 SM 9801. Stockholm: Statistika meddlanden.

Steemers, Jeanette. 1999. "Changing Channels: The Redefinition of Public Service Broadcasting for the Digital Age." Presented at the ECPR joint sessions, Mannheim, April.

Steinmo, Sven. 1993. *Taxation and Democracy: Swedish, British and American Approaches to Financing the Modern State*. New Haven, Conn.: Yale University Press.

Stolle, Dietlind. 1998. "Making Associations Work: Group Characteristics and Membership and Generalized Trust." Presented at the American Political Science Association annual meeting, Boston, September.

———. 2000. "Clubs and Organizations: The Benefits of Joining an Organization." Presented at the ECPR joint sessions. Copenhagen, April.

Strate, John M., Charles J. Parrish, Charles J, Charles D. Elder, Coit Ford III.

1989. "Life Span Civic Development and Voting Participation." *American Political Science Review.* 83:443–64.

Streeck, Wolfgang. 2000. "Citizenship, Production and Redistribution." Presented at the Society for the Advancement of Socio-Economics (SASE) meeting, London, July.

Strömberg, L., and J. Westerståhl. 1984. *The New Swedish Communes: A Summary of Local Government Research.* Stockholm: Liber.

Sundberg, Jan. 1991. "Participation in Local Government: A Source of Social Democratic Deradicalization in Scandinavia," in L. Karvonen and Jan Sundberg eds., *Social Democracy in Transition.* Aldershot, U.K.: Dartmouth.

Svallfors, Stefan. 1995. "Political Trust and Attitudes Towards Redistribution: A Comparison of Sweden and Norway. *European Societies,* forthcoming.

———. 1999. "The End of Class Politics? Structural Cleavages and Attitudes to Swedish Welfare Policies." *Acta Sociologica* 38:53–74.

Svåsand, Lars. 1991. "State Subventions for Political Parties in Norway," in M. Wiberg, M. ed. *The Public Purse and Political Parties: Public Financing of Political Parties in Nordic Countries.* Helsinki: Finnish Political Science Association.

Swank, Duane. 1999. "Social Democratic Welfare States in a Global Economy: Scandinavia in Comparative Perspective," in R. Geyer, C. Ingebritsen and J. W. Moses, eds. *Globalization, Europeanization and the End of Scandinavian Social Democracy?* Basingstoke: Macmillan.

Swedish Budget Statement 1999. Stockholm: Government of Sweden.

Swenson, Peter. 1998. "Efficiency Wages, Welfare Capitalists, and Welfare States: Employers and Welfare State Development in the United States and Sweden." Presented at the American Political Science Association annual meeting, Boston, September.

Teixeira, Ruy A. 1992. *The Disappearing American Voter.* Washington, D.C.: Brookings Institution.

Teorell, J., and A. Westholm. 1999. Att bestämma sig för att vara med och bestämma: Om varfor ve röstar—alt mindre, in SOU 132, *Demokratiutredningens forsharvolym XII,* Stockholm.

Thorndike, R. L. 1973. *Reading Comprehension Education in Fifteen Countries: International Studies in Evaluation,* vol. 3. Stockholm: Almqvist and Wiksell.

Tilton, Tim. 1994. *The Political Theory of Social Democracy.* Oxford: Clarendon.

Times Mirror Center for the People and the Press. 1990. "The Age of Indifference: A Study of Young Americans and How They View the News." Philadelphia: Pew Charitable Trust.

TIMSS International Center for the Study of Testing, Evaluation, and Educational Policy. 1998. *Mathematics and Science Literacy in the Final Year of Secondary School.* Boston: ISC, Boston College.

Tocqueville, Alexis de. (1969). *Democracy in America.* Garden City, N.Y.: Doubleday Anchor.

Torfing, Jacob Blais. 1999. "Workfare with Welfare: Recent Reforms in the Danish Welfare State" *European Journal of Social Policy,* 9:15–29.

Torney-Purta, J. 1999. "Becoming Political in Democracies: Policy Questions and Hypotheses for the Ongoing IEA Civic Education Study." Presented at the IEA seminar, Stockholm, Staskontöret, August.

Torney-Purta, J., A. Oppenheim, A. Farnen. 1975. *Civic Education in Ten Countries: An Empirical Study.* Stockholm: Almquist and Wiksell.

Torney-Purta, J., J. Schwille, and J-A. Amadeo. eds. 1999. *Civic Education across*

Countries: Twenty-four National Case Studies from the IEA Civic Education Project. Amsterdam: Eburon-IEA.

Torney-Purta, J., R. Lehmann, H. Oswald, and W. Schulz. 2001. *Citizenship and Education in Twenty-Eight Countries: Civic Knowledge at Age Fourteen.* Amsterdam: Eburon-IEA.

Tufte, E. 1978. *Political Control of the Economy.* Princeton, N.J.: Princeton University Press.

Turkka, Tapani. 1998. "The Impact of National Information Infrastructure Initiatives on Citizens' Participation in Politics: The Case of Finland and Malasia." Presented at the ECPR joint sessions, Warwick U.K., March.

UNESCO. 1993. *World Education Report.* Paris: Unesco.

UNDP (United Nations Development Programme). 1997, 1998, 1999. *Human Development Report.* New York: Oxford.

United States Department of Commerce. 1999. *Falling through the Net: Defining the Digital Divide:* Third report in the Telecommunications and Information Technology Gap in America series. Washington, D.C.: GPO.

Uslaner, Eric. 1998. "Social Capital, Television, and the "Mean World": Trust, Optimism, and Civic Participation *Political Psychology* 19:441–67.

———. 1999. "Morality Plays: Social Capital and Moral Behaviour in Anglo-American Democracies," in J. W. Van Deth., M. Maraffi, K.Newton, and P. Whiteley, *Social Capital and European Democracy.* London: Routledge.

———. 2000. "Trust, Democracy, and Governance." Presented at the ECPR joint sessions, Copenhagen, April.

Valen, Henry, and Hanne M. 1994. "Government Alternatives, Cross Pressures and Electoral Turnout at the 1993 Storting Election." Paper presented at the European Consortium for Political Research joint sessions, Madrid.

Van den Berg, Axel, Bengt Furåker, and Leif Johanssen. 1997. *Labour Market Regimes and Patterns of Flexibility: A Sweden Canada Comparison.* Lund, Sweden: Arkiv Förlag.

Vandenbrouke, Frank. 1998. Globalization, Inequality and Social Democracy. London: Institute for Public Policy Research.

Van Deth, Jan. 1998. "Political Involvement and Social Capital." Presented at the American Political Science Association annual meeting: Boston, September.

Van Deth, Jan, and Ellen Scarborough, eds. 1995. *The Impact of Values.* Oxford: Oxford University Press.

Vatta, A. 1999. "The Attitude of Employers' Organizations towards Concertation: A Discussion of Explanatory Factors." Presented at the ECPR joint sessions, Mannheim, April.

Verba, S., and M. H. Nie. 1972. *Participation in America.* New York: Harper and Row.

Verba, Sidney, Kay Lehman Schlozman, and Henry E. Brady. 1995. *Voice and Equality: Civic Voluntarism in American Politics.* Cambridge Mass.: Harvard University Press.

Vergunst, Noel P. 1998. "Consensus Democracy, Corporatism and Federalism: Do Institutions Matter?" Presented at the ECPR joint sessions, Warwick U.K., March.

———. 1999. "The Role of Corporatism and Consensus Democracy in Socio-economic Policy Making and Performance: A Comparative Analysis of Twenty Countries." Presented at the ECPR joint sessions, Mannheim, April.

Vogel, Joachim. 1998. "Coping with the European Welfare Mix: Welfare Delivery Services, Family Formation and Material Inequality between Types of Families in the European Union." Presented at the Siena Group meeting, Sidney, December.

Vowles, J. 2000. "Evaluating Electoral System Change: The Case of New Zealand." Presented at the International Political Science Association (IPSA) conference, Québec, Canada, August.

Vowles, J., and E. P. Aimer. 1993. *Voters' Vengeance: The 1990 General Election in New Zealand and the Fate of the Fourth Labour Government*. Auckland: Auckland University Press.

Vowles, J., P. Aimer, H. Catt, J. Lamare, and R. Miller. 1995. *Towards Consensus: The 1993 General Election in New Zealand and the Transition to Proportional Representation*. Auckland: Auckland University Press.

Vromen, Ariadne. 1995. "Paul Keating Is the Prime Minister, but Who Delivers the Mail? A Study of Political Knowledge Amongst Young People." *Australian Journal of Political Science* 30:74–90.

Walker, Tobi. 2000. "The Service/Politics Split: Rethinking Service to Teach Political Engagement." *PS* 33:647–49.

Wallerstein, Michael, and Miriam Golden. 1997. "The Fragmentation of the Bargaining Society: Wage Setting in the Nordic Countries, 1950 to 1992." *Comparative Political Studies* 30:699–731.

Ward, Diana. 1988. "The Structure of the Idea of Democracy in Eastport," in Shawn Rosenberg, Diana Ward, and Stephen Chilton, *Political Reasoning and Cognition : A Piagetian View*. Durham: Duke University Press.

Warren, Mark E. 1996. "Democracy and Trust." Presented at the American Political Science Association, San Francisco.

Wattenberg, Martin. 1998. "Turnout Decline in the U.S. and the Other Advanced Industrial Democracies." Research Paper, Center for the Study of Democracy, University of California, Irvine.

Weinstein, Jeremy M. 1999. "Abandoning the Polity: Political Parties and Social Capital in American Politics." Presented at the American Political Science Associations annual meeting, Atlanta, September.

Wessels, Bernhard. 1996. "System Characteristics Matter: Empirical Evidence from Ten Representation Studies." Berlin: WZB (Social Science Research Center).

Westholm, Anders, Arne Lindquist, and Richard Niemi. 1989. "Education and the Making of the Informed Citizen: Political Literacy and the Outside World," in Ort Ichilov, ed., *Political Socialization, Education and Democracy*. New York: Teachers' College Press.

WFA (West Finland Alliance). 1998. *The Information Society Strategy of the West Finland Alliance*. Tampere: WFA.

Whiteford, Peter. 1998. "Is Australia Particularly Unequal?" in Paul Smyth and Bettina Cass, *Contesting the Australian Way: States, Markets and Civil Society*. Cambridge: Cambridge University Press.

Wiberg, Matti. 1991. "Public Financing of Parties as Arcana Imperii in Finland," in M. Wiberg, ed., *The Public Purse and Political Parties: Public Financing of Political Parties in Nordic Countries*. Helsinki: Finnish Political Science Association.

———, ed. 1997. *Trying to Make Democracy Work: The Nordic Parliaments and the European Union*. Stockholm: Gidlunds Förlag.

Widfeldt, Anders. 1996. "The Swedish European Election of 1995." *Electoral Studies* 15:116–19.

———. 1997. *Linking Parties with People? Party Membership in Sweden, 1960–1994*. Göteborg Studies in Politics #46. Göteborg: Göteborg University.

Wilkinson, Richard G. 1996. *Unhealthy Societies: The Afflictions of Inequality*. London: Routledge.

Wolfinger, Raymond E., and Steven J. Rosenstone. 1980. *Who Votes?* New Haven, Conn.: Yale University Press.

Wolleback, Dag, and Per Selle. 2000. "Voluntary Associations and Social Capital: The Case of Norway." Presented at the ECPR joint sessions, Copenhagen, April.

Wood, Stewart. 1997. "Weakening Codetermination? Works Council Reform in West Germany in the 1980s." Berlin: WZB (Social Science Research Center).

World Bank. 1997. *World Development Report: The State in a Changing World*. New York: Oxford University Press.

Worre, Torben. 1994. "European Integration, Legitimacy and Democratic Representation: Danish Perspectives." Presented at the ECPR joint session of workshops, Madrid, April.

Zaller, John. 1992. *The Nature and Origins of Mass Opinion*. New York: Cambridge University Press.

Index

Adolescents. *See* young people

Ads. *See* advertising

Adult education, 8, 10, 62, 108, 110, 112, 117, 118, 121–129, 138, 143, 159, 164, 165 174, 180, 188, 222, 239, 241. *See also* study circles

Adult literacy, 107, 120, 187, 235

Advertising, 85, 94–101, 110–113, 138, 201, 202, 225, 233, 246, 249, 261. *See also* commercialism

Age (and political knowledge), 47–49, 230, 232, 236, 257

Aging, 41

Aimer, Peter, 44, 138, 139, 203

Alford, Robert, 34

Althaus, Scott, 218

Ambjörnsson, Ronny, 127, 128

Anderson, Christopher, 80, 81

Asp, Kent, 113

Associational density, 3, 18–22, 185, 213, 267

Associational participation, 3, 22, 25, 30, 37, 38, 39, 93, 211, 217, 231

Atkinson, Anthony, 252

Australia, 7, 20, 33–35, 44, 56, 59, 61, 69–72, 79, 100, 110, 136, 137, 150, 191, 198

Austria, 33, 34, 95, 108, 111, 150, 152, 154, 155, 157, 159, 181

Banducci, Susan, 83, 139

Barber, Bernard, 215

Bartels, Lawrence, 28

Belgium, 22, 60, 61, 95, 108, 150, 154–157, 176, 177, 198, 209, 227, 234–237, 241, 252–254, 263

Bennett, Steven, 48, 59, 92, 94, 95

Bergström, Hans, 226

Blais, André, 223

Boiney, John, 98

Bréchon, Pierre, 216

Brehm, John, 212

Bridges, Amy, 67, 171, 172

Britain, 16, 20, 33, 34, 44, 56–59, 61, 83, 84, 94–96, 99, 119, 135–137, 148, 150, 162, 181, 186, 191, 198

Broadcasting, 2, 9, 95, 96, 109, 110, 188, 230, 233, 247. *See also* television, radio

Butts, R. Freeman, 221

Canada, 10, 22, 23, 33, 34, 43, 44, 56–60, 61, 68, 84, 95, 96, 99, 110, 121, 122, 137, 150, 162, 185–188, 194, 198

Cassel, Carol, 255

Carlsson, Ulla, 97, 108

Central banks, 136

Centralization, 168

Children, 91, 129, 195, 210, 230, 231, 251, 252

Churches. *See* religion

Citizen education. *See* civic education

Citizen participation. *See* civic engagement

Citizenship, 1–5, 10, 17, 25, 44, 54, 65, 78, 110, 118, 120, 176, 212, 214, 216, 224, 231, 240

Civic education, 2, 117, 118, 123, 222

Civic engagement, 1, 5, 15–17, 21, 24–26, 29–32, 36, 41–45, 53, 54, 60, 91, 92, 126, 164, 212, 214, 218, 235, 242. *See also* associational participation

Civics Expert Group, 220, 239, 240, 242

Civil society, 5, 116, 136

Clark, Terry, 90

Clinton, Bill, 114

Clubs. *See* voluntary associations

Coalitions, 84, 86, 114, 136, 139, 140–143, 152, 166, 192, 227, 229, 246–249, 259

Coleman, James S., 15

Collective bargaining, 159, 164, 167, 168, 249

Commercialism, 6, 97, 110, 143, 165, 232, 238, 241, 249

Communism, 172

Competitiveness, 67, 68, 256

Compulsory voting, 29, 32–35, 71, 89, 177, 209, 215, 216, 225, 235, 246, 263

Consensual institutions, 7, 10, 81, 85, 87, 89, 174

Consensus democracy, 227

Conservative parties, 46, 66

Constitutions, 45

Continuing education. *See* adult education

Converse, Phillip, 28

Corporatism, 158, 167, 168, 227, 252, 253

Coulson, Tony, 41, 43

Crafts, N. F. R., 137, 162

Crepaz, Marcus, 227

Curtice, John, 44, 96, 234

Cusack, Thomas, 22

Dahl, Robert, 258

Dalton, Russell, 87

Darmofal, David, 87

Dautrich, Kenneth, 94, 232

Deliberative polls, 219

Delli Carpini, Michael, 218

Denmark, 10, 37, 56, 95, 97, 100, 107–111, 113, 115, 121, 131, 132, 150, 151, 157 162, 167, 168, 180, 181, 186

Digital divide, 9, 132, 177, 180, 181, 183, 189

Dimock, Michael, 24, 40, 44

Direct democracy, 237, 253

Downs, Anthony, 27, 28

Dutch. *See* Netherlands

Eagles, Monroe, 224

Easton, Brian, 246

Economic growth, 9, 21, 148, 149, 150, 152, 154, 250

Economic performance, 134, 147–150, 153, 156, 161, 168, 171

Education, 4, 6, 41, 43, 49, 63, 87, 88, 90, 96, 107, 111, 119, 120, 142, 163, 165, 172, 179, 187, 217–221, 226, 231, 233, 240, 247, 251, 260, 261. *See also* adult education, civic education

Edwards, Robert, 210, 213

Eklund, Klas, 165

Election campaigns, 48, 96, 112, 113, 203, 233

Electoral institutions, 2, 9, 10, 42, 113, 133, 138, 184

Electoral reform, 140, 142, 143, 228, 235, 248

Electoral systems, 6–8, 32, 33, 43, 44, 69, 71–76, 81–85, 88, 89, 111, 114, 135–141, 191, 203, 206, 207, 216, 226–229, 239, 247

Electronic media. *See* television

Employment, 129, 130, 135, 167, 240, 251, 257

England. *See* Britain

Entman, Robert, 221

Environment, 10, 20, 86, 125, 141, 180, 181

Equality, 3, 10, 142, 143, 150, 153–156, 158, 161–164, 167, 172, 178, 213, 218, 253–256. *See also* welfare state

EU. *See* European Union

Eurobarometer, 22, 57, 58, 80, 180, 181, 213, 217, 234, 244, 257, 258, 259

European Community. *See* European Union

European economic integration, 167

European integration, 57, 159, 181, 186, 258

European Parliament, 68, 84, 217, 229, 258, 259

European Union, 10, 34, 43, 57, 58, 68, 100, 112, 115, 116, 123, 125, 131, 135, 150, 151, 165, 181–183, 192, 216, 217, 222, 234, 238, 241, 243, 254, 258

Exclusion, 67, 211

Findahl, Olle, 96

Finland, 9, 61, 97, 107–109, 112, 113, 120, 121, 150, 151, 157, 162, 167, 168, 180, 181; information technology in, 131–133

Fiorina, Morris, 28, 40

Fishkin, James, 27, 28, 40

Foley, Michael, 210

France, 15, 16, 22, 23, 33, 58–60, 95, 104, 108, 110, 119, 120, 150, 194

Franklin, Mark, 4, 29, 67, 69, 84

Fukuyama, Francis, 212

Galston, William, 1
Gans, Curtis, 230
Gated communities, 19
Gerbner, George, 92
Germany, 8, 9, 20, 22, 33, 34, 58–61, 95,
	100, 104, 110, 121, 131, 135, 139, 142,
	148, 150, 154, 157, 162, 186, 192, 194,
	198; political knowledge in, 44, 56, 57,
	59, 60, 96, 111
Gini coefficient, 10, 134, 150, 151, 153,
	154, 155, 173, 177
Globalization, 3, 110, 159, 165, 166, 169,
	179, 181, 189, 256
Goldsmith, Michael, 33, 34
Gordon, Stacy, 42, 84
Granberg, Donald, 40
Greeley, Andrew, 18
Green, Donald, 26
Green parties, 123, 141
Gregory, Robert, 142
Gwyn, Richard, 44

Hahn, Carole, 119
Hansen, John, 24, 41, 42
Harrie, E., 97, 108
Harris, Paul, 140
Hartley, Thomas, 94
HDI. See Human Development Index
Health, 20, 142, 145, 176, 185, 211, 240,
	251
Hepburn, Mary, 90
Highton, B., 217
Hjellum, Torstein, 70, 71
Hoffmann-Martinot, Vincent, 229
Holmberg, Sören, 23, 40, 79, 179
Holmsund, 127
Human capital, 214
Human Development Index (HDI), 137,
	187, 246

IALS. See International Adult Literacy
	Survey
IDEA. See Institute for Democracy and
	Electoral Assistance
IEA. See International Association for the
	Evaluation of Educational Achieve-
	ment, 60, 61, 187, 223

Immigration, 114, 172
Inclusion, 30, 99
Income distribution, 10, 134, 150, 154,
	250, 255, 256
Income inequality, 13, 14, 143, 154, 177,
	185, 186, 227, 252, 256, 260
Infant mortality, 154, 255, 261
Information Society, 244
Information technology, 8, 130, 132, 177,
	189
Infotainment, 97, 110
Inglehart, Ronald, 24
Institute for Democracy and Electoral
	Assistance (IDEA), 29, 31, 138
Intellectuals, 10, 163, 166, 253
Interest groups, 156, 255
International Adult Literacy Survey
	(IALS), 13, 49, 54, 60, 63, 65, 101,
	118–122, 137, 138, 168, 188, 195, 197
International Association for the Evalua-
	tion of Educational Achievement
	(IEA), 39, 119, 120, 137
International Center for the Study of
	Testing, Evaluation, and Educational
	Policy (TIMMS). See TIMMS
Interpersonal trust, 3, 5, 7, 16–23, 29, 30,
	37, 38, 91–94, 172, 212, 213, 231, 255,
	261
Ireland, 20, 58–61, 95, 137, 150, 187,
	198, 227, 229, 234, 236, 241, 250, 252,
	254, 258
Irvine, William, 86
Italy, 16, 18, 58, 59, 95, 101, 104, 108,
	110, 111, 137, 150, 176, 177, 187, 209
Iversen, Torben, 159
Iyengar, Shanto, 94

Jackman, Robert, 210
Jamieson, Kathleen, 232
Japan, 58, 101, 131, 148, 157, 186, 200–
	202, 209
Junn, Jane, 32, 41, 44, 45

Kangas, Olli, 236, 260
Karp, Jeffrey, 83
Katz, Richard, 75
Kawachi, Ichiro, 185
Keeter, Scott, 218
Kennedy, Bruce, 185

Kenworthy, Lane, 154, 157, 174
Korpi, Walter, 152, 166
Krouwel, André, 112
Kuklinski, James, 219

Labor markets, 124, 129, 147, 160, 164, 166, 167, 172, 174, 249, 251, 253
Labor-market policies, 20, 124, 164, 166, 179, 182
Labor parties, 66, 80–83, 118, 123, 130, 135, 138, 148, 152, 163, 164, 186, 193, 207, 227, 247, 249, 260. *See also* social democratic parties
Ladner, Andreas, 72
Lane, Jan-Erik, 126, 130
Left-of-center parties, 42, 148
Left-wing parties, 143, 250
Libraries, 9, 109, 118, 120, 127–132, 172, 239, 242, 243, 246
Lidström, Anders, 180
Lifelong learning. *See* adult education
Lijphart, Arend, 41, 69, 81
Lindbeck, Assar, 152
LIS. *See* Luxembourg Income Study
Listhaug, Ola, 112
LO (Swedish Labor Confederation), 123, 164–168, 254
Local elections, 2, 8, 26, 31–36, 64, 101, 209. *See also* voter turnout in local elections, 6–7, 13–17, 26, 38, 53, 64–71, 84, 89, 104, 215–217, 225, 227, 229, 256, 257, 263
Local elites, 87
Local government, 31, 57, 68, 72, 115, 136, 143, 172, 213, 216, 225, 227, 246, 253
Lochner, Kimberly, 185
Lupia, Arthur, 28
Luskin, Robert, 219
Luxembourg Income Study (LIS), 150, 153, 154

Mackerras, Malcom, 215
Macroeconomics, 202
Mair, Peter, 152
Majoritarian system, 7, 78, 81, 86, 143, 226, 228
Marsh, Ian, 79, 80
Mass media, 112, 113

Materialism, 177
McAllister, Ian, 43, 44
McCann, James, 214
McGregor, Judy, 246
Mill, John Stuart, 1, 31, 32, 147
Millard, William, 59
Miller, R. A., 210
Milner, Henry, 72, 109, 121, 160, 163, 166
Minority government, 248
Mishra, Ramesh, 181
MMP, 82, 135, 139–142, 203, 206, 247, 248, 249, 262
Mobility, 63, 126, 164, 242, 252
Mobilization, 41, 70, 71, 74, 75, 80, 176, 218
Morlan, Robert, 34, 35
Mortality, 255, 256, 261
Multi-party systems, 85, 228
Myrdal, Alva, 163, 164
Myrdal, Gunnar, 10, 115, 116, 163–165

Nagel, Jack, 141
Netherlands, 8, 19, 20, 23, 60, 61, 68, 87, 96, 104, 108–111, 121, 150, 154, 157, 162, 180, 194, 198
New Zealand, 9, 19, 20, 34, 43–45, 53–56, 61, 82, 84, 96, 109, 120, 121, 133–143, 148, 150, 186–189, 198, 200–206
Newspapers, 2, 8, 9, 27, 80, 90, 95, 96, 101, 108, 109, 111, 118, 120, 129, 137, 229, 230–232, 236, 239, 242–246, 260, 261, 262; circulation of, 99–101, 137, 176; reading of, 3, 40, 58, 90, 91, 92, 94, 99, 101, 108, 109, 187, 230, 235; readership of, 16, 90, 143, 174, 179, 188, 234
Newton, Kenneth, 22, 23, 34, 92
Nie, Norman, 41, 45, 70
Niemi, Richard, 54
Nonvoting, 44, 215
Nordic countries, 23, 33, 97, 108–115, 121, 133, 150, 159, 166–169, 188. *See also* Scandinavia
Norris, Pippa, 23, 29, 93, 94, 96
Norway, 7–10, 19, 24, 44, 69, 70–73, 83, 95, 97, 108–113, 121, 131, 132, 138, 150–152, 157; sustainable welfare state in, 162, 167, 168, 181, 192

OECD, 4, 49, 60, 63, 119, 121, 131–134, 137, 150, 152–155, 166, 176, 186–188, 194, 195
Olson, Mancur, 170, 171
Ontario, 34, 35

Palme, Olof, 105, 122, 171, 260
Parker, Kimberly, 48
Participatory democracy, 241
Party membership, 26, 112, 179, 188
Periodicals, 108
Petersson, Olof, 23
Pew Center for the People and the Press 48, 95, 97, 230, 232
Polarization, 84
Political culture, 69, 76, 141, 225, 241, 259, 262
Political efficacy, 43, 55, 56
Political engagement. *See* civic engagement
Political institutions, 3, 16, 22–24, 28, 40, 56, 66, 67, 77–80, 90, 119, 126, 158, 159, 179, 181, 182, 186, 215, 222, 230, 249, 252. *See also* electoral systems, electoral institutions
Political involvement. *See* civic engagement
Political knowledge, 1, 2, 7, 19, 23, 28, 32, 38–41, 43–45, 47–49, 53–60, 63–66, 78, 90, 96, 98, 99, 111, 118–120, 213, 218–222, 231, 232. *See also* political sophistication, public affairs knowledge
Political literacy. *See* political knowledge
Political participation, 1, 6, 9, 10, 15, 23, 24, 28, 31, 32, 39, 45, 49, 53, 61, 65, 66, 69, 70, 83, 89, 93, 111, 125, 158, 174, 176, 184, 188, 209, 213, 215, 222, 263. *See also* voter turnout
Political science, 22, 28, 66, 88, 222, 246
Political sophistication, 42, 221
Political trust, 22, 23, 24, 213, 261. *See also* vertical trust
Polls, 23, 31, 33, 42, 66, 67, 74–78, 208, 216, 218, 219, 223–226, 247, 248
Popkin, Samuel, 24, 44
Portugal, 22, 60, 210
Postal voting, 67
Postman, Neil, 97

Poverty, 223
Powell, G. Bingham, 80, 83
Press. *See* newspapers
Proportionality (in electoral outcomes), 69, 81, 83, 84, 141, 225–227
Proportional representation, 44, 69, 83, 188, 191, 227, 248
Public affairs knowledge, 4, 6, 94, 97, 109
Public health, 123, 251
Public interest, 96, 115, 142, 247
Public opinion, 15, 164, 179
Public sector, 95, 143, 252
Public service, 96, 109, 136, 233, 245
Public-service television. *See* television
Public television. *See* television
Putnam, Robert, 1, 3, 5, 7, 11, 15–20, 22, 25, 39, 40, 54, 90–93, 98, 100, 147, 185

Quality of life, 245
Quebec, 34, 35, 186–189
Quirk, Paul, 228

Radio, 99, 108–110, 138, 185, 224, 230, 233, 242
Rahn, Wendy, 212
Rallings, Colin, 217
Rational choice, 158, 214, 223, 253
Reading comprehension, 8, 120
Reading literacy, 110, 235
Reagan, Ronald, 47
Redistribution, 9, 148, 156, 161, 170, 172, 252
Referenda, 123, 217, 235
Refugees, 172
Regional development, 130
Rehn, Gösta, 10, 164–166, 168
Rehn-Meidner model, 164, 254
Reich, Robert, 114, 115
Religion, 5, 18, 19, 76, 107, 126, 137, 163, 180, 211, 214
Rosenstone, Stephen, 24, 41, 42, 56, 67
Rothstein, Bo, 167
Rubensson, Kjell, 121–123
Russia, 58, 223

Scandinavia, 3, 9, 10, 20, 57–60, 101, 108, 121, 126, 130–134, 154, 156, 159–162, 173, 186

Scandinavian model, 9, 109, 134, 152
Schools, 62, 120, 124, 125, 130, 132, 180, 184, 210, 221, 239, 241, 245, 257, 262
School systems, 120, 124
Schuckman, Harvey, 34, 35
Scotland, 137, 217
Second-order elections, 68, 225
Segura, Gary, 42, 84
Semetko, Holli, 96
Service learning, 242
Shapiro, Ian, 26
Skolverket, 180
Smeeding, Timothy, 154
Social capital, 1, 3, 5–8, 15–29, 36, 38–40, 53–55, 90, 91–94, 100, 210–214, 217, 231, 255
Social democratic parties, 105, 116, 123, 126, 163–167, 186, 253
Social policy, 261
Social trust. See interpersonal trust
Sovereignty, 182
Spain, 96, 210, 236
Stolle, Dietlind, 22
Study circles, 8, 9, 98, 110, 112, 121–129, 234, 241
Sustainable welfare state, 10, 148, 155–163, 168, 169–174, 177–181, 183–186 188, 250, 253, 256, 261
Svallfors, Stefan, 24, 161
Svåsand, Lars, 113
Sweden, 2, 8–10, 19, 22–24, 29, 33, 36, 40, 58, 63, 78–80, 83, 84, 87, 95–97; civic education in, 107–116, 138, 148, 151–154, 157; adult education in, 120–134; sustainable welfare state in, 161–171, 174, 177–183, 186, 187, 194, 198
Swedish Model, 167
Switzerland, 7, 33–35, 60, 61, 67–78, 95, 109, 111, 132, 150, 162, 186, 194, 198
SWS. See sustainable welfare state

Teixeira, Ruy, 24, 41
Television, 2, 5–9, 20, 31, 51, 90–102, 107–114, 116, 133, 137–140, 159, 171–176, 180, 185, 224, 230–236, 242, 246, 247, 250, 257, 262; public television 79, 96, 179, 188, 233, 261; public-service television, 95, 96, 108–111, 237
Television dependency (scale), 7, 97–102,

107, 133, 137, 159, 173, 176, 200, 234–237, 249
Thatcher, Margaret, 136
Thrasher, Michael, 217, 229
Times Mirror Center, 48, 95
TIMSS, 61, 120, 187
Tocqueville, Alexis de, 16, 20, 28, 32
Torney-Purta, Judith, 118, 119, 120
Trade unions, 19, 109, 123, 124, 127, 136, 158, 163, 167, 229, 251
TV. See television
TV dependency (scale). See television dependency (scale)

UK. See Britain
Umeå, 8, 125, 126, 127, 128, 129, 130, 131, 132, 241, 242, 243
UNDP, 131, 145, 155, 223, 250, 255, 260
Unemployment, 151, 157, 164, 165, 176, 238, 251
UNESCO, 118, 137, 234, 239, 244, 252
Union density, 159, 253
United Kingdom. See Britain
United Nations, 59, 63, 65, 128, 137, 145, 155, 187, 223, 235
United Nations Development Project. See UNDP
United States, 1, 4–8, 16, 20, 24, 28, 29, 34–36, 40–44, 47, 49, 53, 55, 58–61, 63, 67, 68, 78, 79, 83, 84, 87, 119, 121, 131–133, 137, 138, 147, 148, 150, 154, 158; media consumption in, 90–96, 99–101, 109, 111, 113–115; sustainable welfare state in, 162, 172, 176, 179, 183–187, 195, 198
Uslaner, Eric, 18, 22, 91, 92, 172

Van Deth, Jan, 217
Västerbotten, 126, 127, 130, 242, 243, 244, 253
Verba, Sidney, 45, 70
Vertical trust, 23, 24, 213, 215
Voluntary associations, 2, 16, 18, 20, 23, 38, 60, 185, 210. See also associational participation
Volunteering, 23, 211
Voter turnout 2, 4, 5–7, 14–17, 25, 29, 38–44, 47, 57, 67, 75, 76, 77, 80, 91–94, 107, 112, 138, 179, 185, 186, 214,

218, 223, 246; in local elections 6–7, 13–17, 26, 38, 53, 64, 65, 66–71, 84, 89, 104, 215–217, 225, 227, 229, 256, 257, 263
Vowles, Jack, 44
Vromen, Ariadne, 220

Wage bargaining. *See* collective bargaining
Wage negotiations. *See* collective bargaining
Wallerstein, Michael, 168
Ward, Diana, 220
Warren, Mark, 114
Wattenberg, Martin, 217
Welfare state, 9, 116, 132–136, 152–154, 163–167, 184, 187, 189, 239, 245, 250–253, 256, 260, 261. *See also* sustainable welfare state

West Finland Alliance, 244
Westholm, Anders, 29, 54
Westminster (model), 136, 137, 139, 158, 228, 229, 246, 248
Wolfinger, Raymond, 41, 67
Women, 69, 82, 114, 123, 141, 145, 155, 206, 211, 219, 236, 248, 252
Working hours, 184, 186
World Bank, 18, 244, 260
World Values Survey, 18, 20–23, 29, 30, 37, 87

Young people, 6, 43, 48, 63, 112, 117–120, 147, 165, 179, 211, 218, 227, 230, 236, 240–242

Zaller, John, 221